Footprint story

It was 1921

Ireland had just been partitioned, the British miners were striking for more pay and the federation of British industry had an idea. Exports were booming in South America – how about a handbook for businessmen trading in that far away continent? The Anglo-South American Handbook was born that year, written by W Koebel, the most prolific writer on Latin America of his day.

S.Stolz

1924

Two editions later the book was 'privatized' and in 1924, in the hands of Royal Mail, the steamship company for South America, it became The South American Handbook, subtitled 'South America in a nutshell'. This annual publication became the 'bible' for generations of travellers to South America and remains so to this day. In the early days travel was by sea and the Handbook gave all the details needed for the long voyage from Europe. What to wear for dinner; how to arrange a cricket match with the Cable & Wireless staff on the Cape Verde Islands and a full account of the journey from Liverpool up the Amazon to Manaus: 5898 miles without changing cabin!

Tread your own path

Footprint Handbooks

1939

As the continent opened up, the South American Handbook reported the new Pan Am flying boat services, and the fortnightly airship service from Rio to Europe on the Graf Zeppelin. For reasons still unclear but with extraordinary determination, the annual editions continued through the Second World War.

Surfing Europe

South American Handbook 2011

Updated Annually

1970s

Many more people discovered South America and the backpacking trail started to develop. All the while the Handbook was gathering fans, including literary vagabonds such as Paul Theroux and Graham Greene (who once sent some updates addressed to "The publishers of the best travel guide in the world, Bath, England").

1990s

During the 1990s the company set about developing a new travel guide series using this legendary title as the flagship. By 1997 there were over a dozen guides in the series and the Footprint imprint was launched.

2000s

The series grew quickly and there were soon Footprint travel guides covering more than 150 countries. In 2004, Footprint launched its first thematic guide: *Surfing Europe*, packed with colour photographs, maps and charts. This was followed by further thematic guides such as *Diving the World*, *Snowboarding the World*, *Body and Soul escapes*, *Travel with Kids* and *European City Breaks*.

2010

Today we continue the traditions of the last 89 years that have served legions of travellers so well. We believe that these help to make Footprint guides different. Our policy is to use authors who are genuine experts who write for independent travellers; people possessing a spirit of adventure, looking to get off the beaten track.

Cambodia Handbook

Andrew Spooner

Cambodia is perhaps the most beguiling of all the countries of Southeast Asia. Long associated with the brutal Khmer Rouge, the country has risen above its blood-tinted history to finally take its place as one of the region's pre-eminent tourist destinations. Home to a truly rich mix of travel experiences from ancient monuments and powdery beaches to remote ethnic minority villages and city life, Cambodia never fails to excite the senses.

Ancient Cambodia produced one of world's greatest civilizations at Angkor. But Angkor Wat is merely one temple lying at the heart of a thousand others. The capital, Phnom Penh, retains the sort of landscape most travellers dream of: a skyline punctuated by spires, turrets and pinnacles of royal and religious origin rather than by office blocks.

Further south is Sihanoukville, Cambodia's most popular beach-side town, characterized by long, palm-fringed beaches, comfy deckchairs and gentle, lapping waters. More adventurous souls will be impressed by the outlying islands, which provide the perfect backdrop for snorkelling, diving or fishing trips. Decrepit colonial ruins scattered through a Garden of Eden landscape make Kep the real gem of the south, however. Infinitely more low key than Sihanoukville, the small coastal town, with its blossoming flowers, trees laden with fruit and freshly cooked crab speciality, is truly a slice of paradise.

In stark contrast to the laid-back beaches are the northeastern provinces. Here, tracts of red earth cut through hills, carpeted in jungle and speckled with the thatched huts that are home to a miscellany of minority groups. Elephant rides are the call of the day around Sen Monorom, while those looking for adventure in Ban Lung won't be disappointed by the waterfalls, boat rides and the stunning, bottle-green waters of Yaek Lom Lake.

This page A young girl picking lotus flowers near the Angkor Wat Temple.

Previous page Sandstone and wood carving at the Carving Association and Orphan Career Center, Siem Reap.

THAILAND

Dangrek Mountains

Samrong
Banteay
Chhmar
Thma Pok
Srah Chhuk
Sisophon
Poipet
Mongkol
Borei
BANTEAY
MEANCHEY
Kauk
Kduoch
Kamping Pay
Pailin
Reang
Kesei
Daun
Pruhk
Lem
BATTAMBANG
Moung
Roessei

Anlong
Veng

SIEM REAP-
ODDAR
MEANCHEY
Koh Ker
Kulen
Koh Ker

Thkov
Banteay
Srei
Angkor **3** **4**
Phnom Krom
Prek Toal
Bird Sanctuary
Chong
Khneas
Dam Dek
5
Tonlé Sap
Stoeng
Pursat
Kompong
Luong

6
Battambang

Preah
Vihear
Choam
Ksant
T'Beng
Meanchey
Chaeb

PREAH VIHEAR

Phnom Kulen
Beng Mealea
Bakong
Roluos

Preah Khan
Ta Seng

Voen
Kham
Dom
Kralor
STUNG
TRENG
Stung
Treng

12

Sambor
Prei Kuk
KOMPONG
THOM

KRATIE

Kompong
Thom
Phnom
Santuk

Spoe Tbong

7
Kratie
Mekong

Chhlong

PURSAT

*Phnom Aural
(1813m)* ▲

Cardamom
Mountains

*Phnom Knang
Trapeang
(1210m)* ▲

Hak Lek Cham Yem
Koh Kong

Koh Kong

9

KOH KONG

Kirirom
National Park

Sre Ambel

Koh Rong
Sihanoukville
(Kompong Som)
Koh Prins
Koh Tang

Gulf of Thailand

N

50 km
50 miles

KOMPONG
CHHNANG

Kompong
Chhnang

Oudong

Skon

Kompong
Cham

KOMPONG CHAM

Koh Dach

PHNOM
PENH

1 **2**
Kien
Svay
26
30
KANDAL
Choeung Ek
Kompong
Speu
KOMPONG SPEU
Tonlé Bati
Phnom Tamao
Phnom
Chisor
Angkor
Borei
Takeo
TAKEO

Chhuk

Elephant
Mountains

Bokor Mountain
National Park
Phnom Bokor
Preah Sihanouk
'Ream' National
Park

KAMPOT

Kompong
Trach
Kampot 16
Kep
10
Ha Tien

Caves

Tinh
Bien

PREY VANG

Prey Veng

Kompong
Trabék

SVAY
RIENG
Svay
Rieng

Bavet

M
B

Highlights

LAOS

Highlights

Ta Veng
Veng Xai
Yaek Lom Lake ⑧ Bokeo
an Lung
RATANAKIRI
Lumphat

DULKIRI   *Boos Ra*

Sen Monorom

tang   Dak Dam

VIETNAM

① The Royal Palace and Silver Pagoda are highlights of the capital's concoction of temples, summerhouses and palaces. ▶▶ page 46.

② Visit the Tuol Sleng Museum in Phnom Penh to remember the dead and remind the living. ▶▶ page 51.

③ Marvel at Angkor Wat, the largest religious monument in the world. ▶▶ page 91.

④ The royal City of Angkor Thom and the Bayon are simply awesome. ▶▶ page 95.

⑤ Supporting numerous floating villages, Tonlé Sap is the largest freshwater lake in Southeast Asia. ▶▶ page 123.

⑥ Explore the provincial town of Battambang. The nearby Bamboo Train is Cambodia's most unlikely travel experience ▶▶ pages 149 and 151.

⑦ Use Kratie as a base to see the endangered Irrawaddy dolphins. ▶▶ page 170.

⑧ Take a dip in the crystal-clear volcanic Yaek Lom Lake. ▶▶ page 180.

⑨ Laze on stunning white beaches on Koh Kong Island. ▶▶ page 199.

⑩ A quiet alternative to Sihanoukville, Kep is a wonderful coastal town with beautiful gardens. ▶▶ page 201.

Clockwise from top
Angkor Thom and the Bayon.
Kep.
Tuol Sleng Museum in Phnom Penh.
Kratie and the Irrawaddy dolphins.
Koh Kong Island.

Clockwise from top

Battambang and the Bamboo Train.

Tonlé Sap.

Yaek Lom Lake.

Royal Palace and Silver Pagoda.

Next page Angkor Wat.

Contents

ANGKOR & CENTRAL REGION

NORTHWEST

NORTHEAST

SOUTH

PNOMH PENH

Contents

Footprint features

Essentials

Planning your trip

Where to go

While **Phnom Penh** is not the most sophisticated metropolis, it is a charming, bustling town, with a good selection of early 20th-century modernist architecture, a strong sense of latter 20th-century history and delightful restaurants and bars.

The attractions of **Angkor** hardly need further amplification here but you should look beyond just Angkor Wat and the Bayon. Outlying temples, such as **Banteay Srei** and the **Roluos Group**, are quite easily accessible and even the less well-known ones (for instance **Sambor Prei Kuk** and **Banteay Chhmar**) are worth trying to plan into an itinerary. An alternative route from Phnom Penh to Siem Reap is to journey up the road that skirts the western extremities of the Tonlé Sap lake stopping off enroute at Kompong Chhnang and the emerging elegance of Battambang.

Cambodia's coastline is pretty enough and **Sihanoukville**, with its sweeping white-sand beaches, still hopes to become the nation's resort town, but is presently mired in a period of unsustainable development that is ruining both beaches and sea. The views on the road between Kampot and Kep (including **Bokor Mountain National Park**) and between Sihanoukville and Koh Kong are scenic highlights.

Kratie, in the Mekong provinces of the northeast, is an idyllic riverside town, where one can rest to the slow ebb and flow of the Mekong and catch a glimpse of the rare Irrawaddy dolphins. The surrounding scenery is nothing short of stunning and the bright red sun that sets over the town is truly a highlight of any trip here. Despite the difficulties of getting there, almost all visitors rave about the simple and rustic charms of northeast Cambodia, particularly **Ratanakiri** with its hills, trees and tribal minorities. Colourful and remote, this area appeals enormously to the independent and hardened traveller.

Otherwise, the remaining towns and areas of Cambodia, while imbued with typical Khmer charm and style, cannot be regarded as being so significantly different from the rest as to justify a major diversion. For most visitors Cambodia's tranquil and, dare one say it, timeless way of life is its greatest appeal – something which requires an unhurried schedule in order to be fully appreciated.

Itineraries

If time is limited, by far the best option is to get an open-jaw flight where you fly into one city and out of another or fly into Bangkok, the cheapest point of entry, and use the **Bangkok Airways** regional 'Discovery Airpass', which includes **Siem Reap Airways** routes. Distances between towns are long and roads are not always sealed, making overland journey times lengthy and sometimes tortuous, especially in the wet season.

One week A one-week trip will require careful planning and prioritizing. Either take internal flights, if you want to cover a lot of ground, or limit yourself to just one area. Up to four days could be spent around the exceptional ruins of **Angkor**, with one day in **Phnom Penh** and one in either the laid-back beaches of **Sihanoukville** or in colonial-inspired **Kampot**.

Packing for Cambodia

Travellers usually tend to take too much. In Phnom Penh it is possible to buy most toiletries and other personal items, although they are imported and therefore pricier than elsewhere in the region. Outside the capital the range of products, beyond items like soap, washing powder, batteries, shampoo and the like, is limited. Suitcases are not appropriate if you are intending to travel overland by bus. A backpack, or even better a travelpack (where the straps can be zipped out of sight), is recommended. Travelpacks have the advantage of being hybrid backpacks/suitcases.

In terms of clothing, dress in Cambodia is relatively casual – even at formal functions. However, though formal attire may be the exception, dressing tidily is the norm. Travellers tend to take too many of the same articles of clothing: be aware, laundry services are quick and cheap.

You may want to pack antacid tablets for indigestion; antibiotics for travellers diarrhoea (eg Ciproxin/Ciprofloxacin); antiseptic ointment (eg Cetrimide); anti-malarials (see page 31); mosquito repellents; travel sickness tablets; painkillers; condoms/ contraceptives; tampons/sanitary towels; high-factor sun screen and a sun hat and a blow-up pillow.

For longer trips involving jungle treks take a clean needle pack, clean dental pack and water filtration devices. However, be wary of carrying disposable needles as customs officials may find them suspicious. If you are a popular target for insect bites or develop lumps quite soon after being bitten, carry an Aspivenin kit. This syringe suction device is available from many chemists and draws out some of the allergic materials and provides quick relief.

Make sure your passport is valid for at least six months and take photocopies of essential documents, passport ID and visa pages, insurance policy details and student ID card. Spare passport photos are useful when applying for permits or in case of loss or theft.

Two weeks Building on the one-week options, go from **Phnom Penh**, via **Choeung Ek** and onto **Siem Reap** (**Angkor**) by boat, where you will have more time to visit some of the outlying ruins such as **Koh Ker** and **Beng Melea**. Factor in a couple of nights in Battambang – the boat ride from Siem Reap is one of the most engaging in the country.

One month With one month you can take things a little more slowly. Fly to **Phnom Penh** or **Siem Reap** or go by bus and boat through the **Mekong Delta**. Visit **Angkor** and then, from Phnom Penh, go south to **Sihanoukville** and explore the beaches and outlying islands. A day or two can also be spent visiting **Kampot** and the seaside town of **Kep**, as well as exploring the eerie **Bokor Mountain National Park**. If you are looking for something a bit more active, how about cycling from Ho Chi Minh City in Vietnam to **Angkor** (through the Mekong Delta) or may be trek (on foot or on an elephant) in the ecotourism area of the Virachey National Park in the Ratanaki province.

When to go

If you are intending to travel extensively overland, you should visit in the **dry season**, which spans the months from November until about April. Cambodia's mud and laterite

Mine safety

Visitors should be very cautious when walking in the countryside: landmines and other unexploded ordnance is a ubiquitous hazard. Stick to well-worn paths, especially around Siem Reap and when visiting remote temples. There are said to be more than seven million anti-personnel mines buried around the country and, despite the best efforts of the Halo Trust and other de-mining organizations, many still remain. Very few foreign visitors have been injured, maimed or killed by landmines. However, mines do pose an ever-present danger.

The following is a short checklist of ways to avoid injury taken from a special supplement in the *Phnom Penh Post* published to coincide with Cambodia's first Mine Awareness Day in February 1995:

⊘ Ask local people whether mines are a problem in an area before venturing out by inquiring '*mian min teh?*' Ask more than one local, just to make sure.

⊘ Stick to known safe paths.

⊘ Use a guide wherever possible.

⊗ Do not remove the mine warning signs (some tourists, incredibly, have taken to removing signs as souvenirs).

⊗ Do not touch mines.

⊘ If you find yourself in a mine field retrace your steps exactly, stepping into each of your foot marks.

---

roads are somewhere between difficult and impossible to pass in the **wet season** and travel will be slow and desperately uncomfortable. That said, it is probably when the country is at its most beautiful, a million shades of electric green set against stormy grey skies. It can also be a great time to visit the usually overrun temples at Angkor Wat – the throngs of Korean and Japanese tourists tend to be scared off by any wet-season induced inconvenience. The dry season offers its own challenges as wind-blown dust invades all bodily cavities and from late March to early April it starts to get unbearably hot.

Seasonal festivities are fun to witness but hardly the stuff around which to timetable a holiday. During Khmer New Year it is a lot harder to organize travel as most buses are full and hotels booked up. If you wish to travel during this period you will need to book your transport and accommodation well in advance. For visitors from neighbouring countries with larger Chinese populations, Cambodia offers a pleasant escape from Chinese New Year: it is business almost as usual.

What to do

Cambodia is not as well known for trekking activities as Vietnam and Laos with their stunning mountainous landscape. Likewise other activities, such as rafting, kayaking and cycling, are only slowly emerging and are not as developed as they are in a place like Thailand. Safety is always an issue when participating in adventurous sports: make sure you are fully covered by your travel insurance; check the credentials of operators offering adventure activities; and make sure that vehicles and safety equipment are in a good condition. Note that medical care in Cambodia is very limited, see page 31.

Cycling and mountain biking

Cambodia is offered by several tour agencies with tours centering around Angkor Wat. Some offer longer tours (13 days) starting in Phnom Penh, taking in Angkor and finishing on the coast at Sihanoukville. Many cyclists prefer to bring their own all-terrain bikes (the roads are not suitable for racers) but it's also possible to rent them from tour organizers. Tour operators include **Asia Adventures**, www.asia-adventures.com, and **Intrepid Travel**, www.intrepidtravel.com.

Diving and snorkelling

The dive industry in Cambodia is in its infant years, but the coast boasts lots of pristine coral reefs and unexplored areas. There are several dive operators in Sihanoukville, such as **Scuba Nation Diving Centre**, T012-604680. Koh Kong town is now also emerging as a potential dive destination.

Trekking

In Mondulkiri and Ratanakiri you can go out trekking on an elephant to visit villages in the ethnic minority heartland. Tours, lasting most of a day, offer a unique opportunity to explore surrounding jungle, habitat and villages. Longer two- or three-day treks usually involve camping by a lakeside or in jungle, romantically lit with fireflies.

Many tour operators offer treks in Virachey National Park via the district ranger stations. There are a number of different tours which combine jungle trekking with overnight camping, river journeys and village-based accommodation.

Getting there

Air

International connections with Cambodia are still poor – but improving – and most travellers will need to route themselves through Kuala Lumpur, Singapore or Bangkok, all of which have good onward connections to both Phnom Penh and Siem Reap. There are direct flights only from within the region.

To/from Phnom Penh These airlines currently operate international services to Phnom Penh's Pochentong Airport: **Air Asia** – Kuala Lumpur, Bangkok; **Bangkok Airways** – Bangkok; **China Airlines** – Taipei; **Silk Air** – Singapore; **Dragon Air** – Hong Kong; **Thai** – Bangkok; **Malaysia Airlines** – Kuala Lumpur; **Vietnam Airlines** – Vientiane, Ho Chi Minh City; **Shanghai Air** – Shanghai; **China Southern** – Guangzhou; **Eva** – Taipei; **Jet Star** – Singapore; **Korean & Asiana** – Incheon. New Cambodian national flag carrier **Cambodia Angkor Air** flies to and from Ho Chi Minh City. See Phnom Penh transport, page 72, for contact details for each airline.

To/from Siem Reap There are connections with **Bangkok Airways** – Bangkok; **Air Asia** – Kuala Lumpur; **Malaysia** – Kuala Lumpur; **Vietnam** – Hanoi and Ho Chi Minh City; **Jet Star** – Singapore; **Silk** – Singapore; **Korean & Asiana** – Incheon; **Lao Aviation** – Vientiane.

Getting to Singapore, Kuala Lumpur and Bangkok

Travelling to any one of these three main hubs by air offers up some of the cheapest and best connected flying on the planet. Due to high tourist and business demand pretty much every major airline from every major country in the world flies here. From these three different places a range of budget and short-haul carriers can then link the traveller to Cambodia. Direct flight times into each of these hubs are roughly 12 hours from Europe, 16 hours from the west coast of the USA and eight to 12 hours from Australia and New Zealand.

National flag carrier

Emerging from the destruction of the Pol Pot era has been a long and difficult path for Cambodia. In the post-Khmer Rouge years attempts to establish normalcy floundered and in 2001 the national flag carrying airline, Royal Air Cambodge, folded after running up losses of US$30 million.

In July 2009, after an eight-year absence, another step towards returning to 'normality' occurred when new, national airline, Cambodia Angkor Air, www.cambodiaangkorair.com, was established.

Financed largely by Vietnam and their flag carrier, Vietnam Airlines, Cambodia Angkor Air is presently flying between Siem Reap and Phnom Penh and from both those cities to Ho Chi Minh. A route between Siem Reap and Sihanoukville is also planned for some point in the future.

Singapore

Some 20 km from downtown Singapore, **Changi Airport**, www.changi.airport.com.sg, is Southeast Asia's busiest airport with most major long-haul airlines flying here from throughout the world and almost every major city in the region connected to it by air. This airport has incredible facilities including hotels, cinemas, spas, dozens of places to eat, great shopping, lots of comfortable seating and free Wi-Fi, making it easily the best place in the region to wait in between flights. **Singapore Airlines**, www.singaporeair.com – often voted one of the best in the world – is the national carrier. Another important Singaporean airline is **SilkAir**, www.silkair.com, which flies to numerous short- and mid-range destinations. Changi is also a hub for budget Asian airlines. There is a separate budget terminal – imaginatively named the **Budget Terminal**, www.btsingapore.com. A free shuttle bus service links it with Terminal 2.

Bangkok

Bangkok's **Suvarnabhumi International Airport**, one of the biggest airports in the world, has extensive connections to major cities in Europe, New Zealand and Australia. The USA is less well served, though it is possible to connect to US-bound flights via Taiwan, Japan and Korea. **Thai Airways**, www.thaiairways.com, is the national carrier.

While arriving at Suvarnabhumi is relatively painless, passenger facilities at the airport are poor. In 2007, due to a mixture of runway cracks and lack of working facilities, the old airport, **Don Muang**, 25 km to the north of the city, was forced to re-open for some domestic routes.

Despite the problems, Bangkok is still an excellent hub to reach much of the rest of the region. **Thai Airways** routing is extensive with flights to most major and capital cities in the region. Bangkok is also one of the primary hubs for budget and short-haul carriers. The main players are **Air Asia**, www.airasia.com, **Jetstar**, www.jetstar.com, and **Bangkok Airways**, www.bangkokair.com.

Chiang Mai in the north and Phuket in the south also have international airports with some scheduled short-haul connections, mainly with **Air Asia** and **Thai Airways**.

Kuala Lumpur

The Malaysian capital's **Kuala Lumpur International Airport (KLIA)** is now positioning itself as a major regional hub with the national carrier, **Malaysian Airlines**, among others,

Europe to Cambodia overland

If you've around three weeks to spare, you can travel from Europe to Cambodia overland via the Tran-Siberian Railway. It's safe, comfortable and relatively inexpensive, but good organizational skills are called for!

- London to Moscow takes 48 hours by Eurostar and high-speed train to Cologne; then take a direct Russian sleeping-car from Cologne to Moscow. Fares around £175 one way.
- Moscow to Beijing takes six nights on one of two weekly Trans-Siberian trains;

Train Four every Tuesday via Mongolia and the Gobi Desert; or *Train 20* every Friday via Manchuria. Tickets around £410 one way.
- Beijing to Hanoi (Vietnam) takes two nights on a twice-weekly train leaving every Sunday and Thursday, soft sleeper fare around £200 one way.
- From Hanoi to Ho Chi Minh City there are daily connections by train. Buses will then take you the final leg from HCMC to Phnom Penh.

For more details on overland train travel visit www.seat61.com.

providing long-haul flights from Europe, Australia/New Zealand and the USA and short-haul flights throughout the region. The KLIA airport itself is well run, efficient and comfortable.

For budget travellers there's the nearby **KLIA Low Cost Carrier Terminal** (**LCCT**), 20 minutes by shuttle bus from the main terminal. It offers some of the most extensive budget airline routings in the region, primarily with **Air Asia**, www.airasia.com, which is even now offering budget long-haul flights to the UK and Australia as well as all regional capitals and many other major destinations. Travellers should be aware that the LCCT has the most basic facilities, with long queues and bad service – transiting here can be an ordeal.

Airport departure tax International departure from Cambodia is US$25 for international flights. There is a US$6 departure tax on internal flights.

Road

It is possible to enter Cambodia, overland, from Thailand, Vietnam and Laos. Travellers coming from Thailand usually cross at **Poipet** - the road from here to Siem Reap is now massively improved cutting journey times to two hours. There are other overland entries from Thailand through Pailin (very rough roads), Anlong Veng (reasonably rough roads) and Koh Kong. As ever, the overland route from Vietnam via **Moc Bai** is the slow but cheap option for travellers coming from the east, and the border crossing at **Omsano** has enabled those coming from Vietnam to take the more scenic river route via Chau Doc. There is a brand new scenic border open via Kep between Cambodia and Vietnam (Ha Tien). There is also a crossing between Phnom Penh and Tinh Bien in Vietnam. The border crossing from Laos, close to the town at **Stung Treng**, is open but no visas are issued at the border with Laos. ▶▶ *See also box, page 18.*

Official border crossings

Cambodia–Vietnam
If travelling to Vietnam by road, ensure that your visa is appropriately stamped with the correct entry point or you will be turned back at the border. Don't forget visas for Vietnam are not available at the border.

Bavet (Cambodia)–Moc Bai (Vietnam)
There is a road crossing at Moc Bai on Highway 1 connecting Phnom Penh in Cambodia with Ho Chi Minh City via Tay Ninh Province. Travellers taking the bus from Phnom Penh to Ho Chi Minh City will cross at Bavet in Cambodia.

Kaam Samnor (Cambodia)–Vinh Xuong (Vietnam)
Further south, there is a crossing at Kaam Samnor to Vinh Xuong via Chau Doc in the Mekong Delta by boat. **Capitol** and **Narin** guesthouses organize buses to the Neak Luong ferry crossing on the Mekong from where a fast boat transports passengers to the Vietnamese border. After the border crossing there is a boat to Chau Doc. Departs 0800, arrives Chau Doc 1400, US$12.

Phnom Den (Cambodia)–Tinh Bien (Vietnam)
Further south still there is a road crossing into Vietnam at Phnom Den, approximately 22 km south of Chau Doc.

Kep (Cambodia)–Ha Tien (Vietnam)
Right at the very south of the country there is a new scenic border open at Ha Tien between Cambodia and Vietnam. As this exit/entry point is so new, fares have not been decided on. They should settle at roughly US$5 for a moto and US$10 for a tuk-tuk. Sok Lim Tours are now also offering shared-car transport from US$4. See page 214 for details.

Cambodia–Laos
The official border crossing is Don Kralor-Voem Kham (Laos) an hour north of the town of Stung Treng (see page 171). Visas for both Laos and Cambodia are now available at the border. For Cambodia the usual entry requirements apply: two passport photos and US$20. For Laos, fees vary: US$20 for Chinese citizens, US$30 for Australian citizens, US$35 for most EU nations including UK and US$42 for Canadians. You will need a passport photo as well. The border is open 0800-1700, but they may open before/after for a fee.

Most travellers pass directly through the border on bus services as the crossing point is at a remote location and few facilities are available there. All buses wait for travellers to acquire visas. At present **Sorya**, www.ppsoryatransport.com, runs the best direct service from Phnom Penh to 4000 Islands and Pakse, in Laos. This bus also stops in Stung Treng where you can hop on if there any seats left. From Stung Treng, the tour

Sea/river

There are sailings from **Ho Chi Minh City** (Saigon) to Phnom Penh. Ho Chi Minh City tour cafés run minibuses to **Chau Doc** and on to the border which is crossed on foot. Change to a speed boat which will take you to **Neak Luong** in Cambodia. Disembark here and take a taxi/pickup along Route 1 to Phnom Penh.

company XploreAsia (see page 174) also offers minibus tickets to 4000 Islands and Pakse. It should be noted there is little point arranging your own travel to the border in the hope of picking something else up on the other side as this will work out much more expensive.

Cambodia–Thailand

Cham Yem (Cambodia)–Hat Lek (Thailand)

The border crossing is 12 km from Koh Kong, across the river (15-20 minutes). The trip to the border at Cham Yem inside Cambodia costs ฿60 by moto, ฿50 by shared taxi and US$6 with own taxi. The border is open 0700-2000. There are public minibuses on the Thai side to Trat (84 km, 1¼ hours, until 1800, ฿150. You can find private taxis after 1800 but bidding will start at ฿1000. From Trat buses run to Pattaya, Bangkok and Bangkok airport.

Pruhm (Cambodia)–Daun Lem (Thailand)

There is an international border crossing at Pruhm, 20 km from Pailin. Immigration visas are ฿1000, tourist visa and ฿1500, business visa. They could refuse dollars so ensure you have baht. The crossing is known for scams similar to those found in Poipet. You will need to bring passport photographs with you as there is no photography processing facility here. From Pailin it is ฿50 per person in a shared taxi to the border which is around 20 km away. There are usually motos and taxis at the border crossing to take tourists at Pailin. From the Thai side it is a ฿20 motorbike ride to the *songthaew* station, which has *songthaews* to the nearest bus station at Chantaburi. It takes 1½ hours to reach Chantaburi bus station and it costs ฿35.

Poipet (Cambodia)–Aranya Prathet (Thailand)

The border crossing between Poipet and Thailand is open daily 0730-1700 and is a very popular route for budget-conscious foreigners entering Cambodia. The immigration officials at the Poipet border can be difficult.

Transport from Thailand The bus takes four to five hours, air conditioned ฿160-200, non air conditioned ฿100; buses leave from the northern bus station in Bangkok. Take a motorbike, ฿25, or tuk-tuk, ฿40-50, the 7 km from Aranya Prathet to the Cambodian border. The train takes six to eight hours, ฿100 (US$1), from Bangkok to Aranya Prathet. For travel details from Poipet, see page 156.

O'Smach (Cambodia)–Chong Jom (Thailand)

Fifteen kilometres north of Anlong Veng lies the border crossing at O'Smach. The crossing is open 0830-1600 (1700 at a push). Pick-ups leave from Anlong market early in the morning, 3000 riel. For people travelling from Thailand the best bet is to take public transport to Surin (by bus or train) and then organize a tuk-tuk from there to the border.

Some boats travel from Thailand's Koh Chang/Trat area to Hat Lek for the Koh Kong border crossing but these are mostly seasonal and vary according to demand.

Cruise ships visit the international seaport of Sihanoukville.

Getting around

Air

At the moment the only domestic route within Cambodia that operates safely and with any frequency is between Phnom Penh and Siem Reap with **Siem Reap Airways**, www.siemreapairways.com, and **Cambodia Angkor Air**, www.cambodiaangkorair.com.

Rail

There are two lines out of Phnom Penh: one to Poipet on the Thai border which goes via Pursat, Battambang and Sisophon; the second, which runs south to Sihanoukville on the coast via Takeo, Kep and Kampot. At the time of publication neither were operating.

Road

Over the last few years the road system in Cambodia has dramatically improved. A trunk route of international standards, apart from a few gnarly stretches, now links Stung Treng to Koh Kong. New bridges are being built and other short cuts are being created. Much of the rest of the network is pretty basic and journeys can sometimes be long and labourious. Also, to some parts, such as Ratanakiri, the road is a graded, laterite track, untarmacked and potholed. In the rainy season expect to be slowed down on many roads to slithering muddy crawl. The Khmer-American Friendship Highway (Route 4), which runs from Phnom Penh to Sihanoukville, is entirely tarmacked. The infamous National Highway 6, which runs between Poipet and Phnom Penh, has had extensive work and is tarmacked between Siem Reap and Phnom Penh. National Highway 1 has also been extensively improved. The Japanese in particular have put considerable resources into road and bridge building.

The roads from Phnom Penh are numbered 1-10 in a clockwise order starting from Highway 1, which runs to Ho Chi Minh City. The worst roads in the country are in the central region between Preah Vihear, Kompong Thom and T'Beng Meanchey. Some of the remote northeastern roads, particularly around Mondulkiri and Ratanakiri, can also be a bit rough. The road from Sisophon to Siem Reap is in an appalling condition and can take from four to eight hours depending on the season. In the east the roads have improved in the last couple of years, due to the demands of logging: not the best of reasons. Even so they are still pretty nerve-wracking.

Bus and shared taxi There are buses and shared taxis to most parts of the country. Shared taxis (generally Toyota Camrys) or pickups are usually the quickest and most reliable public transport option. The taxi operators charge a premium for better seats and you can buy yourself more space. It is not uncommon for a taxi to fit 10 people in it, including two sitting on the driver's seat. Fares for riding in the back of the truck are half that for riding in the cab. The Sihanoukville run has an excellent and cheap air-conditioned bus service.

Car hire and taxi A few travel agents and hotels may be able to organize self-drive car hire and most hotels have cars for hire with a driver (US$30-50 per day). There is a limited taxi service in Phnom Penh.

Moto The most popular and sensible option is the motorbike taxi, known as 'moto'. This costs around the same as renting your own machine and with luck you will get a driver who speaks a bit of English and who knows where he's going. Once you have found a good driver stick with him: handing out the odd drink, a packet of cigarettes or an extra dollar or two is a good investment. Outside Phnom Penh and Siem Reap, do not expect much English from your moto driver.

Motorbike and bicycle hire Motorbikes can be rented from between US$5 and US$8 per day and around US$1 per day for a bicycle. If riding either a motorbike or bicycle be aware that the accident rate is very high. This is partly because of the poor condition of many of the cars, trucks and other vehicles on the road; partly because of poor roads; and partly because of horrendously poor driving. If you do rent a motorbike ensure it has a working horn (imperative) and buy some rear-view mirrors so you can keep an eye on the traffic. Wear a helmet (even if using a motodop); it may not be cool but neither is a fractured skull. More experienced motorcyclists can also rent more higher-powered dirt bikes of 250cc and over from about US$25 per day.

River

All the Mekong towns and settlements around the Tonlé Sap are accessible by boat. It is a very quick and relatively comfortable way of travel and much cheaper than flying. The route between Siem Reap and Phnom Penh is very popular while the route between Siem Reap and Battambang is one of the most scenic. For those on a budget it is the best way to go. With the new road opening, boats are no longer used as a main form of transport along the Mekong and in the northeast.

Maps

Regional maps **Bartholomew** Southeast Asia (1:5,800,000); **Nelles** Southeast Asia (1:4,000,000); **Hildebrand** Thailand, Burma, Malaysia and Singapore (1:2,800,000).
Country maps **Gecko Maps** (1:750,000), highly recommended. **Periplus** Cambodia (1:1,100,000); **Nelles** Vietnam, Laos and Cambodia (1:1,500,000); **Bartholomew** Vietnam, Laos and Cambodia (1:2,000,000).
City maps **The Periplus Cambodia** map also has a good map of Phnom Penh (1:17,000) and a detailed map of Angkor (1:95,000). **Gecko Maps** (1:750,000) has a good map of Siem Reap, Sihanoukville and Phnom Penh. There is a 3D map of Siem Reap and Phnom Penh, which is quite good and is distributed for free in restaurants, bars and guesthouses.
Other maps **Tactical Pilotage Charts** (TPC, US Airforce) (1:500,000); **Operational Navigational Charts** (ONC, US Airforce) (1:500,000). Both of these are particularly good at showing relief features (useful for planning treks); less good on roads, towns and facilities.

Sleeping price codes

LL over US$200 **Luxury**: mostly found in Bangkok with some in Ho Chi Minh City, Hanoi, Luang Prabang, Phnom Penh and Siem Reap. Some beach and mountain resorts also fall into this category.

L-AL US$101-200 **First class plus**: there are a number of hotels in this category found in all the major cities and some smaller ones plus resorts across the region. A full range of facilities will be included.

A US$66-100 **First class**: these hotels are increasingly found in towns across Vietnam but less so in Cambodia and Laos. Hotels in this category should offer reasonable business services, a range of recreational facilities, restaurants and bars, although these services will be more limited in Cambodia and Laos.

B US$46-65 **Tourist class**: all rooms will have air conditioning and an attached bathroom with hot water. Other services should include one or more restaurants, a bar and room service. In Bangkok and Vietnamese beach resorts a pool may be available.

C US$31-45 **Economy**: rooms should be air conditioned in Vietnam and Laos but not necessarily in Cambodia and will have attached bathrooms with hot water and Western toilets. A restaurant and room service will probably be available. In Vietnam and Laos a pool may be available.

D-E US$12-30 **Medium budget**: air-conditioned en suite rooms in Vietnam and Laos although not necessarily in Cambodia.

F US$7-11 **Budget/guesthouse**: usually fan-cooled rooms and often shared bathrooms with basic facilities. Bed linen should be provided, towels may not be. Rooms are small and facilities few. In Vietnam, at the higher end, air conditioning will be available.

G US$6 and under **Dormitory/guesthouse-type accommodation**: with shared bathroom facilities, squat or Western toilets, fan-cooled and probably but not necessarily cold-water showers. Cleanliness will vary.

Sleeping

Accommodation standards in Cambodia have greatly improved over the last couple of years. Phnom Penh now has a good network of genuine boutique hotels – arguably they are overpriced and sometimes management can be a bit Fawlty Towers but the bar has certainly been raised. Siem Reap, without doubt, has now become a destination for the upmarket international traveller. The range, depth and quality of accommodation here is of an excellent standard and is on a par with anywhere else in Asia. Even if you travel to some of the smaller, less visited towns, family-run Chinese-style hotels should now provide hot water, air conditioning and cable TV even if they can't provide first-class service. These places are often the best bargains in the country as many of the cheap backpacker places, while very, very cheap, are mostly hovels.

More expensive hotels have safety boxes in the rooms. In cheaper hotels it is not uncommon for things to be stolen from bedrooms. In Phnom Penh this poses a real dilemma for it is more dangerous to take valuables on to the night time streets. Most hotels and guesthouses will accept valuables for safekeeping but do keep a close eye on your cash.

Eating price codes

�y♈♈	Expensive	over US$12
♈♈	Mid-range	US$6-12
♈	Cheap	under US$6

Prices refer to the cost of a two-course meal for one person, excluding drinks or tips.

Eating

For a country that has suffered and starved in the way Cambodia has, eating for fun as opposed to for survival, has yet to catch on as a pastime. There are some good restaurants and things are improving but don't expect Cambodia to be a smaller version of Thailand, or its cuisine even to live up to the standards of Laos. Cambodian food shows clear links with the cuisines of neighbouring countries: Thailand, Vietnam, and to a lesser extent, Laos. The influence of the French colonial period is also in evidence, most clearly in the availability of good French bread. Chinese food is also available owing to strong business ties between Cambodia and China. True Khmer food is difficult to find and much that the Khmers would like to claim as indigenous food is actually of Thai, French or Vietnamese origin. Curries, soups, rice and noodle-based dishes, salads, fried vegetables and sliced meats all feature in Khmer cooking.

Phnom Penh and Siem Reap have the best **restaurants** with French, Japanese, Italian and Indian food being available. But those who want to sample a range of dishes and get a feel for Khmer cuisine should head for the nearest market where dishes will be cooked on order in a wok – known locally as a *chhnang khteak*.

International **soft drinks** are widely available in Cambodia. If there is a national drink in Cambodia, then it has to be **tea** which is drunk without sugar or milk. **Coffee** is also available black or 'crème' with sweetened condensed milk. That ubiquitous and well-known brand of cola is available as well as most other international soft drinks. Soda water with lemon, *soda kroch chhmar*, is a popular drink. **Bottled water** is widely available; local mineral water too. **Fruit smoothies** – known locally as *tikalok* – are found at stalls with that give-away food processor on the counter. If you want to avoid consuming your fruit with horrendous quantities of sugar then make sure you make your intentions clear. Most market stands will serve great fruit smoothies, but again, you might wish to request minimal sweet milk and stipulate whether you want egg or not. Fresh **milk** is hard to find outside of metropolitan areas.

Local and imported **beers** are available. Of the locally brewed beers the three most common are Angkor Beer, Anchor and ABC Stout – available on draught, in bottles and cans. VB or Victoria Bitter is also brewed locally but is much less common. Beer Lao, although imported, is usually the cheapest and also one of the best – popular with cost-conscious visitors.

Fishy business

Every national cuisine has its signature dish and in Cambodia it is *prahok*, a strong, pungent, fermented fish paste that's been used to flavour Khmer dishes for centuries.

Cambodians swear by it and use it in everything from dips and soups, through to a simple accompaniment for rice. Reports suggest that 95% of Cambodians eat the delicacy, so it is no surprise that the practice of making it has passed down from generation to generation.

The Fisheries Department believe that in some areas 10% of fish caught are set aside for the manufacture of *prahok*. The paste is made by stomping on hundreds of small fish and fish heads in a large bucket. Once the fish is transformed into a thick brown paste it's left in the sun for a day to ferment. Salt is then added and the paste is put in jars and sold.

Locals suggest that *prahok* can be eaten after a month of maturation, but most consider the paste to be at its best after a few years. This is a Cambodian delicacy, like sushi or parmesan cheese, and may taste a bit unusual at first, it is something of an acquired taste (if you can get past the smell).

Festivals and events

There are several different public holidays celebrated each year in Cambodia (see page 33). Most are celebrated with parades and special events to commemorate the particular holiday. The largest holidays also see many Khmers – although less than used to be the case – loosing off their guns, to the extent that red tracer fills the sky. The habit of firing weapons also extends to nights with a full moon and the onset of the rainy season. It is best to stay indoors at such times, as the concept of 'what goes up must come down' does not seem to be recognized in Cambodia. Several interesting festivals enliven the Cambodian calendar which festival-goers would be disappointed to miss. The major festivals mark important events in the farming year, determined by seasonal changes in the weather, and are listed below.

January

1 and 7 Jan New Year's Day (public holiday), **National Day** and **Victory over Pol Pot** (public holiday). Celebration of the fall of the Khmer Rouge in 1979. It is also the anniversary of the beginning of the Vietnamese occupation of the country, leading some people to lobby against it being declared a national holiday.
Jan/Feb Chinese and Vietnamese New Year (movable). Celebrated by the Chinese and Vietnamese communities. **Anniversary of the last sermon of Buddha** (movable).

March

8 Mar Women's Day (public holiday). Processions, floats and banners in main towns.

April

13-15 Apr Cambodian New Year or Bonn Chaul Chhnam (public holiday). A 3-day celebration to mark the turn of the year. Predictions are made for the forthcoming year, the celebration is to show gratitude to the departing demi-god and to welcome the new one. Every household erects a small altar to welcome a new demi-god, filled with offerings of food and drink. Homes are spring cleaned. Householders visit temples and traditional games like *boh angkunh* and *chhoal chhoung* are played and ritual festivities are performed.
17 Apr Independence Day (public holiday). Celebrates the fall of the Lon Nol government

(17 April 1975) with floats and parades through Phnom Penh.

Chaul Chhnam (movable). 3-day celebration, which involves an inevitable drenching, to welcome in the new year. A similar festival to Pimai in Laos and Songkran in Thailand.

April/May

Visak Bauchea (movable – full moon, public holiday). The most important Buddhist festival; a triple anniversary commemorating Buddha's birth, enlightenment and his Paranirvana (state of final bliss).

May

9 May Genocide Day (public holiday). To remember the atrocities of the Khmer Rouge in which nearly 2 million Cambodians lost their lives. The main ceremony is held at Choeng Ek, just south of Phnom Penh.

Royal Ploughing Ceremony (movable, public holiday). As in Thailand, this marks the beginning of the rainy season and traditionally is meant to alert farmers to the fact that the job of rice cultivation is set to begin (as if farmers need any advance warning!). Known as *bonn chroat preah nongkoal* in Khmer, the ceremony is held on a field close to the Royal Palace in Phnom Penh. The land is ploughed by a man (King of Meakh) while the seed is sowed by a woman (Queen Me Hour), reflecting the gender division of labour in agriculture and probably also symbolizing fertility. The sacred cows are led to silver trays holding rice, corn and other foods. Depending on their choice of food, this is taken as an omen for the coming year.

June

19 Jun Anniversary of the Founding of the Revolutionary Armed Forces of Kampuchea. Founded in 1951, main parades and celebrations are in Phnom Penh.

28 Jun Anniversary of the founding of the People's Revolutionary Party of Cambodia. Founded in 1951, again, the main parades and celebrations are in Phnom Penh.

July

Chol Vassa (moveable). The start of the rainy season retreat – a Buddhist 'lent' – for meditation. (movable with the full moon), the most important Buddhist festival; a triple anniversary commemorating Buddha's birth, enlightenment and his Paranirvana (state of final bliss).

September

End of Buddhist 'lent' (movable). In certain areas it is celebrated with boat races.

Prachum Ben (movable, public holiday). In remembrance of the dead, offerings are made to the ancestors.

October/November

Oct/Nov Water Festival, Bon Om Tuk (movable, public holiday) or **Festival of the Reversing Current**. To celebrate the movement of the waters out of the Tonlé Sap (see page 123), boat races are held in Phnom Penh. The festival dates back to the 12th century when King Jayavarman VII and his navy defeated water-borne invaders. Most wats have ceremonial canoes which are rowed by the monks to summon the Naga King. Boat races extend over 3 days with more than 200 competitors but the highlight is the evening gala in Phnom Penh when a fleet of boats, studded with lights, row out under the full moon. Under the Cambodian monarchy, the king would command the waters to retreat. The festival was only revived in 1990. In addition to celebrating the reversing of the flow of the Tonlé Sap River, this festival marks the onset of the fishing season. (The Khmer diaspora in Vietnam celebrate the same festival at the same time further down the Mekong in Soc Trang.) The festival coincides with **Ok Ambok** (The Pounding of Rice).

30 Oct-1 Nov King Sihanouk's Birthday (public holiday). Public offices and museums close for about a week and a firework display is mounted by the river close to the Royal Palace in Phnom Penh.

November	December
9 Nov Independence Day (public holiday) Marks Cambodia's independence from French colonial rule in 1953.	**Late Dec Half marathon**. A half marathon is held at Angkor Wat, surely one of the most spectacular places to work up a sweat.

Shopping

Cambodia craftsmanship is excellent and whether you are in search of silverware, colourful *kramas*, hand-loomed sarongs or bronze buddhas you will find them all in abundance. A great favourite for its range and quality of antiques, jewellery and fabrics is the **Russian Market** (Psar Tuol Tom Pong) in Phnom Penh. Silverware, gold and gems are available in the **Central Market** (Psar Thmei). The contents of the shops and markets away from Phnom Penh are leaner and meaner although Siem Reap has a good selection. Until the purchasing power of the provinces picks up, or tourists start fanning out in greater numbers, you are advised to stock up on souvenirs in the two main centres.

Most of the markets in Cambodia, even the tiniest of rural markets, sell gems. For the most part guarantees of authenticity are not readily available – a lot of the sapphires have been heated to create a sparkly blue colour, as have the rubies. When buying gems abide by the philosophy, if it's too good to be true it probably isn't. If you are looking to buy any gems, your best bet is to look into semi-precious stones such as amethyst or zircon.

Responsible travel

Since the early 1990s there has been a phenomenal growth in 'ecotourism', which promotes and supports the conservation of natural environments and is also fair and equitable to local communities. While the authenticity of some ecotourism operators needs to be interpreted with care, there is clearly both a huge demand for this type of activity and also significant opportunities to support worthwhile conservation and social development initiatives by this means. **Green Globe** (T020-7730 4428, www.greenglobe21.com) and **Responsible Travel** (www.responsibletravel.com) offer advice for travellers on selecting destinations and sites focused on conservation and sustainable development.

In addition, the **International Eco-Tourism Society** (www.ecotourism.org), **Tourism Concern** (T020-7753 3330, www.tourismconcern.org.uk), and **Planeta** (www.planeta.com), develop and promote ecotourism projects in destinations all over the world and their websites provide details for initiatives throughout Southeast Asia.

For opportunities to participate directly in scientific research and development projects, contact **Earthwatch** (www.earthwatch.org), **Discovery International** (www.discovery initiatives.com) and the **Nautilus Institute** (www.nautilus.org), which focuses on environmental and sustainability issues in the Asia-Pacific region. See also box opposite and on page 36.

How big is your footprint?

The benefits of international travel are self-evident for both hosts and travellers: employment, increased understanding of different cultures, business and leisure opportunities. At the same time there is clearly a downside to the industry. Where visitor pressure is high or poorly regulated, adverse impacts to society and the natural environment may occur. In order to ensure your contribution to the host nation is a positive one, Tourism Concern has these guidelines on its website, www.tourismconcern.org.uk.

→ Learn about the country you're visiting. Start enjoying your travels before you leave by tapping into as many sources of information as you can.

→ Think about where your money goes – be fair and realistic about how cheaply you travel. Try and put money into local people's hands; drink local beer or fruit juice rather than imported brands, and stay in locally-owned accommodation.

→ Open your mind to new cultures and traditions. It can transform your holiday experience and you'll earn respect and be more readily welcomed by local people.

→ Think about what happens to your rubbish: take biodegradable products and a water filter bottle. Be sensitive to limited resources like water, fuel and electricity.

→ Help preserve local wildlife and habitats by respecting rules and regulations, such as sticking to footpaths, not standing on coral and not buying products made from endangered plants or animals.

→ Use your guidebook as a starting point, not the only source of information. Talk to local people, then discover your own adventure.

→ Don't treat people as part of the landscape; they may not want their picture taken. Put yourself in their shoes, ask first and respect their wishes.

Local customs and conduct

Cambodians are relaxed, easy-going people who are unlikely to take or give offence. Decent behaviour is never going to upset the Cambodians and it is difficult for normal people to offend them unwittingly. Only crass behaviour, such as patting people on the head or invading their homes uninvited, will upset them. One of the sheer joys of Cambodia and the reason for its enduring popularity among travellers is the simplicity of the way of life and the population's tolerance of others.

Temples When visiting a temple do dress respectfully (keep bare flesh to a minimum) and take off your hat and shoes. Put your legs to one side and try not to point the soles of your feet at anyone or the Buddha image. Females are not to touch monks or sit beside them on public transport. Shoes should be removed before entering temples and a small donation is often appropriate.

Greeting Cambodians use their traditional greeting – the 'wai' – bowing with their hands held together. As a foreigner, shaking hands is perfectly acceptable.

In private homes It is polite to take your shoes off on entering the house and a small present goes down well if you are invited for a meal.

HOPE (Harnessing Opportunities through Play and Education)

Identifying and assisting pro-active, savvy grassroot organisations in Cambodia, the UK-based charity **Harnessing Opportunities through Play and Education (HOPE)** is committed to giving Cambodian kids a childhood and young adults a better future, through play, education and development, in order to harness opportunities and permanent, positive change.

Many tourists come to Cambodia and feel an urgent need to help the cute little ones, often street kids that run around shoeless and dirty, but it's easy to forget that little orphans grow up, and need to find sustainable employment to provide for them later on. Without providing for older orphans in terms of education and survival skills, there's little point taking kids into care if all it does is defer the time before the children and young adults are back living off the streets in poverty.

Supporting various young adult programmes, HOPE help vulnerable young adults to integrate into the community by providing them with ongoing financial support (whether at home or with their education), finding vocational skills training opportunities and part-time work. With background from the tourism and hospitality industry, HOPE aims to utilize the many opportunities tourism brings, and, in addition to completing their education, many young adults are already in industry training to benefit from the tourism growth.

Refreshingly, HOPE is not re-inventing the wheel, but simply assisting and supporting existing projects with similar values and long term goals.

For more information about HOPE and how you can help, please visit www.hopeforcambodia.org.uk.

General Displays of anger or exasperation are considered unacceptable and therefore reflect very badly on the individual. Accordingly, even in adversity, Khmers (like the Thais) will keep smiling. Displays of affection are also considered embarrassing and should be avoided in public areas. Try not to pat anyone on the head. To beckon someone, use your hand with the palm facing downwards. Pointing is rude.

Women should **dress appropriately**. Short skirts, midriff-baring and cleavage-exposing tops and tight outfits are deemed clothes that prostitutes wear. If you choose to dress like this then you may unwittingly attract undesirable attention and potentially offend some people.

Essentials A-Z

Accident and emergency

Contact the relevant emergency service and your embassy (see page 74). Make sure you obtain police/medical reports in order to file insurance claims.

Emergency services Police: 117, Fire: 118, Ambulance: 119.

Children

Travelling with children can be a most rewarding experience in Cambodia, and with sufficient care and planning, it can also be safe. Children are often excellent passports into a local culture – the Khmers love babies and children – and you will also receive the best service and help from officials and members of the public when in difficulty if you have kids with you. Be aware that expensive hotels as well as market stalls may have squalid cooking conditions and try to ensure that children do not drink any water (especially important when bathing). Bottled water and fizzy drinks are widely available.

For babies, powdered milk is available in provincial centres, although most brands have added sugar. Breastfeeding is strongly recommended if possible. Baby food can also be bought in some towns – the quality may not be the same as equivalent foods bought in the West, but it is perfectly adequate for short periods. Disposable nappies can be bought in Phnom Penh, but are often expensive.

Customs and duty free

Customs tend to be very relaxed both on arrival and departure. A reasonable amount of tobacco products and spirits can be taken in without incurring customs duty – roughly 200 cigarettes or the equivalent quantity of tobacco, 1 bottle of liquor and perfume for personal use. Taking any Angkorian-era images out of the country is strictly forbidden.

Disabled travellers

Cambodia may have the world's highest incidence of one-legged and no-legged people (because of landmine injuries) but this does not mean that facilities for the disabled are well developed. In short, Cambodia is not an easy country for the disabled traveller: pavements are often uneven, there are potholes galore, pedestrian crossings are ignored, ramps are unheard of and lifts are few and far between. On top of this, numerous other hazards abound, among the most dangerous of which must number the taxi and moto drivers whose philosophy on road safety is eccentric to say the least. However, while there are scores of hurdles that disabled people will have to negotiate, the Cambodians themselves are likely to go out of their way to be helpful. See also Angkor, page 81, for specific information.

Drugs

As Amit Gilboa's book, *Off the Rails in Phnom Penh*, makes clear, drugs are readily available and cheap in Cambodia. Many places use marijuana in their cooking and the police seem to be quite ambivalent to dope smokers (unless they need to supplement their income with your bribe money, in which case – watch out). Drugs (including marijuana) are illegal, so there is always a legal risk if you wish to indulge.

Without exaggeration, one of the biggest dangers for travellers who take drugs in Cambodia today is dying of an overdose. You run a much higher risk of this than of being shot, beaten, blown up by a landmine or other 'dangers' associated with this 'Off the Rails' lifestyle. Travellers are the highest risk group when it comes to drug overdoses (or at least the group most reported). The backpacker areas around the lake in Phnom Penh and Sihanoukville are particularly prone to the problem, with travellers being pulled dead from seedy guesthouses week in week out.

The frequency of overdoses is largely attributed to the fact that the people buying drugs aren't getting what they thought they were. It is believed that most people found dead (by overdose) thought they had bought ecstasy or cocaine but had in fact been given heroin. It is important to note that cocaine and ecstasy do not really exist in Cambodia, despite what you may be told.

Another particularly nasty side effect from the drugs explosion in Cambodia is the introduction of *yaa baa*. Although the drug has been around the region for a while it really has taken a stranglehold on Cambodia, especially in urban areas. It is a particularly nasty amphetamine that is said to have sent numerous people mad and can also be lethal.

In a nutshell: don't buy illicit drugs in Cambodia, it is dangerous.

Electricity

Voltage 220. Sockets are usually round 2-pin.

Embassies and consulates.

A full list of Cambodian embassies and consulates can be found on www.cambodia.gov.kh.
Australia and New Zealand 5 Canterbury Cres, Deakin, Canberra, ACT 2600, T+61-2-6273 1259, www.embassyof cambodia.org.nz/au.htm.
France 4 rue Adolphe Yvon, 75116 Paris, T+33-1-4503 4720, ambcambodgeparis@ mangoosta.fr.

Germany Benjamin-Vogelsdorf Strasse, 213187, Berlin, T+49-30-4863 7901, www.kambodscha-botschaft.de.
Japan 8-6-9, Akasaka, Minato-Ku, Tokyo 1070052, T+81-3-5412 8522, www.cambodianembassy.jp.
Laos Thadeua Rd, KM2 Vientiane, BP34, T+856-2-131 4950, recmlao@laotel.com.
Thailand 185 Rajdamri Rd, Lumpini Patumwan, Bangkok 10330, T+66-2-254 6630, recbkk@cscoms.com.
United Kingdom and **Scandinavian countries**, 64 Brondesbury Park, Willesden Green, London, NW6 7AT, T020-8451 7850, www.cambodianembassy.org.uk.
USA 4500, 16th St, NW Washington, DC20011, T+1-202-726 8042, www.embassy.org/cambodia.
Vietnam 71 Tran Hung Dao St, Hanoi, T844-942 4789, arch@fpt.vn; 41 Phung Khac Khoan, Ho Chi Minh City, T848-829 2751, cambocg@hcm.vmn.vn.

Gay and lesbian

Gay and lesbian travellers will have no problems in Cambodia. Men often hold other men's hands as do women, so this kind of affection is commonplace. Any kind of passionate kissing or sexually orientated affection in public, however, is taboo – both for straight and gay people. The gay scene is just starting to develop in Cambodia but there is definitely a scene in the making. **Linga Bar** in Siem Reap and the **Salt Lounge** in Phnom Penh are both gay bars and are excellent choices for a night out.

Health

See your GP or travel clinic at least 6 weeks before departure for general advice on travel risks and vaccinations. Try phoning a specialist travel clinic if your own doctor is unfamiliar with health conditions in

Cambodia. Make sure you have sufficient medical travel insurance, get a dental check, know your own blood group and if you suffer a long-term condition such as diabetes or epilepsy, obtain a **Medic Alert** bracelet/necklace (www.medicalert.co.uk). If you wear glasses, take a copy of your prescription.

Vaccinations

It is advisable to vaccinate against polio, tetanus, typhoid, hepatitis A, and rabies if going to more remote areas. Yellow fever does not exist in Cambodia, but the authorities may wish to see a certificate if you have recently arrived from an endemic area in Africa or South America. Japanese Encephalitis may be advised for some areas, depending on the duration of the trip and proximity to rice-growing and pig-farming areas.

Health risks

The most common cause of travellers' **diarrhoea** is from eating food contaminated food. Swimming in sea or river water that has been contaminated by sewage can also be a cause; ask locally if it is safe. Diarrhoea may be also caused by viruses, bacteria (such as E-coli), protozoal (such as giardia), salmonella and cholera. It may be accompanied by vomiting or by severe abdominal pain. Any kind of diarrhoea responds well to the replacement of water and salts. Sachets of rehydration salts can be bought in most chemists and can be dissolved in boiled water. If the symptoms persist, consult a doctor. Tap water in the major cities is in theory safe to drink but it may be advisable to err on the side of caution and drink only bottled or boiled water. Avoid having ice in drinks unless you trust that it is from a reliable source.

Mosquitoes are more of a nuisance than a serious hazard but some, of course, are carriers of serious diseases such as **malaria**, which exists in most of Cambodia except Phnom Penh. The choice of malaria prophylaxis will need to be something other than chloroquine for most people, since there is such a high level of resistance to it.

Always check with your doctor or travel clinic for the most up-to-date advice on the best anti-malarials to use. It's also sensible to avoid being bitten as much as possible. Sleep off the ground and use a mosquito net and some kind of insecticide. Mosquito coils release insecticide as they burn and are available in many shops, as are tablets of insecticide, which are placed on a heated mat plugged into a wall socket.

Each year there is the possibility that **avian flu** or **SARS** might rear their ugly heads. Check the news reports. If there is a problem in an area you are due to visit you may be advised to have an ordinary flu shot or to seek expert advice.

There are high rates of HIV in the region, especially among sex workers.

If you get sick

Contact your embassy or consulate for a list of doctors and dentists who speak your language, or at least some English. Doctors and health facilities in major cities are also listed in the Directory sections of this book. Make sure you have adequate insurance (see below). Hospitals are not recommended anywhere in Cambodia (even at some of the clinics that profess to be 'international'). If you fall ill or are injured your best bet is to get yourself quickly to either **Bumrungrad Hospital** or **Bangkok Nursing Home**, both in Bangkok. Both hospitals are of an exceptional standard, even in international terms.

Thailand

Bumrungrad Hospital, Soi 3 Sukhumvit, Bangkok, T+66 2-667 1000, www.bumrungrad. com. The best option: a world-class hospital with brilliant medical facilities.

Useful websites

www.btha.org British Travel Health Association.
www.cdc.gov US government site that gives excellent advice on travel health and details of disease outbreaks.

www.fco.gov.uk British Foreign and Commonwealth Office travel site has useful information on each country, people, climate and a list of UK embassies/consulates.
www.fitfortravel.scot.nhs.uk A-Z of vaccine/health advice for each country.
www.numberonehealth.co.uk Travel screening services, vaccine and travel health advice, email/SMS text vaccine reminders and screens returned travellers for tropical diseases.

Insurance

Always take out travel insurance before you set off and read the small print carefully. Check that the policy covers the activities you intend, or may end up doing. Also check exactly what your medical cover includes, ie ambulance, helicopter rescue or emergency flights back home. Also check the payment protocol. You may have to cough up first before the insurance company reimburses you. It is always best to dig out all the receipts for expensive personal effects like jewellery or cameras. Take photos of these items and note down all serial numbers. You are advised to shop around. **STA Travel**, T0871-230 0040, www.statravel.co.uk, and other reputable student travel organizations offer good value policies. Young travellers from North America can try the **International Student Insurance Service (ISIS)**, available through STA Travel, T1-800-7770112, www.sta-travel.com. Older travellers should note that some companies will not cover people over 65 years old, or may charge higher premiums. Please also note your nation's ongoing travel warnings – if you travel to areas or places that are not recommended for travel your insurance may be invalid.

Internet

Cambodia is surprisingly well connected and most medium-sized to large towns have internet access. Not surprisingly, internet is

a lot more expensive in smaller towns, up to a whopping US$5 per hr. In Phnom Penh internet rates are US$1-2 per hr and in Siem Reap it should be US$1 per hr or under. Most guesthouses and hotels and many cafés and restaurants now have free Wi-Fi access. In the more developed areas you'll now also find an excellent 3G network, often operating at higher speeds than fixed-line internet. See Telephone, page 34, for more details.

Language

In Cambodia the national language is Khmer (pronounced 'Khmei'). It is not tonal and the script is derived from the southern Indian alphabet. French is spoken by the older generation who survived the Khmer Rouge era. English is the language of the younger generations. Away from Phnom Penh, Siem Reap and Sihanoukville it can be difficult to communicate with the local population unless you speak Khmer.

Media

Cambodia has a vigorous English-language press which fights bravely for editorial independence and freedom to criticize politicians. The principal English-language newspapers are the fortnightly *Phnom Penh Post*, which many regard as the best and the *Cambodia Daily*, published 5 times per week. There are also several tourist magazine guides. The **BBC World Service** provides probably the best news and views on Asia (available on 100 FM).

Money

The **riel** is the official currency though US dollars are widely accepted and easily exchanged. At the time of going to press the **exchange rates** were US$1 = 4230, UK£1= 6605, €1 = 5507.

In Phnom Penh and other towns most goods and services are priced in dollars and there is little need to buy riel. In remote rural areas prices are quoted in riel (except accommodation). In many places, particularly near the Thai border, Thai baht can often be used as well.

Money can be exchanged in banks and hotels. US dollar traveller's cheques are easiest to exchange – commission ranges from 1% to 3%. Cash advances on credit cards are available. Credit card facilities are limited but some banks, hotels and restaurants do accept them, mostly in the tourist centres. **ANZ Royal Bank** has recently opened a number of ATMs throughout Phnom Penh and Siem Reap. Machines are also now appearing in other towns and a full ATM network should be established in the next couple of years. Most machines give US dollars only.

Opening hours

Shops Daily from 0800-2000. Some, however, stay open for a further hour or 2, especially in tourist centres. Most markets open daily between 0530/0600 and 1700.
Banks Mon-Fri 0800-1600. Some close 1100-1300. Some major branches are open until 1100 on Sat.
Offices Mon-Fri 0730-1130, 1330-1630.
Restaurants, cafés and bars Daily from 0700-0800, although some open earlier. Bars are meant to close at 2400 by law.

Police and the law

A vast array of offences are punishable in Cambodia, from minor traffic violations through to possession of drugs. If you are arrested or are having difficulty with the police contact your embassy immediately. As the police only earn approximately US$20 a month, corruption is a problem and contact should be avoided, unless absolutely necessary. Most services, including the provision of police reports, will require paying bribes. Law enforcement is very haphazard, at times completely subjective and justice can be hard to find. Some smaller crimes can attract large penalties while perpetrators of greater crimes often get off completely.

Post

International service is unpredictable but it is reasonably priced and fairly reliable (at least from Phnom Penh). Only send mail from the GPO in any given town rather than sub POs or mail boxes. **Fedex** and **DHL** also offer services.

Public holidays

1 Jan National Day and Victory over Pol Pot.
7 Jan Celebration of the fall of the Khmer Rouge in 1979.
8 Mar Women's Day. Processions, floats and banners in main towns.
13-15 Apr Cambodian New Year (Bonn Chaul Chhnam).
17 Apr Independence Day
Apr/May Visak Bauchea.
1 May Labour Day
9 May Genocide Day
1 Jun International Children's Day
18 Jun Her Majesty Preah Akkaek Mohesey Norodom Monineath Sihanouk's Birthday.
Sep (moveable) End of Buddhist 'lent'.
24 Sep Constitution Day
23 Oct Paris Peace Accord
Oct/Nov Water Festival (Bon Om Tuk) or Festival of the Reversing Current.
30 Oct-1 Nov King Sihanouk's Birthday
9 Nov Independence Day (1953)
10 Dec Human Rights Day

Safety

Cambodia is not as dangerous as some would have us believe. The country has really moved forward in protecting tourists and violent crimes towards visitors is comparatively low. Since large penalties have been introduced for those who kill or maim tourists, random acts of violence aren't as common these days. Having said that, night time safety on the streets of Phnom Penh is a problem; robberies and hold-ups are common. Many robbers are armed, so do not resist. As Phnom Penh has a limited taxi service, travel after dark poses a problem. Stick to moto drivers you know. Women are, obviously, particularly targeted by bag snatchers but many bag snatchers will now be chased by the locals, beaten and sometimes even killed. Khmer New Year is known locally as the 'robbery season'. Theft is endemic at this time of year so be on red alert. A common trick around New Year is for robbers to mess around with tourists (usually throwing water and talcum powder in the eyes) and rob them – literally – blind. Leave your valuables in the hotel safe or hidden in your room.

Outside Phnom Penh safety is not as much of a problem. Visitors should be very cautious when walking in the countryside, however, as landmines and other unexploded ordnance is a ubiquitous hazard. Stick to well-worn paths, especially around Siem Reap and when visiting remote temples. Motorbike accidents have serious fatality rates here.

Students

There are no specific student discounts in Cambodia. Anyone in full-time education is entitled to an **International Student Identity Card** (ISIC Association, Box 9048, 1000 Copenhagen, Denmark, T45-3393 9303). These are issued by student travel offices and travel agencies and offer special rates on all forms of transport and other concessions

and services. They sometimes permit free admission to museums and sights, at other times a discount on the admission.

Telephone

It is now relatively easy for foreigners to buy mobile phone simcards in Cambodia. If you have an unlocked handset that allows you to use any simcard this is by far the easiest and cheapest choice for telephony in Cambodia for both local and international calls. Mobile network company **M-Fone** offer a good nationwide coverage and pay-as-you-go service – it is easy to buy top-up for their services via scratch cards of various denominations. They also offer hi-speed mobile internet services via their 3G network for an extra charge – this can often be cheaper, quicker and more reliable than using an internet café.

Landline linkages are so poor in Cambodia that many people and businesses prefer to use mobile phones instead. In 2009 Cambodia liberalized and deregulated their mobile networks and there are now several to choose from depending on your needs. It's not uncommon for some Khmers to have 3 or 4 simcards/numbers. For landlines the 3-digit prefix included in a 9-digit landline telephone number is the area (province) code. If dialling within a province, dial only the 6-digit number. International calls can be made from most guesthouses, hotels and phone booths. Don't anticipate being able to make international calls outside Phnom Penh, Siem Reap and Sihanoukville. Use public **MPTC** or **Camintel** card phone boxes dotted around Phnom Penh to make international calls (cards are usually sold at shops near the booth). International calls are expensive, starting at US$4 per min in Phnom Penh, and more in the provinces. To make an overseas call from Cambodia, dial 007 or 001 + IDD country code + area code minus first 0 + subscriber number. The country code for Cambodia is +855.

Tipping

Tipping is rare but appreciated. Salaries in restaurants and hotels are low and many staff hope to make up the difference in tips. As with everywhere else, good service should be rewarded.

Tourist information

Government tourism services are minimal at best. The Ministry of Tourism, 3 Monivong Blvd, Phnom Penh T023-426876, is not able to provide any useful information or services. The tourism office in Siem Reap is marginally better but will only provide services, such as guides, maps, etc, for a nominal fee. In all cases in Cambodia you are better off going through a private operator for information and price.

Useful websites

www.cambodian-online.com Useful starting point with information ranging from visa requirements to hotel reservations. Site does tend to be a bit out of date.
www.tourismcambodia.com/ Cambodia's National Tourism Authority. Good source of general and practical information on travel, visas, accommodation and so on.
www.embassyofcambodia.org
A remarkably good website set up by the Royal Cambodian Embassy in Washington DC. Informative and reasonably up to date.

www.cambodia.org/ The Cambodian Info Centre. Wealth of information. News, clubs, organizations and politics, photos and facts. Also very good links academic essays, cultural essays, books, etc.
www.khmer440.com Although this site is a tad blokey, the forum is very good for bouncing any specific Cambodia questions to the predominantly expat crowd.
www.gocambodia.com Useful range of practical information.
www.canbypublications.com Good source of up-to-date travel information. Accommodation/eating listings are paid for, so are not independent reviews.

Tour operators

Numerous operators offer organized trips, ranging from a whistle-stop tour of the highlights to specialist trips that focus on a specific activity. The advantage of travelling with a reputable operator is that your transport, accommodation and activities are all arranged for you in advance – particularly valuable if you only have limited time. By travelling independently, however, you can be much more flexible about where you go and what you do. You can explore less visited areas and save money, if you budget carefully. For regional tour operators, such as Asian Trails, www.asiantrails.com, refer to the Activities and tours listings in the guide.

Voluntourism

Despite the relative positive impacts tourism has brought to Cambodia, it is difficult to track how much locals benefit from your tourist dollar. As you arrive, it's striking to see the contrasts between flash five-star hotels next to simple wooden Khmer housing, and when you see street kids running up to you barefoot and filthy, it can be difficult not to feel a little niggle of guilt about how much you just paid for your lunch.

Unfortunately, this emotion is being targeted and abundant rumours are highlighting the unfortunate case that children are being taken or bribed from families to stay in orphanages to increase donations, and children are taken out of school in order to beg for tourist dollars. Therefore, beware of people approaching you in the street who want to take you to a school or NGO that is in desperate need of funds and think twice before giving to begging children.

'Voluntourism' is on the increase and many companies are promoting and selling 'meaningful experiences'. While such experiences can be mutually beneficial for host communities and visitors, it is advised to be selective and use organizations that actively implement child protection policies and be prepared to send a police check if you intend to work with children. Be careful to ask where all your money goes and make sure it ends up where intended.

Lastly, if you come to work, then work; don't fall for the temptations of cheap beers and laid-back lifestyle of Cambodia.

In the UK

Adventure Company, 15 Turk St, Alton, Hampshire GU34 1AG, T0870-794 1009, www.adventurecompany.co.uk.

Audley Travel, 6 Willows Gate, Stratton, Audley, Oxfordshire OX27 9AU, T01869-276219, www.audleytravel.com.

Coromandel, Andrew Brock Travel Ltd, 29A Main St, Lyddington, Oakham LE15 9LR, T01572-821330, www.coromandelabt.com. Tailored individual travel.

Guerba Adventure & Discovery Holidays, Wessex House, 40 Station Rd, Westbury, Wiltshire BA13 3JN, T01373-826611, www.guerba.co.uk.

Magic of the Orient, 14 Frederick Pl, Clifton, Bristol BS8 1AS, T0117-311 6050, www.magicoftheorient.com. Tailor-made holidays to the Far East.

Regent Holidays, 15 John St, Bristol BS1 2HR, T0117-921 1711, www.regent-holidays.co.uk.

Silk Steps, Deep Meadow, Edington, Bridgwater, Somerset TA7 9JH, T01278-722460, www.silksteps.co.uk.

Steppes Travel, 51 Castle St, Cirencester, Glos GL7 1QD, T01285-880980, www.steppestravel.co.uk. Specialists in tailor-made holidays and small group tours.

Symbiosis Expedition Planning, 3B Wilmot Place, London NW1 9JS, T0845-123 2844, www.symbiosis-travel.com.

Trans Indus, Northumberland House, 11 The Pavement, Popes Lane, London W5 4NG, T020-8566 2729, www.transindus.co.uk.

Travelmood, 214 Edgware Rd, London W2 1DH, T0870-001002, www.travelmood.com.

Visit Vietnam (Tennyson Travel), 30-32 Fulham High St, London SW6 3LQ, T020-7736 4347, www.visitvietnam.co.uk. Also deals with Cambodia, www.visitasia.co.uk.

In North America

Adventure Center, 1311 63rd St, Suite 200, Emeryville, CA, T1-800 227 8747, www.adventurecenter.com.

Global Spectrum, 3907 Laro Court, Fairfax, VA 22031, T1-800 419 4446, www.globalspectrumtravel.com. Travel specialists to Southeast Asia.

Hidden Treasure Tours, 162 West Park Av, 2nd Floor, Long Beach, NY 11561, T1-888 889 9906, www.hiddentreasuretours.com.
Journeys, 107 April Drive, Suite 3, Ann Arbor MI 46103, T734-665 4407, www.journeys-intl.com.
Myths & Mountains, 976 Tree Court, Incline Village, NV 89451, T800-670-6984 www.mythsandmountains.com. Organizes travel to Cambodia.
Nine Dragons Travel & Tours, PO Box 24105, Indianapolis, IN 46224, T1-317- 329 0350, T1-800 909 9050 (USA toll free), www.nine-dragons.com.

In Australia and New Zealand
Intrepid Travel, 360 Bourke St, Melbourne, Victoria 3000, T03-8602 0500, www.intrepidtravel.com.
Travel Indochina, Level 10, HCS House, 403 George St, Sydney, NSW 2000, T02-9244 2133, T1300-367666 (toll free), www.travelindochina.com.au. Small-group journeys and tailor-made holidays.

In Southeast Asia
Discovery Indochina, 3A Cua Bac St, Hanoi, Vietnam, T+84 (0)4 716 4132, www.discoveryindochina.com. Private and customized tours covering Cambodia, Vietnam and Laos.
Luxury Travel, 5 Nguyen Truong St, Ba Dinh District, Hanoi, T+84 (0)4 3927 4120, www.luxurytravelvietnam.com. Luxury tours to Vietnam, Cambodia and Laos. Tailor-made itineraries, including golf, family holidays, beach holidays and honeymoons.

Time

7 hrs ahead of GMT.

Visas and immigration

In 2009 Cambodia began an e-visa system which will allow tourists to negotiate arrivals much quicker. The charge is US$20 plus a US$5 admin charge. These visas are valid for 3 months from date of issue for a single entry of 30 days. They can ONLY be used at the following points of entry: Siem Reap Airport, Phnom Penh Airport, Poipet, Koh Kong and Bavet. The usual tourist visas for a 30-day stay are still available on arrival at these and several other entry points. Fill in a form and hand over 1 photograph (4 cm x 6 cm). Tourist visas cost US$20 and your passport must be valid for at least 6 months from the date of entry. More details of the e-visa plus an up-to-date list of border crossings and requirements can be found here http://evisa.mfaic.gov.kh/e-visa/. Cambodia also has missions overseas from which visas can be obtained.

Travellers leaving by land must ensure that their Vietnam visa specifies Moc Bai or Chau Doc as points of entry otherwise they could be turned back. You can apply for a Cambodian visa in Ho Chi Minh City and collect in Hanoi and vice versa.

Extensions can be obtained at the Department for Foreigners on the road to the Airport, T023-581558 (passport photo required). Most travel agents arrange visa extensions for around US$40 for 30 days. Those overstaying their visas are fined US$5 per day, although officials at land crossings often try to squeeze out more.

Weights and measures

Metric.

Women

A woman travelling alone is an unusual sight in Cambodia and can expect a good deal of curious attention. Sexual harassment is not uncommon and many motos/tour guides will try their luck with women but generally it is more macho posturing than anything serious. It is a good idea to dress modestly and travel in the company of others in remote areas and after dark especially Phnom Penh. While women travelling alone can generally face more potential problems than men or couples, these are far less pronounced in Cambodia than in many countries.

Contents

Footprint features

Phnom Penh

★ **Don't miss ...**

PREY VANG

Koh Dach

PHNOM PENH

Kien Svay

Tonlé Sap

Choeung Ek

KANDAL

Oudong

Tonlé Bati

Phnom Tamao

Phnom Chisor

Kompong Speu

KOMPONG SPEU

Kirirom National Park

N

5 km
5 miles

It is not hard to imagine Phnom Penh in its heyday, with wide shady boulevards, beautiful French buildings and exquisite pagodas. They're still all here but are in a derelict, dust-blown, decaying state, surrounded by growing volumes of cars, pickup trucks and motorcyclists. It all leaves you wondering how a city like this works. But it does, somehow.

Although Phnom Penh has a reputation as a frontier town thanks to drugs, gun ownership and prostitution, plus the sometimes overbearing indulgences of a boorish elite, a more cosmopolitan character is being forged out of the chaos. Stylish restaurants and bars now line the riverside, the economy is developing at a dynamic pace, and a sense of pride is returning. Yet the City of Ghosts' history is never far away, with amputees visible on street corners and filthy homeless street children being chased by overzealous security guards. The place also sometimes feels like a holiday camp for NGO workers; its smart bars and cafés largely populated by overpaid and over-here Westerners.

Perhaps the one constant in all the turmoil of the past century has been the monarchy – shifting, whimsical and pliant. The splendid royal palace, visible to all, was a daily reminder of this ultimate authority that even the Khmer Rouge had to treat with caution. The royal palace area, with its glittering spires, wats, stupas, national museum and broad green spaces, is perfectly sited alongside the river and is as pivotal to the city as the city is to the country.

Ins and outs

Getting there

There are flights to Phnom Penh's **Pochentong airport** (www.cambodia-airports.com), 10 km west of the city on Road 4, from Bangkok, Guangzhou, Ho Chi Minh City, Hong Kong, Kuala Lumpur, Shanghai, Singapore, Siem Reap and Vientiane. It is also possible to get to Phnom Penh by boat and bus from Chau Doc in Vietnam and by road crossing at Moc Bai, Vietnam. Visitors travelling from Thailand can take the long overland route or go by sea to Sihanoukville and take a bus from there. A taxi from the airport to town costs US$7 – there's a stand just outside arrivals – a moto should be about US$3 and a tuk-tuk US$5-7 depending on your haggling skills. Expect to pay a little bit more when coming in the reverse direction. ▶▶ *See Transport, page 72, for further details.*

Getting around

Fleets of tuk-tuks (*lomphata* in Khmer) provide the nearest thing to taxis in Phnom Penh. Hotels can arrange car hire around town and surrounding areas. Motorbikes are ubiquitous. Most visitors use the local *motodops* (motorbike taxis where you ride on the back) as a quick, cheap and efficient way of getting around. Be advised that riding a moto can be risky – an accident even at low speed can result in bad and potentially fatal head injuries if you're not wearing a helmet. Some ex-pat residents carry their own helmet with them while getting around town. There are cyclos too, which undoubtedly appeal to many tourists but for regular journeys they prove to be just too slow and expensive. At present there is no public transport system in Phnom Penh. A bus network has been mooted and there's even talk of a futuristic "Skytrain" to link the river with the airport but without any concrete plans in place at this stage both projects seem years away. When travelling on any form of public transport in Phnom Penh be wary of bag snatchers.

Orientation

Navigating Phnom Penh is reasonably straightforward. The map shows a pretty rigid grid pattern with a couple of diagonals and curves thrown in to lighten the picture. Every street is numbered but some major thoroughfares have names too. The key to unlocking Phnom Penh's geography is the simple fact that the horizontal steets (east-west) are evenly numbered and odd numbers (north-south) are used for the vertical ones. The rivers Tonlé Sap and Bassac run north-south and, with the exception of some houses and restaurants over the Japanese Friendship Bridge, all Phnom Penh lies to the west of the river. Monivong and Norodom boulevards are the main roads running north-south, and east-west are Confederation de Russie, Kampuchea Krom and Preah Sihanouk boulevards.

The royal quarter lies to the east of the town not far from the river; north of here is what might be regarded as a colonial quarter with government ministries, banks, hotels, museums and other municipal functions, many housed in French-era buildings (the best colonial architecture is on streets 53, 114, 178, Norodom Boulevard and Samdech Sotheraos Boulevard). Chinatown, the commercial quarter, surrounds the central covered market, Psah Thmei. Sisowath Quay, the street which runs along the riverbank, is where many visitors head to as it has the highest concentration of restaurants and bars.

Tourist information

The main tourist office in Phnom Penh is **Ministry of Tourism** ① *3 Monivong Blvd, T023-426876*, which organizes tours.

Phnom de plume

Legend has it that the city is named after Penh, a rich Khmer lady, who lived on the banks of the Mekong River. Floodwaters are said to have washed a tree onto the riverbank and Penh found four statues of the Buddha hidden inside.

In 1372 she built a monastery to house the statues on a nearby hill – or 'phnom' in Cambodian. The people of Cambodia believed the statues were a sign from the gods that they wanted a new home.

When the Thais invaded in 1431 and after the collapse of Angkor, the capital moved to Oudong and then to a site near the important temple of Phnom Penh. The city lies at the confluence of the Sap, Mekong and Bassac rivers and the French called the junction 'Les Quatre Bras'; in Khmer it is known as the 'Chameon Mon'.

Modern Phnom Penh

Phnom Penh lies at the confluence of the Sap, Mekong and Bassac rivers and quickly grew into an important commercial centre in the early 1700s. The Cambodian capital relies heavily on the river. The Mekong provides the city's water supply and Phnom Penh is the only significant port on the Mekong above Can Tho in the delta. Years of war have taken a heavy toll on the city's infrastructure and economy, as well as its inhabitants. Refugees first began to flood in from the countryside in the early 1950s during the First Indochina War and the population grew from 100,000 to 600,000 by the late 1960s. In the early 1970s there was another surge as people streamed in from the countryside again, this time to escape US bombing and guerrilla warfare. On the eve of the Khmer Rouge takeover in 1975, the capital had a population of two million, but it soon became a ghost town. On Pol Pot's orders it was forcibly emptied and the townspeople frog-marched into the countryside to work as labourers. Only 45,000 inhabitants were left in the city in 1975, a large number of them soldiers. In 1979, after four years of virtual abandonment, Phnom Penh had a population of a few thousand. People began to drift back following the Vietnamese invasion (1978/1979) and as hopes for peace rose in 1991, the floodgates opened: today the population is again around two million.

Phnom Penh has undergone an economic revival since the Paris Peace Accord of 1991. Following the 1998 coup, however, there was an exodus of businesses and investors for whom this was the final straw. With the coup now fading into memory, Phnom Penh is experiencing a mini-boom and property prices are soaring. Still, public health facilities are woefully inadequate – the city's services are overstretched and there are problems with everything from water and electricity supplies to sewage and refuse disposal. Electricity supply is so erratic that every hotel and many private houses have their own generator. The water supply will sometimes stop for a few hours. (The Khmer Rouge saw to it that the plumbing network was completely destroyed before they left.) The capital's streets are potholed and in need of repair. Even if the main thoroughfares are newly metalled, many side streets remain ample justification for the capital's fleets of four-wheel drive vehicles. There are insufficient schools for the city's growing numbers of children: hence, for those that can afford them, private schools and language training centres have appeared.

1 Phnom Penh

To Boat Piers & Route 5

French Embassy

76

78

British Embassy

International Mosque

Calmette Hospital

US Embas

Boeng Kak Lake
Lake being filled in (not complete)

Tropical & Traveller Medical Clinic

Confederation de Russie Blvd

Psar Th (Centr Market)

Kampuchea Krom Blvd

O Russei

Wat Koh

Croix Rc

Olympic Stadium

Wat Moha Montrei

Preah Sihanouk Blvd

Lucky Supermarke

Dragon Air

Thai

Tuol Sleng Museum

To Wat Tuol Tom Pong, Psar Tuol Tom Pong(Russian Market) Rajana &

To Vietnamese Emb

To Choeung Ek

To Phnom Penh Water Park, Airport & Routes 3 & 4

Monireth Blvd

Mao Tse Tung Blvd

Nehru Blvd

Charles de Gaulle Blvd

Monivong Blvd

Sleeping ⬤
Almond **23** *E5*
Amber Villa **24** *D4*
Anise **20** *E4*
Aram **28** *D5*
Billabong **1** *C3*
Boddhi Tree **2** *E3*
Capitol **5** *D3*
Diamond **6** *C3*
Flamingo **8** *C4*
Floating Island **9** *B2*
Golden Gate **10** *D4*
Grandview Guesthouse **12** *A3*
Happy Guesthouse **14** *D3*
Hello Guesthouse **15** *D3*
Himawari **30** *D5*
Holiday Villa **16** *C3*
Imperial Garden Villa **11** *D5*
Intercontinental **18** *E1*
Juliana **19** *C2*
KIDS **7** *C4*
Lazy Fish Guesthouse **21** *B3*
Le Royal **22** *B3*
L'Imprévu **13** *E4*

New York **25** *C3*
Number 10 Lakeside
Guesthouse **27** *B3*
Palm Resort **17** *E4*
Pavilion **38** *D5*
Phnom Penh **29** *A3*
Regent Park **31** *D5*
Royal Guesthouse **39** *C4*
Scandinavia **32** *E4*
Simon 2 Guesthouse **34** *B3*
Sunway **36** *B3*
Velkommen Inn **40** *B4*
Walkabout **37** *C4*

Eating ⬤
Asia Europe Bakery **1** *D3*
Baan Thai **2** *E4*
Boeung Bopha **5** *A4*
The Deli **36** *C4*
Elsewhere **6** *D4*
Family **7** *B3*
Garden Centre Café **4** *E4*
Gasolina **8** *E4*
Green Vespa **18** *B4*
Jars of Clay **11** *E2*
Java **10** *D5*
Khmer Surin **12** *E4*
K'NYAY **20** *D5*
La Marmite **13** *B4*
Lazy Gecko **14** *B3*
La Gourmandise Bleu **31** *E3*
Living Room **29** *E4*
Monsoon **35** *B4*
Mount Everest **15** *D4*
Ocean **32** *E4*
Origami **16** *D5*
Peking Canteen **17** *C3*
Pyong Yang **19** *E3*
Romdeng **37** *C4*
Sam Doo **21** *C3*
Shiva Shakti **22** *D4*
The Shop **24** *D4*
Tamarind **23** *D4*
Tell **25** *B3*
Teukei **33** *D3*
Topaz **28** *E4*
Yumi **38** *E3*

Bars & clubs ⬤
Blue Chilli **39** *C4*
Cathouse **26** *C4*
Heart of Darkness **27** *C4*
Manhattan **30** *A3*
Meta House **39** *D5*
Pontoon **40** *B4*
Sharkys **9** *C4*
Zepplin **34** *C3*

➡ **Phnom Penh maps**
1 Phnom Penh, page 44
2 Sisowath Quay, page 49

Sights

Historic centre → *For listings, see pages 57-75.*

Royal Palace
ⓘ *Daily 0730-1100, 1400-1700, US$3, camera US$2, video US$5.*

Of all the cultural sights in Phnom Penh, the Royal Palace, between Street 184 and Street 240, is the most impressive. The scale of the palace (and adjoining Silver Pagoda) dwarfs the others and, given the rather gloomy recent history that pervades most of the city's sights, the Royal Palace holds nothing nasty in store for its visitors.

Built mainly by the French in 1866, on the site of the old town, the Royal Palace, along with the Silver Pagoda in a pagoda-style compound, has, since November 1991, been home to Prince Norodom Sihanouk and as of October 2004, King Norodom Sihamoni. The entrance is on Samdech Sothearos Boulevard via the Pavilion of Dancers (or Chan Chaya Pavilion). Opposite the entrance are the walls of the royal residence (closed to the public) and the stable of the white elephant (a highly auspicious and sacred animal treasured as a symbol of royal beneficence).

The **Throne Hall**, the main building facing the Victory Gate, was built in 1917 in Khmer style; it has a tiered roof and a 59-m tower, influenced by Angkor's Bayon Temple. The steps leading up to it are protected by multi-headed nagas. It is used for coronations and other official occasions such as the reception of foreign ambassadors when they present their official credentials: scenes from the *Ramayana* adorn the ceiling. Inside stand the sacred gong and French-style thrones only used by the sovereign. Above the thrones hangs Preah Maha Svetrachatr, a nine-tiered parasol, which symbolizes heaven. A huge carpet fills the hall. Woven into the carpet is the pattern found in the surrounding tiles and the steps leading up to the building. There are two chambers for the king and queen at the back of the hall, which are used only in the week before a coronation when the royal couple were barred from sleeping together. The other adjoining room is used to house the ashes of dead monarchs before they are placed in a royal stupa. Only the main throne room is open to the public. Here there are Buddha images in the left nave, before which the kings would pray each day. The chairs closest to the entrance were reserved for high officials and the others were for visiting ambassadors. The yellow chairs were used by visiting heads of state.

Returning to his former abode in November 1991, Sihanouk must have found it much as he had left it – although many of the state gifts from the display cases have sadly been smashed or stolen.

Immediately to the south of the Throne Hall is a small unremarkable building which contains a collection of knick-knacks, curios, swords, small silver ornaments and costumes. There is also a display of the different coloured costumes worn by staff at the royal palace each day of the week.

The **Royal Treasury** and the **Napoleon III Pavillion** – or summerhouse – built in 1866, are to the south of the Throne Hall. The latter was presented by Napoleon III to his Empress Eugenie as accommodation for the princess during the Suez Canal opening celebrations. She later had it dismantled and dispatched it to Phnom Penh as a gift to the king. The elegant building is constructed around a slender wrought iron frame and is packed with bric-a-brac. Programmes of long forgotten, but no doubt memorable, royal command dance performances are strewn in glass cases. Upstairs there are some decidedly third-rate portraits and some rather more interesting historical photographs of the royal family. The prefabricated folly was renovated and refurbished in 1990 and its ersatz marble walls remarbled – all with French money – but the graceful building is still showing signs of age and is much in need of more money. 'Floor condition is under deterioration' reads one melancholy warning sign. Next to the villa are rooms built in 1959 by Sihanouk to accommodate his cabinet. Beyond is the north gate and the Silver Pagoda enclosure.

Silver Pagoda
① *Daily 0730-1100, 1400-1700, US$3, camera US$2, video US$5.*

Often called the Pagoda of the Emerald Buddha or Wat Preah Keo Morokat after the statue housed here, the Silver Pagoda houses something of a magpie collection. The wooden temple was originally built by King Norodom in 1892 to enshrine royal ashes and then rebuilt by Sihanouk in 1962. The pagoda's steps are of Italian marble, and inside, its floor comprises more than 5000 silver blocks (mostly carpeted over to protect them from the bare feet of visitors) which together weigh nearly six tonnes. All around are cabinets filled with presents from foreign dignitaries. The pagoda is remarkably intact, having been granted special dispensation by the Khmer Rouge, although 60% of the Khmer treasures were stolen from here. In the centre of the pagoda is a magnificent 17th-century emerald Buddha statue made of Baccarat crystal. In front is a 90-kg golden Buddha studded with 9584 diamonds, dating from 1906. It was made from the jewellery of King Norodom and its vital statistics conform exactly to his – a tradition that can be traced back to the god-kings of Angkor. The gold Buddha image is flanked by bronze and silver statues of the Buddha. Under a glass cover is a golden lotus – a Buddhist relic from India. At the back of the room there is a jade Buddha and a palanquin used for coronations which required 12 porters to carry it.

The 600-m-long wall enclosing the Silver Pagoda is galleried; its inward face is covered in frescoes, painted in 1903-1904 by 40 local artists, which depict epic scenes from the *Ramayana* and numerous scenes of the Silver Pagoda and Royal Palace itself – the story starts by the east gate. The lower part of the fresco has deteriorated alarmingly under the combined assault of children's fingers and rising damp. To the east of the Silver Pagoda is a statue of King Norodom on horseback (it is in fact a statue of Napoleon III with the head replaced with that of the Cambodian monarch). Beyond the statue is a stupa containing the ashes of King Ang Duong (1845-1859). Beyond the stupa, on the south wall, are pavilions containing a footprint of the Buddha (to the east) and a pavilion for royal celebrations (to the west). Next to Phnom Mondap, an artificial hill with a building covering the Buddha's footprint, in the centre of the south wall is a stupa dedicated to Sihanouk's favourite daughter who died of leukaemia in 1953. On the west wall is a stupa of King Norodom Suramarit with a bell tower in the northwest corner. Beyond the bell tower on the north wall is the *mondap* (library), originally containing precious Buddhist texts. The whole courtyard is attractively filled with urns and vases containing flowering shrubs.

National Museum of Cambodia
① *Daily 0800-1700, US$3, camera US$2, video US$3. Photographs only permitted in the garden. The shop sells reproductions of works from Angkor and a good selection of books, maps and cards. French- and English-speaking guides are available, mostly excellent.*

The National Museum of Cambodia is the desert-red building just north of the palace (entrance is on the corner of streets 13 and 178). It was built in 1920 following the design of French archaeologist and painter, George Groslier, in what, certainly from the outside, appears to be Khmer style. However, closer acquaintance reveals a curious hybrid with

Phnom de guerre

Of the original population of Phnom Penh thousands died during the Pol Pot era so the population of the city now seems rural in character. The population tends to vary from season to season: in the dry season people pour into the capital when there is little work in the countryside but go back to their farms in the wet season when the rice has to be planted.

Phnom Penh has long faced a housing shortage – two-thirds of its houses were damaged by the Khmer Rouge between 1975 and 1979 and the rate of migration into the city exceeds the rate of building. Apart from the sheer cost of building new ones and renovating the crumbling colonial mansions, there has been a severe shortage of skilled workers in Cambodia: under Pol Pot 20,000 engineers were killed and nearly all the country's architects.

Exacerbating the problem is the issue of land ownership as so many people were removed from their homes. These days there are many more qualified workers but sky-rocketing property prices coupled with the confusing issue of land title has created a situation where a great land grab is occuring with people being tossed out of their homes or having them bulldozed to make way for profitable developments.

French colonial influence much in evidence. It is built around a central courtyard and, for admirable reasons of ventilation and light, there are no doors or windows on the interior walls. Unfortunately the bats which live in the ample roof space exploit the open galleries, covering the exhibits with several tons of guano each year. While sales of said guano may help bolster the museum's paltry income it doesn't do the sculptures any good at all. The museum was opened to exhibit works scattered throughout the country and in 1951 it was handed over to the Cambodians to run. The museum contains a collection of Khmer art – notably sculpture – throughout the ages (although some periods are not represented). Galleries are arranged chronologically in a clockwise direction. Most of the exhibits date from the Angkor period but there are several examples from the pre-Angkor era (that is from the kingdoms of Funan, Chenla and Cham). The collection of Buddhas from the sixth and seventh centuries includes a statue of Krishna Bovardhana found at Angkor Borei showing the freedom and grace of early Khmer sculpture. The chief attraction is probably the pre-Angkorian statue of Harihara, found at Prasat Andat near Kompong Thom (see page 264). There is a fragment from a beautiful bronze statue of Vishnu found in the West Baray at Angkor, as well as frescoes and engraved doors. The library at the museum was one of the largest of its type in Southeast Asia but has now been dismantled and sold.

The riverside → For listings, see pages 57-75.

Sisowath Quay is Phnom Penh's Left Bank. A broad pavement runs along the side of the river and on the opposite side of the road a rather splendid assemblage of colonial buildings looks out over the broad expanse of waters of the Quatre Bras. The erstwhile administrative buildings and merchants' houses today form an unbroken chain – almost a mile long – of bars and restaurants, with the odd guesthouse thrown in. While foreign tourist commerce fills the street, the quayside itself is dominated by local Khmer families who stroll and sit in the cool of the evening, served by an army of hawkers.

Wat Ounalom

ⓘ *0600-1800.*

Phnom Penh's most important wat, Wat Ounalom, is north of the museum, at the junction of Street 154 and Samdech Sothearos Boulevard, facing the Tonlé Sap. The first building on this site was a monastery, built in 1443 to house a hair of the Buddha. Before 1975,

Sisowath Quay

Tonlé Sap

Phnom Penh maps
1 Phnom Penh, page 44
2 Sisowath Quay, page 49

N

50 metres
50 yards

Sleeping 🛏
Amanjaya & K-West Restaurant **1**
Bougainvillier **2**
Bright Lotus Guesthouse **3**
Castle **4**
Dara Reang Sey **9**
Foreign Correspondents
  Club of Cambodia (FCCC)
  & Fresco **12**
Indochine 2 **5**
Paragon **6**
Quay **13**
Red Hibiscus **11**
River Star **8**
Sunshine **10**

Eating 🍴
Cantina **3**
Corner 33 **1**
Fortune Pho **15**
Friends **5**
Frizz **11**
Happy Herb Pizza **7**
Khmer Borane **9**
La Croisette **10**
Le Wok **18**
Lemongrass **21**
Metro **12**
Pacharan **2**
Pop Café **8**
Rising Sun **13**
Veiyo **16**

Bars & clubs 🍸
Fly Lounge **4**
Memphis Pub **17**
Riverhouse **14**
Riverside **19**
Salt Lounge **20**

Wat Ounalom △

National Museum
of Cambodia 🏛

Royal Palace

Silver Pagoda △

more than 500 monks lived here but the Khmer Rouge murdered the Patriarch and did their best to demolish the capital's principal temple destroying its famous library in the process. Nonetheless it remains Cambodian Buddhism's headquarters and the complex has been restored since 1979. The stupa behind the main sanctuary is the oldest part of the wat. The main sanctuary, which dates from 1952, now contains only the poorly assembled fragments of a Burmese marble Buddha. On the first level there is a fine bust of the Buddha, while frescoes on the second level represent scenes from the Buddha's life, painted in 1952. There are usually quite a few chatty monks about the place.

Wat Phnom and around → *For listings, see pages 57-75.*

ⓘ *Boulevard Tou Samouth where it intersects St 96, US$1.*

Wat Phnom stands on a small hill at the north end of town and is the temple from which the city takes its name. It was built by a wealthy Khmer lady called Penh (see box, page 43) in 1372. The sanctuary has been rebuilt several times: in 1434, 1890, 1894 and 1926. The main entrance is to the east, the steps guarded by nagas and lions. The principal sanctuary is decorated inside with frescoes depicting scenes from Buddha's life and the *Ramayana*. At the front, on a pedestal, is a statue of the Buddha. There is a statue of Penh inside a small pavilion between the vihara and the stupa, the latter containing the ashes of King Ponhea Yat (1405-1467). The surrounding park is a tranquil, pleasant escape from the madness of the city. However, note that there are monkeys with attitude in abundance here although they tend to fight between themselves.

Wat Phnom is a favourite with the Phnom Penhois and is often teeming with worshippers praying for a dose of good fortune. Vietnamese devotees flock to the shrine of the spirit Preah Chau, north of the main sanctuary. Others buy birds to release in exchange for good luck (not that much luck for the bird though, which will probably be captured again). To the left of the image of Preah Chau is a statue of the Hindu god, Vishnu, 'the preserver', and the shrine is guarded by spirits wielding clubs. The summit affords nice views down Phnom Penh's tree-lined avenues, and there are plans to replant the hill with hundreds of trees to recall how it looked in former times. There is one resident, sad-looking elephant. On the slope behind the wat is an overgrown royal stupa.

West of Wat Phnom is the **National Library** ⓘ *0800-1100 and 1430-1700*, exemplifying the refinement of French colonial architecture. Original construction began in 1924, and the resplendent building was set in blossoming gardens. Not surprisingly and somewhat sacrilegiously, the Khmer Rouge ransacked the building, transforming it into, of all things, a stable. Books were either burnt or thrown out on to the streets. Fortunately many of the discarded books were grabbed by locals who kindly returned them to the library after 1979. There are some antiquated palm-leaf manuscripts, photo documentation from earlier years and some fascinating artworks.

French Embassy

The French Embassy, on the intersection of Monivong Boulevard and Street 76, was recently rebuilt as a low concrete whitewashed complex for the French to occupy once again. This was the building into which 800 expatriates and 600 Cambodians crowded when the Khmer Rouge first occupied the city in mid-April 1975. Within 48 hours of Pol Pot's troops' arrival in Phnom Penh, the French vice-consul was informed that the new regime did not recognize diplomatic privilege. Cambodian women married to foreigners were allowed to stay in the embassy (some marriages were hastily arranged), but all

Cambodian men were ordered to leave. The foreigners were finally escorted out of Cambodia; everyone else was marched out of the compound. Jon Swain, who was caught up in the Khmer Rouge takeover, gives a graphic first-hand account of the sanctuary provided by the French Embassy, in his book, *River of Time*.

Boeng Kak Lake

Boeng Kak Lake, a 10- to 15-minute walk from the Central Market, will appeal to backpackers as it's well supplied with cheap food and guesthouses. The lakeside setting with the all-important westerly aspect – ie sunsets instead of the sunrises of Sisowath Quay – appeals strongly to the nocturnal instincts of guests (some bars and restaurants open 24 hours a day). The lake was quite beautiful but close to the guesthouses it becomes more like a floating rubbish tip and with not much lake left it looks more like a canal. On the water not much differentiates one guesthouse from another – all are of the same ilk. In the eyes of the law, the places on the lake are considered 'squatted' so their future is unsure. The lake has been partially filled and families are being evicted from this area to make way for new development, but many bars and guesthouses are still standing. Local guesthouse owners estimate that it will take another two years to fill the lake completely, but only time will tell how fast it will develop.

Around Independence Monument → *For listings, see pages 57-75.*

South of the Royal Palace and Silver Pagoda, between Street 268 and Preah Sihanouk Boulevard, is **Independence Monument**. It was built in 1958 to commemorate independence but has now assumed the role of a cenotaph.

Wat Lang Ka, on the corner of Sihanouk and Norodom Boulevard (close to Independence Monument), was another beautiful pagoda that fell victim to Pol Pot's architectural holocaust but, like Wat Ounalom, it was restored in Khmer style on the direction of the Hanoi-backed government in the 1980s. It is a really soothing get-away from city madness and the monks here are particularly friendly. They hold a free meditation session every Monday and Thursday night at 1800 and anyone is welcome to join in.

South of the centre → *For listings, see pages 57-75.*

Tuol Sleng Museum

ⓘ *0800-1100, 1400-1700, closed Mon. Public holidays 0800-1800. US$2. There is a free film show at 1000 and 1500 each day. Recommended. The Documentation Centre of Cambodia website, www.welcome.to/dccam, is a Yale University project to investigate the crimes of the Khmer Rouge and document and record their atrocities. This information is available to those who may wish to pursue legal redress for genocide.*

Further southwest from Independence Monument, on Street 113 (close to Street 350), is the Tuol Sleng Museum (or Museum of Genocide). After 17 April 1975 the classrooms of Tuol Svay Prey High School became the Khmer Rouge main torture and interrogation centre, known as Security Prison 21 – or just S-21. More than 20,000 people were taken from S-21 to be executed at Choeung Ek extermination camp. Countless others died under torture and were thrown into mass graves in the school grounds. Only seven prisoners survived because they were sculptors or artists and could turn out countless busts of Pol Pot.

Classrooms were subdivided into small cells by means of crude brick walls (now liable to topple over). In some rooms there is a metal bedstead and on the wall a fuzzy black and white photograph showing how the room was found in 1979 with a body manacled to the bed. Walls on the stairways often have holes knocked in them and one can all too easily imagine the blood and filth that poured down the stairs making these outlets necessary. The school was converted into a 'museum of genocide' by the Vietnamese (with help from the East Germans who had experience in setting up the Auschwitz Museum). One block of classrooms is given over to photographs of the victims. All the Khmer Rouge victims were methodically numbered and photographed. The pictures on display include those of foreigners who fell into the hands of the Khmer Rouge but the vast majority are Cambodians – men, women, children and babies – all of whom were photographed. Some have obviously just been tortured or raped and stare with loathing and disgust into the camera, while others appear to be unaware of the fate that awaits them. The photographs are quite easily the most poignant and painful part of the museum. One block contains the simple but disturbing weapons of torture. It is a chilling reminder that such sickening violence was done by such everyday objects.

South of Tuol Sleung Museum

Wat Tuol Tom Pong, next to a market of the same name (just off Mao Tse Tung Boulevard – the entrance is on Street 135), is a modern pagoda – very bright, almost kitsch. Surrounded by a high wall, it has entrances with mythical animals associated with the Buddha.

Former US Embassy

The former US Embassy, now home to the Ministry of Fisheries, is at the intersection of Norodom and Mao Tse Tung boulevards. As the Khmer Rouge closed on the city from the north and the south in April 1975, US Ambassador John Gunther Dean pleaded with Secretary of State Henry Kissinger for an urgent airlift of embassy staff. But it was not until the very last minute (just after 1000 on 12 April 1975, with the Khmer Rouge firing mortars from across the Bassac River onto the football pitch near the compound that served as a landing zone) that the last US Marine helicopter left the city. Flight 462, a convoy of military transport helicopters, evacuated the 82 remaining Americans, 159 Cambodians and 35 other foreigners to a US aircraft carrier in the Gulf of Thailand. Their departure was overseen by 360 heavily armed marines. Despite letters to all senior government figures from the ambassador, offering them places on the helicopters, only one, Acting President Saukham Khoy, fled the country. The American airlift was a deathblow to Cambodian morale. Within five days, the Khmer Rouge had taken the city and within hours senior officials of the former Lon Nol government were executed on the tennis courts of the embassy.

West of the centre → *For listings, see pages 57-75.*

There are two wats worthy of a visit lying to the west of the city centre. **Wat Koh**, on Monivong Boulevard (between Streets 174 and 178), is popular for its lake. **Wat Moha Montrei**, on Preah Sihanouk Boulevard (between Streets 173 and 163), was used as a rice storage depot by the Pol Pot regime. A brick mosque on Chraing Chamres II, called **An-Nur an-Na'im Mosque**, is much smaller than the one which previously occupied the site. The original building, built in 1901, was destroyed by the Khmer Rouge.

Choeung Ek

ⓘ *US$2. Southwest on Monireth Blvd, about 15 km from town, by moto the return trip should be between US$2-5, in a car it will be around US$10.*

Now in a peaceful setting surrounded by orchards and rice fields, Choeung Ek was the execution ground for the torture victims of Tuol Sleng – the Khmer Rouge interrogation centre, S-21 (see page 51). It is referred to by some as the '**killing fields**'. Today a huge glass tower stands on the site, filled with the cracked skulls of men, women and children exhumed from 129 mass graves in the area (which were not discovered until 1980). To date 8985 corpses have been exhumed from the site, although researchers believe the number of victims buried is closer to double that figure. The site, once an orchard, is peaceful now, with only the odd bird or quacking duck to break the silence – and rather more numerous children begging. Signs attempt to explain the inexplicable: "The method of massacre which the clique of Pol Pot criminals was carried upon the innocent people of Kampuchea cannot be described fully and clearly in words because the invention of this killing method was strangely cruel. So it is difficult for us to determine who they are for they have the human form but their hearts are demons' hearts …". The really sad part is that Choeung Ek is just one of 4973 gravesites uncovered by the Documentation Centre, dedicated to investigating Khmer Rouge atrocities.

Oudong

ⓘ *Take Route 5 north from Phnom Penh, turn left down a track before Oudong town (at Vihea Luong medical centre, by the big Angkor Beer and condom signs); it's approximately 1½ hrs (40 km) by moto. Buses depart hourly from the Central Market with Phnom Penh Public Transport Co. Alternatively, buses going to Kampong Chhnang pass through Oudong (get off at the Oudong billboard). To avoid too much climbing get your moto driver to drop you off at the foot of the steps. Oudong is busy with Phnom Penhois on Sun. There are drink stalls at the foot of the hill.*

Oudong was the royal capital between 1618 and 1866 and only the foundations of the ancient palace remain. The skyward-soaring stupas can be seen from miles away emerging from the forest-clad hills. At the top of the larger of two ridges, just south of Oudong itself, are the ruins of **Phnom Chet Ath Roeus**. The vihara was built in 1911 by King Sisowath to house a large Buddha image, but was destroyed by the Khmer Rouge. Beyond the wat to the northwest is a string of viharas – now in ruins – and beyond them, several stupas, which house the ashes of King Ang Douong (1845-1859) and King Monivong (1927-1941). On the other side of the ridge stands a memorial to those murdered by the Khmer Rouge, whose remains were unearthed from mass graves on the site in the early 1980s. The stupas themselves are nothing special but the views over the vast surrounding plain are spectacular. The town itself is a nondescript, sleepy little place, a short ride north of the temples. Its chief function seems to be washing mud-caked cars and pick-ups coming in from the country so that their occupants can drive in to Phnom Penh with some dignity. Oudong is also home to **Prasat Nokor Vimean Sour**, a kitsch, concrete model of Angkor Wat built in 1998.

Koh Dach (Koh Dait)

ⓘ *There are a few ways to get to the island, 15 km north of the city over the Japanese Friendship Bridge. You can take a moto to the ferry dock on Route 6 and catch a ferry from there (cheapest option) or you can take one of the small tourist boats on the riverfront, north of Street 178, which will do the trip for US$10-20 (for 1 or 2 hrs).*

Koh Dach (also known as Mekong Island) is a fairly touristy yet reasonably serene island jutting from the Mekong. Just 12 km long, it is home to five villages who, for the most part, cultivate beans, corn, sesame seeds, peanuts and banana crops. However, the island is famed for its weaving and visitors are welcome to come and observe the crisscrossed weaving of looms. There are a few hut-style restaurants on the river edge, which make for a good lunch spot. In the dry season, the shore recedes, providing a good sandy beach for swimming.

Kien Svay

① *Kien Svay is about 12 km east of Phnom Penh, off Route 1. Follow Route 1 until you pass L'Imprevu Hotel and turn left 1 km later and follow the road through the archway. There is quite a good Khmer restaurant on the highway before the turn-off. Buses can be caught to Kien Svay from the Central Market (US$0.50).*

The small resort of Kien Svay (also known as Koki Beach) has become the definitive Cambodian picnic spot. Every weekend the folks from Phnom Penh descend on the site, to get a bit of R&R by the small Mekong tributary. The main attraction is the multitude of water houses for rent – small, sheltered bamboo stilt platforms protruding from the water. The huts are accessible via a small boat trip and usually the huts' owner will take you there and back. The plethora of fried insect and bug hawkers could fulfill anyone's monthly nutrition quota but for those not fond of six-legged creatures there are also numerous stalls selling chicken, rice and other Khmer dishes. Longer boat rides around the area can be also organized. The boat trip to the hut and rental of the hut for an hour should cost around US$0.50-1 but this needs to be negotiated from the outset. The trip takes about 40 minutes and a moto from Phnom Penh should cost US$6-7. Possibly more interesting than the riverside itself are the surrounding villages. Most of them are silk weaving centres and provide an insight into Khmer life. This is probably one of the best places to pick up a *kramar* (see page 262).

Tonlé Bati

① *US$3 (includes a free drink), 33 km south of Phnom Penh on Route 2 and about 2.5 km from the main road. If driving yourself, don't go straight over at the Takhmau roundabout or you'll end up at Sa'ong. If you are taking public transport it is best to catch the bus to Takeo, which departs regularly from the Central Market from 0700, several buses a day. There are a number that make the return trip in the afternoon (up until 1300). Make sure you indicate where you wish to hop off (31 km from Phnom Penh) or you could wind up at Takeo, 46 km away. A shared taxi en route to Takeo is also an option.*

This is a popular local weekend picnic site, 33 km south of Phnom Penh. Besides the tranquillity of the Bati River and shady foliage there is the added attraction of the temple of **Ta Phrom**. The temple dates from Jayavarman VII's reign (1181-1201) and, unusually, it is consecrated to both Brahma and the Buddha, though some of the Buddhist iconography is easily recognizable as being modern. The reclining Buddha carved on the front lintel is modern as are the Buddha statues inside. Interestingly two are fixed into Yoni – the Sivaist 'female' pedestal. The temple is made largely of laterite with a central tower of limestone – notice how the carving of Vishnu is superimposed with Buddha images. The temple has been modelled in traditional form: four outer sanctuaries and the central sanctuary in cruciform layout. Each sanctuary contains a linga. There is a smaller temple, **Yeay Peau**, 100 m north of Ta Prohm. Both temples have a number of fine bas-reliefs.

Yeay Peau is steeped in legend and is believed to be named after King Ta Prohm's mother. King Preah Ket Mealea fell in love with a young fisherman's daughter, Peau.

Together they produced a son, Prohm. As the king had to return back to his royal duties he left a ring for his son, to enable the boy to prove his royal lineage. Upon being told that his father was the king, Prohm set off to track him down. After showing his genealogical proof (the ring), Prohm took up residence in his father's court for several years. So much time was spent away that when he returned to Tonlé Bati he didn't recognize his mother. Besotted with her beauty, Prohm demanded that Peau should be his wife. Refusing to believe Peau's pleas that she was his mother, she suggested a contest to settle the dispute. She proposed a 'winner takes all' competition – they were both to build temples and whoever finished first would have the final say in whether the marriage was to proceed. The pair of them undertook their construction at night, the women villagers allied with Peau and the men aided Prohm. Peau called the men's bluff, lighting the sky with a candle and the men, who were easily duped, believed it was daybreak and headed off to bed. The women continued their slog through the night and eventually Peau's temple was completed. Devestated, Prohm conceded defeat and respected Peau's wishes to be known as his mother and not bride-to-be.

The modern **Wat Tonlé Bati** is also nearby and about 10 km from Tonlé Bati is a house belonging to Khmer royalty. Locals climb the hill (Phnom Tamao) on Sundays to make donations to the monks, but it is noisy, crowded and not advised on weekends.

Phnom Tamao

ⓘ *44 km south of Phnom Penh on Route 2 and about 8 km (to the left) off the main road. If driving/riding zero the odometer at the start of the trip and turn left at the sign for the zoo (at 36 km), follow the dirt road until you hit the zoo. On public transport it is best to take the bus to Takeo, which departs regularly from the Central Market from 0700. There are a number that make the return trip in the afternoon (up until 1300). Make sure you indicate where you wish to hop off (36 km from Phnom Penh – you will need a moto or other form of transport to take you up the road to the zoo). A shared taxi en route to Takeo is also an option. Admission US$2.*

Phnom Tamao, 45 km southeast of Phnom Penh, is considered by many to be the country's premier wildlife sanctuary. Asian zoos aren't usually renowned for their humane treatment of animals but this one is markedly better (though there is still a long way to go). The sanctuary stretches over 1200 ha, 80 ha of which have been designated as a sprawling zoo and wildlife rescue centre. The zoo was established to preserve and rescue rare and endangered local species from the grip of poachers and smugglers and it has rescued a vast array of animals including tigers, lions, deers, bears, peacocks, herons, crocodiles and turtles, which can all be seen at here. The Sun Bear enclosure is a definite highlight and is now one of the best of its type in Asia. The enclosure is home to a number of Sun Bears rescued from the smugglers.

Phnom Chisor

ⓘ *55 km south of Phnom Penh on Route 2, the turn-off is marked by Prasat Neang Khmau (the temple of the Black Virgin); Phnom Chisor is approximately 4 km from the main road. Take moto or hire car. For public transport take the Takeo bus and ask to hop off at Prasat Neang Khmau. US$3.*

This phnom (hill) is topped by a large rock platform on which many buildings from different eras have been built and from which there are tremendous views over the surrounding plains. The principal remaining sanctuary (originally called Suryagiri, literally meaning 'Sun Mountain') is dedicated to Brahma and dates from the 11th century. Navigating the steep 55 steps is a bit of a task.

Kirirom National Park

ⓘ *The best way to get to the park from Phnom Penh is by hired motorbike (US$5-8 per day) or car (US$30 per day). To take a moto (ie motorbike taxi) could cost you up to US$15 but should be less depending on your bargaining skills. From Phnom Penh head out on the Pochentong Airport road along Route 4. The entrance to the park is 78 km from the airport, passing first through the major town of Kompong Speu. As you near the park bundles of firewood can be seen for sale along the roadside. The other option is to take the bus to Sihanoukville and ask to be let off at Kirirom (or Preah Suramarit Kossomak Park in Khmer). From there you will have to arrange your own transport. Note that motorbikes aren't permitted in certain areas of the park.*

The Preah Suramarit Kossomak Park, better known as Kirirom National Park, is a wooded upland area which has become deservedly famed for its huge and beautiful trees and its tranquillity. Capitalizing on its beauty, King Sihanouk established a settlement here in 1944 called Chuolong City. After the return of the French in 1945-1946, it became a hideout for the Khmer Issarak guerrillas fighting for independence. During the 1960s Chuolong City became an exclusive holiday retreat for the French and Khmer élite. The Khmer Rouge destroyed the villas in the 1970s, but some ruins still remain. Amazingly, it was not until 1992 that the Khmer Rouge were finally dislodged from the area.

Kirirom, which covers 35,000 ha of upland forest set in the Elephant Mountain Range, was designated a national park in 1993. In the higher elevations of the park the predominant tree is the pine tree (*Pinus merkuzi*). A 1995 survey of the area mentions muntjac deer, sambar deer, tigers and leopards. The higher altitude (675 m above sea level) offers a wonderful climate change, particularly in the hotter seasons and the park has become very popular as a weekend getaway (it has been cleared of mines and so is also suitable for hiking). Pick-up trucks piled high with young Khmers and motorbikes with whole families squeezed on the back form a convoy to the park on weekends so it is considerably more peaceful to visit on a weekday when the park regains some of the tranquillity for which it became popular in the first place. Just before entering the park, near the ranger's office, there is a sign pointing to a waterfall (to the right, approximately 10 km). These falls are arguably more magnificent than those heralded as the best in Kirirom – with water roaring down a 25-m drop into the natural pool below.

Inside the park, a metalled road leads to an intersection with some food stalls. The road to the right marked 'Liu Shaq Qi' leads up a small hill to one of the villas laid waste by the Khmer Rouge. The ruins are covered in Khmer and Vietnamese graffiti. There are good views from here of the surrounding countryside and a large lake. The lake can be reached on foot by returning to the intersection but since it has been severly polluted it is probably best viewed from a distance. For those who wish to take their chance, locals hire life jackets and inner tubes for 1000 riel. Further along on the same road are some popular picnic and bathing spots near river rapids. Thatch huts can be rented for a nap/picnic for US$1. There are plenty of walks and tracks to explore. **O Traw Sek Resort** is a series of rapids within the resort although 'rapid' perhaps isn't the best term since the waters are quite slow moving, particularly in the dry season. Nonetheless, it is a tranquil area with lush greenery, a still, green pool perfect for a dip and swarms of dragonflies flitting around. Wat Kirirom is a small but pleasant enough place.

Hotel and guesthouse prices

LL over US$200	L US$151-200	AL US$101-150
A US$66-100	B US$46-65	C US$31-45
D US$21-30	E US$12-20	F US$7-11
G under US$7		

Restaurant prices

¶¶¶ over US$12	¶¶ US$6-12	¶ under US$6

● Sleeping

Phnom Penh boasts a wide range of accommodation, from good 4- to 5-star standard to lowly guesthouse dormitories. For general ease of access to restaurants and bars, Sisowath Quay is hard to beat but with Phnom Penh being as compact as it is, location is not a major issue. Many taxis will try and take you to a 'preferred' destination – as they get commissions. To avoid this, you can organize an airport pick up with your hotel; 80% of the hotels here offer this service.

Historic centre *p46, map p44*
This is a good place to base yourself – prices are a little lower than on the riverfront though facilities are comparable.
A Aram, St 244, T012-565509, www.boddhi tree.com. Nice little guesthouse tucked away in a small street near the palace. The stylish rooms are a bit small and overpriced.
A-D Diamond, 172-184 Monivong Blvd, T023-217221/2, diamondhotel@online. com.kh. Hotel in a good central location. A little overshadowed by some of the newer and better hotels but staff are exceptionally helpful and friendly. Rooms are clean with TV, bath and IDD telephone.
A-D Holiday Villa, 89 Monivong Blvd, T023-990888, www.holidayvilla.com.my. A bit 1970s but well appointed, with bath, internet, TV, safe deposit box, IDD phone. Breakfast included. Restaurant serving Halal.
A-D Regent Park, 58 Samdech Sothearos Blvd, T023-427131, regentpark@online. com.kh. The well-designed lobby belies a collection of ordinary rooms and apartment-

style suites. Still, it's reasonable value and in a good location. Thai and European restaurant. Price includes breakfast.
B-C Billabong, No 5 St 158, T023-223703, www.thebillabonghotel.com. Reasonably new hotel, well appointed, though small rooms. Breakfast included. Swimming pool, poolside bar and de luxe rooms with private balconies overlooking the pool. Internet.
C-D Flamingo Hotel, No 30 St 172, T023-221640, reservation@flamingo.com.kh. Reasonably new hotel, bit garish from the outside but good facilities. Well fitted rooms with all the usual amenities, including a bath. Free internet, gym and restaurant.
D-F KIDS Guesthouse, No 17A St 178, T012-410406, ryan@ryanhem.com. Rather a good find. Welcoming guesthouse of the Khmer Internet Development Service (KIDS) set in a small tropical garden, spotted with a couple of cabana-style internet kiosks. A couple of rooms are a decent size, quite clean and equipped with a huge fridge. Discount on internet use for guests. Good deals for guests staying 4 nights or more. Has opened a new coffee shop.
D-G Walkabout Hotel, corner of St 51 and St 174, T023-211715, www.walkabouthotel. com. In the heart of Phnom Penh, a popular Australian-run bar, café and guesthouse. Has 23 rooms ranging from small with no windows and shared facilities to large with own bathroom and a/c. Rooms with bathrooms are okay but lower-end rooms are a little gloomy and cell-like. 24-hr bar downstairs, so often noisy and quite a bit of traffic, clientele mostly there for the females that hang around till dawn looking for a suitor.

The riverside *p48, maps p44 and p49*
Can be a bit noisy but the frenetic activity, cool breezes and sense of space makes the riverside of the best spots in town.
L Naga World, Samdech Techo Hun Sen Park, T023-218026, www.nagaworld.com. Mammouth hotel newly opened with casino,

entertainment centre, karaoke lounges and over 500 bedrooms across 14 storeys.

L-A Cambodiana, No 313 Sisowath Quay, T023-426288, www.hotelcambodiana.com. Originally built for Prince (as he then was) Sihanouk's guests. This eyesore of a building has a more than a few communist touches and it's not surprising that in a former life, under the Lol Non regime, it was a military base. The place is reedemed by its vista, which overlooks the confluence of the Mekong, Tonlé Sap and Bassac rivers. 300 rooms every one of which is equipped with an internet connection. Exceptional facilities: 2 restaurants (French and Chinese), pool, tennis courts, health centre, boutique, business centre and a particularly good book shop (many French titles).

L-A Himawari, 313 Sisowath Quay, T023-214555, www.himawarihotel.com. With luxurious designer apartments/suites, the Himawari offers an upmarket spot on the river. The usual a/c, cable TV and en suite facilities enhance great river views. Good restaurants, gym and nice pool.

AL Amanjaya, corner St 154 and Sisowath Quay, T023-214747, www.amanjaya.com. Gorgeous rooms with full amenities, beautiful furniture and creative finishing touches. The balconies have some of the best views on the river. Service can be a little ragged – you'll be asked to pay in full when you check-in – but they get enough right to make this probably the nicest place by the river. Free wireless internet and awesome breakfast are both included in the room rate. Good location. K-West restaurant downstairs. Recommended.

AL-A Imperial Garden Villa and Hotel, 315 Sisowath Quay, T023-219991, www.imperialgarden-hotel.com. Another unsightly architectural development. The term 'garden', in this context, seems to refer to an area of concrete with the odd plant chucked in for good measure. The rooms (and suites) have a reasonably good view over the river, with wide screen TV, safe and all modern conveniences. Swimming pool, tennis, massage centre, restaurant.

AL-A The Quay, 277 Sisowath Quay, T023-224894, www.thequayhotel.com. Brand new hotel from the FCC people set on the riverfront in a re-modelled colonial property. It aspires to create a designer feel which it partly pulls off, although this is undone by a patchy cheap finish. Big bath tubs, colour flatscreen TVs, a/c, free Wi-Fi and a good location. Also claims to be an 'eco-hotel' though it's not certain if these claims can be substantiated.

A Bougainvillier Hotel, 277G Sisowath Quay, T023-220528, www.bougainvillier hotel.com. Lovely riverside boutique hotel, rooms decorated in a modern Asian theme, with a/c, safe, cable TV, and mini bar. Good French restaurant. Recommended.

A Castle Hotel, 4-6 St 148, T023-211425, www.hotelcastle.com.kh. Comfortable hotel with good size swimming pool to cool down in and conveniently located.

A Foreign Correspondents Club of Cambodia (FCCC), No 363 Sisowath Quay, T023-210142, www.fcccambodia.com. Known locally as the FCC. 3 decent sized rooms are available in this well known Phnom Penh landmark. Not far to stagger home from the bar and handy for breakfast.

C River Star Hotel, T023-990501, www.riverstarhotel.com. Decent hotel on the riverfront. The only thing extraordinary about the rooms is the view. All rooms have a/c, bathroom and seating area.

C-D Red Hibiscus, 277c Sisowath Quay, T023-990691, www.redhibiscus.biz. Stylish rooms, some with river views, in an excellent location. All a/c, en suite and with tv.

C-F Paragon Hotel, 219b Sisowath Quay, T023-222607, info_paragonhotel@ yahoo.com. The Paragon gets the simple things right – it's a well-run and friendly hotel. The best and priciest rooms have private balconies overlooking the river – uncomplicated decoration with enough elegant touches to give it character. The cheaper rooms at the back are dark but still some of the best value in this part of town. Each room has colour TV, hot water and private shower or bath, a/c or fan. Recommended.

D-F Bright Lotus Guesthouse, No 22 St 178 (near the museum), T023-990 446, sammy_lotus@hotmail.com. Fan and a/c rooms with private bathroom and balconies. Restaurant.

D-F Indochine 2 Hotel, No 28-30 St 130, T023-211525. Great location and good, clean, comfortable rooms.

D-G Sunshine, No 253 Sisowath Quay, T023-725684. 50 rooms, a few of which have a glimpse of the river. Facilities, from a/c to fan, in accordance with price.

E-F Royal Guesthouse, 91 St 154, hou_heng @yahoo.com. Small family-run guesthouse. Some rooms are much better than others. Ask for the top-floor balcony rooms with a/c at US$12 they are worth paying extra for.

Wat Phnom and around
p50, maps p44 and p49

The area around Wat Phnom is now blighted by the unnecessarily huge and overbearing US Embassy. It still retains some leafy charm though. The area down by the lake is now being developed and while some guesthouses still remain at the time of publication their future is not assured.

LL Le Royal, St 92 (off Monivong Blvd), T023-981888, www.raffles-hotelleroyal.com. This is a grand colonial-era hotel built in 1929. Now owned by the Raffles group, both this hotel and the **Grand Angkor** in Siem Reap have reputations for handling labour disputes in a heavy handed manner and were subject to boycotts by international workers' organizations. Parts of the hotel have been beautifully restored though rooms can be on the small side (and plumbing also has a reputation for being a bit dodgy). The hotel has passable bars and restaurants, a delightful tree-lined pool, a well stocked bookshop and the **Elephant Bar**, one of Phnom Penh's most legendary watering holes.

LL-A Phnom Penh Hotel, 54 Monivong Blvd, T023-724851, www.phnompenh.hotel.com. 407 well-appointed rooms with TV, a/c, internet, room safe. Health club, spa

and an outdoor swimming pool. Within walking distance to the lake's cheap restaurants and bars.

L-A Sunway, No 1 St 92, T023-430333, asunway@online.com.kh. Overlooking Wat Phnom, this is an adequate hotel in an excellent location. 140 ordinary though well-appointed rooms, including 12 spacious suites, provide comfort complemented by facilities and amenities to cater for the international business and leisure traveller.

D Dara Reang Sey Hotel, Corner St of St 13 and 118 Phsar Chas, T023-428181, darareangsey@cannet.com. Busy hotel with popular local restaurant downstairs, clean rooms with hot water and some rooms have baths.

D-E Velkommen Inn, 23 St 104, T092-177710, www.velkommeninn.com. A friendly Norwegian and his Khmer wife run Velkommen Inn. Its located 50 m from **Angkor Express** and **Mekong Express** bus stations near the riverside and boat docks. Has clean rooms.

E-F Simon 2 Guesthouse, the road in front of the lake T012-608892. This place has the largest, cleanest rooms.

F Floating Island, on the lake (formerly **Shanti**), T012-949343, chumkanthavy@gmail.com. Rooms emulate the feeling of being in a caravan, a small one. Some rooms have their own bathroom. Nice, breezy deck upstairs.

G Lazy Fish Guesthouse and Restaurant, No 16 St 93, lakeside, T012-703358 or T016-533913, lazyfishlakeside@hotmail.com (although the owner admits he's lazy and never checks it). Very basic guesthouse with shared bathroom facilities. Has small veranda area but no lake left outside to look at.

G No 10 Lakeside Guesthouse, No 10 St 93, Boeng Kak Lake, T012-725032, phanna2005@gmail.com. Similar to Number 9. It is rather dingy and stuffy. Hammocks, pool table and lockers.

G-F Grandview Guesthouse, just off the lake, T023-430766, www.grandview.netfirms.com. This place is streets ahead of local competition. Clean, basic rooms with a/c for a few extra bucks. Rooftop restaurant with good sunset views, serving large breakfast menu, pizza, Indian and Khmer food (all under US$2). Travel services and internet.

G-F Happy Guesthouse and Restaurant, No 11 St 93, lakeside, T023-430833, www.happy11ghcambodia.com. If your idea of good accommodation is staying in a cupboard, then this is the place for you. 40 basic rooms, most with shared facilities but a few with private bathroom. Restaurant, free pool table and lovely veranda area.

Around Independence Monument
p51, map p44

Referred to by the locals as "NGO-land" this part of town is quiet, leafy and filled with small villas that were once home to dozens of NGOs. The local services grew up to feed the well-paid foreign workers who lived here.
A The Pavilion, 227 St 19, T023-222280, www.pavilion-cambodia.com. A popular and beautiful small, 10-room hotel set in a old French colonial villa. Each room is unique with a/c, en suite and TV. The restaurant also serves decent food. However, the management has a reputation for being extremely prickly and a penchant for banning organizations and individuals. Children are completely banned (unless friends of the owner) – we've had several reports of the management abruptly and unceremoniously asking women with children to leave the restaurant.
A-B Almond Hotel, 128F Sothearos Bvld, T023-220822, www.almondhotel.com.kh. Stylish, new hotel in upmarket part of town though still offers good value for facilities. The more expensive rooms offer the best deal and come with huge balconies – the cheaper ones have no windows. A/c, en suite and TV through-out. Breakfast and Wi-Fi included.
B-C Amber Villa, 1a St 57, T023-216303, www.amber-kh.com. This small, friendly, family-run hotel is often full so book ahead – rooms include breakfast, laundry and internet – all have a/c and en suite facilities. The best have TV/DVD and balconies.

B-D Scandinavia Hotel 4 St 282, T023-214498, www.hotel-scandinavia-cambodia.com. The **Scandinavia** is slowly gaining a reputation as one of the best boutique hotels/guesthouses in Phnom Penh. Very friendly service is married to stylish, well-designed rooms (some are a bit dark, though), all with a/c, en suite facilities, internet, cable TV. The roof-top restaurant serves decent food and the small pool, filled with huge inflatable toys, is as funky as they come. The owner has also turned much of the public space into a gallery for international and contemporary art. Recommended.
C-E Anise, 2c St 278, T023-222522, www.anisehotel.com. Excellent value in the heart of a busy area. All rooms are en suite with cable TV, a/c. Pay a little more and you'll get a room with bathtub and private balcony. Included in the is price laundry, internet and breakfast. Recommended.
C-E Golden Gate Hotel, No 9 S 278 (just off St 51), T023-721161, goldengatehtls @hotmail.com. Very popular and comparatively good value for the facilities offered. Clean rooms with TV, fridge, hot water and a/c. Within walking distance to restaurants and bars. Visa/MasterCard.

South of the centre *p51, map p44*
C-E Boddhi Tree, No 50 St 113, T016-865445, www.boddhitree.com. A tranquil setting which belies its location just metres from the Tuol Sleng prison. Lovely old wooden building with rooms offering simple amenities, fan only, some with bathroom. Great gardens and fantastic food at very reasonable prices.
C-E L'Imprévu, on Highway Number 1, 6 km past the Monivong Bridge, T023-360405, imprecas@everyday.com.kh. French-run. Lovely bungalows with TV, fridge and hot water. Good pool and garden. Tennis court, petanque, snooker, table tennis and a gym.
C-E Palm Resort, on Route 1, 5 km out of Phnom Penh, T023-308 6881. Beautiful

bungalows surrounded by lush gardens and a very large swimming pool. A/c rooms with very clean bathrooms. Excellent French restaurant. Recommended.

West of the centre p52, map p44
LL-A Intercontinental, 296 Mao Tse Tung Blvd, T023-430766, www.intercontinental.com. A 350-room hotel at the southern end of town. Bit unsightly from the outside and not a great location but comfortable with large, luxurious bathrooms and highly regarded by business guests. Cantonese restaurant, coffee shop and Clark Hatch fitness centre with aerobics room. Offers most of the facilities business visitors require as well as a large swimming pool. Probably the best international business hotel in town. Recommended.
A Juliana, No 16 St 152, T023-880530, www.julianacambodia.com.kh. A very attractive resort-style hotel with 91 rooms, and decent sized pool in a secluded garden which provides plenty of shade; His and Hers, popular haircut and Thai massage centre and several excellent restaurants. Recommended.
B-C New York Hotel, 256 Monivong Blvd, T023-214116, www.newyorkhotel.com.kh. The rooms aren't going to set the world on fire but the facilities are good for the price – massage centre, sauna, restaurant and in-room safe.
E-F Spring Guesthouse, No 34 St 111 (next to the German Embassy), T015-888777, www.springguesthouse.hostel.com. Decent friendly guesthouse in good location. Rooms are a mix of fan and a/c, with cable TV, en suite hot showers and Wi-Fi. Also run some tours, etc.
E-F Capitol, No 14 St 182, T023-364104, www.capitolkh.com. 'A Phnom Penh institution', as they say. What, in 1991, was a single guesthouse has expanded to 5 guesthouses all within a stone's throw. All are aimed at the budget traveller and offer travel services as well as a popular café and internet access. There are a number of other cheap guesthouses in close proximity, such as **Happy Guesthouse** (next door to Capitol

Guesthouse) and **Hello Guesthouse** (No 242 St 107) – all about the same ilk.

Kirirom National Park p56
E-F Kirirom Restaurant and Guesthouse, turn left before the intersection at the large Johnnie Walker sign about 10 km from the entrance to the park, T018-815403. 5 large twin rooms in a motel-style chalet, all rooms come equipped with ceiling fan, furnishings and attached cold water shower and toilet, tranquil with excellent views of the park, English spoken, electricity from 1500-2300. Adjacent restaurant serves Khmer and Western food, US$15 per person.

🍴 Eating

A whole swathe of upmarket, stylish and pricey eateries are establishing themselves by the river and in NGO-land in the St 57 area. They mostly serve Phnom Penh's burgeoning yuppies and well-paid ex-pats and NGO workers. It has to be said though, that the standard of food is remarkably high in these establishments – most are excellent value as well, offering some of the best priced upmarket cuisine in Southeast Asia. If you want to go 'local' most other places are relatively inexpensive – around US$3-6 per head. A bowl of noodles from a street stall will be even cheaper but be warned that street food in Cambodia doesn't have the same hygiene standards as in Thailand and Vietnam.

Historic centre p46, map p44
🍴 **The Deli**, near corner of St 178 and Norodom Blvd, T012-851234. Great cakes, bread, salads and lunch at this sleek little diner. Sandwich fillings, for the price, are a bit light, though.
🍴 **Tamarind**, No 31 St 240, T012-830139. Stylish bar and restaurant specializing in Mediterranean food: great kebabs and couscous. Also serves tapas. Atmospheric.

Ψ **Peking Canteen**, No 393 St 136, T011-909548. Open until 2200. Hole-in-the-wall Chinese restaurant famous for its cheap dumplings (which come either steamed or fried). Very busy at lunchtime. Short walk from Psar Thmei.

Ψ **Sam Doo**, 56 Kampuchea Krom Blvd, T023-218773. Open until 0200. Late-night Chinese food and the best and cheapest dim sum in town.

Ψ **The Shop**, No 39 St 240, T012-901964. Owned and managed by a Belgian ex-pat, this is an excellent deli and bakery offering imaginative sandwiches, juices, superb smoothies, fruit teas, salads and light lunches. As you'd expect from a Belgian, they also serve up fabulous chocolates and have just opened up a purpose-built chocolatier 2 doors down, 0900-1800. Recommended.

The riverside *p48, maps p44 and p49*

ΨΨΨ **Bougainvillier Hotel**, 277G Sisowath Quay, T023-220528. Upmarket French and Khmer food. Superb foie gras and you can even find truffles here. Fine dining by the river. Recommended.

ΨΨΨ **Foreign Correspondents Club of Cambodia (FCCC)**, No 363 Sisowath Quay, T023-724014. 0700-2400. A sunrise breakfast overlooking the river in this superb colonial building is an essential Phnom Penh experience although ironically, this is the last place in Phnom Penh most local journalists dine. The 2nd floor bar and restaurant serves an extensive international menu. It's a bit pricey and standards have dipped of late but there's Wi-Fi and wonderful photography exhibitions.

ΨΨΨ **K-West**, Amanjaya Hotel, corner of St 154 and Sisowath Quay, T023-213772. Open 0630-2200. Beautiful, spacious restaurant offering respite from the outside world. Khmer and European food plus extensive cocktail list. Surprisingly, the prices aren't that expensive considering how upmarket it is. Come early for the divine chocolate mousse – it sells out quickly. Great salads as well. Free Wi-Fi. Recommended.

ΨΨΨ **Origami**, No 88 Sothearos Blvd, T012-968095. Best Japanese in town, delectable, fresh sushi and sashimi. Pricey – one local describes it as where "good things come in very small, expensive packages".

ΨΨΨ **Pacharan**, 389 Sisowath Quay, T023-224394. Excellent Spanish tapas and main courses in a old colonial villa with views across the river and an open kitchen. Stylish Mediterranean feel to it. While the tapas are good value the prices of the main courses are about the highest in town. Part of the FCC empire. 1100-2300. Recommended.

ΨΨΨ **Riverhouse**, corner of St 110 and Sisowath Quay, T023-212302, www.riverhouse cambodia.com. Happy hour 1700-1900, restaurant closes at 2200, bar at 2400. Mediterranean/Thai restaurant in a lovely restored building overlooking the river. Brilliant food, particularly the steak, which is cooked to perfection. Upstairs is a comfortable lounge bar which also serves light meals. Recommended.

ΨΨΨ-ΨΨ **Corner33**, 33 Sothearos Blvd. T09-299 8850, www.corner33.com. Open daily 0700-2200. Set on the upper floors of a building on the corner of St 178 just back from the river, the big sofas and large windows are perfect for views of the palace. Thai and Asian food along with some pasta, coffee and cakes. Free Wi-Fi with coffee.

ΨΨ **Cantina**, No 347 Sisowath Quay, T023-222502. Great Mexican restaurant and bar opened by long-time local character, Hurley. Fantastic food made with the freshest of ingredients. The restaurant attracts an eclectic crowd and can be a source of great company. Terrific photography exhibition, featuring pictures from war-time photographers. Interestingly, the restaurant's sign is a sculpture crafted from old guns. Seating inside and on the street. Very popular. Recommended.

ΨΨ **Green Vespa**, No 95 Sisowath Quay, T012-877228. Open 0630-late. Serving the best Sunday roast dinners in Cambodia, the best you are going to get away from home.

ΨΨ **Khmer Borane**, No 389 Sisowath Quay, T012-290092. Open till 2300. Excellent Khmer restaurant just down from the **FCC**. Wide selection of very well prepared Khmer and Thai food, try the *amok*.

ⓜ La Croisette, No 241 Sisowath Quay, T023-220554. Authentically French and good value hors d'oeuvres and steak. Sit on the broad pavement dining contentedly with Edith Piaf singing softly in the background. Good selection of wines.

ⓜ Lemongrass, No 14 St 130, T012-996707. Open 1000-2200. Khmer Thai restaurant classical atmosphere and surroundings with reasonably priced menu. Opt for the rice pudding and mango.

ⓜ Le Wok, 33 St 178, T09-821857. Open daily 0900-2300. French-inspired Asian food served in this friendly little restaurant located on fashionable street 178 a short stroll from the river front. Daily fixed-lunch menus and a la carte.

ⓜ Metro, corner of Sisowath and St 148. Open 1000-0200. Huge, affordable tapas portions make this a great spot for lunch or dinner. The creme brulée smothered in passion fruit is life-affirming. Free Wi-Fi. Recommended.

ⓜ Pop Café, 371 Sisowath Quay, T012-562892. Open 1100-1430 and 1800-2200. Almost perfect, small, Italian restaurant sited next door to the FCC. Owned and managed by Italian ex-pat Giorgio, the food has all the panache you'd expect from an Italian. The home-made lasagne is probably one of the best value meals in town. Recommended.

ⓜ Rising Sun, No 20 St 178 (just around the corner from the FCC) T012-970719. English restaurant with possibly the best breakfast in town. Good bacon and hash browns, plus, they'll use 2 teabags in a pot if you ask nicely. Ginormous roast and excellent iced coffee. Recommended.

ⓜ Riverside, corner St 148 and Sisowath Quay, T023-766743. Enjoy omelettes and burgers while dining inside or out.

ⓜ Romdeng, No 74 St 174, T092-2153 5037, romdeng@mithsamlanh.org. Open 1100-2100. Sister restaurant to **Friends**, helping out former street kids. Serves just Khmer foods. Watch out for specials like fried tarantula with chili and garlic. Highly recommended.

ⓜ Veiyo (River Breeze), No 237 Sisowath Quay, T012-847419. Pizza and pasta, etc along with Thai and Khmer cuisine.

ⓨ Chiang Mai Riverside, No 227 Sisowath Quay, T012-832369. Open until 2200. Riverfront location for this small but successful Thai restaurant. Simple picture menus (always a turn-off but common in Cambodia where little English is spoken). Endorsed by the Thai government.

ⓨ Fortune Pho, St 178, just behind the FCC. Open 0800-2100. Great Vietnamese noodles in this small shop. Unfortunately your eating experience can sometimes be ruined by dreadful service.

ⓨ Friends, No 215 St 13, T023-426748. Non-profit restaurant run by street kids being trained in the hospitality industry. The food is delicious and cheap. Highly recommended.

ⓨ Frizz, 335 Sisowath Quay, T023-220953. Awesome Khmer food. Friendly service and great location. One of the best spots to eat local food on the riverside. Incredibly cheap as well. Offers cooking classes too. Recommended.

ⓨ Happy Herb Pizza, No 345 Sisowath Quay, T023-332349. Another Phnom Penh institution, open for over 10 years. Watch out for the 'happy' pizza full of hash – it has a nasty kick. Free pizza delivery.

Cafés and bakeries

Fresco, 365 Sisowath Quay, T023-217041. Just underneath the FCC and owned by the same people. They have a wide selection of sandwiches, cakes and pastries of mixed quality and high price.

Wat Phnom and around *p50, map p44*

Thankfully the restaurants at the lake are a notch above the accommodation standards. All of the restaurants here are exceptionally cheap, almost half the price of places in the city. All of the guesthouses on the lake have restaurants, most with identical Western-Khmer-Thai menus and prices.

¶¶¶ **Tell**, No 13 St 90, T023-430650. Restaurant closes at 2300, bar at 2400. Swiss German specials including excellent raclette, fondue and wurst. Generous portions authentically prepared. Imported German beer. Owners maintain high standards in the kitchen and in the chalet-esque dining room. There's another branch in Siem Reap.

¶¶ **La Marmite**, No 80 St 108 (on the corner with Pasteur), T012-391746. Excellent value French food – some of the best in town.

¶¶ **Monsoon**, No 17 St 104, T016-355867. Open 1000-0200. They serve a damn fine curry at this funky South Asian restaurant-cum-wine bar. The drinks list is also pretty good and the soft furnishings should lull you into a state of somnolence. Recommended.

¶ **Boeung Bopha**, Highway 6 (over the Japanese Friendship Bridge), T012-928353. Open until 2300. Large Khmer restaurant with huge menu which includes a number of Khmer dishes and buffet.

¶ **The Family Restaurant**, St 93, lakeside. A small, family-run, Vietnamese restaurant serving brilliant (and quite adventurous) food at ridiculously low prices. Great service, lovely owners. Highly recommended.

¶ **Lazy Gecko**, St 93, lakeside. Popular, chilled out restaurant/café/bar offering a good selection of sandwiches, burgers and salads in large portions. Good home-cooked Sun roast. Affable owner, Juan, is a good source of information. Selection of new and used books for sale. Good trivia night on Thu.

Around Independence Monument
p51, map p44

¶¶¶ **Comme à la Maison**, No 13 St 57, T023-360801. Great French delicatessen-type restaurant-cum-café. Good pizzas and pastries and the breakfast is exceptional.

¶¶¶ **Elsewhere**, No 175 St 51, T023-211348. An oasis in the middle of the city offering delectable modern Western cuisine. Seats are speckled across wonderful tropical gardens, all topped off by a well-lit pool.

¶¶¶ **Ocean Restaurant**, No 11 St 288, T017-766690. Open 1100-2200. Good Italian food. Serves a variety of Mediterranean and seafood dishes in a/c.

¶¶¶ **Shiva Shakti**, 70 Sihanouk Blvd, T012-813817. Open until 2230, closed Mon. Facing the Independence Monument. Indian and Moghul specials, vegetarian and meat dishes. The option of pavement eating does not appeal by the side of this busy boulevard but the calm and aromatic atmosphere of the interior is enormously attractive. Quite expensive for Phnom Penh but a good range of excellent food. Selection of cigars.

¶¶¶ **Topaz**, 182 Norodom Blvd, T012-333276. Open 1200-1400, 1800-2300. Has set its sights on being the most upmarket place in town – a/c restaurant or outside dining, upstairs bar and cigar room. Recommended if you can afford it.

¶¶¶ **Yi Sang**, ground floor of **Almond Hotel** (see Sleeping), daily. Serving up excellent Cantonese food in 3 sittings: 0630-1030 dim sum and noodles, 1130-1400 dim sum and à la carte, 1730-2200 sea food and à la carte - the newly opened **Yi Sang** is hoping to offer some of the best grub in town. Very good quality and great value.

¶¶ **Baan Thai**, No 2 St 306, T023-362991. Open 1130-1400, 1730-2200. Excellent Thai food and attentive service at this popular restaurant that has been running for 13 years. Main dishes US$4-5. Garden and old wooden Thai house with sit-down cushions.

¶¶ **Gasolina**, No 56/58 St 57, T012-373009. Open 1100-late. Huge garden and decent French-inspired food await in this friendly, relaxed restaurant. The owner also arranges tai chi and capoeira classes. They normally have a BBQ at the weekends.

¶¶ **K'NYAY**, 25k Soramit Blvd (St 268), T023-225225, www.knyay.com. Tue-Fri 1200-2100, Sat 0700-2100, Sun 0700-1500. As one of the only places in Phnom Penh that advertises itself as selling vegan food and set in a villa, complete with stylish interior, K'NYAY even has a pretentious name. Unfortunately, despite creating a hip image the food doesn't match. Very average but if you're a veggie, a god-send.

Living Room, No 9 St 306, T023-726139. Tue-Thu 0700-1800, Fri-Sun 0700-2100. The Japanese owner has done a superlative job at this pleasant hangout spot, set in a villa amid a lot of soothing greenery. The food and coffee is spot-on and the set plates are great value but it's the laid-back, calming vibe that is the clincher. Bring a book, curl up on the sofa and forget the chaos. There's a purpose-built kids play area downstairs. Free Wi-Fi if you spend over US$3. Highly recommended.

Mount Everest, 98 Sihanouk Blvd, T023-213821. Open 1000-2300. Has served acclaimed Nepalese and Indian dishes for 5 years, attracting a loyal following.

Talking to a Stranger, No 21 St 294, T012-798530. Wed-Sun. Fantastic bar and restaurant set in an old colonial building high on atmosphere and with a brilliant photography display. Excellent antipasti platter and delectable chocolate cake dessert. Popular with the expat crowd who, at times, aren't the most engaging lot but the owners are good company.

Khmer Surin, No 9 St 57, T023-363050. Closes 2230. Set in an attractive building with some traditional Thai-style seating on cushions, this quiet restaurant is a little way south of Sihanouk Blvd.

Yumi, No 29a St 288, T092-163903. Open 1100-1400 and 1700-2200. Recommend its Sushi. Run by a lively Japanese guy.

Cafés/bakeries

Asia Europe Bakery, No 95 Sihanouk Blvd, T012-893177. Western-style café/bakery. Delicious pastries, cakes and excellent breakfast and lunch menu. Recommended.

Garden Centre Café, No 23 St 57, T023-363002. Popular place to go for lunch and breakfast, perhaps not surprisingly, the garden is nice too.

Java, No 56 Sihanouk Blvd. Contenders for best coffee in town. Nice use of space – open-air balcony and pleasant surroundings. Delightful food. Features art and photography exhibitions on a regular basis. Good place to come and eavesdrop on some NGO talk.

Le Gourmandise Bleue, 159 St 278, T023-994019. Tue-Sun 0700-2000. Sweet little French-North African bakery serving up almost perfect cakes and coffee. Famous for its macaroons and also does couscous dishes.

The Shop, No 39 St 240 and No St 38, T023-986964. Open 0700-1900. Popular sandwich joint – fresh salads. Closes early on Sun at 1500.

T&C Coffee World, numerous branches – 369 Preah Sihanouk Blvd; Sorya Shopping Centre; 335 Monivong Blvd. Vietnamese-run equivalent to **Starbucks**, but better. Surprisingly good food and very good coffee. Faultless service.

South of the centre *p51, map p44*
Boddhi Tree, No 50 St 113, T016-865445, www.boddhitree.com. Kitchen closes 2100. Bang opposite the Tuol Sleng Museum. A delightful garden setting and perfect for lunch, a snack or drink. Delicious salads (US$2-3) and sandwiches, the barbecue chicken and cheddar is exquisite. Well run and managed and a great deal of care spent on preparation, presentation and service. Very good Khmer food in a very therapeutic garden setting.

Cafes and bakeries
Jars of Clay, No 39 St 155 (beside the Russian Market). Fresh cakes and pastries.

West of the centre *p52, map p44*
Teukei, No 23 St 111, T012-707609. Good European food.

Foodstalls
According to a survey by the Ministry of Health, 75% of the street food tested contained high levels of bacteria. If locals with money avoid such places there is no good reason for visitors to patronize them. Those wishing to try should ensure their hepatitis

antibody count is high. **Central Market**, just off Monivong Blvd (at the intersection of St 118 and Charles de Gaulle Blvd). Also good food stalls around the **Capitol Hotel** on St 182. Several Vietnamese stalls on St 242 and around most city markets. At the **Russian Market** on St 182, in the corner of the food hall area, is a stall with a sign saying 'best iced coffee in Phnom Penh'. They're right.

◑ Bars and clubs

The vast majority of bars in Phnom Penh attract prostitutes.

Blue Chilli, No 36 St 178, T012-566353. Open 1800-late. Gay bar with DJ and dancing. Drag show on Sat.

The Cathouse, corner of St 51 and St 18. Open till 2400. Around since the UNTAC days of the early 1990s and one of the oldest running bars in the city. Not a bad place to have a beer and wonder what it would look like full of UN soldiers getting drunk and fighting.

Elephant Bar, Le Royal Hotel. Open until 2400. Stylish and elegant bar in Phnom Penh's top hotel, perfect for an evening gin. 2 for 1 happy hour everyday with unending supply of nachos, which makes for a cheap night out in sophisticated surroundings. Potentially the best drinks in town.

Elsewhere, No 175 St 51, T023-981888. Atmospheric, up-market bar set in garden with illuminated pool and candlelit seating. Great cocktails and wine. Very popular with the expats, who have been known to strip off for a dip. Good for a drink before heading somewhere else or a late night spot for engaging conversation. Livens up on the last Sat of every month, when it has parties.

The Fly Lounge, No 21a St 148, T089-509007. Open 1700-0200. Cool hangout with in-house pool. Serves great cocktails and plays chill out music.

Foreign Correspondents Club of Cambodia (FCCC), 363 Sisowath Quay. Satellite TV, pool, *Bangkok Post* and *The Nation* both available for reading here. Happy hour 1700-1900.

Perfect location overlooking the river, excellent food.

Green Vespa, No 95 Sisowath Quay, T012-877228. Open 0630-late. British-run pub, expat hang-out. Happy hour between 1800-1900.

Heart of Darkness, No 26 St 51. Heaving with people. Reasonable prices, friendly staff and open late. Has been Phnom Penh's most popular hangout for a number of years. Absolutely full of prostitutes, but your best bet for a night of dancing. There have been many violent 'incidents' here, so it is advisable to be on your best behaviour in the bar as they do not tolerate any provocation.

La Croisette has live music every Thu and Fri. See Eating, page 63.

Manhattan, in the rather dubious **Holiday International Hotel**, St 84, T023-427402. One of Phnom Penh's biggest discos. Security check and metal detectors at the door prevent you from bringing in small arms.

Memphis Pub, St 118 (off Sisowath Quay). Open till 0200. Small bar off the river. Very loyal following from the NGO crowd. Live rock and blues music from Tue to Sat.

Metro, corner Sisowath and St 148, T023-217517. Open 1000-0200. As well as serving fine grub **Metro** is also home to a fabulous bar. A/c and smooth surroundings make it popular with rich Khmers and expansive ex-pats. Recommended.

Pontoon, on the river at end of St 108, T012-572880. 1200-2330 weekdays, until late at weekends. Great little spot for a drink and dance. Hosts international DJs and serves good cocktails. Gay nights Thu and Fri. Sat Club night. Recommended.

The Rising Sun, No 20 St 178, T023-970719. Open til 2400. Just around the corner from the FCCC. An English pub whose emphasis is just as much on food as beer.

Riverhouse Lounge, No 6 St 110 (Sisowath Quay). Open 1600-0200. Upmarket, cocktail bar and club. Good wine, cocktails and cigars. Nice views of the river and airy open balcony space. Live music (Sun) and DJs (Sat) with good music and crowd. Great restaurant attached. Atmospheric. Recommended.

Riverside Bar, 273a Sisowath Quay. Great riverfront bar. Tasty food. Recommended.
Salt Lounge, No 217 St 136, T012-289905, www.thesaltlounge.com. Relatively new, funky minimalist bar. Very atmospheric and stylish. Gay friendly.
Sharkys, No 126 St 130. 'Beware pickpockets and loose women' it warns. Large, pool tables and food served until late. Quite a 'blokey' hangout and advertised as the longest running rock and roll bar in Cambodia.
Talking to a Stranger, see Eating, page 64. Great cocktails and relaxed atmosphere. In the throes of developing a cocktail lounge at the time of publication. Recommended.
Zepplin Bar aka Rock Bar, No 128 St 136 (just off Monivong beside the Central Market). Open until late. Hole in the wall bar owned by a Taiwanese man named Joon who has over 1000 records for customers to choose from. Cheap beer and spirits. Truly unique concept and an excellent choice for rocking to your favourite songs.

◉ Entertainment

There are always events in Phnom Penh – the best bet is to pick up a copy of the *Cambodia Daily* and check out the back page which details up-and-coming events.

Casinos
Casinos are illegal within a 100-km radius of Phnom Penh. Those who think it surprising to find 2 in the heart of the city are clearly new to Cambodia.
Holiday International Hotel, St 84. This Singaporean-owned hotel opened the only casino in town in Nov 1994 – the first to begin operating since 1970. Roulette, blackjack and usual entertainments.
Naga is a floating casino moored near **Cambodiana Hotel**. Scarcely a week passes without a newspaper reporting the Naga's imminent closure due to non-payment of rent or some other misdemeanour. It is open 24 hrs a day and continues to flourish.

Cambodia Asia Bank on the ship never shuts, even on public holidays (cash advances on Visa only).

Dance
National Museum of Cambodia, St 70 in the north of the city. Folk and national dances are performed by the National Dance group. Contact the National Museum directly or the **Ministry of Information and Culture**, 395 Monivong Blvd.
Sovanna Phum Theatre, No 111 St 360 (on the corner of St 105), T023-987564, sovannaphum@camintel.com. Shadow puppets, traditional dance and circus. Every Fri and Sat 1930, US$4.

Films and art
Check the *Cambodia Daily* for details.
MTV Video Studio, 1 block down from **Lucky Supermarket** on Sihanouk Blvd. 20 private, a/c rooms which can be rented to watch movies. Hundreds of DVDs to choose from. US$4 for 2 hrs.
Meta House, 6 St 264, T012-607465, www.meta-house.com. Fri-Sat, 1800-2400. This is one of the newest contemporary art places in town. Installations, film and video happenings, light shows and Southeast Asian and international art. Recommended.

◯ Shopping

Art galleries
There is plenty of promising artistic talent coming out of Cambodia, with some tremendous works both in traditional and contemporary styles.
Apsara Art Gallery, No 170A St 450, next to Russian Market, T012-867390. Open 0700-1800. Paintings, posters bronzes and a framing service. Studios of local work on St 178. Cambodian landscapes, Angkor and attractive ladies are the most commonly churned out themes but the quality is disappointing.
Asasax Gallery, No 192 St 178, T012-877795. Open 0800-2000. Mixed media artist and

sculptor using colourful modern materials to develop work based on traditional themes (apsaras and the sort).

Happy Painting, 363 Sisowath Quay (FCC), www.happypainting.net. The gallery is owned by French-Canadian artist Stéphane Delaprée. His work is colourful in that naïve art kind of way. It is a shame that a foreigner is one of Cambodia's most famous artists. The Cambodian royal family, among many others, has bought his work.

Meta House, T012-607465, www.meta-house.com, due to change location check website for details. Fri-Sat 1800-2400. Interesting international art – some of which is for sale.

New Art Gallery, No 20 St 9, T012-824570. Contemporary paintings by local artists.

Reyum Institute of Arts and Culture, No 47 St 178 (across from the National), T023-217149, www.reyum.org. Open 0800-1800. A great place to start for those interested in Cambodian modern art. Some absolutely world-class artists have been mentored and exhibit here.

Sala Artspace, 339 Sisowath Quay, www.sala-artspace.org. Mon-Sat 0800-2200. Nice little gallery that serves up a few snacks along with some reasonable art.

Scan Gallery, at Scan Hotel, 4 St 282, T023-214498, www.hotel-scandinavia-cambodia.com. Decent array of international and local contemporary art – it is usually well-hung and everything is for sale.

Books/maps/music/DVDs

Cambodia is still a hub of pirated DVDs and music.

DVD Shop, St 178, just behind the FCC. Probably the best and biggest range of fake DVDs in town. Everything from arthouse classics through to the latest box set of 24.

D's Books, No 79 St 240 and No 12 St 178. Second-hand books and new (copied books). There is also a branch up from the Rising Sun.

The International Stationary and Book Centre, 37 Sihanouk Blvd. Better on stationery than international books. Lots of text books.

Monument Books, 111 Norodom Bvld, T023-217617. Open 0730-2030. Best and most extensive range of English-language newspapers, magazines and books in town. They also do a damn fine cup of coffee.

Rogue, No 1c St 278, T012-709096. Open 0900-2100. Run by a British ex-pat, **Rogue** (formerly **Boom Boom Room**) cuts out the hassle of Limewire and sells stolen music to you at knock-down prices. Re-fill your ipod from a choice of over 4000 albums.

Handicrafts and clothes

Many non-profit organizations have opened stores to help train or rehabilitate some of the country's underprivileged. St 240, just to the south of the Palace is now becoming a hub of creative activity.

Ambre, No 37 St 178, T012-688608. Mon-Sat 1000-1800. Internationally renowned high-end women's fashion. Prices, given the quality, are also excellent value. Recommended.

Bare Necessities, No 46 St 322, T023-996664. Selling a range of bras and underwear which fit western sizes, from maternity to sporty to sexy. A social enterprise raising money to support awareness and treatment of breast cancer for poor, rural Cambodian women.

Disabled Handicrafts Promotion Association (DHPA), No 106 St 51. Open 0700-1700. Handicrafts and jewellery made by people with disabilities and widows.

Friends @ 240, 240 St, T012-802072. Open 0900-1800. Small studio selling creative fashion in the form of accessories and clothing. Recommended.

Jasmine, No 73 St 240, T023-223103. Open 0730-1800. Boutique selling Cambodian-made feminine clothes and accessories.

The National Centre for Disabled People (NCDP), 3 Norodom Blvd, T023-210140. Great store with handicrafts such as pillow cases, tapestries and bags made by people with disabilities. Recommended.

National Museum of Arts, corner of St 19 and St 184 (behind the National Museum). Sells reproductions of Khmer statues, prints and frescoes of Angkor.

Nyemo, No 71 St 240 between St 63 and Monivong Blvd, www.nyemo.com. This is non-profit shop with a wide range of silk products.

Orange River, 367 Sisowath Quay (under FCC), T023-214594. Open 0900-2200. Has a selection of beautifully designed decorative items and a very good stock of fabrics and silks which will leave many wishing for more luggage allowance. Pricier than most other stores.

Rajana, No 170 St 450, next to the Russian Market. Open 0700-1715. Traditional crafts, silk paintings, silver and jewellery.

Silk & Pepper, No 33 St 178 (next door to Le Wok, see Eating). Contemporary, sleek, Khmer-inspired fashions and silks, Also sells Kampot pepper in little china pots.

Markets and shopping malls

Central Market (Psar Thmei), just off Monivong Blvd. Distinguished by its central art deco dome (built 1937), it is mostly full of stalls selling silver and gold jewellery, old coins and assorted fake antiques. Around the main building more mundane items are for sale, including, of course, *kramas*, the famous Cambodian checked scarf. The main gates into the Central Market are lined with stalls selling touristy items.

Old Market (Psar Chah), between St 13, St 106 and St 110. Sells stationery, clothes, jewellery, fabrics and *kramas* intended for locals rather than tourists.

O Russei Market, St 182. Sells mainly fruit and vegetables but also some terrible ladies' fashions.

Tuol Tom Pong, between St 155 and St 163 to east and west, and St 440 and St 450 to north and south, close to the pagoda of the same name. Known to many as the Russian Market. Sells antiques (genuine articles and fakes) and jewellery – nearby is an antique furniture market – as well as clothing, pirate CDs and computer software, videos, sarongs, fabrics and an immense variety of tobacco – an excellent place for buying souvenirs, especially silk. Most things at this market are

about half the price of the Central Market. There are also several food stalls here.

Sorya Shopping Centre, St 63, beside the Central Market. 7-floor, a/c shopping centre with goods ranging from shoes to plasma-screen TV. It even has a skating rink. Great view of the city from the look-out deck at the top.

Photography

City Colour Photo, 123 Monivong Blvd. Reasonably good photo processing. Stocks new and old cameras. Camera repairs.

Nikon Centre, 208 Preah Monivong. The most professional photographic shop.

Silverware and jewellery

Old silver boxes, belts, antique jewellery can be found along Monivong Blvd. Samdech Sothearos Blvd, just north of St 184, has a good cluster of silver shops.

Cambodiana Hotel also has a good silver shop. There are plenty of jewellery stalls in the central covered market. Most modern silverware is no more than 80% silver.

Rachana, No 6B St 118, T023-211290, has nicely made silver animals and other crafts.

Tuol Tum Pong (Russian Market), which is recommended for gold and setting gems.

Supermarkets

There are a number of petrol stations (**Star** and **Caltex**) which also serve as mini-marts – some are open 24 hrs.

Big A, Monivong Blvd. Good range.

Lucky Supermarket, 160 Sihanouk Blvd, and another branch in the **Parkway Centre**. Excellent French and Australian wine starting at US$5 per bottle (Cambodia has the cheapest wine in Southeast Asia). **Lucky** sells various English-language newspapers' weekly international editions.

Pencil Supercentre, St 214 and Norodom Blvd. Good range of products.

Sharky Mart. No 124 St 130 (below **Sharkys Bar**), T023-990303. 24-hr store stocking everything from condoms and beer through to junk food. Dubious hamburgers but a

reasonably good selection of sandwiches. Free delivery during the day.
Veggy's, No 23 240 St, T023-211534. An excellent green-grocer selling fresh vegetables and salads as well as a range of good imported food.

▲ Activities and tours

Badminton/squash
Cambodiana Hotel, US$10 per hr for court hire.
International Youth Club, No 51 St 96.

Golf
Cambodia Golf and Country Club, Route 4, 35 km south of Phnom Penh, T023-363666. There is a driving range on the roof of the Parkway Centre.

Gym
All the top hotels have gyms and sports clubs which are usually open to non-members and non-guests for a fee.
Amrita Spa, Hotel Le Royal, T023-981888. Offers a gym, steam room, jacuzzi and pool.
Clark Hatch Fitness Centre, Hotel Inter-Continental, corner of Mao Tse Tong and Monireth blvds, T023-424888. Aerobics, gym, sauna, swimming pool, kick boxing.

Running
Cinder track at the **Olympic Stadium**.
Hash House Harriers meet 1500 Sun at the railway station.

Shooting
There's a gun-range about 5 km past the airport off the road to Kompong Som – look out for the Go Kart track signs on the right. You can shoot everything from pistols to fully-automatic AK47s. Should you feel the urge you can even throw a grenade for US$30. You may need to be escorted out here by a known local (eg a tuk-tuk or moto driver) as they often don't let in uninvited foreigners.

Spectator sports
The 1960s Olympic Stadium is the centre of sport. Basketball (able-bodied and wheel-chaired), volleyball and training sessions of Tai-kwondo can be watched. University and schools football league play from Nov-Apr. A semi-professional league plays Jan-Jun. The standard is good. Crowds reach several thousand for the big games. Worth a look even if nothing is going on there.

Swimming
Some of the large hotels allow non-residents to use their pool for a fee: **Inter-Continental**, **Juliana** and so on.
International Youth Club, No 51 St 96, 50-m pool, US$10.
Phnom Penh Hotel, Monivong Blvd.
Phnom Penh Water Park, Confederation de Russie Blvd (airport road), Mon-Fri 1030-1830, weekends 0900-2000. Entrance US$7 or US$5 for children under 1 m. What a disappointment. Shoddy finish, complete absence of shade, poor rides and shocking mismanagement at a horrendous price. Take care of your children.

Tennis
Hotel Cambodiana, US$5-15 per hr.
International Youth Club, No 51 96 St. US$10 per hr.
L'Imprévu, see Sleeping, page 60. Tennis court US$5 per hr.

Therapies and alternative exercise
Gasolina, 56/58 St 57, T012-373009. Capoeira and tai chi classes are both held here (see Eating, page 65) every Tue and Thu. They can also arrange yoga tuition.
Seeing Hands, on Norodom Blvd, or on St 178 behind the FCC, is the place to go for a therapeutic massage. All masseurs are blind. There are several other branches around town. For US$5 you can't go wrong.

Tour operators
Most travel agencies or hotels can organize plane tickets, bus tickets and so forth. Some

of the tour operators listed here also have offices in Siem Reap, see page 139.

Asia Pacific Travel, No 19-20E0, St 371, T023-884432, www.angkortravelcambodia.com. Also has offices in Siem Reap. Arranges tours in Cambodia, Vietnam and Laos.

Asian Trails, No 22 St 294, Sangkat Boeng Keng Kong 1, Khan Chamkarmorn, T023-216555, www.asiantrails.travel. Offers a broad selection of tours: Angkor, river cruises, remote tours, biking trips.

Diethelm Travel, No 65 St 240, T023-219151, www.diethelm-travel.com. Well-known Southeast Asian tour operator, operating within Cambodia and regionally.

Exotissimo Travel, 6th floor, SSN Center66 Norodom Blvd, T023-218948, www.exotissimo.com. Wide range of day trips and classic tours covering Angkor, Sihanoukville, etc. Also offers tailor-made trips.

Hanuman Tourism-Voyages, No 128 Norodom Blvd, T023-218356. Offering a diverse selection of short and long tours across the country. Also boat trips.

Heritic Asia Travel, No 6D off St 169, Veal Vong Kan 7 Makara, T012-955440, www.heriticasia.com.

Local Adventures Cambodia, No 146 St 376, T023-990460, www.cambodia.nl. Modestly price tours to some more off the beaten track locations. Recommended for intrepid travellers, excellent Khmer guides.

PTM Tours, No 333B Monivong Blvd, T023-219161, www.ptm-travel.com. Reasonably priced package tours.

⊖ Transport

Air

Siem Reap Airways and new national carrier, **Cambodia Angkor Air** have connections with **Siem Reap**. See page 15 for details. Flights should be booked in advance.

Airline offices Most airline offices are open Mon-Fri 0800-1700, Sat 0800-1200. **Air Asia**, Room T6 Phnom Penh Airport, T023-890035, www.airasia.com. **Asiana Airlines**, Room A16, Domestic Arrival Terminal, Phnom Penh Airport, T023-890441, www.flyasiana.com. **Bangkok/Siem Reap Airways**, No 61A St 214, T023-722545, www.bangkokair.com. **China Airlines**, 32 Norodom, T023-222056, www.china-airlines.com. **Cambodia Angkor Air**, 1-2/294, Mao Tse Tung, T023-666 6786, www.cambodiaangkorair.com. **Dragon Air**, Unit A3, 168 Monireth Blvd, T023-424300, www.dragonair.com. **Jet Star Asia**, 333b Monivong, T023-220909, www.jetstar asia.com. **Lao Airlines**, 111 Sihanouk Blvd, T023-222956. **Malaysian Airlines**, 35-37 Samdech Pan, St 214, T023-218923. www.malaysiaairlines.com. **Silk Air**, 219B Himawari Hotel, T023-426806, www.silkair.net. **Thai**, T023-214359, www.thaiairways.com. **Vietnam Airlines**, No 41 St 214, T023-990840, www.vietnamairlines.com.vn.

Helicopter flights For charters, Helicopters Cambodia, No 10 St 310, T023-213706, www.helicopterscambodia.com, including rides over Angkor (see page 81).

Bicycle

Hire from guesthouses for around US$1 per day. The city is mostly flat, so not too exhausting. Bicycles can be bought cheaply (around US$40) from the shops that cluster on St 107.

Boat

Fast boats to **Siem Reap** depart from the tourist boat dock on Sisowath Quay at the end of 106 St. Ferries leave from wharves on the river north of the Japanese Friendship Bridge. Moto drivers get paid commission by the ferry companies so it should be possible to get a free ride to the boat. Fast boat connections (5 hrs) with Siem Reap, US$35. All boats leave at 0700 or earlier. Most hotels will supply ferry tickets.

International It is possible to get to **Vietnam** (crossing at Chau Doc) by bus and boat, see page 18 for details.

Bus

Most buses leave southwest of Central Market (Psar Thmei) by the Shell petrol station and all companies run a service between Phnom Penh and **Siem Reap**.

Capitol Tours, No 14 St 182, T023-217627. **GST Buses**, T012-895550, depart from the southwest corner of the Central Market (on the corner of St 142). **Neak Krohorm**, 127 St 108, T023-219496. **Mai Linh**, 391 Sihanouk Blvd, T023-211888. **Mekong Express**, 87 Sisowath Quay, T023-427518. **Phnom Penh Public Transport Company** (formerly Ho Wah Genting Bus Company), T023-210359, departs from Charles De Gaulle Blvd, near the Central Market. **Sorya Transport Company**, Central Bus Station, T023-210359.

To **Battambang**, Capitol, Sorya, and Neak Krorhorm run frequent buses daily, starting from 0600, US$4-5, approximately 5 hrs from the Central Market; **Kompong Cham**, Sorya run buses every hour from 0630 to 1600, US$3.50; **Kompong Chhnang**, over 5 buses a day, 2-3 hrs, US$3. You can also get a minibus, US$1.60, pick-up, US$1.05, or shared taxi, US$2, to Kompong Chhnang (2 hrs). Most **Siem Reap**-bound buses will stop in **Kompong Thom** but you will usually be forced to pay the full fare; to **Kratie**, Sorya, 2 buses per day, US$5.25; **Sihanoukville**, Sorya and Mekong Express run frequently between Sihanoukville and Phnom Penh, 0700-1430, 4 hrs, US$5; **Takeo**, 6 buses a day, 3 hrs, departures from 0700-1400. **Kompong Speu**, 10 buses departing hourly from 0600; **Neak Leung**, 10 buses from 0600, 2 hrs. **Capitol Tours** runs a bus to **Kampot** departing 0700 and

1300, US$3.50. GST Buses, runs 3 trips a day to Pursat, US$2.50. Phnom Penh Public Transport Buses, leave for Pursat 3 times daily, 0645, 0730, 1230, 10,000 riel. Sorya, Neak Krorhorm and GST Buses, run frequently to Sisophon between 0630 and 1230, 18,000 riel. The Sorya buses leave for Kratie at 0715, US$5.25, 7 hrs. Virak Buntham Express Travel, St 106, on the riverfront opposite the Night Market, T012-322302 run buses to and from Koh Kong, 0800. To Stung Treng the Sorya bus leaves Phnom Penh at 0715, US$10. The Sorya bus also leaves for Banlung, Ratanakiri at 0700.

Phnom Penh Public Transport Co has buses to Takeo hourly between 0700-1600, 6000 riel, 2½ hrs. Neak Krohorm travels to Siem Reap, Sisophon, Battambang and Poipet.

International See also pages 18 and 17. The bus from Phnom Penh to Ho Chi Minh City depart daily (Phnom Penh Public Transport Co, Capitol Tour, Sorya, Mekong Express), 8 hrs, US$9-12 per one-way ticket. Sorya and Mekong Express run a daily bus to Bangkok from Phnom Penh, 0630 and 0730, US$9. Sorya also runs frequent routes to Laos and leaves Phnom Penh for Pakse every morning at 0645, US$27.

Car

Chauffeur-driven cars are available at most hotels from US$25 per day upwards. Several travel agents will also hire cars. Prices increase if you're venturing out of town.
Mr Vanny, a local English-speaking guide and driver, offers an excellent fast and safe service to pretty much anywhere in Cambodia – T09-285 0989/01-197 7328.

Cyclo

Plentiful but slow. Fares can be bargained down but are not that cheap – a short journey should be no more than US$1. A few cyclo drivers speak English or French. They are most likely to be found around the big

hotels and can also be hired for the day (around US$7).

Motorcycle

From guesthouses and some hotels (US$5-7 per day). Quite a few shops rent larger dirt-bikes from US$7-10 a day (depending on where you are going and for how long). You might want to book a big bike in advance, often if you turn up on the day there isn't a great selection. It should be pointed out that riding a powerful dirt-bike into the wilds of Cambodia should only be attempted with the right equipment and experience. While spending the extra on a helmet, good boots and other protection may seem expensive if you're on a budget, sucking your food through a straw in one of Phnom Penh's notoriously bad hospitals is a worse option. If your budget doesn't stretch to protective equipment don't even attempt to go off-road. Also remember that if you don't have a valid driving licence to ride a motorcycle in your own country you are unlikely to be covered by insurance.
Angkor Motorcycle Rentals, No 92 St 51, T012-916824. Highly reputable bike rental company.
The Bike Shop, No 31 St 302, T012-851776. Run by a French dirtbike legend, these guys easily have the best off-road bikes in town. They are the most expensive but reliability is second to none and they will also collect you if your bike breaks down. Bernard can also organize tours. Recommended.

Moto

Motos or 'motodops' are 50-100cc motorbike taxis and the fastest way to get around Phnom Penh. They are ubiquitous and you will be inundated by offers if you are anywhere that tourists might be remotely inclined to visit. Standard cost per journey is around US$0.50 for a short hop but expect to pay double after dark. If you find a good English speaking moto driver, hang on to him and he can be yours for US$8-10 per day.

Shared taxi

These are either Toyota pick-ups or saloons. For the pick-ups the fare depends upon whether you wish to sit inside or in the open; vehicles depart when the driver has enough fares. For **Vietnam**, take a taxi from Psar Chbam Pao, just over Monivong Bridge, on Route 1. For **Sihanoukville**, **Battambang**, **Siem Riep** and **Thailand** take a shared taxi from the Central Market. Leave early (0500-0600). Prices will vary depending on the number of passengers in the car but expect to pay around US$2-3. To **Koh Kong**, 5-6 hrs, leaves from the market, US$10 per person (6 people per car), US$60 own car, from 0600 onwards.

Taxi

There are only a few taxis in Phnom Penh as the risk of being held up at gunpoint is too high. **Taxi Vantha**, T012-855000/023-982542, is available 24 hrs.

Train

The railway station is a fine old 1930s art deco French edifice, recently restored. Quite why is not readily apparent as the station's main function is to provide a place for the homeless to doss down. The station is on Monivong Blvd between 106 and 108 streets. There are 2 lines – the southern line to Sihanoukville and the northern line to **Battambang**. In mid-2010 there were no rail services running in Cambodia though plans are emerging for routes to re-open.

ⓘ Directory

Banks Most banks are now charging 1-2% commission on credit card advances. **ANZ Royal Bank**, Russian Blvd, 20 Kramuon Sar (corner of St 67) has now opened ATMs across the city: also near the Independence Monument and at 265 Sisowath Quay. **Cambodia Asia Bank**, No 252 Monivong Blvd, T023-722105. Western Union money wire. Branch also at the Naga Casino, which is

open 24 hrs. Cash advances on credit cards. **Cambodia Commercial Bank** (CCB), No 130 Monivong Blvd (close to the Central Market), T023-426208. Cash advance on credit cards, TCs and currency exchange. **Canadia Bank**, No 126 Charles de Gaulle Blvd, T023-214668, and 265-269 Ang Duong St, T023-215286. Cash advances on credit cards. **Singapore Banking Corporation** (SBC), No 68 St 214, T023-214466; No 203 Monivong Blvd, T023-882878; No 315 Sisowath Quay, T023-990688. Western Union money transfer and currency exchange. **Union Commercial Bank** (UCB), No 61 St 130, T023-724931. Most banking services, no charge on credit card cash advances. **Embassies and consulates** Australia, No 11 St 254, T023-213470, www.cambodia.embassy.gov.au. Belgium, Hotel Cambodiana, T023-214024. Canada, No 11 St 254, T023-213470. China, 156 Mao Tse Tung, T023-720920, kh.china-embassy. org. France, 1 Monivong Blvd, T023-430020. www.ambafrance-kh.org. Germany, No 76-78 St 214, T023-216381. Japan, 194 Norodom Blvd, T023-217161-4, eojc@online. com.kh. Laos, 15-17 Mao Tse Tung Blvd, T023-997931. Thailand, 196 Norodom Blvd, T023-726306-10, www.mfa.go.th. United Kingdom, No 29 St 75, T023-427124, ukincambodia.fco.gov.uk. USA, No1 St 96, T023-728000, cambodia.usembassy.gov. Vietnam, 436 Monivong Blvd, T023-362531, embvnpp@camnet.com.kh. **Emergency services** Ambulance, T119 (from 023 phones) or T023-723840 or T023-724891. Fire, T118 (from 023 phones) or T023-723555 or T012-786693. Police, T117, T112 (from 023 phones) and T012-999999 or for tourist police T097-7780002. To report child abuse T023-720555 or T023-997919. **Internet** Nearly every café, restaurant, guesthouse and hotel now has free Wi-Fi. In addition Phnom Penh has an excellent mobile 3G network which can often be quicker than fixed line, cable internet. Internet cafés/shops are also extremely cheap and ubiquitous. Rates can be as low as US$0.50 per hr. **Khmer Web**, 150 Sihanouk Blvd, T023-219240 (has another store on St 182). **KIDS**, No 17A St 178, T023-218690, also a guesthouse (see page 57). **Mittapheap Cybercafé**, on the corner of Monivong Blvd and St 174. **Medical services** You are advised to try and get to Bangkok if you are seriously ill or have injured yourself. **Bumrungrad Hospital** and **Bangkok Nursing Home** in Bangkok are state-of-the-art modern hospitals. Highly recommended. **Bumrungrad Hospital Office**, 113 Mao Tse Tumg Blvd, T023-221103, is the local service office for the private hospital in Bangkok. **Calmette Hospital**, 3 Monivong Blvd, T023-426948, is generally considered the best, 24-hr emergency centre. **European Dental Clinic**, 160 Norodom Blvd, T023-854408. French-run. **International SOS Medical and Dental Clinic**, No 161 St 51, T023-216911 or T012-816911. **Pharmacy de la Gare**, 81 Monivong Blvd, T012-805908. There is also another good pharmacy opposite the **Rising Sun Restaurant/bar**. **Royal Optic**, 220 Monivong Blvd. **Tropical and Travellers Medical Clinic**, No 88 St 108, T0023-306802. English doctor. **Post office and courier services** Main post office, St 13. Open 0700-2100. Possible to make international telephone calls from here. **DHL**, 28 Monivong Blvd, T023-427726. **FedEx**, 701D Monivong Blvd, T023-216712. **TNT**, No 151F St 154, T023-211880. **UPS**, No 27 St 134, T023-427511. **Visa extensions Foreign Ministry**, Sisowath Quay, at the intersection of St 240.

Contents

Angkor & the Central Region

THAILAND

Chong Jom

O Smach

Dangrek Mountains

Preah Vihear

Samrong

Anlong Veng

Choam Ksant

SIEM REAP-ODDAR MEANCHEY

Koh Ker 7

Kulen

T'Beng Meanchey

PREAH VIHEAR

Phnom Kulen

Banteay Srei 4

Beng Mealea

12

1 2 3 Angkor

Siem Reap

Preah Khan 6 Ta Seng

Phnom Krom

Bakong

Roluos

Dam Dek

Sang Ker

Prek Toal Bird Sanctuary

Chong Khneas

Sambor Prei Kuk

5

Tonlé Sap

KOMPONG THOM

Stoeng

Kompong Thom

Phnom Santuk

Pursat

Kompong Luong

N

PURSAT

Kompong Chhnang

6

20 km
20 miles

An enormous and elaborately detailed complex, the ancient temple city of Angkor Wat has remained the heart and soul of Cambodia for almost two millennia. And, despite its popularity with ever-growing throngs of visitors, this is still a historical site that exceeds expectation. Included in the gargantuan complex lie legions of magical temples which attest to the ability of bygone artisans, from the intricate Banteay Srei, with its detailed carvings to the beaming faces of the Bayon. Visitors also flock to jungle-clad Ta Prohm, where tentacle-like foliage entwined around the temple provides an insight into how earlier explorers would have discovered it.

The town of Siem Reap has graduated from Angkor's service centre to an international tourist hub, teeming with modern restaurants and upmarket hotels. Fortunately, the settlement still retains much of its original charm, with old colonial shopfronts, misty lamp-lit streets and a bustling market area. A short trip from Siem Reap is the Tonlé Sap, Southeast Asia's largest freshwater lake, scattered with many floating villages.

North of Siem Reap is Anlong Veng, the hauntingly beautiful former stronghold of the Khmer Rouge. Although short on tourist sites, the town will be of interest to history buffs.

If you travel by road from Angkor to Phnom Penh you'll pass through Kompong Thom and Cambodia's central region. This is certainly a place for the more independent-minded traveller who will put up with tough roads and sparse public transportation in order to be rewarded with amazing temples, beautiful jungle scenery and some of the friendliest small villages in the country.

Angkor and around

The huge temple complex of Angkor, the ancient capital of the powerful Khmer Empire, is one of the archaeological treasures of Asia and the spiritual and cultural heart of Cambodia. Henri Mouhot, the Frenchman who rediscovered it, wrote that "it is grander than anything of Greece or Rome". Its architectural wonders are, to those that know them, unsurpassed by anything in Europe, Asia or Latin America.

The jungle around Angkor is scattered with many temple complexes which are also covered in this section. The former Khmer Rouge stronghold of Anlong Veng is found north of Siem Reap – the large town that serves the area.

In the central region both Kompong Thom and the less easily accessible T'Beng Meanchey provide hubs to visit the remote archaeological remains of Koh Ker, Sambor Prei Kuk and Preah Khan. You'll also find the more spectacular Preah Vihear in this central region, pressed up tight against a disputed part of the Cambodian-Thai border. Due to recent fighting we recommend visitors heed their home governments' warnings on travel to Preah Vihear and exercise extreme caution. ▸▸ *For listings, see pages 128-142.*

Ins and outs

Getting there and around.

Angkor is served by the airport at Siem Reap, 7 km from town. Boats also travel from Phnom Penh and Battambang. Buses and shared taxis also ply the route from the capital.
▸▸ *See Transport, page 140.*

Most of the temples within the Angkor complex (except the Roluos Group) are in an area extending across a 25 km radius roughly 8 km north of Siem Reap. The Roluos Group are 13 km east of Siem Reap and Banteay Srei 32 km. Cars with drivers and guides are available from larger hotels for US$25-30 per day plus US$25 for a guide. An excellent guiding service by car is provided by Mr Hak, T012-540336, www.angkortaxidriver.com, who offers a variety of packages and tours around Angkor and the surrounding area. Expect to pay US$10-12 per day for a moto unless the driver speaks good English in which case the price will be higher. This price will cover trips to the Roluos Group but not to Banteay Srei. There is no need to add more than a dollar or two to the price for getting to Banteay Srei unless the driver is also a guide and can demonstrate to you that he is genuinely going to show you around.

Tuk-tuks (remork in Khmer) and their ilk have appeared on the scene in recent years and are quite a popular option for two people, US$14-17 a day (maximum of two people). **Bicycle hire** costs US$2-3 per day from most guesthouses and is a good option for those who feel reasonably familiar with the area as the roads are pretty good. The White Bicycles scheme, set up by Norwegian ex-pats (see Transport, page 141), offers bikes for US$2 per day with US$1.50 of that going straight into local charities and no commission to the hotels and is recommended. If you are on a limited schedule and only have a day or two at the temples you won't be able to cover an awful lot of them on a pedal bike as the searing temperatures and sprawling layout can limit even the most advanced cyclists. Angkor Wat and Banteay Srei have official parking sites, 1000 riel (US$0.25), and at the other temples you can quite safely park and lock your bikes in front of a drink stall.

For those wishing to see Angkor from a different perspective it is possible to charter a **helicopter**. In many ways, it is only from the air that you can really grasp the size and scale

Angkor tips

These days avoiding traffic within the Angkor complex is difficult but still moderately achievable.

As it stands there is a pretty standard one-day tour itinerary that includes: Angkor Wat (sunrise), Angkor Thom, Bayon, etc (morning), break for lunch, Ta Prohm (afternoon), Preah Khan (afternoon) and Phnom Bakheng (sunset).

If you reverse the order, peak hour traffic at major temples is dramatically reduced. As many tour groups trip into Siem Reap for lunch this is an opportune time to catch a peaceful moment in the complex, just bring a packed lunch or eat at 1100 or 1400.

To avoid the masses at the main attraction, Angkor Wat, try to walk around the temple, as opposed to through it. Sunset at Phnom Bakheng has turned into a circus fiasco, so aim for Angkor or the Bayon at this time as they are both relatively peaceful.

Sunrise is still pretty quiet at Angkor, grab yourself the prime position behind the left-hand pond (you need to depart Siem Reap no later than 0530), though there are other stunning early-morning options, such as Srah Srang or Bakong. Bakheng gives a beautiful vista of Angkor in the early-mid morning.

of Angkor and a short flight will certainly be a memorable experience. Try **Helicopters Cambodia**, T063-963316, www.helicopterscambodia.com, who offer flights from US$75 per person. **Elephants** are stationed near the Bayon or at the South Gate of Angkor Thom during the day. In the evenings, they can be found at the bottom of Phnom Bakheng, taking tourists up to the summit for sunset.

The Angkor site can be a real struggle for **disabled or frail persons**, the stairs are 90 degrees steep and semi-restoration of areas means visitors will sometimes need to climb over piles of bricks. Still, many people manage to do it. Hiring an aide to help you climb stairs, etc, is a very good idea and costs around US$5-10 a day.

Kompong Thom provides a convenient stop-off point halfway between Siem Reap and Phnom Penh on the continually improving National Highway 6 and all buses travelling between the two destinations will stop in Kompong Thom. The rest of the central region contains some of the country's worst roads making the area a little tricky to navigate. Public transport is limited and in some of the more remote areas it is almost non-existent. In larger towns, like Kompong Thom, there are a range of options from shared taxi to buses but in other spots you might find yourself hopping in the back of someone's tractor. To access sites like Preah Khan or Koh Ker a larger dirt bike or 4WD is the best option. Most roads are constructed from dirt, so travelling to the temples or smaller towns becomes very difficult, or near impossible, in the wet season. The region is still littered with mines, many of which aren't marked, so stay on clearly marked tracks.

Best time to visit

Angkor and the central region's busiest period coincides with the dry season, November to February. Not only is this the driest time of year it is also the coolest (although it can still be unbearably hot). Be advised that this time of year is also incredibly busy and you may find yourself experiencing the drama of Angkor along with hundreds of Korean and Chinese tour groups. The monsoon lasts from June to October/November. It can be incredibly wet and muddy at this time of year but you may find you have an entire temple to yourself.

Angkor, Siem Reap & Roluos

➡ **Angkor maps**
1 Angkor, Siem Reap & Roluos, page 82
2 Angkor Wat, page 93
3 Angkor Thom, page 98
4 Siem Riep, page 120
5 Siem Riep market area, page 122

Guides can be invaluable when navigating the temples, with the majority being able to answer most questions about Angkor as well as providing additional information about Cambodian culture and history. Most hotels and travel agents will be able to point you in the direction of a good guide. The **Khmer Angkor Tour Guide Association** ① *T063-964347, www.khmerangkortourguide.com*, has well-trained guides. Most of the guides here are very well briefed and some speak English better than others. The going rate is US$20-25 per day.

Angkor Conservation is a specialist research institution, just off the main road to Angkor and about 1 km from the Grand Hotel (signed Conservation d'Angkor). Many statues, stelae and linga found at Angkor are stored here to prevent theft. It is accessible by special appointment only. Contact the Ministry of Culture in Phnom Penh for a written invitation which needs to describe the research objectives of the visitor.

To Banteay Srei (10 km) & Phnom Kulen

Wat Phnom Bok

Phnom Bok (212m)

Prasat To

Pradak

Banteay Samre

Prei Pasat

Pasat Komnap

Rolung River

To Chau Srei Vibol Temple Complex (5km approx)

To Phnom Penh

Kuk Taleh

Prasat Pou Teng

Lolei

Prasat O Kaek

Preah Ko

Bakong

Roluos

Prahu

Prasat Prei Monti

Svay Pream

Prasat Totoeng O Thngai

Prasat Trapeang Phong

Temple fees and opening hours
A one-day pass costs US$20, three-day pass US$40, seven-day pass US$60. The seven day pass is valid for any seven days (doesn't have to be consecutive) one month from the purchase date. Most people will be able to cover the majority of the temples within three days. If you buy your ticket after 1715 the day beforehand, you get a free sunset thrown in. The complex is open daily 0530-1830. You will need to pay additional fees if you wish to visit Beng Melea (US$5), Phnom Kulen (US$20) or Koh Ker (US$10) - payable at the individual sites.

Safety
Landmines were planted on some outlying paths to prevent Khmer Rouge guerrillas from infiltrating the temples; they have pretty much all been cleared by now, but it is safer to stick to well-used paths. Wandering anywhere in the main temple complexes is perfectly safe. Be wary of snakes in the dry season. The very poisonous Hanuman snake (lurid green) is fairly common in the area.

The destruction of Cambodia's heritage

The empire of Angkor produced some of the finest art that the world has seen. But Cambodia's heritage is in danger of being obliterated by art thieves intent on stealing anything that might have a market.

In January 1999 King Norodom Sihanouk remarked "It is very, very sad that Cambodian people were so masterful and skilful but now plunder their own history."

Khmer Rouge guerrillas moved into Angkor Wat in 1971, lit fires in the galleries, installed rocket launchers on Phnom Bakheng, looted temples and sliced the heads off sculptures. Like other guerrilla groups after them, they sold the extracted pieces on the black market in neighbouring Thailand to help finance their war efforts.

From the mid-1970s, ancient Khmer sculptures began to resurface in private art collections in the West, and on the floors of leading auction houses. But the real destruction only began with the onset of peace in 1993. Ironically, when the Khmer Rouge controlled much of the heartland of the former Angkorian kingdom the temples were safe from attack by all but Khmer Rouge guerrillas. With the pacification of the area it became a free-for-all.

In 1992 and 1993 there were reported thefts from many of the temples and from the conservation office in Siem Reap where about 7000 of the most valuable artefacts were stored. Between February and April 1993, there was a series of carefully organized break-ins into the conservation office; many priceless statues were stolen. In the most dramatic raid, in February 1993, thieves used machine guns to enter the conservation centre, shot one of the guards, fired a rocket-propelled grenade at the storeroom door and left with 11 of the most valuable statues. UN and local officials said they had been smuggled into Thailand. They also alleged that all four political factions were behind the thefts as well as soldiers "from a neighbouring country". And there was strong evidence that some of the thefts were orchestrated by conservation office staff themselves.

Despite the publicity that these thefts received, the destruction has continued on a truly monumental scale and, just like the destruction of Cambodia's forests, the army, it seems, has been closely involved in the pillage. Local villagers reported that at the end of 1998 at Banteay Chhmar more than 100 soldiers descended on the temple and used heavy equipment, including pneumatic drills, to remove nearly 50 sq ft of heavily carved relief work depicting the Hindu epics and decapitate scores of statues. So thorough was their work that the main temple at the site is in imminent danger of collapse.

Photography

Don't forget to ask the permission of the people who you wish to include in your shots. In general, the best time to photograph most temples is before 0900 and after 1630.

Itineraries

The temples are scattered over an area in excess of 160 sq km. There are three so-called 'circuits'. The **Petit Circuit** (17 km) takes in the main central temples including Angkor Wat, Bayon, Baphuon and the Terrace of the Elephants. The **Grand Circuit** (26 km) takes a wider route, including smaller temples like Ta Prohm, East Mebon, Pre Rup and Neak Pean. The **Roluos Group Circuit** ventures further afield still, taking in the temples near Roluos: Lolei, Preah Ko and Bakong. The order of visiting is a matter of opinion; here are some options:
Half day South Gate of Angkor Thom, Bayon, Angkor Wat.

The main smuggling route for the pieces is across the border into Thailand, although some are shipped from the Cambodian ports of Kompong Som and Koh Kong to Bangkok and Singapore. In early 1999 a 10-wheeler truck was intercepted on the Thai border with 117 pieces stolen from Banteay Chhmar. Today Angkorian antiquities can be viewed and purchased in the air-conditioned antique shops of Bangkok's shopping complexes or Singapore's Tanglin Shopping Centre. There was even evidence that wealthy, but unethical, Western art buyers have been able to place orders for busts and sculptures of their choice through some of these shops. There are persistent rumours pointing to the existence of 'catalogues', containing detailed photographs of Angkorian statues and bas-reliefs. Shopkeepers will surreptitiously offer to 'organize' the acquisition of specific pieces.

Dealers in the antiquities-smuggling racket are reported to have links with organized crime. The underworld's labyrinthine networks – used in the trafficking of narcotics – facilitate the movement of statues around the world. 'Licences' for the illegal export of ancient works of art can be readily procured in Bangkok by dealers with good connections. Although Thailand does its best to prevent the smuggling of its own cultural treasures, it has refused to sign the UN's 1970 convention for preventing antiquities trafficking. This allows Bangkok dealers to trade Burmese and Cambodian pieces with impunity.

It is said that when Cambodia's Prime Minister, Hun Sen, booked into a Bangkok hotel all the Khmer artefacts of doubtful provenance were hastily removed from public display. Having survived 1000 years of warfare and weather, many of Angkor's remaining statues are doomed to decapitation. The heads of many dancing apsaras – the most famous motif of Angkor's temples – have disappeared. As a rule of thumb, the more remote the site the easier it has been for art thieves to help themselves to Cambodia's heritage. Growing cultural consciousness – combined with uneasy consciences of some Western collectors – may allow for some of this invaluable loot to be returned in the years to come. But for the present, Cambodia is losing tonnes of its cultural and artistic heritage to unscrupulous dealers and collectors.

Heritage Watch, www.heritagewatch. org, is an organization dedicated to stopping the illicit trade in Cambodian antiquities.

One day Angkor Wat (sunrise or sunset), South Gate of Angkor Thom, Angkor Thom (Bayon, Terrace of the Elephants, Royal Palace) and Ta Prohm. This is a hefty schedule for one day; you'll need to arrive after 1615 and finish just after 1700 the following day.
Two days The same as above but with the inclusion of the rest of the Angkor Thom, Preah Srah Srang (sunrise) and at a push, Banteay Srei.
Three days – Day 1 Sunrise at Angkor Wat; morning South Gate of Angkor Thom, Angkor complex (aside from Bayon); Ta Prohm; late afternoon-sunset at Bayon. **Day 2** Srah Srang; morning Banteay Kdei and Banteay Srei; late afternoon Preah Khan; at Angkor Wat. **Day 3** Sunrise and morning Roluos; afternoon Ta Keo and sunset either Bakheng or Angkor Wat.

Those choosing to stay one or two days longer should try to work Banteay Samre, East Mebon, Neak Pean and Thomannon into their itinerary. A further two to three days warrants a trip to Prasat Kravan, Ta Som, Beng Melea and Kbal Spean.

History

Khmer Empire

Under Jayavarman VII (1181-1218) the Angkor complex stretched more than 25 km east to west and nearly 10 km north to south, approximately the same size as Manhattan. For five centuries (9th-13th) the court of Angkor held sway over a vast territory. At its height, according to a 12th-century Chinese account, Khmer influence spanned half of Southeast Asia, from Burma to the southernmost tip of Indochina and from the borders of Yunnan to the Malay Peninsula. Khmer monuments can be found in the south of Laos and East Thailand as well as in Cambodia. The only threat to this great empire was a riverborne invasion in 1177, when the Cham used a Chinese navigator to pilot their war canoes up the Mekong. Scenes are depicted in bas-reliefs of the Bayon temple.

The kings and construction – the temples and the creators

Jayavarman II (AD 802-835) founded the Angkor Kingdom, then coined Hariharalaya the capital to the north of the Tonlé Sap, in the Roluos Region (Angkor), in AD 802. Later he moved the capital to Phnom Kulen, 40 km northeast of Angkor, where he built a Mountain Temple and Rong Shen shrine. After several years he moved the capital back to the Roluos Region.

Jayavarman III continued his father's legacy and built a number of shrines at Hariharalaya. Many historians believe that he was responsible for the initial construction of the impressive laterite pyramid, Bakong, considered the great precursor to Angkor Wat. Bakong, built to symbolize Mount Meru, was later embellished and developed by Indravarman. Indravarman (AD 877-889) overthrew his predecessor violently and undertook a major renovation campaign in the capital Hariharalaya. The majority of what stands in the Roluos Group today is the work of Indravarman. Among his architectural feats are Preah Ko Temple, built in AD 880, and the remodelling of Bakong (with sandstone cladding). His greatest creation, initiated five days after his coronation, was the 'Sea of Indra', a massive baray (waterbasin), 3.8 km long by 800 m wide. Indravarman is credited with establishing many of the architectural 'norms' for the period that followed. A battle between Indravarman's sons destroyed the palace and the victor and new king Yasovarman I (AD 889-900) moved the capital from Roluos and laid the foundations of Angkor itself. Prior to the move, he constructed Lolei Temple at Roluos on an island in the baray his father built. He dedicated the temple to his ancestors. His new capital at Angkor was called Yasodharapura ('glory-bearing city'), and here he built 100 wooden ashramas (retreats), all of which have disintegrated today. Yasovarman selected Bakheng as the location for his temple-mountain and after flattening the mountain top, set about creating another Mount Meru. The temple he constructed was considered more complex than anything built beforehand – a five-storey pyramid with 108 shrines. A road was then built to link the former and present capitals of Roluos and Bakheng. Like the kings before him, Yasovarman was obliged to construct major waterworks and the construction of the reservoir – the East Baray (now completely dry) – was considered an incredible feat. The baray is eight times larger than his father's 'Sea of Indra' and historian, Claude Jacques, believes it would have taken no less than six million man days to construct. Some also suggest that Yasovarman constructed the temples of Phnom Bok and Phnom Krom.

After Yasovarman's death in AD 900 his son Harshavarman (AD 900-923) assumed power for the next 23 years. During his brief reign, Harshavarman is believed to have built Baksei Chamkrong (northeast of Phnom Bakheng) and Prasat Kravan (the 'Cardamom

Sanctuary'). His brother, Ishanarvarman II, resumed power upon his death but no great architectural feats were recorded in this time. In AD 928, Jayavarman IV moved the capital 120 km away to Koh Ker (see page 127). Here he built the grand state temple Prasat Thom, an impressive seven-storey sandstone pyramid. Over the next 20 years as king he undertook the construction of some smaller temples in the Koh Ker area and a baray. Many of the sculptures from his reign are in the National Museum in Phnom Penh.

Following the death of Jayavarman things took a turn for the worse. Chaos ensued under Harshavarman's II (AD 941-944) weak leadership and over the next four years, no monuments were known to be erected. Jayavarman's IV nephew, Rajendravarman, took control of the situation and it's assumed he forcefully relocated the capital back to Angkor. Rather than moving back into the old capital Phnom Bakheng, he marked his own new territory, selecting an area south

(see page 127)

Angkor's rulers

Jayavarman II (802-835)
Jayavarman III (835-877)
Indravarman (877-889)
Yasovarman (889-900)
Harshavarman (900-923)
Ishnavarman II (923-928)
Jayavarman IV (928-941)
Harshavarman II (941-944)
Rajendravarman (944-968)
Jayavarman V (968-1001)
Udayadityavarman I (1001-1002)
Suryavarman (1002-1049)
Udayadityavarman II (1050-1066)
Harshavarman III (1066-1080)
Jayavarman VI (1080-1107)
Dharanindravarman I (1107-1112)
Suryavarman II (1113-1150)
Yasovarman II (c. 1150-1165)
Tribhuvanadityavarman (c.1165-1177)
Jayavarman VII (1181-1218)

of the East Baray as his administrative centre. Here, in 1961, he constructed the state temple – Pre Rup and constructed the temple, East Mebon (AD 953), in the middle of the baray. Srah Srang, Kutisvara and Bat Chum were also constructed, with the help of his chief architect, Kavindrarimathana. He also took to task the restoration of Baksei Chamkrong, a temple he held in the highest regard. It was towards the end of his reign that he started construction on Banteay Srei, considered one of the finest examples of Angkorian craftsmanship in the country. Rajendravarman's son became the new king Jayavarman V (AD 968-1001) and he took the royal reigns. The administrative centre was renamed Jayendranagari and yet again, relocated. A new state temple, Ta Keo, was built west of the East Baray. The temple is believed to be somewhat cursed as it was struck by lightening during its construction and never completed. More than compensating for the unfinished Ta Keo was Jayavarman's V continued work on Banteay Srei. Under his supervision the splendid temple was completed and dedicated to his father.

Aside from successfully extending the Khmer Empire's territory King Suryavarman I (1002-1049), made a significant contribution to Khmer architectural heritage. He presided over the creation of a new administrative centre – the Royal Palace (in Angkor Thom) and the huge walls that surround it. Also built under his instruction was the colossal West Baray, still in use, measuring 8 km by 2 km (so large, it can be seen from outer space) and the sanctuary atop Preah Vihear. The next in line was Udayadityavarman II (1050-1066), the son of Suryavarman I. The Baphuon temple mountain and West Mebon (in the West Baray) were built during his relatively short appointment.

Jayavarman VI (1080-1107) never settled at Angkor living instead in the northern part of the kingdom. He constructed temples outside of the main Angkor region including Wat

Phou (in southern Laos) and Phimai (in Thailand). After overthrowing his great-uncle Dharanindravarman, Suryavarman II (1113-1150), the greatest of Angkor's god-kings, came to power. His rule marked the highest point in Angkorian architecture and civilization. Not only was he victorious in conflict, having beat the Cham whom couldn't be defeated by China, he was responsible for extending the borders of the Khmer Empire into Myanmar, Malaya and Siam. This aside, he was also considered one of the era's most brilliant creators. Suryavarman II was responsible for the construction of Angkor Wat, the current day symbol of Cambodia. Beng Melea, Banteay Samre and Thommanon are also thought to be the works of this genius. He has been immortalized in his own creation – in a bas-relief in the South Gallery of Angkor Wat the glorious King Suryavarman II sits on top of an elephant. After a period of political turmoil, which included the sacking of Angkor, Jayavarman VII seized the throne in 1181 and set about rebuilding his fiefdom. Historian, Dawn Rooney, suggests that Jayavarman VII was the greatest builder, "constructing more monuments, roads, bridges and resthouses than all the other kings put together."

Jayavarman VII created a new administrative centre – the great city of Angkor Thom, a 3-km block, surrounded by a moat and laterite wall. The mid-point of Angkor Thom is marked by his brilliant Mahayana Buddhist state temple, the Bayon. It is said that the Bayon was completed in 21 years. Jayavarman took thousands of peasants from the rice fields to build it, which proved a fatal error, for rice yields decreased and the empire began its decline as resources were drained. The temple consists of sculptured faces of Avolokiteshvara (the Buddha of compassion and mercy) which are often said to also encompass the face of their great creator, Jayavarman VIII. He was also responsible for restoring the Royal Palace, renovating Srah Srang and constructing the Terrace of Elephants, the Terrace of the Leper King and the nearby baray (northeast of Angkor Thom), Jayataka reservoir. At the centre of his reservoir he built Neak Pean.

Jayavarman VII adopted Mahayana Buddhism and so Buddhist principles replaced the Hindu pantheon, and were invoked as the basis of royal authority. This spread of Buddhism is thought to have caused some of the earlier Hindu temples to be neglected. The king paid tribute to his Buddhist roots through his monastic temples: Ta Prohm and Preah Khan. Further afield in northwestern Cambodia he constructed Banteay Chhmar. He also built 102 hospitals throughout his kingdom, as well as a network of roads, along which he constructed resthouses. But because they were built of wood, none of these secular structures survive; only the foundations of four larger ones have been unearthed at Angkor.

Henri Mouhot's rediscovery of Angkor

Thai ascendency and their eventual occupation of Angkor in 1431 led to the city's abandonment and the subsequent invasion of the jungle. Four centuries later, in 1860, Henri Mouhot, a French naturalist, stumbled across the forgotten city, its temple towers enmeshed in the forest canopy. Locals told him they were the work of a race of giant gods. Only the stone temples remained; all the wooden secular buildings had decomposed in the intervening centuries. Mouhot's diaries, published in the 1860s, with his accounts of 'the lost city in the jungle', fired the imagination of archaeologists, adventurers and treasure hunters in Europe. In 1873 French archaeologist Louis Delaporte removed many of Angkor's finest statues for 'the cultural enrichment of France'.

French 'restoration'

In 1898, the École Française d'Extrême Orient started clearing the jungle, restoring the temples, mapping the complex and making an inventory of the site. Delaporte was later to write the two-volume *Les Monuments du Cambodge*, the most comprehensive Angkorian inventory of its time, and his earlier sketches, plans and reconstructions, published in *Voyage au Cambodge* in 1880 are without parallel. Henri Parmentier was chief of the school's archaeological service in Cambodia until 1930. Public interest was rekindled in the 1920s when French adventurer and novelist André Malraux was arrested in Phnom Penh, charged with stealing sculptures from one of the temples, Banteay Srei at Angkor. He published a thriller, *The Royal Way*, based on his experiences. Today around 400 sandstone, laterite and brick-built temples, walls, tombs and other structures remain scattered around the site.

Plundering of Angkor

Colonial souvenir hunters were not the first – or the last – to get their hands on Angkor's treasures. The great city's monuments were all subjected, at one time or another, to systematic plundering, mainly by the warring Cham (from South Vietnam) and Thais. Many temple pedestals were smashed to afford access to the treasure, hidden deep in pits under the central sanctuaries. Other looters knocked the tops off towers to reach the carefully concealed treasure chambers.

Centuries of entanglement in the jungle also took their toll on the buildings – strangler figs caused much structural damage and roots and vines rent roofs and walls asunder. In 1912, French writer Pierre Loti noted: "The fig tree is the ruler of Angkor today... Over the temples which it has patiently prised apart, everywhere its dome of foliage triumphantly unfolds its sleek pale branches speckled like a serpent's skin." Even today, some roots and trees remain stubbornly tangled in the ancient masonry – affording visitors a Mouhot-style glimpse of the forgotten city. Between 1953 and 1970, the Angkor Conservancy – set up jointly by the French and Cambodian governments – maintained and restored the ruins. But when war broke out, the destructive forces of the Khmer Rouge – and other guerrilla factions – were unleashed on what the jungle had spared and the French archaeologists, such as Bernard Grosslier, had restored.

Restoration of Angkor

As if the conservation and protection of the complex was not already fraught with difficulties, a threat emerged in the mid-1980s, from the most unlikely of sources. The Vietnamese-backed administration enlisted the services of Indian archaeologists to begin where the Angkor Conservancy had left off. They were given a six-year contract to clean and restore the galleries and towers of Angkor Wat itself. Prince Sihanouk is reported to have burst into tears when he heard that the Indians, using unskilled Cambodian workmen, had begun their concrete and chemical-assisted restoration effort. The cleaning agents stripped off the patina which for a millennium had protected the sandstone from erosion by the elements. Bas-reliefs depicting scenes from the *Ramayana* were scrubbed and scraped until some were barely discernible. Cement was used with abandon. Archaeologists around the world, who, since 1970, have only been dimly aware of the rape of Angkor, now consider the gimcrack restoration programme the last straw after two decades of pillage and destruction.

Whether the Indian team of archaeologists and conservators have really caused untold damage to the monuments of Angkor through insensitive restoration and the use of untested solvents is a source of some dispute. Certainly most press reports in the West have taken the line that their work rather than helping to restore and preserve the monuments has helped to further ruin it. Cement has been used to fill in cracks, where

Western archaeologists would probably have left well alone. New stone has been cut and fitted where, again, other specialists might have been happy merely to have done sufficient restoration to prevent further degeneration. The Indian team also used chemical cleaning agents – an unorthodox and contentious approach to restoration. However, although some of the methods used by the Indian team do seem rather crude and insensitive to the atmosphere of the place, the carping of some Western archaeologists seems to have been motivated as much by professional envy as anything else. The Indians were called in by the government in Phnom Penh at a time when most Western countries were boycotting the country, in protest at the Vietnamese occupation. French archaeologists in particular must have been pacing their offices in indignation and pique as a country with such 'primitive' skills took all the glory.

In 1989 UNESCO commissioned a Japanese art historian to draw up an Angkor plan of action. The top priority in its restoration, he said, was to underpin the foundations of Angkor Wat, Bayon, Baphuon, Preah Khan, Neak Khan and Pre Rup. Once the Paris Peace agreements had been signed in 1991, the Ecole Française, the New York based World Monuments Fund and the Japanese started work. UNESCO is coordinating the activities of the various teams and Angkor was declared a World Heritage site. Some temples are closed or partially closed for restoration work.

Whether the Japanese are any more sensitive than the Indians in their restoration work is an interesting subject for debate. For while the Indians may have been criticized for unsuitable techniques at least they were merely patching up. The Japanese approach is nothing less than renovation. Thus, while the traditional tools of the architect were brushes and hammers, visitors will be surprised to see huge cranes and lifts putting temples back as Japanese archaeologists think they once looked. Concrete and laterite blocks as well as newly carved sandstone are used to replace decayed stonework. Interestingly, in 2002 Indian archaeologists were again invited back to take part in the restoration process.

Documentation of Angkor

Sanskrit and Khmer inscriptions

About 900 inscriptions have been found in Indochina that give a jigsaw set of clues to Angkor civilization. Those written in Sanskrit are largely poetic praises dedicated to gods and kings; Khmer-language ones give a much more focused insight into life and customs under the great kings. Some give a remarkably detailed picture of everyday life: one documents a ruling that pigs had the right to forage in rice fields, another dictates that ginger and honey should be used in the preparation of ritual foods. Most of the inscriptions have now been deciphered. Contemporary palm-leaf and paper documents which would have added to this knowledge have long since rotted away in the humid climate.

Bas-reliefs

Bas-reliefs carved into Angkor's temple walls also give a fascinating pictorial impression of life in the great city. Its citizens are shown warring, hunting, playing and partying and the reliefs present a picture which is often reassuringly normal in its detail: men played chess, old women read palms and people ate and drank and gossiped while musicians provided entertainment. Young men went hunting and young women evidently spent hours at the Angkorian equivalent of the hairdressers and boutiques.

Chou Ta-kuan's account

The most complete eyewitness account of Angkor was written by Chou Ta-kuan, an envoy from the Chinese court, who visited Cambodia in 1296, around 75 years after the death of Jayavarman VII, the last great conqueror of the Angkor period. Chou Ta-kuan wrote detailed accounts of an outsider's observations and impressions during this time. He cast Angkor as a grand and highly sophisticated civilization, despite the fact that it was, by then, well past its heyday. His descriptions of daily life actually seem quite comparable with Khmer life today. Ordinary people generally built their houses out of wood and leaves and their homes, like today, were raised on stilts. He described a society highly suspicious of evil spirits, where parents would call their children 'ugly' names, like dog, in order to deflect the attention from the evil spirits (see page 220 for further accounts).

French interpretation

What the French archaeologists managed to do, with brilliance, was to apply scientific principles to deciphering the mysteries of Angkor. The French, and by extension the West, nonetheless managed to 'invent' Angkor for its own interests, moulding the Angkorian Empire and its art so that it fitted in with the accepted image of the Orient. (This notion that Europeans invented the Orient is most effectively argued in Edward Said's seminal book *Orientalism*, first published in 1978 and now widely available in paperback. It is a book that does not deal specifically with Angkor but much of the argument can be applied to the French appropriation of Angkor and the Khmers.) Much that has been written about the ruins at Angkor and the empire and people that built them says as much about what the French were trying to do in Indochina, as about the place and people themselves. What is perhaps ironic is that Cambodians then reappropriated the French vision and made it their own. Today, French invention and Cambodian 'tradition' are one. Cambodia, lacking the cultural integrity to resist the influence of the French, became French and in so doing they took on board the French image of themselves and made it their own.

Angkor Wat → *For listings, see pages 128-142.*

The awe-inspiring sight of Angkor Wat first thing in the morning is something you're not likely to forget. Constructed between 1113 and 1150, it is believed to be the biggest religious monument ever built and certainly one of the most spectacular. British historian Arnold Toynbee said in his book *East to West* that: "Angkor is not orchestral; it is monumental." That sums it up. The temple complex covers 81 ha and is comparable in size to the Imperial Palace in Beijing. Its five towers are emblazoned on the Cambodian flag and the 12th-century masterpiece is considered by art historians to be the prime example of Classical Khmer art and architecture. It took more than 30 years to build and is contemporary with Notre Dame in Paris and Durham Cathedral in England. The temple is dedicated to the Hindu god Vishnu, personified in earthly form by its builder, the god-king Suryavarman II, and is aligned east to west.

Angkor Wat differs from other temples primarily because it is facing westward, symbolically the direction of death, leading many to believe it was a tomb. However, as Vishnu is associated with the west, it is now generally accepted that it served both as a temple and a mausoleum for the king. The sandstone was probably quarried from a far-away mine and floated down the Siem Reap river on rafts. Like other Khmer temple mountains, Angkor Wat is an architectural allegory, depicting in stone the epic tales of Hindu mythology. The central sanctuary of the temple complex represents the sacred

Who owns Angkor Wat?

The Cambodian Constitution states that all of Cambodia's heritage sites are owned by the state and its people. However, the ticketing rights to Angkor are a completely different story. Cambodia's largest corporation, Sokimex, has held ticketing rights to Angkor since 1999. The company, which runs a huge chain of Cambodian petrol stations and hotels, struck a lucrative deal with the government in May 1999. This deal has persisted until this day and is obviously very lucrative for all concerned.

From that point onward, a huge amount of myths have grown-up around the temples being owned by either Hun Sen or the Vietnamese (the owner of Sokimex is a Cambodian citizen – his partial Vietnamese ethnicity is often called into question). In fact, as stated earlier the temples are owned wholly by the people and government of Cambodia.

Mount Meru, the centre of the Hindu universe, on whose summit the gods reside. Angkor Wat's five towers symbolize Meru's five peaks; the enclosing wall represents the mountains at the edge of the world and the surrounding moat, the ocean beyond.

Angkor Wat was found in much better condition than most of the other temples in the complex because it seems to have been continuously inhabited by Buddhist monks after the Thais invaded in 1431. They were able to keep back the encroaching jungle. A giant stone Buddha was placed in the hall of the highest central tower, formerly sacred to the Hindu god, Vishnu. Three modern Buddhist monasteries flank the wat.

The temple complex is enclosed by a **square moat** – more than 5 km long and 190 m wide – and a high, galleried wall, which is covered in epic bas-reliefs and has four ceremonial tower gateways. The main gateway faces west and the temple is approached by a 475-m-long road, built along a **causeway**, which is lined with **naga balustrades**. There are small rectangular barays on either side of the roadway. To either side of the balustrades are two isolated buildings, thought to have been **libraries** – there are two more pairs of them within the temple precincts on the first and second terraces.

At the far end of the causeway stands a **cruciform platform**, guarded by stone lions, from which the devaraja may have held audiences; his backdrop being the three-tiered central sanctuary. Commonly referred to as the **Terrace of Honour**, it is entered through the colonnaded processional gateway of the outer gallery. The transitional enclosure beyond it is again cruciform in shape. Its four quadrants formed galleries, once stocked full of statues of the Buddha. Only a handful of the original 1000-odd images remain. Each gallery also had a basin which would originally have contained water for priests' ritual ablution. The second terrace, which is also square, rises from behind the **Gallery of a Thousand Buddhas**. It has a tower at each corner.

The cluster of **central towers**, 12 m above the second terrace, is reached by 12 steep stairways which represent the precipitous slopes of Mount Meru. Many historians believe that the upwards hike to this terrace was reserved for the high priests and king himself. Today, anyone is welcome but the difficult climb is best handled slowly by stepping sideways up the steep incline. The five lotus flower-shaped sandstone towers – the first appearance of these features in Khmer architecture – are believed to have once been covered in gold. The eight-storey towers are square, although they appear octagonal, and give the impression of a sprouting bud. Above the ascending tiers of roofs – each jutting gable has an elaborately carved pediment – the tower tapers into a circular roof. A quincunx shape is formed by the towers with four on each corner and another marking the centre. The central tower is dominant, and is the Siva shrine and principal sanctuary, whose pinnacle rises more than 30 m above the third level and 55 m above ground level. This sanctuary would have contained an image of Siva in the likeness of King Suryavarman II, as it was his temple-mountain. But it is now a Buddhist shrine and contains statues of the Buddha. The steps leading up to the third level are worn and very steep. On the south side the steps have a hand rail (not recommended for vertigo sufferers).

Over 1000 sq m of bas-relief decorate the temple. Its greatest sculptural treasure is the 2-m-high **bas-relief**, around the walls of the outer gallery. It is the longest continuous bas-relief in the world. In some areas traces of the paint and gilt that once covered the carvings can still be seen. Most famous are the hundreds of figures of devatas and apsaras in niches along the walls. The apsaras – the celestial women – are modelled on the god-king's own bevy of bare-breasted beauties and the sculptors' attention to detail provides an insight into the world of 12th-century haute couture. Their hair is often knotted on the crown and bejewelled – although all manner of wild and exotic coiffures are depicted. Jewelled collars and hip-girdles also are common and bracelets worn on the upper arms. Sadly many of the apsaras have been removed in recent years.

The bas-reliefs narrate stories from the *Ramayana* and *Mahabharata*, as well as legends of Vishnu, and are reminiscent of Pallava and Chola art in southeast India. Pious artisans and peasants were probably only allowed as far as Angkor Wat's outer gallery, where they could admire the bas-reliefs and pay homage to the god-king. In the open courtyards, statues of animals enliven the walls. Lions stand on guard beside the staircases. There were supposed

② Angkor Wat

➡ **Angkor maps**
1 Angkor, Siem Reap & Roluos, page 82
2 **Angkor Wat, page 93**
3 Angkor Thom, page 98
4 Siem Riep, page 120
5 Siem Riep market area, page 122

Anti-clockwise round Angkor Wat's bas-reliefs

1 West gallery, southern half represents a scene from the Hindu *Mahabharata* epic. The Battle of Kurukshtra shows the clash between the Pandavas (with pointed headdresses, attacking from the right) and the Kauravas. The two armies come from the two ends of the panel and meet in the middle in a ferocious battle. Above the war scene is Bhima, head of the Kauravas, wounded and lying atop a pile of arrows, surrounded by grieving followers and loved ones. The centre of the sculpture reveals the chief of the Pandavas in his war chariot. (The larger the figure the more important the person.) The southwest corner has been badly damaged – some say by the Khmer Rouge – but shows scenes from Vishnu's life.

2 South gallery, western half depicts Suryavarman II (builder of Angkor Wat) leading a procession. He is riding a royal elephant and carrying an axe, giving orders to his army before leading them into battle against the Chams. Shade is provided to him by 15 umbrellas, while a gamut of servants cool him with fans. The rank of the army officers is indicated by the number of umbrellas. Other troops follow on elephants. While trailing behind them are musicians and priests bearing holy fire. The undisciplined, outlandishly dressed figures are the Thais helping the Khmers in battle against the Chams.

3 South gallery, eastern half was restored in 1946. It depicts the punishments and rewards one can expect in the afterlife. On the left-hand side, the upper and middle levels show the dead waiting for their moment of judgement with Yama (Judge of the Dead) and his assistants, Dharma and Sitragupta, as to whether they will go to either the 37 heavens or 32 hells. On the left, lead two roads one to the heavens (above), and the other to hell (below). The damned, depicted in the bottom row, are in for a rough ride: the chances of their being savaged by wild animals, seized by demons or having their tongues pulled out (or any combination thereof) are quite high. Yama was tough and some might suggest that the crime didn't exactly fit the punishment: those who damaged others' property received broken bones; gluttons were sawn in half, and those who picked Shiva's flowers had their heads nailed. The blessed, depicted in the upper two rows, are borne along in palanquins surrounded by large numbers of bare-breasted apsaras dancing on lotuses.

4 Eastern gallery, southern half, is a 50-m-long panel that's probably to be 300 of them in the original building. Part of the bas-reliefs were hit by shrapnel in 1972, and some of its apsaras were used for target practice.

One of the great delights of Angkor, particularly at Angkor Wat, are the glorious trees. Huge tropical trees grow in Angkor's forests – a reminder of how much of Cambodia used to look. Driving out to Angkor from Siem Reap, the flat landscape is largely bare of trees but inside the protected area forests flourish. High in the treetops birds sing and call to each other all day. The wildlife, whose motto seems to be 'always watching: always waiting', are an integral part of Angkor. Keeping the prising tentacles and smothering creepers at bay requires constant vigilance and a sharp blade. A great deal of archaeology is still concealed in the embrace of the forest and exploring the less beaten paths often reveals some unknown and unmapped ruin.

Angkor's best known. The Churning of the Sea of Milk, portrays part of the Hindu legend, Bhagavata-Pourana. On the North are 92 deva (gods) and on the South 88 asura (demons) battling to win the coveted ambrosia (the nectar of the gods which gives immortality).

The serpent, Vasuki, is caught, quite literally, in the centre of their dispute. The asura hold onto the head of the serpent, whilst the devas hold the tail. The fighting causes the waters to churn, which in turn produces the elixir. In the centre, Vishnu commands. Below are sea animals (cut in half by the churning close to the pivot) and above, apsaras encouraging the competitors in their fight for the mighty elixir. Eventually (approximately 1000 years later) the elixir is won by the asuras until Vishnu appears to claim the cup.

Shortly before Cambodia collapsed into civil war in 1970, French archaeologists, who were repairing the roof and columns of the east gallery, dismantled the structure. Because they were unable to finish the job, the finest bas-reliefs have been left open to the elements.

5 Eastern gallery, northern half is unfinished and depicts the garuda-riding Krishna (Vishnu's incarnation) overcoming a wall of fire, with the help of a Garuda, to claim victory over Bana, the demon king. Having captured Bana and the ambrosia, Kailasa, Parvati and Ganesh, plead with Krishna to spare Bana's life. The gate in the centre of the east gallery was used by Khmer royalty and dignitaries for mounting and dismounting elephants.

6 North gallery, eastern half shows Garuda-riding, Krishna claiming victory over the demons. Shiva is shown in meditation with Ganesh, Brahma and Krishna. Most of the other scenes are from the *Ramayana*, notably the visit of Hanuman (the monkey god) to Sita.

7 North gallery, western half pictures another battle scene: demons versus gods. Twenty-one gods are pictured including Varuna, god of water, standing on a five-headed naga; Skanda, the god of war (several heads and a peacock with arms); Yama, the god of dead (chariot drawn by oxen): and Suva, the sun god (standing on a disc).

8 Western gallery, northern half has another scene from the *Ramayana* depicting another battle between the devas and asuras – this time in the form of Rama and Ravana. The demon king Ravana, who rides on a chariot pulled by monsters and commands an army of giants, has seduced and abducted Rama's beautiful wife Sita. The battle takes place in the centre of the relief.

The royal city of Angkor Thom

Construction of Jayavarman VII's spacious walled capital, Angkor Thom (which means 'great city'), began at the end of the 12th century: he rebuilt the capital after it had been captured and destroyed by the Cham. Angkor Thom was colossal – the 100-m-wide moat surrounding the city, which was probably stocked with crocodiles as a protection against the enemy, extended more than 12 km. Inside the moat was an 8-m-high stone wall, buttressed on the inner side by a high mound of earth along the top of which ran a terrace for troops to man the ramparts.

The area within the walls was more spacious than that of any walled city in medieval Europe – it could easily have encompassed the whole of ancient Rome. Yet it is believed that this enclosure, like the Forbidden City in Beijing, was only a royal, religious and administrative centre accommodating the court and dignitaries. The rest of the population lived outside the walls between the two artificial lakes – the east and west barays – and along the Siem Reap River.

Four great gateways in the city wall face north, south, east and west and lead to the city's geometric centre, the Bayon. The fifth, Victory Gate, leads from the royal palace (within the Royal Enclosure) to the East Baray. The height of the gates was determined by the headroom needed to accommodate an elephant and howdah complete with parasols. The flanks of each gateway are decorated by three-headed stone elephants and each gateway tower has four giant faces, which keep an eye on all four cardinal points.

Five causeways traverse the moat, each bordered by sculptured balustrades of nagas gripped, on one side, by 54 stern-looking giant gods and on the other by 54 fierce-faced demons. The balustrade depicts the Hindu legend of the churning of the sea (see box, page 101).

Some stone buildings survived the sacking of the city by the Cham, such as the temples of Phimeanakas and Baphuon, and these were incorporated by Jayavarman in his new plan. He adopted the general layout of the royal centre conceived by Suryavarman II.

Inside Angkor Thom

The **South Gate** provides the most common access route to Angkor Thom, predominantly because it sits on the path between the two great Angkor complexes. The gate is a wonderful introduction to Angkor Thom with well-restored statues of asuras (demons) and gods lining the bridge. The figures on the left, exhibiting serene expression, are the gods, while those on the right, with grimaced, fierce-looking heads, are the asuras. The significance of the naga balustrade, across the moat, is believed to be symbolic of a link between the world of mortals, outside the complex, to the world of gods, inside the complex. The 23-m-high gates feature four faces in a similarly styled fashion to those of the Bayon.

The **Bayon** is one of Angkor's most famous sights and most people visiting Cambodia are familiar with the beaming faces before even stepping foot in the temple. The Bayon was Jayavarman VII's own temple-mountain, built right in the middle of Angkor Thom; its large faces have now become synonymous with the Angkor complex. It is believed to have been built between the late 12th century to early 13th century, around 100 years after Angkor Wat. Unlike other Khmer monuments, the Bayon has no protective wall immediately enclosing it. The central tower, at the intersection of the diagonals city walls, indicates that the city walls and the temple were built at the same time.

The Bayon is a three-tiered, pyramid temple with a 45-m-high tower, topped by four gigantic carved heads. These faces are believed to be the images of Jayavarman VII as a Bodhisattra, and face the four compass points. They are crowned with lotus flowers, symbol of enlightenment, and are surrounded by 51 smaller towers each with heads facing north, south, east and west. There are over 2000 large faces carved throughout the structure. Although the Bayon seems a complex, labyrinthine structure, its overall layout is quite basic. The first two of the three levels feature galleries of bas-relief (which should be viewed clockwise), a circular central sanctuary dominates the third level.

When Pierre Loti, the French writer, first saw these towers in 1912 he was astounded: "I looked up at the tree-covered towers which dwarfed me, when all of a sudden my blood curdled as I saw an enormous smile looking down on me, and then another smile on another wall, then three, then five, then 10, appearing in every direction". The facial features are striking and the full lips, curling upwards at the corners, are known as 'the smile of Angkor'.

Even the archaeologists of the École Française d'Extrême Orient were not able to decide immediately whether the heads on the Bayon represented Brahma, Siva or the Buddha. There are many theories. One of the most plausible was conceived in 1934 by George Coedès, an archaeologist who spent many years studying the temples at Angkor. He postulated that the sculptures represented King Jayavarman VII in the form of Avaloketsvara, the Universal Buddha, implying that the Hindu concept of the god-king had been appended to Buddhist cosmology. Jayavarman VII, once a humble monk who twice renounced the throne and then became the mightiest of all the Khmer rulers, may be the smiling face, cast in stone, at the centre of his kingdom. The multiplication of faces, all looking out to the four cardinal points, may symbolize Jayavarman blessing the four quarters of the kingdom. After Jayavarman's death, the Brahmin priests turned the Bayon into a place of Hindu worship.

The Bayon has undergone a series of facelifts through its life, a point first observed by Henri Parmentier – a French archaeologist who worked for L'École Français d'Extrême Orient – in 1924 and later excavations revealed vestiges of a former building. It is thought that the first temple was planned as a two-tiered structure dedicated to Siva, which was then altered to its present form. As a result, it gives the impression of crowding – the towers rise right next to each other and the courtyards are narrow without much air or light. When Henri Mouhot rediscovered Angkor, local villagers had dubbed the Bayon 'the hide and seek sanctuary' because of its complex layout.

The **bas-reliefs** which decorate the walls of the Bayon all seem to tell a story but are much less imposing than those at Angkor Wat. The sculpture is carved deeper but is more naive and less sophisticated than the bas-reliefs at Angkor Wat. They vary greatly in quality, which may have been because the sculptors' skills were being overstretched by Jayavarman's ambitious building programme. The reliefs on the outer wall and on the inner gallery differ completely and seem to belong to two different worlds. The relief on the outside depicts historical events; those on the inside are drawn from the epic world of Hindu gods and legends, representing the creatures who were supposed to haunt the subterranean depths of Mount Meru. In fact the reliefs on the outer wall illustrating historical scenes and derring-do with marauding Cham were carved in the early 13th century during the reign of Jayavarman; those on the inside were carved after the king's death when his successors turned from Mahayana Buddhism back to Hinduism. In total, there are over 1.2 km of bas-reliefs, depicting over 11,000 characters.

Two recurring themes in the bas-reliefs are the powerful king and the Hindu epics. Jayavarman is depicted in the throes of battle with the Cham – who are recognizable thanks to their unusual and distinctive headdress, which looks like an inverted lotus flower. The naval battle pictured on the walls of Banteay Chhmar are almost identical. Funnily enough, there's a bas-relief in the north section of the west gallery depicting a huge fish eating a deer, a complimentary inscription says "the deer is its food", an artistic directive, which the carver obviously forgot to remove. The other bas-reliefs give an insight into Khmer life at the time: the warrior elephants, oxcarts, fishing with nets, cockfights and skewered fish drying on racks; vignettes show musicians, jugglers, hunters, chess-players, people nit-picking hair, palm readers and reassuringly down-to-earth scenes of Angkor citizens enjoying a drink. In the naval battle scenes, the water around the war canoes is depicted by the presence of fish, crocodiles and floating corpses.

The **Royal Enclosure**, to the north of the Bayon, had already been laid out by Suryavarman I: the official palace was in the front with the domestic quarters behind, its gardens surrounded by a laterite wall and moat. Suryavarman I also beautified the royal city with ornamental pools. Jayavarman VII simply improved his designs.

③ In & around Angkor Thom

Terrace of the Elephants **1**	Tep Tranam **6**	Chau Say Tevoda **11**
Royal Enclosure **2**	Preah Pithu Group **7**	North Kleang **12**
Phimeanakas **3**	Preah Palilay **8**	South Kleang **13**
Terrace of the Leper King **4**	Victory Gate **9**	
Prasats Suor Prat **5**	Thommanon **10**	Artificial lakes

In front of the Royal Enclosure, at the centre of Angkor Thom, Suryavarman I laid out the first Grand Plaza with the recently renovated **Terrace of the Elephants** (also called the Royal Terrace). The 300-m-long wall derives its name from the large, lifelike carvings of elephants in a hunting scene, adorning its walls. The 2.5-m wall also features elephants

➡ **Angkor maps**
1 Angkor, Siem Reap & Roluos, page 82
2 Angkor Wat, page 93
3 **Angkor Thom, page 98**
4 Siem Riep, page 120
5 Siem Riep market area, page 122

flanking the southern stairway. Believed to once be the foundations for the royal reception hall, lead tiles were found here in more recent years. This discovery corroborates Chinese diplomat Chou Ta-kuan's evidence that "the tiles of the king's main apartment are made of lead". Royalty once sat in gold-topped pavilions at the centre of the pavilion, and here there are rows of garudas (bird-men), their wings lifted as if in flight. They were intended to give the impression that the god-king's palace was floating in the heavens like the imagined flying celestial palaces of the gods. At the end of the terrace is an impressive sculpture of a five-headed horse. Also in front of the Royal Enclosure are the stately **North** and **South Kleangs**, which sit on the east side of the central square (opposite the Terrace of the Elephants). Although Kleang means 'storeroom', a royal oath of allegiance carved into one of the doorways indicates that they may have served as reception areas for foreign envoys. The North Kleang was originally constructed in wood under Rajendravarman II; Jayavarman V reconstructed it with stone and Jayavarman VII later added 12 laterite victory towers, called the **Prasat Suor Prat**. The function of the towers is steeped in controversy. While some say they were intended as anchors for performing acrobats and clowns, Chou Ta-kuan stated that they were used to settle disputes between performing men (to see who could last the longest seated on a tower without illness or injury). Henri Mauhot disagreed with both theories, suggesting that the towers were created to hold the crown jewels.

At the northeast corner of the 'central square' is the 12th-century **Terrace of the Leper King**, which may have been a cremation platform for the aristocracy of Angkor. Now rebuilt it is a little too fresh and contemporary for some tastes. The 7-m-high double terrace has bands of bas-reliefs, one on top of the other, with intricately sculptured scenes of royal pageantry and seated apsaras as well as nagas and garudas which frequented the slopes of Mount Meru. Above is a strange statue from an earlier date, which probably

The Bayon

Bas-reliefs depicting legends on inner walls

North Gate

Library

Pool

West Gate

East Gate

1st level

2nd level

Library

Pool

N

South Gate

Central tower with 4 gigantic carved heads facing 4 compass points

Bas-reliefs depicting historical events on outer walls

50 metres
50 yards

The Churning of the Sea

The Hindu legend, the Churning of the Sea, relates how the gods and demons resolved matters in the turbulent days when the world was being created.

The elixir of immortality was one of 13 precious things lost in the churning of the cosmic sea. It took 1000 years before the gods and demons, in a joint dredging operation aided by Sesha, the sea snake, and Vishnu, recovered them all.

The design of the temples of Angkor was based on this ancient legend. The moat represents the ocean and the gods use the top of Mount Meru – represented by the tower – as their churning stick. The cosmic serpent offered himself as a rope to enable the gods and demons to twirl the stick.

Paul Mus, a French archaeologist, suggests that the bridge with the naga balustrades which went over the moat from the world of men to the royal city was an image of the rainbow. Throughout Southeast Asia and India, the rainbow is alluded to as a multi-coloured serpent rearing its head in the sky.

depicts the god of death, Yama, and once held a staff in its right hand. The statue's naked, lichen-covered body gives the terrace its name – the lichen gives the uncanny impression of leprosy. Opposite the Terrace of the Elephants, on the south side of the Terrace of the Leper King, are the remains of an earlier wall, carved with bas-reliefs of demons. These reliefs were found by French archaeologists and had been intentionally concealed. This illustrates the lengths to which the Khmers went to recreate Mount Meru (the home of the gods) as faithfully as possible. According to Hindu mythology, Mount Meru extended into the bowels of the earth; the bas-relief section below ground level was carved with weird and wonderful creatures to symbolize the hidden depths of the underworld. The second layer of carving is the base of Mount Meru on earth. Flights of steps led through these to the lawns and pavilions of the royal gardens and Suryavarman's palace.

The **Phimeanakas** (meaning Celestial or Flying Palace in Sanskrit) inside the Royal Enclosure was started by Rajendravarman and used by all the later kings. The structure stands close to the walls of the Royal Palace, none of which exists today. Suryavarman I rebuilt this pyramidal temple when he was renovating the Royal Enclosure. It rises from the centre of the former royal palace. Lions guard all four stairways to the central tower which was originally covered in gold, as the Chinese envoy Chou Ta-kuan related in 1296: "The king sleeps in the summit of the palace's golden tower. All the people believe that the tower is also inhabited by the Lord of the Sun, who is a nine-headed serpent. Every night the serpent appears in the form of a woman with whom the king sleeps during the first watch. None of the royal wives are allowed in the tower. The king leaves at the second

Barays and the Jayavarman conundrum: the case *for* irrigation

By founding his capital at Roluos, just southeast of Angkor, in the middle of an arid plain annually plagued by drought and flash floods, Jayavarman II bequeathed to scholars a geo-climatic conundrum: what possessed him to site the nerve centre of Khmer civilization at such an environmentally unfriendly spot and how did the great city sustain itself through the centuries?

Archaeologists have postulated that the Khmers engineered a complex irrigation system to grow enough rice to feed the city's population. In this view, Angkor was a classic hydraulic society.

In *The Art of Southeast Asia*, Philip Rawson wrote: "Angkor was a capital filled with temples and supporting many inhabitants. But its nucleus was a splendid irrigation project based on a number of huge artificial reservoirs fed by the local rivers and linked to each other by means of a rectangular grid system of canals." The barays, or man-made lakes, fed an intricate network of irrigation channels. The first baray was Lolei, built by Indravarman at the city of Roluos. "The engineering involved at Angkor," Rawson said, "… was vaster and far more sophisticated than anything seen before in that part of the world." Lolei was more than 3.5 km long and 800 m wide. The East Baray was twice the size of Lolei and the West Baray, built during Udayadityavarman II's reign, is thought to have held about four million cu m of water when full.

The barays were constructed by building dykes above the level of the land and waiting for the monsoon flood. Because the resultant reservoirs were higher than the surrounding land, there was no need to pump the water to flood the paddy fields: a gap was simply cut in the dyke. The water stored in the barays would have been replenished by each monsoon, making it possible to irrigate the ricelands. With their land being watered year round, the Khmers would be able to grow three crops of rice a year.

The barays were central to the health and vigour of Khmer civilization but because they were sitting targets for enemy saboteurs, they may also have played a part in its downfall. During successive Siamese invasions the irrigation system would have been irreparably damaged and essential maintenance neglected through lack of manpower. The precarious, and artificial, balance of man and nature was disturbed and the irrigation channels cracked and dried up along with the mighty Khmer Empire.

Why Angkor should have gone into decline from about the 13th century has exercised the minds of historians for years. Apart from the destruction of the fragile irrigation system, several other explanations as to Angkor's downfall have been suggested: climatic change, the shift of trade from land to sea-based empires and the corruption of a system which, like the Roman emperors, made the king a demi-god. Some think the builder King Jayavarman VII bankrupted the empire with his vast and ambitious building schemes.

watch to go to his wives and concubines. If the naga spirit does not appear one night, it is a sign that the king's death is imminent. Should the king fail to visit the naga for a single night, the welfare of the kingdom will suffer dire consequences." The Phimeanakas represented a genuine architectural revolution: it was not square, but rectangular and on

Barays and the Jayavarman conundrum: the case *against* irrigation

When the first Westerners stumbled upon the Khmer ruins at Angkor – the lost city in the jungle – in the middle of the 19th century, they judged it to be the finest example of a civilization based upon the massive control of water for irrigation. The sheer size of the monuments, the vast barays storing millions of gallons of water, all seemed to lend force to the notion that here was the finest example of state-controlled irrigation. In Karl Marx's words, the Khmer Kingdom was a society based upon the Asiatic mode of production. The upshot of this was that, by necessity, there needed to be a centralized state and an all-powerful king – leading, in Professor Karl Wittfogel's famous phrase, to a system of 'Oriental Despotism'. Such a view seemed hard to refute – how could such enormous expanses of water in the baray be used for anything but irrigation?

However, in the past decade, archaeologists, irrigation engineers and geographers have challenged the view of the Khmer Kingdom as the hydraulic civilization par excellence. Their challenge rests on four main pillars of evidence. First, they point out that if irrigation was so central to life in Angkor, why is it not mentioned once in over 1000 inscriptions? Second, they question the usual interpretation of Angkorian agriculture contained in the Chinese emissary Chou Ta-kuan's account, *Notes on the customs of Cambodia*, written in 1312. This account talks of "three or four rice harvests a year" – which scholars have assumed means irrigated rice agriculture. However, the detractors put a different interpretation on Chou Ta-kuan's words, arguing that they in fact describe a system of flood retreat agriculture in which rice was sown as the waters of the Great Lake, the Tonlé Sap, receded at the end of the rainy season. Third, they note that aerial photographs show none of the feeder canals needed to carry water from the barays to the fields nor any of the other irrigation structures needed to control water.

Finally, the sceptics draw upon engineering evidence to support their case. They have calculated that the combined storage capacity of all the barays and reservoirs is sufficient to irrigate only 400 ha of riceland – hardly the stuff on which great civilizations are built.

The geographer Philip Stott maintains that flood retreat agriculture would have produced the surplus needed to feed the soldiers, priests and the court of the Khmer god-king, while postulating that the barays were only for urban use. He writes that they were "just like the temple mountains, essentially a part of the urban scene, providing urban symbolism, beauty, water for bathing and drinking, a means of transport, and perhaps a supply of fish as well. Yet, not one drop of their water is likely to have fed the rice fields of Angkor."

The East Baray is now dry but the West Baray is used for fish cultivation.

---

the upper terrace, surrounding the central tower, there was a gallery with corbelled vaults, used as a passageway.

The **Srah Srei**, or the women's bath, to the north of Phimeanakas is also within the walled enclosure. Chou Ta-kuan appears to have enjoyed watching Angkor's womenfolk bathe, noting that, "To enter the water, the women simply hide their sex with their left hand". The Phimeanakas is linked by the **Avenue of Victory** to the Eastern Baray.

South of the Royal Enclosure and near the Terrace of the Elephants is the **Baphuon**, built by Udayadityavarman II. The temple was approached by a 200-m-long sandstone causeway, raised on pillars, which was probably constructed after the temple was built. The platform leads from the temple-mountain itself to the east gopura – an arched gateway leading to the temple courtyards. The Baphuon is not well preserved as it was erected on an artificial hill which weakened its foundations. Only the three terraces of its pyramidal, Mount Meru-style form remain and these give little indication of its former glory: it was second only to the Bayon in size. Chou Ta-kuan reported that its great tower was made of bronze and that it was "truly marvellous to behold". With extensive restoration, the temple is starting to shape-up. Most of the bas-reliefs were carved in panels and refer to the Hindu epics. Some archaeologists believe the sculptors were trying to tell stories in the same way as the shadow plays. It is believed that the fourth level wall on the western side was originally created in the form of a large, reclining Buddha, though it is hard to make out today. There is a wonderful view from the summit. South of the Baphuon, returns you back to the Bayon.

Preah Palilay, just outside the north wall of the Royal Enclosure, was also built by Jayavarman VII. Just to the east of this temple is **Tep Tranam**, the base of a pagoda, with a pool in front of it. To the east of Tep Tranam and the other side of the Northern Avenue is the **Preah Pithu Group**, a cluster of five temples.

South of Angkor Thom

Phnom Bakheng and Baksei Chamkrong

ⓘ *To get up to the ruins, either climb the steep and uneven hill where the vegetation has been cleared (slippery when wet), ride an elephant to the top of the hill (US$15) or walk up the gentle zig-zag path the elephants take.*

Phnom Bakheng, Yasovarman's temple-mountain, stands at the top of a natural hill, 60-m high, affording good views of the plains of Angkor. There is also a roped off Buddha's footprint to see. It is just outside the south gate of Angkor Thom and was the centre of King Yasovarman's city, Yasodharapura – the 'City Endowed with Splendour'. A pyramid-temple dedicated to Siva, Bakheng was the home of the royal lingam and Yasovarman's mausoleum after his death. It is composed of five towers built on a sandstone platform. There are 108 smaller towers scattered around the terraces. The main tower has been partially demolished and the others have completely disappeared. It was entered via a steep flight of steps which were guarded by squatting lions. The steps have deteriorated with the towers. Foliate scroll relief carving covers much of the main shrine – the first time this style was used. This strategically placed hill served as a camp for various combatants, including the Vietnamese, and suffered accordingly. Today the hill is disfigured by a radio mast.

Baksei Chamkrong was built by Harshavarman I at the beginning of the 10th century and dedicated to his father, Yasovarman I. It lies at the foot of Phnom Bakheng (between Bakheng and Angkor Thom), the centre of Yasovarman's city, and was one of the first temples to be built in brick on a stepped laterite base. An inscription tells of a golden image of Siva inside the temple.

East of Angkor Thom

Chau Say Tevoda and Thommanon

There is a close group of temples just outside the east gate of Angkor Thom. Chau Say Tevoda, built by Suryavarman II, is the first temple outside the east gate and is dwarfed by Ta Keo. The temple is dedicated to Siva but many of the carvings are of Vishnu. It is similar in plan to Thommanon, next door, whose surrounding walls have completely disappeared, leaving only the gateways on the east and west ends and a ruined central tower. Originally both temples would have had a hall linked to the central tower and enclosing walls with elaborate gateways. A library, to the southeast, is the only other building in the complex. There are repeated pediments above the doorways.

Ta Keo and Ta Nei

Ta Keo, begun during Jayavarman V's reign and left unfinished, stands east of the Royal Palace and just off the Avenue of Victory. The pyramid-temple rises over 50 m, its five tower shrines supported on a five-tiered pyramid. It was one of the first temples to be built entirely of sandstone. Previous tower sanctuaries had entrances only on the east side but Ta Keo has openings on all four sides. It was originally surrounded by a moat.

Deeper in the forest, 600 m north of Ta Keo, is Ta Nei. Built by Jayavarman VII the building has appropriated the Bayon's style but on a much smaller scale. Much of the building still remains in the collapsed state but ongoing work from the Apsara Authority means the building is being used for training purposes. It is an overgrown temple with lichen-covered bas-reliefs.

Ta Prohm

For all would-be Mouhots and closet Indiana Joneses, the temple of Ta Prohm, to the south of Ta Keo, is the perfect lost-in-the-jungle experience. Unlike most of the other monuments at Angkor, it has only been minimally cleared of undergrowth, fig trees and creepers and so retains much of its mystery. Widely regarded as one of Angkor's most enchanting and beautiful temples, it is an absolute 'must-see'.

Ta Prohm was built to house the divine image of the Queen Mother and was consecrated in 1186 – five years after Jayavarman VII seized power. The outer enclosures are somewhat obscured by dense foliage but reach well beyond the temple's heart (1 km by 650 m). The temple proper consists of a number of concentric galleries featuring corner towers and the standard gopuras. Other buildings and enclosures were built on a more ad hoc basis. The temple marked the end of an architectural style in which the temple's structure lay on a single plane with rising towers alluding to the notion of elevation rather than comprising multiple levels.

It underwent many transformations and an inscription gives detailed information on the complex. Within the complex walls lived 12,640 citizens. It contained 39 sanctuaries or prasats, 566 stone dwellings and 288 brick dwellings. Ta Prohm literally translates as the Royal Monastery and that is what it functioned as, home to 18 abbots and 2740 monks. By the 12th century temples were no longer exclusively places of worship – they also had to accommodate monks so roofed halls were increasingly built within the complexes. According to contemporary inscriptions, the temple required 79,365 people for its upkeep, relying on the income of 3140 villages to subsidize the 2740 officials and 615 dancers. The list of property it owned was on an equally impressive scale. It included 523 parasols, 35 diamonds and 40,620 pearls.

The French writer Elie Lauré wrote: "With its millions of knotted limbs, the forest embraces the ruins with a violent love". Creepers entwine themselves around ancient stones like the tentacles of a giant octopus. Trunks and roots pour off temple roofs like lava flows. It was decided by the École Française d'Extrême Orient to leave the temple in its natural state. The trees are predominantly the silk-cotton tree and the aptly-named strangler fig. The plants are believed to have spawned in the temple's cracks from seeds blown in or dropped by birds. Naturally, the roots of the trees have descended towards the soil, prying their way through foundations in the process. As the vegetation has matured it has forced its way further into the temple's structure, damaging the man-built base and causing untold destruction. This has created a situation where the structures now rely on the trees for support. Herein lies the dilemma – if the trees die or are damaged, the now damaged and loose temple walls could easily crumble or collapse. Venerable trees weighing several tonnes growing on temple roofs also cause unimaginable stress, slowly shattering the stones.

In recent years a colossal tree was struck by lightening and fell on a gallery, causing quite serious damage. This reignited a campaign to 'save Ta Prohm' and a project is underway to prune some of the smaller trees and larger branches.

Banteay Kdei, Srah Srang and Prasat Kravan

The massive complex of **Banteay Kdei**, otherwise known as 'the citadel of cells', is 3 km east of Angkor Thom and just to the southeast of Ta Prohm. Some archaeologists think it may be dedicated to Jayavarman VII's religious teacher. The temple has remained in much the same state it was discovered in – a crowded collection of ruined laterite towers and connecting galleries lying on a flat plan, surrounded by a galleried enclosure. It is presumed that the temple was a Buddhist monastery and hundreds of buried Buddha statues have been excavated from the site. In recent times a community of monks has used the site but this is less common now due to the strict restrictions imposed by temple management. The temple area is enclosed by a large laterite wall, 700 m by 500 m, and has three main enclosures. Like Ta Prohm it contains a Hall of Dancers (east side), an open roof building with four separate quarters. The second enclosure runs around the perimeters of the inner enclosure. The third, inner enclosure contains a north and south library and central sanctuary. The central tower was never finished and the square pillars in the middle of the courtyard still cannot be explained by scholars. There are few inscriptions here to indicate either its name or purpose, but it is almost certainly a Buddhist temple built in the 12th century, about the same time as Ta Prohm. It is quite similar to Ta Prohm in design but on a much smaller scale. Historians Freeman and Jacques believe that it was probably built over the site of another temple. The temple is being restored, slowly but surely. However, the 13th-century vandalism of Buddha images (common to most of Jayavarman's temples) will prove a little more difficult to restore. This temple offers a few good examples of Mahayanist Buddhist frontons and lintels that escaped the desecration.

The lake or baray next to Banteay Kdei is called **Srah Srang** ('Royal Bath') and was used for ritual bathing. The steps down to the water face the rising sun and are flanked with lions and nagas. This sandstone landing stage dates from the reign of Jayavarman VII but the lake itself is thought to date back two centuries earlier. A 10th-century inscription reads 'this water is stored for the use of all creatures except dyke breakers', ie elephants. This design is believed to be characteristic of that adopted in the Bayon. The Baray, which measures 700 m by 300 m, has been filled with turquoise-blue waters for over 1300 years.

With a good view of Pre Rup across the lake, some archaeologists believe that this spot affords the best vista in the whole Angkor complex. The green landscape around the baray and beautiful views offer a tranquil and cool resting place, perfect for a picnic lunch.

On the road between Angkor Wat and Banteay Kdei, on the small circuit, is **Prasat Kravan**. The temple, built in AD 921, means 'Cardamom Sanctuary' and is unusual in that it is built of brick. (By that time brick had been replaced by laterite and sandstone.) It consists of five brick towers arranged in a line. The bricklayers did a good job, especially considering they used a vegetable composite as their mortar. The temple's bas-reliefs are considered a bit of an anomaly as brick was hardly ever sculpted upon. In the early 10th century, temples were commissioned by individuals other than the king; Prasat Kravan is one of the earliest examples. It was probably built during the reign of Harshavarman I.

The Hindu temple, surrounded by a moat, is positioned in a north-south direction. Two of the five decorated brick towers contain bas-reliefs (the north and central towers). The central tower is probably the most impressive and contains a linga on a pedestal. The sanctuary's three walls all contain pictures of Vishnu; the left-hand wall depicts Vishnu disguised as Vamana the dwarf. The incarnation of Vamana was used to dupe the evil demon king, Bali, into letting the unassuming dwarf take a small space to meditate. Instead the mighty Vishnu rose up, taking three important steps – from a pedestal, across the ocean, to a lotus – in order to reclaim the world from the evil demon king. On the right-hand wall again is the mighty Vishnu riding his Garuda. Common to both the bas-reliefs is the four-armed Vishnu waving around a number of objects: disc, club, conch shell and ball – these are all symbolic of his personal attributes and power. On the opposing wall is Vishnu, this time with eight arms standing between six rows of people meditating above a giant reptile.

The Northern tower is devoted to Lakshimi, Vishnu's wife. Like her consort, she is also baring her personal attributes. The best light to view the relief is in the morning.

The Cardamom Sanctuary is named after a tree that grew on the grounds. Ironically, its ruin has been largely due to the roots of trees growing beneath it. The French have been involved in the temple's reconstruction. The temple's twin, Prasat Neang Khamau (the Black Lady Sanctuary), can be found outside Phnom Penh.

Pre Rup

Northeast of Srah Srang is Pre Rup, the State Temple of King Rajendravarman's capital. Built in AD 961, the temple-mountain representing Mount Meru is larger, higher and artistically superior than its predecessor, the East Mebon, which it closely resembles. In keeping with the tradition of state capitals, Pre Rup marked the centre of the city, much of which doesn't exist today. The pyramid-structure, which is constructed of laterite with brick prasats, sits at the apex of an artificial, purpose-built mountain. The temple is enclosed by a laterite outer wall (127 m by 117 m) and inner wall (87 m by 77 m) both which contain gopuras in the centre of each wall. The central pyramid-level consists of a three-tiered, sandstone platform, with five central towers sitting above. This was an important innovation at Pre Rup and East Mebon, that the sanctuary at the top was no longer a single tower – but a group of five towers, surrounded by smaller towers on the outer, lower levels. This more complicated plan reached its final development at Angkor Wat 150 years later. The group of five brick towers were originally elaborately decorated with plaster, but most of it has now fallen off. However, the corners of each of the five towers contain guardian figures – as per tradition, the eastern towers are female and the western and central towers are male. The shrine has fine lintels and columns on its doorways. But the intricate sandstone carvings on

Motifs in Khmer sculpture

The **kala** is a jawless monster commanded by the gods to devour his own body – it made its first appearance in lintels at Roluos. The monster represented devouring time and was an early import from Java.

Singhas or lions appeared in stylized forms and are often guardians to temples. The lions lack realism probably because the carvers had never seen one.

The **makara** was a mythical water monster with a scaley body, eagles' talons and an elephantine trunk.

The **naga** or sacred snakes play an important part in Hindu mythology and the Khmers drew on them for architectural inspiration. Possibly more than any other single symbol or motif, the naga is characteristic of Southeast Asia. The naga is an aquatic serpent, the word being Sanskrit for snake, and is intimately associated with water (a key component of Khmer prosperity). In Hindu mythology the naga coils beneath and supports Vishnu on the cosmic ocean. The snake also swallows the waters of life, these only being set free to reinvigorate the world after Indra ruptures the serpent with a bolt of lightning. Another version has Vishnu's servants pulling at the serpent to squeeze the waters of life from it (the so-called churning of the sea). The naga permeates Southeast Asian life from royalty to villager. The bridge across the Bayon to Angkor Wat features nagas churning the oceans; men in Vietnam, Laos and

Singha

Naga

the doors of the upper levels are reproductions. The upper levels of the pyramid offer a brilliant, panoramic view of the countryside.

Eastern Baray, East Mebon and Banteay Samre

The **Eastern Baray** – or Baray Orientale – was built by Yasovarman I and fed by the Siem Reap River. This large reservoir (7 km by 1.8 km), now dried up, was the labour of love for Yasovarman I. Historian Dawn Rooney believes it took 6000 workers more than three years

Thailand used to tattoo their bodies with nagas for protection; water, the gift of life in a region where wet rice is the staple crop, is measured in Thailand in terms of numbers of nagas; while objects from boats to water storage jars to temples to musical instruments are decorated with the naga motif throughout Southeast Asia.

The **garuda** appeared relatively late in Khmer architecture. This mythical creature – half man, half bird – was the vehicle of the Hindu god, Vishnu and the sworn enemy of the nagas.

The **apsaras** are regarded as one of the greatest invention of the Khmers. The gorgeous temptresses – born, according to legend, 'during the churning of the Sea of Milk' – were Angkor's equivalent of pin-up girls and represented the ultimate ideal of feminine beauty. They lived in heaven where their sole raison d'être was to have eternal sex with Khmer heroes and holy men. The apsaras are carved with splendidly ornate jewellery and, clothed in the latest Angkor fashion, they strike seductive poses and seemingly compete with each other like models on a catwalk. Different facial features suggest the existence of several races at Angkor – it is possible that they might be modelled on women captured in war. Together with the five towers of Angkor Wat they have become the symbol of Khmer culture. The god-king himself possessed an apsara-like retinue of court dancers – impressive enough for Chinese envoy Chou Ta-kuan to write home about it in in 1296.

Garuda

Apsaras

to complete. The baray was Yasovarman I's first major work. To keep the punters on side he needed to provide a reliable water supply to his new kingdom, Yasodharataka. And that he did. At full capacity the baray could hold around 45-50 million cu m of water. He named the baray Yasodharataka and declared it protected by the goddess Ganga (overseen by abbots from the ashramas south of the baray). The four corners are marked by stelae.

Today, a boat isn't required to reach the middle of the Eastern Baray, where the flamboyant five towers of the **East Mebon** are located. Intrepid traveller Helen Churchill

Candee remarked of the temple: "Could any conception be lovelier, a vast expanse of sky-tinted water as wetting for a perfectly ordered temple."

The Hindu pyramid structure consists of three tiers. Guarding the corners of the first and second levels are carefully sculpted elephants and sculptures (the best one is in the southeast corner). The inner enclosure contains eight smaller towers and skilfully carved lintels upon the gopuras featuring Lakshmi being watered down by two elephants and Vishnu in his man-lion guise, Narasimha. The upper terrace contains the five towers, the northwest tower features Ganesha riding his own trunk; the southeast tower shows an elephant being eaten by a monster and the central sanctuary's lintels depict Indra on his mount and Varuna the Guardian.

Finished in AD 952, Rajendravarman seems to have followed the Roluos trend and dedicated East Mebon to his parents. The East Mebon and Pre Rup were the last monuments in plaster and brick; they mark the end of a Khmer architectural epoch. The overall temple construction utilizes all materials that were available at the time: plaster, brick, laterite and sandstone. Although many believe East Mebon to be a temple-mountain, that wasn't its original intention, it just appears that way now that surrounding waters have disappeared. The Siem Reap River is said to have been diverted while the temple was built.

Banteay Samre lies further to the east, around 500 m past the east end of the East Baray. It is a Hindu temple dedicated to Vishnu, although reliefs decorating some of the frontons (the triangular areas above arches) portray Buddhist scenes. It is thought to have been built by Suryavarman II and has many characteristics of Angkor Wat such as stone-vaulted galleries and a high central tower. The bas-reliefs are in fine condition.

North of Angkor Thom

Preah Khan

Northeast of the walled city of Angkor Thom, about 3.5 km from the Bayon, is the 12th-century complex of Preah Khan. One of the largest complexes within the Angkor area, it was Jayavarman VII's first capital before Angkor Thom was completed. The name Preah Khan means 'sacred sword' and probably derives from a decisive battle against the Cham, which created a 'lake of blood', but was inevitably won by Jayavarman VII.

Preah Khan is not uniform in style. It is highly likely that Jayavarman VII's initial very well-organized and detailed city plans went slightly pear-shaped during the working city's life. A number of alterations and buildings were added, in addition to a vast civilian habitation (huts and timber houses), which all came together to create a complex labyrinth of architectural chaos. It is similar in ground plan to Ta Prohm (see page 105) but attention was paid to the approaches: its east and west entrance avenues, leading to ornamental causeways, are lined with carved stone boundary posts. Evidence of 1000 teachers suggests that it was more than a mere Buddhist monastery but most likely a Buddhist university. Nonetheless an abundance of Brahmanic iconography is still present on site. Around the rectangular complex is a large laterite wall surrounded by large garudas wielding the naga (each over 5 m in height). The theme continues across the length of the whole 3-km external enclosure, with the motif dotted every 50 m. Within these walls lies the surrounding moat.

The city is conveniently located on the shores of its own baray, Jayataka (3.5 km by 900 m). Some foundations and laterite steps lead from the reservoir, where two beautiful gajasimha lions guard the path. It is best to enter the temple from the baray's jetty in order to experience the magnificence of the divinities and devas of the Processional Way (causeway leading across the moat).

The construction's four walls meet in the centre creating two galleries and likewise, two enclosures. The outer enclosure contains the traditional four gopuras (adorned with stately bas-reliefs) and the Hall of Dancers. This hall contains an elaborate frieze of dancing apsaras and was used, in recent times, to host charity performances to help fund the area's restoration. Within the enclosure there are also a few ponds, libraries and supplementary buildings, most notably, a two-storey pavilion (north of the performance hall) which is believed to have housed the illustrious 'sacred sword'.

The second and innermost walls run so closely together that it is possible to pass through the following enclosure without realizing you had entered it (this is probably due to an expansion undertaken very early on in the piece to offer additional protection to the shrines).

The inner enclosure is a bewildering array of constructions and shrines. Holes in the inner walls of the central sanctuary of Preah Khan suggest they may once have been decorated with brass plates – an obvious target for looters. One inscription implies that up to 1500 tonnes was used within the edifice. The temple was built to shelter the statue of Jayavarman VII's father, Dharanindravarman II, in the likeness of Bodhisattva Avatokitsvara, which has now probably been smashed. A stela was discovered at the site glorifying the builder, Jayavarman VII and detailing what it took to keep the place ticking over. The inventory mentions that for Preah Khan's upkeep, the services of 97,840 men and women, 444 chefs, 4606 footmen and 2298 servants were required. Preah Khan's

Preah Khan

inscriptions also refer to the existence of 515 other statues, 102 royal hospitals of the kingdom, 18 major annual festivals and 10 days' public holiday a month.

The temple was starting to deteriorate, but clearing and careful conservation have helped remedy this. During the dry season, the World Monuments Funds (WMF), based in New York, undertakes archaeological site conservation activities here.

Preah Neak Pean, Ta Som and Krol Ko

To the east of Preah Khan and north of the Eastern Baray are two more Buddhist temples built by Jayavarman VII: Preah Neak Pean (the westernmost one) and the ruins of Ta Som. The exquisite temple of **Neak Pean** was also a fountain, built in the middle of a pool, representing the paradisiacal Himalayan mountain-lake, Anaavatapta. Two nagas form the edge of the island and their tails join at the back. In modern Khmer it is known as the *Prea-sat neac pon* – the 'tower of the intertwined dragons'. The colossal image of the horse is the compassionate Bodhisattva who is supposed to save sailors from drowning. The temple pools were an important part of the aesthetic experience of Preah Khan and Neak Pean – the ornate stone carving of both doubly visible by reflection. Such basins within a temple complex were used for religious ritual, while the larger moats and barays were used for bathing, transport and possibly for irrigation.

Located north of the East Baray is the pretty **Ta Som**. This mini temple has many of the same stylistic and design attributes of Ta Prohm and Banteay Kdei but on a much smaller scale. Unlike the larger constructions of Jayavarman VII, Ta Som's layout is extremely simple – three concentric enclosures and very few annex buildings. The main entrance is to the east, which would indicate some urbanization on the eastern side of the temple. The two inner enclosures are successively offset to the west. The outer (third) enclosure (240 m x 200 m) is pierced by two cruciform gopuras; the eastern one is preceded by a small terrace bound by naga balustrades. The current entry is through the western gopura as this faces the road between East Mebon and Preah Neak Pean and cuts across the moat.

Krol Ko sits north of Preah Neak Pean and about 2 km past Ta Som. The tower was built in the late 12th to early 13th century. Referred to as the Oxen Park, Krol Ko is a single, laterite tower which is about 30 m sq. The two frontons represent bodhisattva Lokesvara, to whom it is believed the temple is dedicated.

West of Angkor Thom

Western Baray, West Mebon and Ak Thom

① *Take Highway 6 west. About 3 km west of the airport turning a track leads north. It is 4 km from Highway 6 to Western Baray. Boats can be hired from the beach on the south of the Western Baray. The boat trip to West Mebon takes about 15 mins.*

The **Western Baray** was built by Udayadityavarman II possibly to increase the size of the irrigated farmlands. In the centre, on an island, is the West Mebon, where the famous bronze statue of Vishnu was discovered (now in the National Museum at Phnom Penh, see page 47). Today, the eastern end of the Western Baray is dry but the scale remains astonishing, more than 2 km across and 9 km long with an average depth of 7 m. It is believed that the reservoir could hold around 123 million cubic litres of water.

South of the Western Baray is **Ak Thom**, marking the site of Jayavarman II's earlier city. It is the oldest surviving temple in the Angkor region and although little remains, it is worth a visit. The central towers are constructed mostly of brick cemented together with a mortar of vegetable sap, palm sugar and termite soil.

Outlying temples

It is possible to visit the other ancient Khmer sites dotted around the main temples at Angkor. Most of these temples can be reached by motos (motorbike taxi) or by car.

The Roluos Group

The Roluos Group, some 16 km southeast of Siem Reap, receives few visitors but is worth visiting if time permits. Jayavarman II built several capitals including one at Roluos, at that time called Hariharalaya. This was the site of his last city and remained the capital during the reigns of his three successors. The three remaining Hindu sanctuaries at Roluos are **Preah Ko**, **Bakong** and **Lolei**. They were finished in AD 879, AD 881 and AD 893 respectively by Indravarman I and his son Yashovarman I and are the best preserved of the early temples.

All three temples are built of brick with sandstone doorways and niches. The use of human figures as sculptural decoration in religious architecture developed around this time – and examples of these guardian spirits can be seen in the niches of Preah Ko and Lolei. Other sculptured figures which appear in the Roluos Group are the crouching lion, the reclining bull (Nandi – Siva's mount) and the naga. The gopura – an arched gateway leading to the temple courtyards – was also a contemporary innovation in Roluos. Libraries used for the storage of sacred manuscripts appeared for the first time, as did the concentric enclosures surrounding the central group of towers. Preah Ko and Lolei have characteristics in common: both were dedicated to the parents and grandparents of the kings who built them. Neither temple has a pyramid centre like Bakong as the pyramid temples were built exclusively for kings.

Preah Ko, meaning 'sacred ox', was named after the three statues of Nandi (the mount of the Hindu god, Siva) which stand in front of the temple. Orientated east-west, there is a cluster of six brick towers arranged in two rows on a low brick platform, the steps up to which are guarded by crouching lions while Nandi, looking back, blocks the way. The front row of towers was devoted to Indravarman's male ancestors and the second row to the female. The ancestors were represented in the image of a Hindu god. Only patches remain of the once magnificent stucco relief work, including a remnant of a kala – a motif also found on contemporary monuments in Java.

Indravarman's temple-mountain, **Bakong**, is a royal five-stepped pyramid temple with a sandstone central tower built on a series of successively receding terraces with surrounding brick towers. It may have been inspired by Borobudur in Java. Indravarman himself was buried in the temple. Bakong is the largest and most impressive temple in the Roluos Group by a long way. A bridge flanked by a naga balustrade leads over a dry moat to the temple. The central tower was built to replace the original one when the monument was restored in the 12th century and is probably larger than the original. Local children will point out to you that it is just possible to catch a glimpse of Angkor Wat from the top. The Bakong denotes the true beginning of classical Khmer architecture and contained the god-king Siva's lingam. The most important innovations of Indravarman's artists are the free-standing sandstone statues – such as the group of three figures, probably depicting the king with his two wives, who are represented as Siva with Uma, a Hindu goddess and consort of Siva, and Ganga, goddess of the Ganges River. The corners of the pyramid are mounted with statues of elephants and the steps guarded by crouching lions. Nandi watches the steps from below. The heads of all the figures are now missing but the simplicity of the sculpture is nonetheless distinctive; it is a good example of early Khmer craftsmanship. The statues are more static and stockier than the earlier statues of Chenla. There is now a Buddhist monastery in the grounds – originally it was dedicated to Siva.

Lolei was built by Yashovarman I in the middle of Indravarman's baray. The brick towers were dedicated to the king's ancestors, but over the centuries they have largely disintegrated; of the four towers two have partly collapsed. Much of the decoration has worn away but the inscriptions carved in the grey sandstone lintels and door jambs remain in good condition.

Phnom Krom and Phnom Bok

Today, Phnom Krom, 12 km southwest of Siem Reap, is the base for nearby boat trips out to the Tonlé Sap's floating villages. However, at the top of the 140-m-high mountain, stands a ruined temple believed to have been built in the late 9th-10th century by Yasovarman I but there are no inscriptions giving exact details. The square laterite enclosure (50 m by 50 m) features a gopura in the middle of each outer wall and includes 10 halls, now mostly crumbled, that make an almost continuous inner square. On a lower platform are three stone sanctuary towers, aligned north to south, dedicated to Shiva, Vishnu and Brahma. The temple affords amazing 360-degree panoramic views, which extend across to the Western Baray and Tonlé Sap's floating villages.

Phnom Bok is the brother temple to Phnom Krom and features almost an identical layout to Phnom Krom. The carvings and decorative features here remain in far better condition due to their more protected location and relatively recent discovery. Approximately 15 km northwest of Siem Riep, the temple sits at the pinnacle of the 235-m-high hill. It is the most elevated of the three temple peaks of Angkor; with Phnom Krom at 137 m and Phnom Bakheng at only 60 m (the hill that is climbed the most by tourists being by far the smallest). All three temples were built by Yasovarman I; Phnom Bakheng was the first.

The ascent of Phnom Bok is a difficult climb but well rewarded, as the 20- to 30-minute hike up the southern slope reveals a limitless horizon, broken only to the north by the view of Phnom Kulen.

Banteay Srei ('Citadel of Women')

① *It is 25 km from Ta Prohm along a decent road and takes about 35-40 mins by motorbike. The way is well signed. There are lots of food and drink stalls.*

Banteay Srei, to the north of Angkor, is well worth the trip. This remarkable temple was built by the Brahmin tutor to King Rajendravarman, Yajnavaraha, grandson of Harshavarman (AD 900-923), and founded in AD 967. The temple wasn't discovered until 1914, its distance from Angkor and concealment by overgrown jungle meaning that it wasn't picked up in earlier expeditions. At the time of discovery, by geographic officer Captain Marec, the site was so badly damaged that mounds of dirt had covered the main structure and foliage had bored its way through much of the site. It wasn't until 1924 that the site was cleared and by 1936 it had been restored.

Banteay Srei translates as 'Citadel of Women', a title bestowed upon it in relatively recent years due to the intricate apsara carvings that adorn the interior. While many of Angkor's temples are impressive because of their sheer size, Banteay Srei stands out in the quality of its craftsmanship. The temple is considered by many historians to be the highest achievement of art from the Angkor period. The explicit preservation of this temple reveals covered terraces, of which only the columns remain, which once lined both sides of the primary entrance. In keeping with tradition, a long causeway leads into the temple, across a moat, on the eastern side.

The main walls, entry pavilions and libraries have been constructed from laterite and the carvings are in pink sandstone. The layout was inspired by Prasat Thom at Koh Ker. Three beautifully carved tower-shrines stand side by side on a low terrace in the middle of a quadrangle, with a pair of libraries on either side enclosed by a wall. Two of the shrines, the southern one and the central one, were dedicated to Siva and the northern one to Vishnu. Both had libraries close by, with carvings depicting appropriate legends. The whole temple is dedicated to Brahma and many believe this temple is the closest to its Indian counterparts. Beyond this inner group of buildings was a monastery surrounded by a moat.

In 1923 controversy surrounded the temple when it was targeted by famous French author André Lalraux for a major looting expedition. The author of *The Royal Way* (1930) shamefully attempted to pillage Banteay Srei of its treasures, having read that the temple not only contained a series of brilliant carvings in excellent condition but that it was also unexcavated (which he took to mean abandoned). He travelled to Angkor and proceeded to cut out one tonne of the finest statues and bas-reliefs. Fortunately, he was arrested trying to leave the country with the treasures and was sentenced to three years in prison (a term that he did not serve). One of the best known statues from this site is a sculpture of Siva sitting down and holding his wife, Uma, on his knee: it is in the National Museum of Arts in Phnom Penh.

Having been built by a Brahmin priest, the temple was never intended for use by a king, which goes some way towards explaining its small size – you have to duck to get through the doorways to the sanctuary towers. Perhaps because of its modest scale Banteay Srei contains some of the finest examples of Khmer sculpture. Finely-carved pink sandstone ornaments roofs, pediments and lintels, all magnificently decorated with tongues of flame, serpents' tails, gods, demons and floral garlands.

Banteay Srei

Phnom Kulen

ⓘ *It takes a good 2 hrs by moto to get to Phnom Kulen from Siem Reap; it is more than 1 hr beyond Banteay Srei. At the height of the wet season the road will be virtually impassable. Entering the park costs foreigners an extra US$20 (or US$12 from the Angkor City Hotel beforehand) plus a fee for a motorbike or car (US$25-30) and it is not covered by the Angkor ticket scheme.*

Phnom Kulen – or Mount Mohendrapura – 28 km northeast of Angkor and 48 km from Siem Reap, is a sandstone plateau considered sacred by the Khmers. The site is the mythical birthplace of the Cambodian Kingdom. At the hill's summit is the largest reclining Buddha in the country – over 900 years old. Jayavarman II built his first brick pyramid temple-mountain – to house the sacred golden Siva-lingam – here at the beginning of the ninth century. Today the temple is only visible in fragments although, over a millennium later, the phallic emblem is said to be still on display in the Phnom Kulen complex. The temple is best known for its carved lintels and bas-reliefs. There are also some remains of ninth-century Cham temples in the area.

Today the hill is clothed in forest and the nights here are cold and the days fresh and invigorating. As with most of the other sites on Phnom Kulen it is necessary to have a guide to point them out as they are small and well concealed in the forest. Khmer visitors to the area seem only to be interested in the reclining Buddha.

Phnom Kbal Spean

ⓘ *Kbal Spean is 50 km northeast of Siem Reap and should cost no more than US$10 by moto (last entry 1530). Upon arrival, follow the path for 1.5 km for about 40 mins up the narrow path. The ideal time to visit is at the end of the wet season, when the fast flowing water gushes around, but doesn't submerge most of the carvings.*

The intriguing spot of Kbal Spean is rich in both style and purpose. The name of the river, and the mountain from which it springs, translates loosely to Headwater Bridge, referring to a natural sandstone arch, marking the beginning of the 150 m of carvings, upstream from the bridge. It is the downstream part, from the bridge to the waterfall, that gives the river its Sanskrit name Sahasralinga, 'River of a Thousand Lingas'.

Phnom Kbal Spean is regarded as highly auspicious so it is not surprising that the remarkable 11th-century riverbed rock carvings display a gallery of gods and celestial beings including Vishnu reclining on the serpent Anata, Shiva, Brahman, Lakshmi, Rama and Hanuman. Some of the carvings are submerged by the river, while a few have been hacked away by unscrupulous looters. The visibility of all carvings is really dependent on the time of year.

Downstream from the carvings are thousands of sculpted lingas in the river bed and a large underwater representation of a yoni (womb). The lingas stretch approximately 6 m downstream from the bridge, to 30 m upstream. Carved from the coarse sandstone from the riverbed, some protrude as much as 10 cm from the bed; others have been worn away by the flowing water. Finnish journalist Teppo Turkki, who visited the site for the *Phnom Penh Post*, wrote at the beginning of 1995: "The lingas, some of which date back to the ninth century, are about 25 cm sq and 10 cm deep and lined in a perfect grid pattern. The river runs over them, covering them with about 5 cm of pristine water." He continued: "The holy objects are designed to create a 'power path' for the Khmer kings." More likely the water which would have fed Angkor was being sanctified before it entered the holy arena of the temples. Beyond the series of carvings is a 15-m waterfall to a crystal-clear pool.

Chau Srei Vibol

ⓘ *Turn east off the road from between Phnom Bok and Roluos, about 5 km south of Phnom Bok. Follow the road over several old bridges until you reach the compound of Wat Trach and the laterite wall at the bottom of the hill.*

The remote, 11th-century hilltop temple of Chau Srei Vibol is now in ruins but at least three major sandstone structures, a sanctuary and two libraries with decorative carvings, are readily identifiable. A couple of broken lions flank the steep eastern entrance gate.

Whilst viewing this small ruined temple in near silence it's worth reflecting on the building boom that occurred under the reign of Suryavarman I, a highpoint in the Khmer Empire. Suryavarman ruled a huge empire, covering much of southern Vietnam, Thailand, Laos and the Malay Peninsula.

Beng Mealea

ⓘ *Beng Mealea is a full day trip from Siem Reap. There is an entrance fee of US$20.*

Beng Mealea, a huge 12th-century temple complex, 40 km east of the Bayon and about 7 km southeast of Phnom Kulen, is completely ruined even though it was built at about the same time as Angkor Wat. Its dimensions are similar but Beng Mealea has no central pyramid. It is widely believed that this temple acted as the 'blueprint' for Angkor. Most of the Buddhist temples built under Jayavarman VII – Preah Khan, Banteay Kdei, Ta Som and Ta Prohm – were modelled after this complex.

Further temples of interest include Sambor Prei Kup, see page 124; Preah Khan, see page 125; Koh Ker, see page 127 and Preah Vihear, see box, page 126.

Anlong Veng and around → *For listings, see pages 128-142.*

From the outset Anlong Veng seems like your average Cambodian dusty, one-street frontier town with a towering mountain range in its midst. But the façade is deceiving. This small, unassuming town was once home to some of the country's most dangerous residents including Pol Pot, his right-hand man, Son Sen and Ta Mok, otherwise known as the "Butcher". These days the place gets a pretty bad rap by locals and expats alike but does have its merits: the people, for the most part, are tremendously friendly and it's surrounded by beautiful countryside and very hospitable rural villages. The town is also a good launching pad for a trip to Preah Vihear Temple (see box, page 126), as the road between Anlong Veng and the temple is in relatively good shape (in the dry season).

Sights

There aren't many 'tourist' attractions per se but the town will appeal to those interested in Khmer Rouge history as it contains a number of sites decisive to the movement's downfall. The most popular destination around Anlong Veng is **Oh Chit**, Ta Mok's hauntingly beautiful lake, which was initially built as a moat for his house. A maniacal dam builder, Ta Mok (aka Brother Number Three) flooded much of the area while trying to develop the lake. Today the dead tree stumps, tranquil waters, grassy knolls and beautiful patches of lotus flower actually create a very beautiful but eerie atmosphere. On any given day packs of small kids swim in the lake while beneath the surface it is believed that the grisly remains of hundreds of people lie. You can visit **Ta Mok's Villa** ⓘ *US$2, which includes entrance to Pol Pot's residence*, the Khmer Rouge's last official headquarters after Pol Pot was overthrown. It was also the place where Pol Pot was tried by his own men, led

The end of the line

Anlong Veng proved to be, quite literally, the end of the line for Pol Pot and marked an important point in the demise of the Khmer Rouge.

In 1996 an internal conflict between high-ranking Khmer Rouge officials marked the disintegration of Pailin, the principal Khmer Rouge outpost. The conflict saw most of the movement's high-ranking officials relocate to Anlong Veng. Times were tough in the mountains without the riches (gems and timber) found in Pailin to bankroll the militia. Paranoia swelled.

Pol Pot ordered his cronies, Ta Mok, Son Sen and Nuon Chea to visit Pailin and settle the dispute. Their mission was a failure and Pol Pot, furious and suspicious that they were collaborating with the government, ordered the three of them to house arrest.

The Cambodian government, aware of the major chasm, struck a deal with those left in Pailin, offering amnesty to those who defected. On 6 November, 15,000 Khmer Rouge soldiers defected, including Ieng Sary, former Khmer Rouge deputy premier.

On 9 June 1997, Pol Pot, believing that Son Sen and his wife were conspiring against him through collusion with Hun Sen, ordered their brutal execution. Son Sen, his wife Yun Yat, and nine of their children and grandchildren were shot. Troops then crushed their skulls with a pickup.

Fearing the same fate, Ta Mok launched an anti-Pol Pot propaganda campaign generating the necessary military support to chase and capture Pol Pot in the surrounding jungle.

In July 1997, Ta Mok put Pol Pot on trial at the local "People's Court", charging him with the murder of Son Sen and the attempted murder and detention of Ta Mok and Nuon Chea. Having ousted Pol Pot, Ta Mok became the new leader of the Khmer Rouge and ordered him to be put under house arrest. On 15 April 1998 it was said that Pol Pot, aged 73, died of a heart attack and was cremated shortly after on a pyre of rubbish and tyres. Rumours surrounding his death are rife: some believe that he killed himself with malaria pills and tranquilizers after learning he was to be turned over to the USA. Others suggest that Ta Mok had Pol Pot executed to protect himself. Locals around Anlong Veng suggest it is most likely that someone (presumably Ta Mok) had been replacing his critical medication with placebos. When asked whether Pol Pot had been murdered, Mei Meakk, Pailin's cabinet chief and confidante said to the *Cambodia Daily*: "Pol Pot was cremated on a bed of tires. What do you think?".

Ta Mok's leadership was short-lived. He was captured by the government forces in 1998 but fled into the jungle. In 1999 he was recaptured and he died in jail in Phnom Penh in 2006.

by Ta Mok. The villa is quite barren these days, looted by government officials, but still bares a few horrific reminders of the old days, including animal-like cages where prisoners were held captive. Inside the building there is a map marking Khmer Rouge territory and a few utopian paintings of Cambodia through the eyes of the regime. Across the lake is **Pol Pot's residence** (now reduced to a bathroom) accessed by a turn-off on the right further from town on the same road heading north, where he was kept under house arrest under Ta Mok's direction. Some of the people working at the site are former Khmer Rouge, employed by Ta Mok. The villa and lake can be accessed by following the main road through town and turning right at the signpost.

About 8 km along Anlong Veng's main street is the bottom of **Dongrek mountain range**. The Dongrek Enscarpment is a site in itself, with spectacular, panoramic views from the cliffs over to Thailand, however, half way up the mountain is an old **Khmer Rouge checkpoint**. Here there are several life-size sculptures of Khmer Rouge troops (with AK47S, kramas and grenades). Considering that the Khmer Rouge were not purveyors of artistic culture these sculptures are particularly detailed (and headless since the government decapitated them). As you move further along this road a small military house marks a path to **Pol Pot's cremation site**, where in 1998 he was burnt on a pyre of rubbish. The gravesite is accessible and marked although a sombre lonely place. (Try and stay to the marked path as some of this area remains mined.) Strangely enough some Khmers visit the site in the belief that winning lottery numbers will be bestowed upon them by greater forces. There will probably be a government official on site procuring some sort of entrance fee.

Further along in the mountains, in a heavily mined area, are the former homes of Pol Pot, Son Sen and Ta Mok, all in close proximity to the border in case a quick get-away was required. It is probably no coincidence that the modern day houses of Nuon Chea and Khieu Samphan also sit on the Thai border, near Pailin (see page 153). Thankfully, when the time came for their arrest, they were unable to use any escape route.

Siem Reap and around → *For listings, see pages 128-142.*

The nearest town to Angkor, Siem Reap is a bustling tourism hub with a growing art and fashion crowd, however it's still true to say that without the temples few people would ever find themselves here. Siem Reap is also an easy place to stay for volunteers looking to do a stint in saving the world, but perhaps too many nights spent in crowded bar street distracts from the task in hand. Visitors exhausted by the temple trail might care to while away a morning or afternoon in Siem Reap itself. The town has developed quite substantially in the past couple of years and, with the blossoming of hotels, restaurants and bars, it is now a pleasant place in its own right. Hotel building has pretty much kept pace with tourist arrivals so the town is a hive of activity.

The town is laid out formally and because there is ample land on which to build, it is pleasantly airy. Buildings are often set in large overgrown grounds resembling mini wildernesses. The current level of unprecedented growth and development is set to continue, so this may not be the case five years from now. The growth spurt has put a great strain on the city's natural resources.

Ins and outs
See under the Angkor section, page 80.

Sights
The town proper has a romantic, French colonial feel, sprawling across a 10 km radius and carved apart by a pleasant lamp-lit river. The most popular tourist areas are around the Old Market (Psah Chas), the Wat Bo part of town and along the Airport Road.

The **Old Market** area is the most touristed part of the town with a gamut of restaurants, bars and boutiques catering for a wide range of tastes. Staying around here is recommended for independent travellers and those staying more than two or three days. A fair proportion of the buildings around here, particularly on the road south to Tonlé Sap, are built of wood and raised off the ground on stilts. (The distance from Siem Reap to the

To ⑦ ㉘ , Jayavarman VII Hospital,
Angkor National Museum & Angkor

To ① ⑧

To ㉓

⑬

Royal
Independence
Gardens

Provincial &
Khmer Angkor
Tour Guide
Association

To Roluos Group

㉜

Yoted
Shrine

Route 6

Caltex

Royal
Villa

⑥

㉖
㉕

㉝

To ② ⑨ ⑪ ⑤ ⑰ ① Star MartBangkok/
Siem Reap Airways, Vietnam Airlines, Exotissimo,
Airport, Cambodian Cultural Village, Dietheim Travel
& War Museum

Ⓢ Krong Thai

Oum Chhay St

④

⑱

㉛ ⑫

㉚ ⑭

⑧ Oum Khun St

㊳

㉗

Pokambor Ave

Siem Reap River

Wat Bo St

㉟

㊱

Sivatha St

⑤

② C

Angkor Hospital
for Children

Samdech Tep Vong St

Ⓢ ANZ

⑨

River Rd

⑫

Wat Bo

⑥
⑩

To ② ㉗ ⑨ ⑪

Central

⑤

㊶

㊵

Provincial
Hospital

㊲

To ㉑

Psar Chars

㉒

Chantiers Écoles &
Artisans d'Angkor

To Chong Khneas
& Tonlé Sap

②

㉞

③

N

|100 metres|
|100 yards|

Sleeping

Angkor Palace Resort
  & Spa **17** *A1*
Angkor Village Resort **1** *A3*
Aspara Angkor **2** *A1*
Bopha **5** *D3*
Bou Savy **19** *B1*
Borann **6** *A3*
Casa Angkor **8** *B1*
Earthwalkers **10** *B1*
Empress Angkor **11** *B1*
European Guesthouse **12** *B3*
FCC Angkor **4** *B2*
Golden Banana B&B **34** *E2*
Green Garden Home
  Guesthouse **35** *B1*
Heritage Suites **23** *A3*
Home Sweet Home **14** *B3*
Jasmine Lodge **15** *B1*
Kazna **24** *C1*
La Noria **26** *A3*
La Residence D'Angkor **3** *C3*
Le Meridien Angkor **7** *A2*
Mahogany Guesthouse **18** *B3*
Mekong Angkor Palace **36** *C1*
Neak Pean **20** *B1*
Ombrello & Kimono **37** *D3*
Passaggio **22** *E3*
Paul Dubrule **9** *B1*
Raffles Grand Hotel d'Angkor
  13 *A2*
Rosy Guesthouse **25** *A3*

Royal Bay Inn Angkor
  Resort **38** *B2*
Salabai **39** *D1*
Shadow of Angkor II **40** *D3*
Shinta Mani **27** *B2*
Sokha Angkor **21** *A1*
Sofitel Royal Angkor **28** *A1*
Soria Moria **41** *D3*
Sweet Dreams
  Guesthouse **31** *B3*
Ta Prohm **29** *E2*
Two Dragons Guesthouse
  30 *B3*
Victoria Angkor **32** *A1*
The Villa **42** *D1*
Villa Kiara **43** *E3*
Yakhom Angkor
  Lodge **33** *A3*

Eating

Abacus **1** *B1*
Barrio **2** *C1*
Butterflies Garden **12** *D3*
Curry Walla **5** *C1*
L'Oasi Italiana **8** *A3*
Moloppor Café **6** *C3*
Sugar Palm **9** *D1*

Bars & clubs

Fresh at Chilli Si Dang **10** *C3*
Zone One **11** *C1*

edge of the lake fluctuates by many kilometres; the highest water levels occurring towards the end of October at the end of the wet season.)

Across the river, the area has taken on the name of Siem Reap's oldest pagoda, **Wat Bo** (built in the 18th century), which can be found at the end of Achamean Street. This area has recently become a popular place to stay with a range of accommodation available. It's not as crowded as the old market area and less traffic than airport road.

The **Airport Road** area has been earmarked for mass tourism and wields countless cumbersome hotels and chains, geared towards package tourists, with packaged meals and packaged tours to go. You can still get into town from these hotels but it is a fair hike, especially at night. Still, this area holds appeal for those that want to fly in and out of Siem Reap and visit Angkor without sticking around for too long.

Yet while Siem Reap is a pleasant enough place to hang out for a few hours, the main places of interest lie outside the town. On the road 6 km south of Banteay Srei temple is the small **landmine museum** ⓘ *0730-1730, US$2; follow the Angkor Wat road north out towards Banteay Srei and you will find the museum on the right hand-side.* The museum exhibits a vast collection of defused mines, bombs, ammunition and other ordinance. Former deminer, Mr Akira, commendably opened the museum in 1997 to create awareness about the insidious effect of mines and help fund his work with landmine victims. When on site, he goes to great lengths to explain the carnage caused by each type of mine (such as what part of the body they are aimed at) and often speaks openly of his experiences as a child conscript during the Khmer Rouge period and later Vietnamese occupation.

On the Airport Road, near the airport, is the **War Museum** ⓘ *daily 0730-1730, US$3.* This government-run museum houses a collection of old tanks, guns and other war paraphernalia collected from the provinces. It's not as absorbing as the mine museum but is worth a trip for those interested in war artillery and machinery.

Cambodian Cultural Village ⓘ *6 km from Siem Reap on the Airport Rd, T063-963098, daily 0900-2100, US$12,* is a park featuring smaller renditions of ancient Cambodian architectural feats and models, slightly on the kitsch side, of the various ethnic housing styles. The traditional dancing and wedding shows will be a hit if you have children with you.

There is now an **Angkor National Museum** ⓘ *daily 0830-1800, US$12, www.angkornationalmuseum.com,* on the road to the temples a short walk from the town centre. Due to the high entry price this museum is usually empty and it does seem rather incongruous that the artefacts on display here are not actually still in situ at the temples themselves. Having said that this isn't a bad museum and a lot of useful information about the development of Angkor can be gathered from here. There are also some

② Siem Reap market area

➡ **Angkor maps**
1 Angkor, Siem Reap & Roluos, page 82
2 Angkor Wat, page 93
3 Angkor Thom, page 98
4 Siem Riep, page 120
5 **Siem Riep market area, page 122**

Sleeping 🛏
Hotel de la Paix **5**
Jim's Place **2**

Eating 🍴
Blue Pumpkin **1**
Curry Walla II **2**
Molly Malone's **3**
Neth Socheata **4**
Shadow of Angkor I **6**
Steung Siem Reap **7**
Dead Fish Tower **5**
Khmer Kitchen **3**
Le Malraux **4**
Le Tigre de Papier **6**
Red Piano **7**
Singing Tree **8**
Soup Dragon **11**
Tell **12**

Bars & clubs 🍸
Angkor What? **13**
Laundry **14**
Linga **15**
Miss Wong **9**
Temple Club **16**
Warehouse **10**
X Rooftop Bar **17**

intriguing background details such as the 102 hospitals built during the reign of Jayavarman VII and the 1960 boxes of hemorrhoid cream that were part of their annual provisions. There are also some displays of what clothes the average Angkorian wore but it's a shame there isn't more about the daily lives of these ancients.

Tonlé Sap

The Tonlé Sap, the Great Lake of Cambodia, is one of the natural wonders of Asia. Uniquely, the 100-km-long Tonlé Sap River, a tributary of the mighty Mekong, reverses its flow and runs uphill for six months of the year. Spring meltwaters in the Himalayas, coupled with seasonal rains, increase the flow of the Mekong to such an extent that some is deflected up the Tonlé Sap River. From June the lake begins to expand until, by the end of the rainy season, it has increased in area four-fold and in depth by up to 12 m. At its greatest extent, the lake occupies nearly a seventh of Cambodia's land area, around 1.5 million ha, making it the largest freshwater lake in Southeast Asia. From November, with the onset of the dry season, the Tonlé Sap River reverses its flow once more and begins to act like a regular tributary – flowing downhill into the Mekong. By February the lake has shrunk to a fraction of its wet season size and covers 'just' 300,000 ha.

This pattern of expansion and contraction has three major benefits. First, it helps to restrict flooding in the Mekong Delta in Vietnam. Second, it forms the basis for a substantial part of Cambodia's rice production. And third, it supports perhaps the world's largest and richest inland fishery, yielding as much as 10 tonnes of fish per square kilometre. It is thought that four million people depend on the lake for their subsistence and three out of every 4 kg of fish caught in the country come from the Tonlé Sap.

Because of the dramatic changes in the size of the lake some of the fish, such as the 'walking catfish', have evolved to survive several hours out of water, flopping overland to find deeper pools. Hok yue – or elephant fish – are renowned as a delicacy well beyond Cambodia's borders. Large-scale commercial fishing is a major occupation from February to May and the fishing grounds are divided into plots and leased out. Recent lack of dredging means the lake is not as deep as it was and fish are tending to swim downstream into the Mekong and Tonlé Sap rivers. The annual flooding covers the surrounding countryside with a layer of moist, nutrient-rich mud which is ideal for rice growing. Farmers grow deep-water rice, long-stalked and fast growing – it grows with the rising lake to keep the grain above water and the stem can be up to 6 m long. The lake also houses people, with communities living in floating villages close to the shore.

Chong Khneas ⓘ *boats can be hired and trips to floating villages are offered, expect to pay about US$10-15 per hr; take a moto from Siem Reap (US$2), boats from Phnom Penh berth at Chong Khneas*, is 10 km south of Siem Reap. This consists of some permanent buildings but is a largely floating settlement. The majority of the population live in houseboats and most services – including police, health, international aid agencies, retail and karaoke – are all provided on water. A trip around the village is testimony to the ingenuity of people living on this waterway with small kids paddling little tubs to each other's houses.

Chong Khneas gets hundreds of visitors every day. For a more authentic, less touristy experience head out a bit further, 25 km east, to the village of **Kompong Phluk**. Costs to get to these villages are pretty high (up to US$50 per person) but are brought down if there are more passengers on the boat. See **Terre Cambodge** or **Two Dragon's Guesthouse** under Activities and tours to organize a tour.

Also on the Tonlé Sap Lake is the **Prek Toal Biosphere** – a bird sanctuary which is home to 120 bird species, including cranes, stalks and pelicans. Boats can be organized from

Chong Kneas to visit the Prek Toal Environment Office, US$30 return, one hour. From here you can arrange a guide and another boat for around US$20. **Terre Cambodia**, www.terrecambodge.com, runs boat tours upwards of US$80, as do **Osmose**, T012-832812, osmose@bigpond.com.kh, and the **Sam Veasna Center for wildlife and conservation**, T063-761597, info@samveasna.org. There is basic accommodation at the Environment Office.

Kompong Thom and around → *For listings, see pages 128-142.*

Kompong Thom is Cambodia's second largest province and the provincial capital is more like a city than a town. It can be quite chaotic as it is a major thoroughfare for people going to Siem Reap and the regions further north. The town was severely bombed by the USA in the 1970s and large craters spotted in the area are testament to this. The Sen River divides the town into two distinct areas with the compact city area to the south and a more sprawling, industrial area to the north. There are plenty of sites to explore around town including the magnificent former capital, Sambor Prei Kuk and Phnom Santuk.

Sambor Prei Kuk

① *Motos will do the return trip for US$8-10, tuk tuks about US$12 and taxis for US$25 per car. There is a great route (about 1 hr) via some beautiful rural villages, rice paddies and farming lots; follow NH6 towards Siem Reap for 5 km until the road veers into a much worse road, NH64 (the road to T'Beng Meanchey); follow this for another 10 km and turn right at the big colourful archway and follow the road through to the temples (another 19 km). There are food and drink stalls within the temple complex on the main road. A small entrance fee, US$3 per person is charged at the tourist information centre at the complex gates and you are required to pay extra to take the bike through.*

Sambor Prei Kuk is a group of over 100 temples which lies 28 km north of Kompong Thom. This ancient Chenla capital, dating from the seventh century, was built by King Ishanavarman I (AD 616-635) and dedicated to Shiva. Sambor Prei Kuk is believed by many to be Southeast Asia's first temple city. The main temples are square or octagonal brick tower-shrines on high brick terraces with wonderful ornamentation in sandstone, especially the lintel stones. The finely sculptured brick has an obvious Indian influence, for example the use of lion sculptures, an animal which didn't exist in Cambodia. The temples are divided into three geographical groups: the Prasat Sambor Group, the Prasat Tao Group and the Prasat Yeay Peu Group. All of the temples are dedicated to Shiva. Some highlights include the inner lingas in the temples of the Prasat Sambor Group (try looking up from the sanctuary to the sky); and the lions guarding the temple of Prasat Tao (unfortunately they are reproductions).

It is believed that there were originally between 180 and 200 monuments but many of these were completely shattered during the US bombardment and craters left by American bombing during the war are still visible. Paradoxically, even the park's conservation centre has been destroyed, so much so that one can consider it as one of Sambor Prei Kuk's ruins. However, given that these are some of the oldest temples in the country – 200 years before Angkor was built, they are well preserved and now that the area is safe, they are really worth visiting, especially for the forested solitude they afford. There are some amazing trees, some which look as old as the structures themselves. Botanists have been through the area and have put little identification signs on most foliage. There is a tranquil atmosphere and very few visitors, unlike Angkor.

Phnom Santuk

ⓘ *Motos that congregate around the taxi stand and Arunreas Hotel will do the trip 20 km southeast of Kompong Thom for US$5-6 (roundtrip).*

The 980 steps to the pagoda at the top of Phnom Santuk Mountain is a great trip to do around noon in order to later catch the brilliant sunset and stunning panoramic views of the countryside. The holy mountain is the most significant in the region and around the brightly painted pagoda are some fascinating Buddha images carved out of large stone boulders. Though many tourists might see the temple as a bit garish or kitsch, the site is hugely popular with the Khmers, who believe it to be somewhat auspicious. There are several vendors around the area, including a gamut of people touting traditional medicines and therapies.

T'Beng Meanchey and around → *For listings, see pages 128-142.*

T'Beng Meanchey is a small, dusty, non-descript town whose future hinges on the development of the roads between the remote temple sites of Koh Ker, Preah Khan and Preah Vihear – if this happens, in all likelihood it will become a major gateway to these remote temples. At the time of writing only a dribble of tourists were making it here, and the place has a more remote feel than areas such as Ban Lung or Sen Monorom. Aside from being a 'gateway' to major temples in the region, T'Beng Meanchey also pierces the junction of some of the country's worst roads. However, the good news is that the roads are being overhauled courtesy of an Asian Development Bank loan so hopefully this will change in years to come.

Sights

The town itself doesn't have a whole lot of tourist attractions apart from the Joom Noon Silk Project and Wat Chey Preuk. The **Joom Noon Silk Project** is a local initiative started by Vietnam veteran, Bud Gibbons, to help rehabilitate people with disabilities through silk weaving projects. These days Bud has handed over the reins to internationally acclaimed weaver, Carol Cassidy. This organization can be credited with producing some of the country's finest silk products which are available nationwide. The **Wat Chey Preuk** compound is almost opposite the hospital. It includes the few remaining structures of an ancient Pre-Angkorian temple built on the site, though it really isn't worth a trip out of your way to see.

Preah Khan

ⓘ *Visiting Preah Khan is a long day trip for die-hard motorcyclists or temple enthusiasts. It is not easy as the sandy roads make for a very uncomfortable trip there. A very early start is required to make it there and back to T'Beng Meanchey in a day. It is advisable to take a mosquito net, hammock and torch (which can be hung in the temple) in case you get stuck out here for the night. Only walk on well-trodden tracks as the area is still heftily mined. There is a small village about 5 km from the site where it is possible to pick up a drink or snack. There are no official guides.*

Preah Khan ('sacred sword'), known as 'Bakan' to most locals, ranks as one of the most remote temples in Cambodia. Surrounded by dense foliage that's presumably speckled with mines and near-impassable roads, a trip to Preah Khan is not for the faint-hearted. Its development is highly mysterious, though most believe that the complex was built in the ninth century and was home to both Suryavarman II and Jayavarman VII at some point

Buddhist temple wars and beyond

The stunning temple complex at **Preah Vihear**, pressed up tight on the remote regions of northern Cambodia, has long been a source of contention between Thailand and the Khmers. Since the colonial-era borders were established, back in the early 20th century, Thailand has made repeated attempts to annex the area. However, in 1962, the argument was arbitrated by the International Court of Justice in The Hague which ruled that the temple fell within the boundaries of Cambodia. Unfortunately this was not the last the international community saw of the dispute. Over the years Preah Vihear has been at the centre of tensions between the two countries.

In the 1990s Thailand suddenly denied access to the site, citing the illegal use of the border. In January 2003 there was further escalation of tensions after the misinterpretation of remarks allegedly made by a Thai actress insinuating that Thailand should regain control of the area. The Thai embassy in Phnom Penh was badly damaged in rioting along with many Thai-owned businesses. In May 2005 both countries deployed troops to the border surrounding Preah Vihear and the situation remained fragile.

Fast forward to 2008 and a long-standing application for Preah Vihear to be placed on the UNESCO World Heritage Site list came to fruition. Initially the Thai government supported the move, even though this meant accepting the contested areas were inside Cambodian territory. The thinking at the time was that the site could now benefit both nations.

With huge pressure coming to bear on the then Peoples' Power Party (PPP) government from the extreme fascist nationalists of the Peoples' Alliance for Democracy (PAD), Thailand withdrew its support for UNESCO status and reneged on its promise to finally recognize Cambodia's claims. Nonetheless, UNESCO declared Preah Vihear a World Heritage Site on 8 July 2008. Much sabre rattling ensued, with shots fired and military units mobilized. Thai nationalists were arrested by the Cambodians as they tried to plant a Thai flag in the Preah Vihear's grounds and bizarre black magic rituals were claimed to have been enacted by both sides. With the Thai foreign minister

(possibly during the Cham invasion). The temples were originally built for Hindu worship and later were transformed into a Buddhist complex. Scholars believe that the laterite and sandstone complex is the largest single enclosure ever constructed during the Angkor period, even superseding the mighty Angkor Thom. Preah Khan was originally linked to Angkor Wat via an ancient super-highway constructed of laterite and there are a number of fantastically carved stone bridges between the two points that still exist today.

The first temple most will see on approach is Prasat Preah Stung, with the Jayavarman VII trademark of large Bayon-like smiling faces peering out over the jungle. To the east is a massive 3-km-long baray and east of this is a petite ninth-century temple, Prasat Preah Damrei. This intricate pyramid is also known as Elephant Temple due to the two regal carved elephants gracing it. The main temple structure is now in ruins and is about 400 m from Prasat Preah Stung. Disappointingly, this temple has been so severely looted that no semblance of its former glory exists whatsoever and much of the building, aside from the outer walls, has collapsed upon itself. Looting has long been a problem here: the recidivist French looter, Louis Delaporte, carted off forced to resign and Thailand completely entrenched, a conflict seemed inevitable.

In October 2008 the fighting started in earnest with a mini-battle taking place that left several soldiers on both sides dead or injured. Thai nationals were advised to leave Cambodia by the Thai government and war seemed imminent. Fortunately, after intervention by the international community, both sides saw sense and pulled back from the brink.

In 2009 the situation continued to be tense, not least because the extremists of the PAD once again entered the fray holding a series of violent protests at the border. At one point they even threatened to storm the temple but the Cambodian government made it very clear they would shoot to kill if this took place. Skirmishes between both nations' armies then took place in April with several soldiers being killed. The PAD backed down and the situation was temporarily relieved.

Yet, there was worse to come. In late 2009 Cambodian prime minister Hun Sen declared the Thai prime minister, Thaksin Shinawatra, who was deposed in a 2006 military coup, an economic adviser to Cambodia. For the ruling Thai Democrat Party government and their PAD allies, both of whom supported the military coup in 2006, this was a deliberate provocation by Hun Sen. Thailand recalled its ambassador, trade agreements were ripped up and the right-wing Thai press went into hysterics. For a short while it seemed like full-blown war might take place but, once again, both parties, amid calls for restraint from the international community, pulled back from the brink.

In mid-2010 the relationship between Thailand and Cambodia was still a long way from being normalized. Thailand's ongoing internal political problems have the potential to stir things up between the nations and there have been continued skirmishes throughout the year.

Quite clearly visiting Preah Vihear is not advisable until this situation is at least partially resolved. Most foreign governments are also advising against travel to the temple. If you do plan to visit we would recommend, at the very least, you take good advice from locals about the situation at time of travel and also use the services of a reputable tour operator or guide.

thousands of kilograms of artefacts to the Guimet Museum in Paris and recently a couple of looters were killed when part of the building collapsed on them. The main structure is in a ruinous state and it's hard to distinguish many of its features as a result, though some bas-reliefs on the outer walls are quite good.

Cows graze freely within the temple's walls and exploring the temples has a real Indiana Jones-caught-in-the-middle-of-nowhere feel. You'll usually have the temples to yourself, aside from a few inquisitive village children.

Koh Ker
ⓘ *Kulen, 32 km away, is the closest village to Koh Ker. You can also access Koh Ker from Siem Reap via Beng Melea. A new toll road has been established which makes the 61 km from Beng Melea, and 146 km from Siem Reap, a breeze. If hiring a car or moto for this trip expect to pay upwards of US$50 and US$30 respectively.*

Koh Ker (pronounced *Koh Care*) is the site of the old capital of Jayavarman IV (AD 928-942). Historians today still do not understand exactly why Jayavarman IV moved the capital from Angkor to Koh Ker, but after a feud with his family the capital was relocated. One inscription reads of Jayavarman IV and Koh Ker "founded by his own power, a city which was the seat of prosperities of the universe". It was a short-lived prosperous seat of the universe, however, as Koh Ker only remained the capital for 24 years. The main ruin here is **Prasat Thom**, an overgrown, seven-storey, stepped period in a pyramid style. The surrounding land was irrigated by baray, similar to, but smaller than, the ones at Angkor. The **Rahal Baray**, east of the pyramid, is 1200 m long by 560 m wide and made out of existing stone. The sculptors used sandstone for most of their carvings and were able to create great detailed scenes of movement that were not previously created in this era. Many of the carvings, such as the fighting monkey men, are now kept in the National Museum of Phnom Penh. De-miners have been working a lot in this area and it is believed that over 80 ruined temples lie in the area.

◉ Angkor and around listings

For Sleeping and Eating price codes and other relevant information, see Essentials pages 22-23.

● Sleeping

Anlong Veng *p117*
There is quite a lot of accommodation on the main road in town.

E 23 October Guesthouse (or Questhouse as it is misprinted on their business card), right at the roundabout past **Lucky Star** and on the opposite side of the road, T012-228993. Concrete building and lacking atmosphere.

E Lucky Star, right at the only roundabout on the main road just after the police HQ on right hand side. Newly built looking like a US motel with more than 40 rooms. Has the **New Lucky** restaurant next door and rooms have a/c.

E-F Monorom Guesthouse and Restaurant, on the main road towards the lake, T011-766428. Rooms are very clean and include a/c, fan, attached bathroom, free water and a pineapple! In the middle of expansion at time of printing, so currently a little disorganized, but should be ready at the end of 2010.

E-G Bot Oddom Guesthouse, right at the only roundabout on the main road just after the police HQ on left hand side, T012-779495. In addition to the typical local guesthouse with US$7 rooms there is a new modern-style hotel with large public balcony areas with views over Ta Mot's lake and the mountainous border. Up

to US$15 with a/c, these are large rooms with 2 double beds and TV. Recommended.

F Dorng Rek Hill Accommodation, literally on the hill looking out over the Cambodian plains, T012-444067. This isolated spot is an unusual place to stay, but the views are worth it. Rooms are basic, with Khmer-style shower in the en-suite bath rooms. Unfortunately, the building itself is not very aesthetic with its surroundings.

F Sokha Rith Guesthouse, on main road over the roundabout towards lake, T017-242404. Typical Khmer decor and clean with option of a/c or fan rooms.

G Pnom Dorngrek Guesthouse, T092-228847. With rooms starting at US$400 this place is not too bad, it has a real local feel as if you are staying with a family and is adorned with family wedding portraits. It is home to many dogs. Rooms are a little pokey but are clean and have a fan. Rooms with attached Western-style bathroom are also available.

Siem Reap *p119, maps p120 and p122*
Hotel accommodation in Siem Reap has expanded dramatically in the past couple of years reflecting the huge surge in demand.

Accommodation is spread across 3 main areas – east of the river in **Wat Bo Village** (cheaper accommodation), on the **airport road** (luxury hotels and others that cater to package tourists), and around the **Old Market** (the main bar and restaurant area). There are also quite a few hotels on the road to Angkor.

It is not uncommon for taxi, moto and tuk tuk drivers to tell new arrivees that the guesthouse they were booked into is now closed or full. They will try to take you to the place where they get the best commission. One way around this is to arrange for the guesthouse or hotel to pick you up from either the bus station or other arrival point – many offer this service for free or a small fee.

Town centre and east of river

LL Heritage Suites, behind Wat Po Lanka, T063-969100, www.heritage.com.kh. Super luxurious and exclusive villas, rooms and suites in this stylish property secreted away behind a temple. Much is made with traditional materials and the top-end rooms come with private steam baths and gardens. A super-splurge but well worth it. Expect all the usual amneties for such a top-end establishment.

LL-A Villa Kiara, just outside eastern edge of town, Sala Kamroeuk village, T063-764156, www.villakiara.com. Set in a very peaceful, private garden compound a couple of kilometres east of town this 17 room/suite "boutique" resort is unpretentious yet stylish. There's free breakfast, Wi-Fi, a restaurant and complimentary transfers to and from town. The pool is cute as well. All rooms are, of course, a/c with TV and en suite hot-water facilities. Recommended.

L-AL Angkor Village Resort, T063-963561, www.angkorvillage.com. Opened in 2004, the resort contains 80 rooms set in Balinese-style surroundings. The accommodation pays homage to traditional Asian architecture with lovely fittings, especially in the bathrooms. Traditional massage services, 2 restaurants, theatre shows and lovely pool. Elephant, boat and helicopter rides can be arranged. Recommended.

L-AL La Residence D'Angkor Hotel, River Rd, T063-963390, www.residence angkor.com. With its beautifully laid out rooms all lavishly furnished with marble and hardwoods this reassuringly expensive hotel could persuade the most principled among us to sell their souls to the corporate beast. Each room has a huge, free-form bathtub – which is the perfect end to a day touring the temples. The pool is lined with handmade tiles in a variety of green hues and, like the rest of the hotel, is in true Angkor style. This and the Victoria hotel go head-to-head as offering the best room in town.

L-AL Le Meridien Angkor, Charles de Gaulle Blvd, Khum Svay Dang Hum (main road towards temples), T063-963900, www.lemeridien.com/angkor. From the outside this 5-star hotel resembles a futuristic prison camp – severe, angled architecture with small, dark slits for windows. Walk into the lobby and it is immediately transformed into space and light, becoming, in a flash, a pretty decent place to lay your hat. Rooms are nicely designed and sized and all come with a/c, en suite and cable TV. Other facilities include spa, restaurants and pool. The garden is a lovely spot to take breakfast. Recommended.

L-AL Raffles Grand Hotel d'Angkor, 1 Charles de Gaulle Blvd, T063-963888, www.raffles.com. Certainly a magnificent period piece from the outside, Siem Reap's oldest (1930) hotel fails to generate ambience, the rooms are sterile and the design of the huge new wings is uninspired (unforgivable in Angkor). Coupled with this is a history of staff lock-outs and mass sackings that have caused the Raffles brand damage. However, it does have all the mod-cons, including sauna, tennis, health and beauty spa, lap pool, gym, 8 restaurants and bars, nightly traditional performances, landscaped gardens, 24-hr valet service and in-house movie channels. Disappointing.

L-AL Sofitel Royal Angkor, Charles de Gaulle Blvd, T063-964600, www.sofitel.com. A large 238-room hotel in a garden-like setting, a large attractive swimming pool and 5 restaurants (including Asian, International and French) and bars. Other perks include an open-air jacuzzi, health and beauty spa. Rates include buffet breakfast and dinner. Not as intimate as some of the other hotels in this price range.

L-AL Sokha Angkor, Sivatha St, T063-969999, www.sokhahotels.com. One of the few Cambodian-owned 5-star hotels in the country, the rooms and services here are top notch, even if the decor is a little gaudy (if you can't afford to stay here, do come and check out the incredibly over-the-top swimming pool, complete with faux temple structures and waterfalls). Also home to an excellent Japanese restaurant. Recommended.

L-AL Victoria Angkor Hotel, Route 6, T063-760428, www.victoriahotels-asia.com. Perfection. A beautiful hotel with that 1930s, East-meets-West style that exemplifies the French tradition of Art de Vivre. The superb facilities make you feel like you are staying in another era – each room is beautifully decorated with local fabrics and fantastic furniture (some Japanese style others more Indian). Swimming pool, open-air salas, jacuzzi and spa. It's the small touches and attention to detail that stands this hotel apart from the rest. Highly recommended.

AL Shinta Mani, Oum Khum and 14th St, T063-761998, www.shintamani.com. This 18-room boutique luxury hotel is wonderful in every way: the design, the amenities, the food and the service. The hotel also offers a beautiful pool, library and has mountain bikes available. Provides vocational training to under-privileged youth. Listed in *Gourmet Magazine* as one of the 'World's Best Hotel Dining Rooms'. Recommended. At time of writing this hotel is undergoing major re-furbishment and is due to re-open early 2011.

AL-A FCC Angkor, near the post office on Pokambor Av, T063-760280, www.fcc cambodia.com. The sister property of the famous FCC Phnom Penh this is a cute hotel set in the grounds of a restored, modernist villa. Rooms offer contemporary luxury and plenty of space but be warned – there is a massive generator at one end of the complex running 24/7 so make sure you are housed well away from here. Also tends to trade more on its reputation so service and food can be decidedly ropey.

AL-A Royal Bay Inn Angkor Resort, Oum Khon St, T063-760500, www.royalbayinnangkor.com. All rooms have balconies facing onto a huge swimming pool in this new resort, set in nice gardens. Expect the usual upmarket trimmings of a/c, multi-channel TV and good service.

A-B Ombrelle & Kimono, 557 Wat Bo Rd. T09-2774313, www.ombrelle-et-kimono.com. Only 5 rooms in this minute villa complete with pool and arty gardens. The rooms are a little pretentious but the welcome is friendly. All en-suite, a/c and with private terrace.

A-D Casa Angkor, corner of Oum Chhay St and Oum Khun St, T063-966234, www.casaangkorhotel.com. This is a good looking, pleasant and well-managed 21-room hotel in a central location. 3 classes of room, all a decent size, well appointed and with cool wooden floors. Friendly reception and efficient staff. Restaurant, beer garden and reading room. Like all Siem Reap hotels this one offers the full range of tour services, airport run, etc.

A-D Passaggio, near the Old Market, T063-760324, www.passaggio-hotel.com. 15 double and 2 family rooms, spacious, a/c, minibar and cable TV, internet, laundry service, bar and restaurant, outdoor terrace.

A-D Soria Moria, Wat Bo Rd, T063-964768, www.thesoriamoria.com. Excellent, well-run small hotel that has a rooftop bar and a decent restaurant. Rooms – all en suite, with contemporary Asian flourishes, a/c and colour TVs – are quiet, and the upper ones have nice airy views the town. Highly recommended.

B-D Kazna Hotel, market end of Taphul Rd, T063-969313, www.kaznahotel.com. Decent, clean well-run mid-range hotel in good location. Every room has a/c and private hot-water bathrooms, TV and rate includes Wi-Fi and breakfast. The better, pricier rooms have balconies. Nice wooden floors and intriguing colour schemes add to the vibe.

B-D La Noria, on road running on east side of the river, just past the 'stone' bridge, T063-964242, www.lanoriaangkor.com.

Almost perfect riverside setting for this gorgeous small resort. Tranquil gardens, a small pool and a real away-from-it-all vibe seduces guests who stay in brightly coloured a/c and en suite rooms each with their own balcony. No TV, very quiet and decent restaurant. Recommended.

C-D Borann, T063-964740, borann@bigpond.com.kh. Attractive hotel in a delightful garden with a pool. A short way down a quiet lane it is secluded and private. 5 small buildings each contain 4 comfortable rooms with terracotta floors and a lot of wood. Some rooms have a/c, some fan only: price varies accordingly. Restaurant.

C-D The Villa, 153 Taphul St, T063-761036, www.thevillasiemreap.com. From the outside this place looks like a funky little guesthouse but some of the rooms are small and dark. All have a/c, TV and shower while the more expensive deluxe rooms are spacious and spotless.

C-E Bopha, on the east side of the river, slightly up from Passagio, T063-964928, bopharesa@everyday.com.kh. Stunning hotel. Good rooms with all the amenities, decorated with local furniture and fabrics. Brilliant Thai-Khmer restaurant.

D Mekong Angkor Palace Hotel, 21 Sivatha Rd, T063-963636, www.mekongangkorpalaces.com. Excellent mid-range hotel in good central location. All of the spotless rooms, are trimmed with a contemporary Khmer vibe, free Wi-Fi, a/c, hot-water bathrooms and TVs. Room rates also include breakfast and there's an excellent swimming as well. Great value and recommended.

D Shadow of Angkor II, Wat Bo Rd, T063-760363, www.shadoworangkor.com. Set on quiet Wat Bo Rd this is the sister guesthouse of **Shadow of Angkor I** located on the market side of the river. This is another place offering well-located, good-value, well-run mid-range accommodation. As well as being clean and comfortable most rooms have balconies and all have a/c, free Wi-Fi, TVs and hot water.

D-E Golden Banana Bed and Breakfast, Wat Damnak Area (past **Martini Bar**), T012-

885366, info@golden-banana.com. Good, clean rooms and decent restaurant.

D-E Home Sweet Home, T063-963245, sweethome@camintel.com. Popular guesthouse and a favourite of the moto drivers (who get a kickback). Regardless, it is still quite good accommodation. Good clean rooms, some with TV and a/c.

D-E Salabai, 155 Taphul Rd, T063-963329, www.salabai.com. Part of an NGO programme that trains disadvantaged young Cambodians to work in the hospitality industry. The rooms are decent enough, in a good location and the suite is an excellent deal. Cheaper rooms have fan, pricier ones a/c, all have private hot water showers. Gets booked up so reserve in advance.

D-E Two Dragons Guesthouse, Wat Bo Village, T012-868551, www.twodragons-asia.com. Well-run mid-range budget guesthouse. All the spotless rooms come with a/c, private en suite hotwater facilities, cable TV and free Wi-Fi. They also pride themselves on giving up-to-date information about everything and anything Siem Reap.

D-E Yaklom Angkor Lodge, Wat Bo St, T012-983510, www.sawasdee-angkor.com. An attractive site and friendly, competent staff who speak good English. The 10 small, simple bungalows are built slightly too close, together. Try to negotiate a discount. Breakfast and airport transfer included. Sawasdee Thai restaurant.

E-F European Guesthouse, T012-582237 www.european-guesthouse.com. 12 fan rooms in a quiet lane off Wat Bo St occupied by 3 guesthouses.

E-F Green Garden Home Guesthouse, down a small lane off Sivatha St, T012-890363. Price varies according to facilities required. A/c or fan, hot water or cold water, etc, cable TV. Garden not as great as their PR would suggest.

E-F Rosy Guesthouse, east side of river before Noria, T063-965059, www.rosy guesthouse.com. Good, clean rooms with bathroom. Very popular.

E-F Sweet Dreams Guesthouse, off Wat Bo St, T012-783013, homesweet home@every day.com.kh. Clean and well-kept rooms in this small guesthouse in a quiet cul-de-sac. A favourite of the motos who obviously get a commission for bringing you here. Restaurant.

F-G Mahogany Guesthouse, Wat Bo St, T063-963417/012-768944, proeun@big pond.com.kh. Fan and now some a/c. An attractive and popular guesthouse, lovely wooden floor upstairs (try to avoid staying downstairs), coffee-making facilities and a friendly crowd of guests.

Around the Old Market (Psar Chars)
LL-AL Hotel de la Paix, corner of Achemean and Sivatha, T063-966000, www.hotelde lapaixangkor.com. Owned by the same company that also runs Bangkok's famous **Bed Supper Club**, this is probably Siem Reap's best-value luxury hotel. The rooms offer simple contemporary design with giant bathtubs and plump bedding – all a/c and with cable TV. The pool is a maze of plinths and greenery and makes for a perfect spot to laze. Can feel a bit urban for Siem Reap but still a great hotel. Recommended.

LL-A Steung Siem Reap Hotel, St 9, T063-965167, www.steungsiemreaphotel.com. This new-build colonial-era-styled hotel is an excellent addition to the central market area of Siem Reap. The pleasant rooms come with cooling wooden floors and many overlook a verdant and very quiet swimming pool. There are all the trimmings you'd expect in this price range, including gym, sauna, free Wi-Fi and free breakfast, huge bathtubs and good, friendly service. Recommended.

A Ta Prohm, T063-380117, www.angkor hotels.org/ta_prohm_hotel. 95 large rooms in a well-kept and long-established property overlooking the river. Bathroom with bathtub. It is a touch overpriced but fair by Siem Reap standards. From the outside it can be difficult to tell whether the hotel is actually open but it is. Restaurant and tourist services.

A-C Neak Pean, 53 Sivatha St, T063-924429, neakpean @camintel.com. 100

rooms, many in large wooden bungalows behind the main building. Swimming pool and garden. Large restaurant.

A-D Molly Malone's, across from **Red Piano** in Old Market area, T063-963533. Fantastic rooms with 4-poster beds and good clean bathrooms. Irish pub downstairs. Lovely owners. Recommended.

D-E Shadow of Angkor I, 353 Pokambor Av, T063-964774, www.shadowofangkor.com. Big old colonial-era house, overlooking the river, the better rooms have balconies, a/c, hot water, and TV. The cheaper rooms, while equally spotless, come with fans. There is also free Wi-Fi and a communal terrace to sit and ponder the river. Run by the same friendly Khmer family who own its sister hotel across the river, **Shadow of Angkor II**.

E Jim's Place, St 9, T063-764005, www.jim place.net. Every room here comes with hot water, en suite bathrooms, cable TV, a/c and free Wi-Fi. They are spotless, though basic but some have rather eccentric toilet designs. Friendly and in good location.

E Neth Socheata, 10, St 2 Thnou, T063-963294, www.angkorguesthouseneth socheata.com. One of the Siem Reap's best deals, this small newly built budget guesthouse, tucked away down a quiet small alley opposite the market, has very nice, clean, pleasantly decorated rooms. All have en suite hot-water facilities and the price varies according to if you choose a/c or fan. The best rooms have small balconies while others are windowless. There's free Wi-Fi and a friendly welcome. Recommended.

On the airport road

The numbers of hotels springing up here are hard to keep track of. Most of them are also aimed at Korean, Chinese and Japanese package tourists, so facilities, food and even languages spoken will reflect this.

LL-A Angkor Palace Resort & Spa, Airport Rd, T063-760511, www.angkorpalace resort.com. Set back from the road in huge, private gardens this is one of the better

choices for upmarket accommodation on the airport road. The rooms are luxurious affairs, complete with daybeds, balconies and silks. There's huge bathtubs, nice big TVs, a/c and a good choice of eating options including a decent café. Khmer-owned and themed add to the attraction.

LL-A Apsara Angkor Hotel, Route 6 (between the airport and town), T063-964999, www.apsaraangkor.com. Pretty standard hotel for the money they are asking. Well-appointed rooms with all amenities but they are rather kitsch. Facilities include gym, internet, swimming pool. Visa/MC/AMEX.

LL-A Empress Angkor, Airport Rd, opposite cultural village, T063-963999, www.empress angkor.com. One of the newest luxury hotels in town..The wooden interior is much nicer than you'd expect from the outside. 207 cosy guestrooms with all the usual inclusions, plus cable TV and balcony. Hotel facilities include restaurant (international and local cuisine), bar, massage, gym, swimming pool, jacuzzi spa and sauna. Visa/AMEX/MasterCard/JCB.

C-E Paul Dubrule Hotel and Tourism School, airport road about 3 km from town centre, T063-963672, www.ecolepaul dubrule.org. Set up by its namesake and founder of the **Accor** hotel group, the Paul Dubrule school has to be one of the best bargains in town. Sure, you'll be looked after by wide-eyed trainees and there's only a skeleton staff after 1800, but the rooms, themed on the local hotels that help sponsor the project, are excellent value. There are only 4 to choose from, the most expensive representing the best deal. All are a/c, with TV, hot water and including breakfast. Recommended.

D-G Jasmine Lodge, Airport Rd near to town centre, T012-784980, www.jasmine lodge.com. One of the best budget deals in town Jasmine is often fully booked, and with good reason. The super-friendly owner Kunn and his family go out of their way to make this a superlative place to stay – there's free internet and Wi-Fi, breakfast can be included in the rate upon request, huge shared areas for sitting, book exchange, tour bookings, bus tickets, etc. There is a huge spread of rooms from basic fan rooms with shared facilities all the way up to sparkling new accommodation with a/c, TV and hot water bathrooms. Highly recommended.

E-G Bou Savy, just outside town centre just off the main airport road, T063-964967, www.bousavyguesthouse.com. One of the best budget options in town this tiny and very friendly family-owned guesthouse is set in soothing gardens and offers a range of rooms with fan or a/c. They also offer breakfast, cheap internet and have some nice public areas. Recommended.

E-G Earthwalkers, just off the Airport Rd, T012-967901, mail@earthwalkers.no. Popular European-run budget guesthouse. Good gardens and pool table. Bit far out of town.

Kompong Thom and around *p124*

A-B Sambor Village, Brocheatebatey or Democrat St, 10-min walk from junction with road No 6, T062-961391, www.sambor village.com. Kompong Thom's most upmarket place is not a bad effort. The pleasant tiled rooms come with 4-poster beds, private terraces, hot water bathrooms, a/c, free Wi-Fi and cable TV. There's a small pool set in a nice garden and free bicycles for guests. Breakfast is also included.

D Stung Sen Royal Hotel, T062-961228. Friendly place with good-sized a/c rooms in a quiet location overlooking the river. For the price things are a little basic but still a good option.

E Mittapheap Hotel, on NH6 just before you cross the bridge into the town centre, T062-961213. The usually clean though musty rooms set in this Khmer villa come with a/c, hot water and TV. It's sited by the river and one of the rooms also has a balcony.

E-F Arunreas Hotel, on the corner, beside the market, on NH6, T062-961294. The accommodation is quite out of place in the town with lifts, Las Vegas-style lights and bell-hops. Rooms are clean with a/c, hot water and cable TV. Make sure you

get a room towards the top of the hotel as the karaoke can be absolutely heinous, particularly if you are tired from a day exploring the temples. Cheaper rooms can be had with fans at the sister guesthouse next door, **Arunreas Guesthouse**.

T'Beng Meanchey and around *p125*

Accommodation here is pretty basic.

F-G Phnom Meas, opposite the taxi stand, T012-632017. Small, clean rooms with fan, attached bathroom and TV. The friendly staff have opted to paint the rooms a nauseating shade of green.

F-G Prum Tep Guesthouse, on the main road about 2 km from the Vishnu traffic circle T012-964645. Clean, hospital-like rooms with a/c, fan and bathroom. Recommended.

G 27 May Guesthouse, on the main road beside the market, T011-905472. Concrete building with pokey rooms with fan or a/c.

🍴 Eating

Angkor Wat *p91*

Outside the entrance to Angkor Wat is a large selection of cafés and restaurants, including the sister restaurant to the **Blue Pumpkin** in Siem Reap, serving good sandwiches and breakfasts, ideal for takeaway. Near the pond there are a number of cheap food and drink stalls, bookshops and posse of hawkers selling film, souvenirs, etc.

††† **Chez Sophéa**, outside Angkor Wat, T012-858003 is a unique place in the evening serving Khmer and French cuisine. Romantic setting. Closes around 2100, but later if you want to stay for a digestif.

Anlong Veng *p117*

Rumour has it that between here and T'beng Meanchey lots of chickens used for cooking have died of starvation (which one could guess from looking at the mere carcasses). And it is also advisable to avoid fish as some (but not all) have probably been caught at Ta Mok's Lake, believed to contain human remains at some point in time (not particularly threatening these days but still unpleasant).

The small town shuts down relatively early so try to get in for dinner before 1900. At all restaurants most meals will be under US$4.

† **Chom No Tror Cheak**, across from Ta Mok's Lake. Has the best variety of food in town. Mixed Thai and Khmer food. English menu.

† **Darareaksmei Restaurant**, on the main road near the roundabout, T011-559171. Whether you like this restaurant or not might depend on how you rate Khmer singing as it doubles as a local entertainment venue (provided by a synthesizer and local talent). In this case, whoever invented karaoke has a lot to answer for. The music aside, this is one of the better restaurants in town with an English menu and Thai and Khmer food. Soup, quail, lok lok. A bit pricier than other places but that covers your entertainment for the night!

† **Lapia**, on the main road as you enter town. This little restaurant offers soup-style meals on individual cookers placed at each table. There is no English menu but with a few instructions the children that run the restaurant can prepare something tasty. The noodles are fantastic.

† **Restaurant 168**, overlooking Ta Mot's Lake, T092-225544. Very popular Khmer restaurant right on the shore of the lake. Individual fairy huts have been built so diners can eat in privacy and enjoy the view. Good local food available at reasonable prices.

Siem Reap p119, maps p120 and p122
Thanks to the growth in mainly foreign-owned restaurants there is now an excellent selection of eating places. Thai, Indian and Asian are particularly well represented but a good number of French and other European restaurants also now compete for the traveller's dollar. Siem Reap is markedly more expensive than Phnom Penh (often double the price). The Old Market area has, over the last few years, become the main area to eat and drink, though the choice of hotels in this area is severely lacking.

Town centre

††† **Barrio**, Sivatha St, away from the central area. T012-756448. 1000-late. Fantastic French and Khmer food. A favourite of the expats. Recommended.

††† **FCC**, Pokamber Av, T063-760280. Sister to the Phnom Penh restaurant, this one is a bit more schmick. Good range of world-class food and drinks, nice surroundings, great armchairs, sophisticated.

††† **Le Malraux**, Sivatha Blvd, T063-966041, www.le-malraux-siem-reap.com. Daily 0700-2400. Sophisticated French cuisine served in this excellent restaurant. Also do some Khmer and Asian dishes, great wine list and good cognacs. Patio or indoor seating. Recommended.

††† **L'Oasi Italiana**, long way up East River Rd, T092-418917. 1100-1400 and 1800-2200 (closed Mon lunchtimes). Attractive leafy location with high-quality Italian menu.

†††-†† **Sala Bai Restaurant School**, Taphul Rd, T089-590864, booking@salabai.com. Taking in students from impoverished backgrounds from the poorest areas of Cambodia, **Sala Bai** trains students in hotel and restaurant skills and places them in establishments around town. Service is not the best as students are quite shy practising their English, but a little bit of patience will help them through. Open for breakfast and lunch only. Highly recommended.

†††-†† **Soria Moria Fusion Kitchen**, Wat Bo Rd, T063-964768. 0700-2200, serves a range of local, Scandinavian and Japanese specialties. Wed nights is the popular US$1 night where all tapas dishes and drinks including cocktails cost US$1 each.

†† **Bopha**, on the east side of the river, slightly up from Passagio, T063-964928. Fantastic Thai-Khmer restaurant in lovely, tranquil garden setting. One of the absolute best in town. Recommended.

†† **Butterflies Gardens**, just off Wat Bo Rd, T063-761211, www.butterfliesofangkor.com. Daily 0800-2200. Tropical butterflies flit around a koi-filled pond in this slightly odd eatery. The food is Khmer/Asian and is average but the setting is well worth a visit.

Le Tigre de Papier, Bar St, T012-659770. Best pizzas in town and offer Khmer cooking classes with profits benefiting a local hotel training school.

The Sugar Palm, Taphul Rd, T012-818143. Closed Sun. Sophisticated Khmer restaurant, immaculate service with casual ambience.

Viroth's Restaraunt, No 246 Wat Bo St, T012-826346. 1100-1400 and 1900-late. Upmarket place offering very good modern Khmer cuisine plus a few Western staples. Looks more expensive than it actually is and is good value.

Curry Walla, Sivatha St and next door to the noon till night market, T063-965451. Best Indian cuisine in town at very good prices. 2 locations in town, no difference in style or menu, ambiance varies. Recommended.

Khmer Kitchen, opposite Old market and Alley West, T063-964154. Tasty cheap Khmer dishes service can be a little slow, but the food is worth waiting for. Sit on the alley side for good people watching. Recommend their pumpkin pies (more of an omelette than a pie!).

Moloppor Café, east of the river, near **Bopha Hotel**. Good cheap Japanese and pizzas.

Around the Old Market (Psar Chars)

There are some cheap market-stall type restaurants around the Old Market and further up Sivatha St, near the Central Market, across from Sokimex petrol station.

The Blue Pumpkin, Old Market area, T063-963574. Western and Asian food and drinks. Sandwiches, ice cream, pitta, salads and pasta. Candidate for 'least likely eatery to find in Siem Reap' with its white minimalist decor. Good breakfasts and cheap cocktails. Eat on the 2nd level. So popular they can be seen at various locations around town and across from Angkor. Recommended if you need a retreat for half an hour.

Dead Fish Tower, Sivatha Blvd, T012-630377. 0700-late. Thai and Khmer restaurant in a fantastically eclectic modern Thai setting. Multiple platforms, quirky decorations, sculptures, apsara dance shows, small putting

green and a crocodile farm all add to the atmosphere of this popular restaurant.

Molly Malone's, T063-963533. Lovely Irish bar and restaurant offering classic dishes like Irish lamb stew, shepherd's pie, roasts and fish and chips.

The Red Piano, northwest of the Old Market, T063-963240. An institution in Siem Reap, based in a 100-year-old colonial building. Coffee, sandwiches, salad and pastas. Cocktail bar, offering a range of tipples, including one dedicated to Angelina Jolie (who frequented the establishment while working on Tomb Raider).

Singing Tree, Alley West, Old market area, T012-2589846, www.singingtreecafe.com. 0730-2100. Serves tasty European and Khmer home cooking, with plenty of veggie options and great fruit shakes.

Soup Dragon, T063-964933. Serves a variety of Khmer and Vietnamese dishes but its specialty is soups in earthenware pots cooked at the table. Breezy and clean, a light and colourful location sitting on a corner terrace surrounded by plants. Upstairs bar, happy hour 1600-1930.

Tell, 374 Sivatha St, T063-963289. Swiss, German, Austrian restaurant and bar. Branch of the long established Phnom Penh restaurant. Serves excellent fondue and raclette, imported beer and sausages. Reasonable prices and generous portions.

Airport Road

There's now a seemingly endless run of Asian restaurants on this road. Some are quite good though you may struggle to find a menu in English.

Abacus, off airport road behind Aceleda bank, T012-644286, wwwcafeabacus.com. Open daily 1100-late. A little further out from the main Old Market area, this place is considered one of the best restaurants in town. Offering French and Cambodian, everything is fantastic here. The fish is superb, the steak is to die for. Highly recommended.

Paul Dubrule Hotel and Tourism School, airport road about 3 km from town centre,

T063-963672, www.ecolepauldubrule.org. As well as being a great place to stay, the school also offers a pretty good set lunch. It can be hit and miss but the quality is often very high and they are always eager to keep their guests happy. Your money will also go to support an excellent vehicle for development – some of the school's graduates have gone on to be well-paid chefs at some of Asia's top hotels and restaurants.

Kompong Thom *p124*

♥♥ Stung Sen Royal Restaurant, attached to the hotel of the same name. The best pick for food in town. It is set up for tour groups with white linen and silver service. It feels a bit weird going in there to eat when you are the only diners (with 4 people waiting on you). Excellent Khmer food and some Western dishes (omelettes, etc). Good value

♥ Arunreas Restaurant. Despite smelling like a wet dog this place serves reasonably cheap, quick Chinese and Khmer food from a large menu. Okay service but the waitresses are usually run off their feet dealing with locals.

♥ Lay Kim Seng Restaurant, behind the market. Also doubles as a bus stop so turns out food very quickly. Large, cheap menu with Asian staples, noodles, rice, soups, etc. There is often a hawker selling pretty good steamed pork rolls outside.

T'Beng Meanchey *p125*

There isn't a huge selection of restaurants in T'Beng Meanchey but the few there are offer Khmer food at very cheap prices (a meal and drinks under US$4). There is a row of Khmer restaurants all offering pretty much the same fare in town, on the road towards the Naga Traffic Circle.

♥ Chan Reas Restaurant, a block south of the Acleda Bank. Friendly restaurant with palatable Khmer food.

♥ Dara Reah Restaurant, on the corner, near the Vishnu roundabout. Despite the unfortunate name, this is probably the best place to eat in town, with an English menu

and good selection of Khmer food. Its forte is dinner. Recommended.

♥ Market Restaurant, on the right-hand side of the market. This place is hugely popular with the locals who like to have a cuppa and tune into the wrestling. Worth a visit if only for the bizarre sight of watching what seems like the entire male population of the town 'ooohh' and 'ahhh' over the wrestling. Its coffee is much better than its food.

♥ Mlop Dong Restaurant, opposite the taxi stand. Cute little restaurant offering good coffee, omelettes and noodles alongside other Cambodian fare. Good option for breakfast.

🍸 Bars and clubs

Siem Reap *p119, maps p120 and p122*
Angkor What?, on street known as 'Bar Street', Old Market Area, T012-490755. Open early evening to early morning. Bar run by friendly staff, popular with travellers and young expats.

Fresh at Chilli Si Dang, East River Rd, T017-875129, 0800-late. Laid-back atmosphere, friendly service away from the tourist drag. Happy hour between 1700 and 2100.

Laundry, near the Old Market, turn right off 'Bar St', T012-246912. Open till late. Funky little bar.

Linga, Laneway behind 'Bar St', T012-246912. Gay-friendly bar offering a wide selection of cocktails. Great whiskey sours.

Miss Wong, The Lane (behind Pub St) T092-428332. 1700-0100. Cute little bar serving sharp cocktails in an Old Shanghai setting.

The Red Piano, Old Market Area, T063-963240. A comfortable bar/diner furnished with large wicker armchairs. The good international menu is fairly priced. Happy hour 1600-2100.

Temple Bar, on 'Bar St', T015-999909. Popular drinking hole, dimly lit, good music. Not related to its seedier counterpart in Phnom Penh.

The Warehouse, opposite Old Market Area, T063-964600. 1000-0300. Popular bar, good service and Wi-Fi.

X Rooftop Bar, Top of Sivataha St (you'll see the aluminous X from most high-rise buildings in town), T092-207842. 1600-sunrise. The latest closing bar in town. Happy hour between 1600-1730.

Zone One, Taphul Village, T012-912347. 1800-late. Place to go to experience local nightlife.

⊕ Entertainment

Siem Reap *p119, maps p120 and p122*
Dance performance
A number of hotels, notably **Le Grand**, **Sofitel** and **Angkor Village**, stage Khmer dancing performances in the evening. There are a few dance shows performed by local children from orphanages; be aware that sometimes these kids are dancing every night to tourists. They may look cute but one might consider whether they should be working late 7 days a week.

Cambodian Cultural Village, on the airport road, 6 km from town. Tickets US$12.

Music concerts
A popular Sat evening attraction is the one man concert put on by Dr Beat Richner (Beatocello), founder of the Jayavarman VII hospital for children. Run entirely on voluntary donations the 3 hospitals in the foundation need US$9 million per year in order to treat Cambodian children free of charge. He performs at the hospital, on the road to Angkor, just north of the **Sofitel** hotel, at 1915 every Sat, lasts about 1 hr, free admission but donations gratefully accepted. A worthwhile experience.

Shadow puppetry
Shadow puppetry is one of the finest performing arts of the region and is an absolute must for visitors to the area. **Bayon Restaurant**, Wat Bo St. Has regular shadow puppet shows in the evening.

Krousar Thmey, a local NGO, often tours its shadow puppet show to Siem Reap. The show is performed by underprivileged children (who have also made the puppets) at **La Noria Restaurant** on East River Rd. Wed at 1930 but check as they can be a tad irregular. Highly recommended. Donations accepted.

⊙ Shopping

Anlong Veng *p117*
With 2 shiny new shopping plazas complete with fast food, escalators and a/c and Alley West smartening up with cheeky chic boutiques, Siem Reap is fast improving its reputation of being more than just a temple stopover. Anything and everything can be obtained from the bustling markets (a relatively new addition to a town that was forbidden to trade in anything too Western or modern during the Khmer Rouge days).

Siem Reap *p119, maps p120 and p122*
Art
Happy Cambodia, Old Market area. Sells the works of French Canadian Stéphane 'Stef' Delaprée. Colourful, cheerful images of everyday Khmer sights and scenes. Originals up to US$385, good-quality prints US$25-40, cards and t-shirts.

Books
Street booksellers (usually people with disabilities) are in abundance, selling copied versions of the old favourites.
Blue Apsara, near the Old Market, carries the best variety of used books in town.

Clothes
Rogue, Old Market area, T012-703264. Sells a range of easy-to-wear casual clothing.
Wanderlust, Alley West, T012-529924. Colourful clothing with ethical flair. The American fashion designer has strong fair trade principals.
Wild Poppy, Sivatha St, T077-568874. Classic comfortable clothing, locally made.

Handicrafts

Chantiers Écoles, down a short lane off Sivatha St, T063-963330. School for orphaned children which trains them in carving, sewing and weaving. Products are on sale and raise 30% of the school's running costs. Outlets selling the school's products are dotted around town under the name **Les Artisans d'Angkor**. There is a silk production centre 15 km out of town, T063-380369, open daily 0730-1730.
Senteurs d'Angkor, opposite Old Market, T063-964860. Sells a good selection of handicrafts, carvings, silverware, silks, handmade paper, cards, scented oils, incense, pepper and spices.

Markets

Outside Phnom Penh, Siem Reap is about the only place whose markets are worth browsing in for genuinely interesting souvenirs. Old Market (Psar Chars) is not a large market but stall holders and keepers of the surrounding shops have developed quite a good understanding of what tickles the appetite of foreigners. All manner of Buddhist statues and icons are on sale. Reproductions of Angkor figures are also available in various degrees of craftsmanship. There is a selection of silk and cotton fabrics, kramas and sarongs, nice silverware, books, CDs and DVDs. Leather puppets and rice paper rubbings of Angkor bas-reliefs are unusual mementos.

In the night market area, off Sivatha St, you will find bars, spas and cafés. The original night market, towards the back, has more original stalls, but is slightly more expensive.

Supermarket

Angkor Market, Sivatha St, T063-767799. Everything you need or miss can be found here, even marmite.
ATC – Angkor Trade Center, Pokambor Av behind the Old Market area. Well stocked convenient shopping on way back from town to Wat Bo area.
Star Mart, the supermarket attached to Caltex petrol stations, is very well stocked. Open 24 hrs.

▲▲ Activities and tours

Siem Reap *p119, maps p120 and p122*
Therapies
Khmer, Thai, reflexology and Japanese massage are readily available. Many masseuses will come to your hotel.
Frangipani, Hup Guan St near Angkor Hospital for Children, T063-964391, www.frangipani siemreap. Aromatherapy, reflexology and other professional treatments.
Mutita Spa, at Borei Angkor Resort and Spa on Route 6, T63-964406. Offers unique J'Pong thearpy a traditional Cambodian heat and relaxation treatment using herbal steam.
Seeing Hands. Massage by seeing impaired individuals. US$3 per hr. Highly recommended.

Tour operators
Many hotels and guesthouses can organize and recommend tour guides and services on arrival.
Asia Pacific Travel, No 100 Route 6, T063-760862, www.angkortravelcambodia. com. Also has offices in Vietnam and Laos.
Exotissimo Travel, No 300 Airport Rd, T063-964323, or head office (Phnom Penh), T023-218948, www.exotissimo.com. Tours of Angkor and sites beyond.
Hidden Cambodia Adventure Tours, Trang Village, House No 1, Slokram Commune, T012-655201, www.hidden cambodia.com. Specializing in dirt bike tours to remote areas and off the track temple locations. Recommended for adventurers. For example: to Koh Ker, 4 hrs.
Journeys Within, on the outskirts of Siem Reap towards the temples, T063-966463, www.journeys-within.com. Specializes in private, customized tours that allow visitors to enjoy the temples as well as go further afield to see the everyday lives of Cambodians.
PTM Tours, No 552, Group 6, Mondul 1, T063-964388, www.ptm-travel.com. Reasonably-priced package tours to Angkor and around Phnom Penh. Also offers cheap hotel reservations.

Terre Cambodge, on Huap Guan St near Angkor Hospital for Children, T092476682, www.terrecambodge.com. Offers tours with a twist, including cruises on an old sampan boat. Not cheap but worth it for the experience.

Two Dragons Guesthouse (see page 132) can also organize some off-the-beaten-track tours. The owner Gordon Sharpless is a very knowledgeable and helpful fellow.

World Express Travel, St No 11 (Old Market area), T063-963600. Can organize tours all over Cambodia. Also books local and international air/bus tickets. Good place to extend visa. Friendly service.

WHL Cambodia, Wat Bo Rd, T063-963854, www.angkorhotels.org. Local website booking hotels and tours with a responsible tourism approach.

☉ Transport

Anlong Veng *p117*
From Anlong to **Siem Reap**, **T'beng Meanchey** or **Kompong Thom**, one must endure enormously potholed roads and broken bridges. Shared taxis/pickups leave in the morning for **Siem Reap**, US$3-4, 3-4 hrs. The road between Anlong Veng and **Preah Vihear** (90 km) is comparatively smooth for this region (in the dry season) and pickups leave from the market around 0700, U$S2.

There is a **border crossing** 15 km north of Anlong Veng at **O'Smach** that is open to foreigners between Thailand and Cambodia, see page 18.

Siem Reap *p119, maps p120 and p122*
Air
The airport (REP), T063-963148, is 7 km from Siem Reap. There are flights from **Phnom Penh, Ho Chi Minh City, Hanoi, Bangkok, Singapore, Kuala Lumpur, Pakse** and **Vientiane**. The airport has a taxi service, café, internet access, phone service and gift shop. A moto into town is US$1, taxi US$7. Guesthouse owners often offer free rides. There is US$25 departure tax at Siem Reap airport.

Airlines Bangkok Airways, Airport Rd, www.bangkokair.com, 6 flights a day to **Bangkok**. Jetstar Asia, www.jetstarasia.com, flies to **Singapore** 3 times a week. Malaysian budget airlines **Airasia**, T023-890035, www.airasia.com, to **Kuala Lumpur**, daily flights. Helicopters Cambodia, 658 St Hup Quan, near Old Market, T063-963316. New Zealand company offering chartered flights around the temples. Lao Airlines, T/F063-963283, Mon-Fri 0800-1700, Sat 0800-1200. To **Vientiane**, 3 flights a week via **Pakse**. Malaysia Airlines, T063-964135, 3 times a week to **Kuala Lumpur**. Vietnam Airlines, Airport Rd, T063-964488, www.vietnamairlines.com. To **Ho Chi Minh City**. Silkair, T063-426808, www.silkair.com, daily flights to **Singapore**.

Boat
Boat to and from **Phnom Penh**, US$35, 5-6 hrs. The trip is fantastically atmospheric and a good way to kill 2 birds with 1 stone and see the mighty Tonlé Sap Lake. The boat is a less appealing option in the dry season when low water levels necessitate transfers to small, shallow draft vessels. In case of extremely low water levels a bus or pickup will need to be taken for part of the trip. The mudbank causeway between the lake and the outskirts of Siem Reap is hard to negotiate and may necessitate some walking (it is 12 km from Bindonville harbour to Siem Reap). Boats depart from the Phnom Penh Port on Sisowath Quay (end of 106 St) 0700, departing Siem Reap 0700 from Chong Khneas on the Tonlé Sap Lake. Tickets and enquiries T012-581358.

To **Battambang** the fast boat takes 4 hrs, US$25. Note that there are frequent mechanical breakdowns and in the past occasional reports of boats being shot at by irate fishermen whose nets have been snagged.

Bus/pick-up/shared taxi
The a/c buses are one of the most convenient and comfortable ways to go to and from

Phnom Penh, US$6-11, 6 hrs. Almost every guesthouse or hotel sells the tickets although it is easy enough to pick up from the bus stations/terminal. Companies include **GST**, **Mekong Express** and **Capitol**. Most buses depart between 0630-0800 near the Old Market. The best service is the Mekong Express, US$11 if you buy in advance. It has the quickest service, 5 hrs and a/c with a little bit of info over the mike.

In peak periods, particularly Khmer New Year, it is important to purchase tickets a day or 2 prior to travel. A shared taxi to Phnom Penh will cost you US$10, minimum 4.

To **Battambang**, most guesthouses can organize a ticket for US$10, 7 hrs.

To **Anlong Veng**, roughly 3-4 hrs via NH67 on the way to Banteay Srei. Shared taxis/pickups leave from the market daily but not regularly, US$103-104. Siem Reap motodops will usually quote the price at US$30 a day for the trip but one should be discerning as you need a bike and driver who will be able to cope with the harsh roads. **Hidden Cambodia**, does tours with both dirt bike and 4WDs of the area (**Anlong Veng, Preah Vihear, Preah Khan**, etc) for around US$100-130 per day.

Car and bicycle

Most hotels and guesthouses rent cars with drivers and US$2 per day for bicycles. **The White Bicycles** scheme has been set up by ex-pat Norwegian NGO workers as a way to provide not only a source of income and work for locals but also to develop a charitable fund that supports children and teenagers in Cambodia. The bikes cost US$2 a day to rent with US$1.50 going to the charitable fund and US$0.50 going to sustain and repair the bikes by employing and training locals. The White Bicycles can be found at several hotels and guesthouses throughout Siem Reap, www.thewhitebicycles.org.

Kompong Thom *p124*

Kompong Thom is 146 km from Siem Reap and 162 km from Phnom Penh. To the north,

T'Beng Meanchey is 151 km of mainly rough road with the turn-off to Preah Khan about 90 km from Kompong Thom. The taxi/bus station is just a block east of the main road in the centre of town. Shared taxis depart all morning for **Siem Reap**, US$6, **Phnom Penh**, 3 hrs, US$5, and the occasional one to **T'Beng Meanchey**, US$6-8. GST Bus Company runs 3 buses a day between **Phnom Penh** (from the Central Market) and Kompong Thom (from Pich Chenda Restaurant). The bus departs from both places at 0645, 0745, 1200, US$5. **Phnom Penh Public Transport Buses** depart from the Central Market at 0645, 0730, 1215, US$3.

T'Beng Meanchey *p125*

Almost every way you approach T'Beng Meanchey is tough. T'Beng Meanchey is 151 km north of Kompong Thom and the road is not in great shape. The trip will take at least 4 hrs in the dry season and considerably more during the rains. A shared taxi to **Kompong Thom** is US$6-8 If you want to visit Koh Ker or Preah Khan from here there are numerous motos at the taxi stand who will take you. Expect to pay between US$10-20 per day. Even if you have your own motorbike it's worthwhile hiring one of the motos to guide you as the tracks can by labyrinthal.

⊙ Directory

Anlong Veng *p117*
Banks **Acelda**, turn right at the only roundabout on the main road, bank is just after Lucky Hotel, T092-466546. **Telephone** If you wish to make a phone call some of the local 'phone-boxes' (ie someone with a mobile) will let you make calls within Cambodia for 600 riel per min.

Siem Reap *p119, maps p120 and p122*
Banks ATMs can be found all over town. **ANZ Royal**, Old Market and Tep Vong St, T06-3969700. Efficient friendly service. **Cambodia Commercial Bank**, 130 Sivatha St, 0900-1600. Open Sat and Sun. Currency and

TC exchange. Advance on Visa, MasterCard, JCB, AMEX. **Canadia Bank**, Old Market Area, T063-964808, Mon-Fri 0800-1500. Moneygram, MasterCard advances, currency and TC exchange. **Krong Thai Bank**, 10-11 Sivatha Blvd. Mon-Fri 0800-1500, Sat 0800-1200. Currency exchange, TCs. **Mekong Bank**, 43 Sivatha St, T063-964417, Mon-Fri 0830-1600, Sat 0830-1200. US dollars TCs cashed, 2% commission, cash advance on Visa and JCB cards only. Western Union services. **Union Commercial Bank**, north of Old Market, Mon-Fri 0800-1530, Sat 0800-1200. Cash advance on MasterCard and Visa, cashes TCs and has an ATM. **Internet** Rates vary but should be around 3000-4000 riel per hr. Most internet places now offer internet calls. Most bars, restaurants, cafés and guesthouses have complimentary Wi-Fi for those utilizing their services. **Medical services** Medical facilities are okay here and improving but by no means of an international standard. In most cases it is probably best to fly to Bangkok. **Royal International Hospital**, Airport Rd, T063-39911. Good standard and costs can be claimed back from most international insurance companies. **Children's hospitals: Jayavarman VII Hospital**, on the road to Angkor Wat. **Angkor Hospital for Children**, Achamean St. Provincial hospital north of Old Market. Pharmacies: opposite the entrance of the provincial hospital. **Post office** On Pokamber Av, west side of Siem Reap River, but it can take up to a month

for mail to be delivered. 0700-1700. **DHL**, Sivatha St (opposite petrol station), will send urgent letters for US$50, guaranteed 4-day delivery. **Telephone** Sim cards are readily available to purchase with a passport in most phone shops for US$10-25 and will let you call overseas.

Kompong Thom *p124*

Banks Acleda Bank, NH6, before the bridge, does Western Union transfers (no credit card advances). There are a number of money changers in front of the market.
Internet There are 2 internet shops on NH6 before the bridge, on the right-hand side of the road and a couple of other places around the market. Internet is quite expensive and ranges from US$2-4 per min. **Post office** There is quite a good post office, a block from the market, which can deliver international mail. **Telephone** There are a number of local 'phone-boxes' (people who will rent you their mobile phone) sprinkled around town, particularly in the market area. Overseas calls can be made at most internet shops for around 800 riel per min.

T'Beng Meanchay *p125*

Communications There isn't a whole lot of access here – the post office is nothing more than a 2-way radio and mobile phones don't have great coverage. **Buddhist for Development** has set up an internet café where you can make international calls for around 1000 riel per min; internet, US$2 per hr.

Contents

Footprint features

The Northwest

THAILAND

Chong Jom
O Smach
Samrong

Dangrek Mountains

Choam
Ksant

T'Beng
Meanchey

Kulen

Preah
Vihear

Koh Ker

SIEM REAP-
ODDAR
MEANCHEY

Anlong
Veng

PREAH VIHEAR

Ta Seng

Preah
Khan

Phnom Kulen

Beng Mealea

Dam Dek

Banteay
Srei

Angkor

Roluos

Sakong

Chong
Khneas

Siem Reap

Phnum Krom
Prek Toal
Bird Sanctuary

Tonlé Sap

KOMPONG
THOM

Sambor
Prei Kuk

Phnom
Santuk

Kompong
Thom

Stoeng

Kompong
Luong

KOMPONG
CHHNANG

Kompong
Chhnang

Pursat

PURSAT

Poipet

Sisophon

Srah Chhuk

Thkov

Phnum
Liep

Mongkol
Borei

Kouk
Kduoch

Thma Pok

Banteay
Chhmar

Knach
Roméas

Kamping
Poy

Battambang

Reang
Kesei

Moung
Roessei

BATTAMBANG

BANTEAY
MEANCHEY

Pailin

Daun
Lem

Pruhm

Sangke

★ Don't miss ...

1 Battambang, page 149.

2 Wat Ek, page 151.

3 Bamboo train, page 151.

4 Phnom Khieu Waterfall,
page 154.

5 Banteay Chhmar, page 156.

20 km

N

Head northwest up Route 5 from Phnom Penh and you'll be introduced to one of Cambodia's most charming and authentic regions. The sleepy but handsome town of Kompong Chhnang should be your first stop off with its links to Southeast Asia's biggest freshwater lake, the Tonlé Sap, floating villages, and its splendid French colonial-era architecture. Equally soporific is nearby Pursat where there's little to do but watch river-life unfold and plot expeditions into the nearby Cardamom Mountains.

After Pursat is the centrepiece of the region – the riverside conurbation of Battambang, complete with elegant French colonial buildings, a smattering of nearby ruins and one of the most bizarre forms of rail transport on the planet – the bamboo train. There's also little doubt that Battambang is now re-emerging as an important and prosperous provincial city that exudes a special kind of relaxing charm. Battambang's proximity to the Thai border helps and the nearby border towns of Pailin and Poipet – both complete with nefarious reputations of scams, Khmer Rouge hang-outs and other unsavoury matters – have done little to damage this emerging city's economic standing.

If you want to take in best of the region's sites Sisophon can provide a suitable temporary base to visit the spectacular archaeological remains at stunning Banteay Chhmar. It should also be noted that this was one of the most bitterly contested territories during the civil war. Thousands of civilians fled northwest from the advancing Khmer Rouge and sought refuge in the border areas of Thailand. Until recently places such as Battambang and Banteay Chhmar were Khmer Rouge strongholds; but with the Khmer Rouge trials now in session their influence, if not their impact, is waning.

Battambang and around

Cuddled into various rivers, the laid-back towns of Kompong Chhnang and Battambang provide a lovely backdrop to sit back and soak up the atmosphere of Khmer life. Pursat is the gateway to the Tonlé Sap and the Cardamom Mountains. Battambang oozes charm with its lovely colonial buildings and outlying sites. With most travellers heading to Siem Reap up the eastern side of the Tonlé Sap this part of Cambodia is still relatively undiscovered making it a perfect antidote to the backpacker haunts found elsewhere. ▶▶ *For listings, see pages 157-164.*

Towards Battambang → *For listings, see pages 157-164.*

Heading north from Phnom Penh on Route 5 early in the morning the traveller quickly passes the ancient capital of Oudong, see page 53. The road is comfortable and fast and the scenery enchanting. In the wet season all hues of green predominate with flashes of red – soil, newly tiled roofs and kramas (Khmer scarves) – but the lakes and rivers are thick with brown silt. Ninety kilometres after leaving Phnom Penh, the attractive little town of Kompong Chhnang hoves into view.

Kompong Chhnang

The sprawling lakeside town has plenty of colonial charm and for those with a day to spare, makes a pleasant break from the dust and grime of Phnom Penh, or even a pleasant stopover point en route to Battambang. The word Kompong comes from the Khmer meaning 'town on the water', a reference to its position alongside the Tonlé Sap and in some parts on the river (floating villages). Chhnang means clay pot, the manufacture of which the area has been famous for, for four centuries. This represents one use, at least, for the sticky riverine mud which threatens to swallow the unwary pedestrian. No visitor will fail to spot the oxen-carts loaded up with clay pots trundling the tracks around town.

The main part of town called **Psar Leu** (upper market) is on Route 5 which is where visitors arriving by bus or shared taxi will be dropped off. A moto will take you pretty much anywhere in town for 2000 to 3000 riel. A typical Victory monument built after the Vietnamese 'liberation' of 1979 dominates the central square. Despite this monstrosity, this is the beautiful part of town. There are plenty of walks north of the square along shady tree-lined roads with well-preserved colonial buildings running alongside. Kompong Chhnang is underestimated by tourists – it is the perfect place to get a hit of quintessential Cambodian life. On one hand you have the heart and soul of Tonlé Sap life: the daily grind of the fishermen, buoyant homes drifting with the tide, merchants donning their archetypal conical hats and an endless stream of boats gliding through. On the other, you have the town: large, leafy boulevards, faded yellow buildings gathered in the French Quarter, the citizen's languid tempo and the even slower pace of meandering cows, and the town's parks which you must scour for a good stretch of grass. Some of the colonial-era town centre is now being renovated, the highlight being the grandiose Provincial Hall – while this is not officially open to tourists you should be able to wander the pleasant grounds. If you do go walking anywhere be prepared to encounter monkeys – they can sometimes be aggressive so don't feed them and watch your valuables as they can steal cameras, sunglasses, etc. Kompong Chnnang is an amalgam of the country's diversity – Cambodia, Vietnam and France; the verve of the river and life on the land; rural and urban all rolled into one area. This place generates a feeling of simple, content, harmonious country life (although below the surface it has had a tumultuous history and still faces many problems – disputes between fishing villages, for example). It does evoke another place and another time: this town could well be one of Cambodia's friendliest spots, with locals literally flocking to simply say hello.

The pier is at **Psar Kraom** (lower market) on the lakeside which is where visitors arriving by boat will land. It is at the end of a 2-km causeway over the lake from the main part of town. Although this is the shabbier side of the town there is much to see here.

Kompong Chhnang

Ferry connections to Phnom Penh & Siem Reap

Tonlé Sap

PSAR KRAOM

To Battambang

Shell

Children's Monument

Tela

Nagas Statue

Statue of 3 Soldiers

2 km Causeway

Football Field

Small

PSAR LEU

Sokimex

Provincial Hall

Royal Army

Park

Victory Monument

School

Women's Centre

Orphanage

Acleda

To 1 3 & Phnom Penh

N
Not to scale

Sleeping
Asia 1
Samrongsen 2

Sokha Guesthouse 4
Sovann Phum 3

Eating
Soksen 1

The lake is very beautiful and there are now several established tourist boats offering tours – rates are about US$15 for a covered ten-seater but you might be able to haggle with a local fisherman to take you out for less. The market activity on the lakeside – much of it taking place from boats – is interesting. You can buy fruit, meat, vegetables, cigarettes, clay pots and clothes. There is also a brightly painted wat on the corner of the causeway facing the lake. There are some huge floating villages here – many of the inhabitants are Vietnamese.

Kompong Chhnang's claim to fame is its pottery and roadside **pottery** stalls line Route 5, particularly towards Battambang. A higher grade of pottery can be found at **Ban Chkol Village**, 6 km south of town. An NGO has actively been training the villagers in the art of pottery and the results are evident to see. To get there follow Route 5 until you see the turn-off for the village.

Five hundred metres from the airport is **Tareak Cave** ① *round trip by moto US$5*, a man-made construction also developed under the Khmer Rouge's auspices. Intended as a hideout, the cave was built by forced labour and required the indigent workers to carve a 2.5-m-high and 6-m-wide hole into a solid rock face. Like most developments under the brutal regime, many people lost their lives while working on this site. Neither of these sights hold great tourist appeal but might peak the curiosity of war buffs.

Across the river are the double peaks of **Mount Kong Ray**, the appellation deriving from the the legend of Kong Ray, a woman murdered when stuck in the middle of a dispute between her husband and mother-in-law. Many believe that the woman's spirit created the mountain, which today resembles a corpse, with feet to the north and hair to the south.

For the more intrepid travellers there are a few pre-Angkorian ruins across the river. The sites are scattered amongst small villages and bush land and are hard to find, so a good guide/moto is required for navigation. **Prasat Srei**, 'Girl Temple', is a seventh- to eighth-century Chenla-era structure. Like many of its kind, the temple has been severely looted. Swamped by bushes the structure features a single tower, with three artificial doors, stony stairs and crumbling lintels. **Prasat Broh**, 'Boy Temple', was constructed during the same period of brick and is in a pretty bad state of repair. There are several other Sambor-inspired temples in the area including **Prasat Srey Bee**, 'Twin Girl Temples', two identical temples sitting atop a beautiful mountain. The return boat trip, including waiting time, will cost around US$25 in one of the 10-seater boats mentioned above. The temples span an area about 15 sq km – you should be able to pick up a moto on the other side for US$10 to show you around.

On the road south to Phnom Penh next to the orphanage there is a Women's and Veterans' Centre. They run an outlet shop where local women make and sell crafts including woven fabrics and pottery. **Phnom Reabat** mountain temple 10 km from Kompong Chhnang probably affords the best view of the collection of temples around the area. The view from the top is nothing short of spectacular, with an outlook extending across to the Cardomom Mountains, and the Tonlé Sap River. The signpost marking the site sums it up, reading: "Attractive 750 metres".

Pursat → *For listings, see pages 157-164.*

Pursat is a town of major indifference to most travellers on the southern side of the Tonlé Sap between Phnom Penh and Battambang. The petite town is special in its own way with a sinuous river slowly lurching through the centre and little, leafy streets dotted by the odd cyclist or vehicle. Pursat doesn't quite have the bustling city feel of other riverine towns but has the facilities and population putting it miles ahead of most rural villages. The place is just right, particularly for those who would like a couple of days to unwind in an authentic, untouristed part of the country.

The province of Pursat is notable for its natural beauty and scenery, but unfortunately little is visible from the road. Pursat is the gateway to the fruitful Tonlé Sap and the Cardomom Mountain Range and the settlement is surrounded by some truly spectacular countryside. Pursat town is renowned for its marble carvings (the province supplies the majority of Cambodia's marble). In the centre of town, between Road 1 and Road 2 (off Route 5), is a **marble carving workshop**, where visitors can see the artisans at work. Cambodia's highest summit, Mount Aoral (1813 m – although no two maps seem to agree), has been included in the province by a slip of the cartographer's hand – and it has recently been opened to hikers. The Cardamom Mountains are thickly clad in forest and provide a source of considerable wealth. So too does the Tonlé Sap, which is fished intensively. Around 79% of the population in this area are either fishermen or farmers. There is quite a large Vietnamese population and they have established a trade in fingerlings (immature fish) with Vietnam. It is estimated that one to two billion fingerlings are exported each year, causing grave concern to environmentalists. Many Vietnamese live in floating villages on the lake. The **floating village** of **Kompong Luong** can be reached via Krakor, which is 35 km east on Route 5. The area is rich in birdlife and the daily waterway life can be completely captivating. Over 10,000 people live in this permanently floating town, with floating bars, restaurants, pool tables, school and medical clinics. The villagers here face the difficulty of relocating homes and businesses twice a year due to the seasonally shifting water levels. During the wet season, they move closer to the riverbanks to be protected from heavy storms. In the dry season they move towards the centre of the river where deeper water levels exist. The dwellings require between 1 m and 4 m of water beneath them in order to float. Visitors can hire a boat for US$5 an hour and venture to the other floating villages of Raing Til, Kompong Thkol and Dey Roneat.

Pursat town has a small museum, on the west side of the bridge over Pursat River, containing ancient artefacts from the region.

Battambang → For listings, see pages 157-164.

Cambodia's second largest city lies 40 km west of the Tonlé Sap at the centre of a fertile plain. Battambang, which translates as 'disappearing stick', is named after a magical stick that the king used to ensure his power. Battambang lies on the lovely Sangkei River and retains a lot of charming early 20th-century buildings as well as 16 wats, some – so it is said – dating back to the Angkor period, which are scattered around the city and surrounding lush countryside. The town itself is quite beautiful, with a number of old colonial buildings sitting around the misty, river area. A large number of NGOs working in the northwest region have offices here so the town has quite good amenities and restaurants. With its proximity to the Thai border and the trade opportunities that come with that, Battambang is slowly emerging as a prosperous, very liveable provincial city. A new university is soon to open, the streets are mostly clean and well-kept and there is a discernable feeling of pride emanating from the city's leafy streets. More notably, some of the riverside colonial buildings are now being beautifully restored, something which only adds to the relaxed upbeat vibe.

Ins and outs

Getting there and around Pick-ups and buses connect with Phnom Penh, Poipet and Pailin. Daily connections by boat with Siem Reap provide the most scenic and enjoyable way to get to Battambang and if you take a slow boat it's a perfect way to enjoy the bucolic charms of the Cambodian countryside. The road to Siem Reap is now markedly improved and taking a bus or shared taxi is the quickest and easiest form of transport between the two towns. Motos can be used to get around town. ▶▶ *See Transport, page 163.*

Sights

In 1975 the Khmer Rouge captured the town and made it a rebel stronghold. Much of the surrounding area was **mined** and it took many years for the area to be swept of ordnance which contributed to a sharp decline in harvests. Yet, with most mines having been removed the area is returning to its former role as a rice basket.

Battambang retains almost all its original French **colonial architecture** including the splendid Governor's Residence. The original planners sited this grand building perfectly at the northern end of the main river crossing creating an imposing spectacle to impress the governor's visitors arriving from Phnom Penh. Most of the town's buildings are **shophouses**: business downstairs, residence upstairs. They were built to the same

Battambang

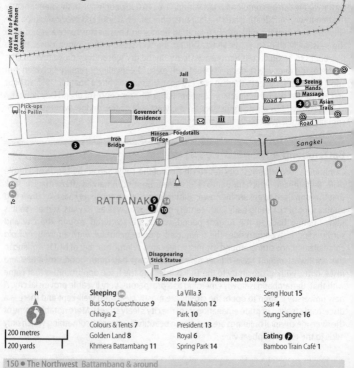

Sleeping		
Bus Stop Guesthouse 9	La Villa 3	Seng Hout 15
Chhaya 2	Ma Maison 12	Star 4
Colours & Tents 7	Park 10	Stung Sangre 16
Golden Land 8	President 13	
Khmera Battambang 11	Royal 6	Eating
	Spring Park 14	Bamboo Train Café 1

formula the British introduced into Malaya with a covered 5-ft walkway to provide shade and shelter for pedestrians. A number of occupants have 'privatized' the walkway by extending their side walls across the pavement down to the road. Most buildings on Street 2 remain as built, many with the original wooden doors and shutters.

The town has a small **museum** which contains a few items from local Khmer temples but the most pleasant way to spend your time here is to stroll along the riverfront or potter around the back streets reflecting on the irony that while the Khmer Rouge may have been savages to their compatriots, the colonial architectural heritage couldn't have been in safer hands.

Around Battambang

Around Battambang are the 11th-century temple of Wat Ek, the Bamboo train also known as the funny train, the lake of Kamping Poy, a mass grave of the Khmer Rouge and a 10th-century mountain-top temple and cave.

Wat Ek (or Ek Phnom) ① *11 km downriver from Battambang, Take a moto on the road that follows the river; US$10 for full-day trip around these sites and others in the area.* It is a nice green drive past trees, shrubs, villages and covered bridges (the local architectural speciality, but of

no great antiquity) to the 11th-century temple, built in 1027. It was built of huge sandstone blocks by Suryavarman and is now a pleasantly abandoned ruin with one central tower leaning precariously. Many smaller structures and gateways have toppled or look as though they are about to topple. There are some carved lintels but nothing more. Local Buddhists are dutifully and busily staking out their own patch next door, as they are across the country, in an effort to pretend that they and their religion were authors of the site and its contents. The process is no different from what occurred in Europe as early Christian churches were established on existing pagan sites.

Battambang's Bamboo Train ① *US$5-15,* has now, quite rightly, become one of the areas biggest tourist attractions. A simple bamboo platform on wheels powered by a small petrol engine, the 'train' follows the railway track for approximately 40 km through the country-side stopping off at villages along the way (with two official 'train stations' at the 12 km and 6 km mark). There are several of these "trains" available and they can be quickly dismantled – takes about one minute – which means should two meet on the single track they simply take the whole

City Café **5**
Espresso Coffee **7**
Madison Corner **8**
Mariyan Pizza **9**
Pkay Proek **2**
Riverside Balcony Bar **3**

Sunrise Coffeehouse **6**
Tho Ny **10**
White Rose **4**

The tears of the Gods: rubies and sapphires

Major deposits of two of the world's most precious stones are found distributed right across mainland Southeast Asia: rubies and sapphires. They are mined in Thailand, Myanmar, Vietnam, Cambodia and Laos.

During the civil war in Cambodia, thousands of Thais were mining gems in Khmer Rouge-controlled territory (especially around Pailin) – with the protection of the vilified Khmer Rouge and the support of the Thai army. Bangkok has become one of the centres of the world's gem business and Thailand is the largest exporter of cut stones.

Rubies and sapphires are different colours of corundum, the crystalline form of aluminium oxide. Small quantities of various trace elements give the gems their colour; in the case of rubies, chromium, and for blue sapphires, titanium. Sapphires are also found in a spectrum of other colours including green and yellow.

Rubies are among the rarest of gems, and command prices four times higher than equivalent diamonds.

The colour of sapphires can be changed through heat treatment (the most advanced form is called diffusion treatment) to 1500-1600°C (sapphires melt at 2050°C). For example, relatively valueless, colourless geuda sapphires from Sri Lanka turn a brilliant blue or yellow after heating. The technique is an ancient one: Pliny the Elder described the heating of agate by Romans nearly 2000 years ago while the Arabs had developed heat treatment into almost a science by the 13th century. Today, almost all sapphires and rubies are heat treated. The most valued colour for sapphires is cornflower blue. Dark, almost black, sapphires command a lower price. The value of a stone is based on the four 'C's: Colour, Clarity, Cut and Carat (1 carat = 200 mg).

There may be some good gem deals to be had in both Pailin and Battambang (around the central market area) if you know what you are doing. Watch out for artificially coloured gems (bright blues and reds are a tell-tale sign).

---

thing apart and carry it past the oncoming "train." These vehicles do work as an official means of public transport carrying local villagers, young and old, women and men, who share the limited space with a smattering of farm animals and foreign tourists. Moto and tuk-tuk drivers will take you to Ban Odomboing where several bamboo train operators gather from whom you can rent your own private "train" for about US$10 a return trip to a nearby village. It's certainly a fun ride bumping along through rural Cambodia and this is a highly recommended trip. The **Bamboo Train Café** (see Eating, page 160) was offering a tuk-tuk and train ride package for about US$15 per tuk-tuk.

Kamping Poy ① *36 km west of Battambang; take a motorbike; many moto drivers will include it on a day trip of the area, US$6,* is the site of a lake and dam (spanning 8 km) which was built by the prisoners of the Khmer Rouge. Half of Battambang Province's population were involved in its construction and thousands are said to have perished. On weekdays this is a peaceful area where people go to swim and fish – and the horrors of its construction lie lost beneath the still waters. However, in a poignant twist, at the weekend it turns into a massive water playground and picnic area for the local population. The army, who help with its upkeep, dish out rubber rings to both adults and children.

Phnom Sampeu is 20 km southwest from town on Route 10 and 10 km from Kamping Poy, along a very poor road. The mountain is the site of some mass graves where victims of the Khmer Rouge were killed and dumped. There are two caves on site. The first one,

Lang La'Coun (meaning **Punishment Cave**), was used as a torture ground during the Khmer Rouge days where people were beaten to death with sticks, stabbed or electrocuted. The second cave is much larger and houses a reclining Buddha (built in 1998). Many prisoners who were killed were thrown down the cave's 15-m-deep hole. A memorial holding some of the victims' remnants has been created. On the moutainside are two old government guns and some bunkers (which were supplied by the Russians). The guns are facing the former Khmer Rouge-controlled **Crocodile Mountain**, named due to its bizarre crocodile-like shape. The site was a major outpost during the war and much cross-fire took place between the two mountains. At the top of the mountain is a tiny wat which was used as a prison during the Khmer Rouge era. Another wat was built in 2002 to promote a newer, more positive future. The new wat deviates from traditional style and has eight doors instead of the usual three or four. The eight doors symbolize the eight directions forward, all peaceful and positive. It is paradoxical that the mountain, with such a horrific history, is so serene and stunning today.

Phnom Banon (entry US$2), a mountain with a 10th-century temple at the top, is also worth a visit. The 80-m-high mountain, 25 km out of Battambang, is a 359-step hike to the top. The temple is believed to have been built by Suryavarman II and completed by Jayavarman VII and perhaps not surprisingly has an Angkorian feel with five prominent towers peeking above the roof line. Like most other temples of this era, many of the apsaras have been removed by looters. On the other side of the mountain is **L'Ang But Meas Cave**, where locals believe Holy Waters are stored. The small, dark entrance leads into a large cave where a large jar is kept – at the last time of visiting a local man had wired up some lights into the cave and was charging a 2000 riel entry. Don't grumble too much as he is impoverished and will also guide you into the cave. At the bottom of the mountain is a 150-year-old pagoda which is still in use today.

Pailin → See listings, pages 157-164.

Pailin lies just 24 km from the Thai border on the edge of the Cardamom Mountain Range (Phnom Kravanh in Khmer). On the surface, Pailin belies its recent bloody history as it looks like any other town. The mountains surrounding the town and dust hanging in the air give this town an almost mystical feel (despite the serious lack of mysticism), especially from the higher ground of Wat Phnom Yaat. The roads around the town are in quite poor condition – dusty and potholed, so expect a bumpy ride if you came from either the border or Battambang. Gem shops line its quiet streets, which can almost feel like a ghost town by day. It livens up at night when the populace come out to eat and drink. The town itself contains a peculiar mixture of citizens: gem dealers are in abundance, prostitutes are on the high side, there is a fair sprinkling of former Khmer Rouge, as well as the odd genocidal mass murderer. Because of its proximity to the border most prices are quoted in Thai baht and the exchange rate from riel to US dollar is generally below the norm.

Sights

Beautiful **Wat Phnom Yaat** marks the entrance to the town. The temple is steeped in legend as it is renowned around the area and afar to bring good luck. During the war people would come here to pray to Madame Yaat (the patron and former nun in residence) for their lives to be spared. A brightly painted staircase flanked by two many-headed nagas leads up to a pagoda, temple and the monks' quarters. In the late afternoon, music rings out from the mountain top as a small band of local musicians meet for rehearsal. There are scenes from

Scam central

Besides being known as a casino-filled frontier town, Poipet has become eponymous with the words 'tourist scam'. The ploys are usually pretty wily and at times can be very convincing. Don't be fooled (although sometimes it's unavoidable).

Overpriced bus tickets from Bangkok Private bus companies and travel agents in Bangkok (particularly around Khao San Road) routinely sell tickets to Poipet for nothing short of exorbitant prices. Not only are they seriously overcharging, but the trip can take up to double the normal travel time, sometimes 12 hours. Another drawback with using these companies is that they have been known to take tourists to other border crossings, such as Pailin, which, believe it or not, is a much more difficult crossing and is a lot further away from Siem Reap. Avoid going with private bus companies from Bangkok. Public buses leave every half hour or so from Bangkok's Northern Bus Terminal (Morchit), ฿180-200. The trip takes approximately five hours and is a quarter of the price.

Bad exchange rate scam Upon arriving at Poipet many tourists are told US currency is no longer accepted and that a kindly money changer/gift shop/restaurant will exchange all your cash to riel/baht. The con artists are crafty and appear as if they are saving you trouble, suggesting the king has outlawed the US dollar or that the exchange rate in Siem Reap is weak. People have been known to lose up to 30% of their money through the dodgy exchange rate offered in Poipet. The US dollar is still widely used in Cambodia, so don't be duped. Traveller's cheques can be cashed in Phnom Penh and Siem Reap. Baht is widely used in Thai border areas and riel is good for smaller transactions.

Corrupt border officials More often than not border officials will overcharge on visas. It could be that they want to see proof of your medical insurance/vaccinations/SARS form, charging a fee when the relevant paperwork can't be provided. Or it could be blatant, outright corruption where they simply overcharge on the visa price or exit stamp (which should be free). Some people suggest obtaining your visa in Bangkok (but more often than not they will still find a hidden charge somewhere). Keep your cool. Try asking for a receipt. Others have suggested feigning a phone call to an embassy/tourist office has helped. The normal border fee should not be more than US$25/฿1000.

---

both Hindu mythology and Buddha's life depicted on the walls.

At the bottom of the hill is another important wat which dates back 570 years. The entrance gate is inscribed with Burmese characters (evidence of early Burmese colonists in this area). There is a rendition of the Churning of the Sea, in red stone along the perimeter wall.

There are some small waterfalls about 8 km from town. Most notable of these is the **Phnom Khieu (Blue Mountain) Waterfall** ① *the route is difficult as it follows dirt tracks and means entering an area which is sensitive militarily, so it is advisable to take a moto and, more importantly, a guide, US$10-15 per person*, which tumbles down several levels. The waterfall is 4-5 km into the jungle and up the mountain along a narrow winding path. Most of the obviously dangerous animals in the jungle have been hunted to oblivion but snakes, including cobras, are common. There are also landmines laid close to the path –

Touts Most tourists will encounter a flock of hassling touts offering every service from carrying your bags through to helping you get your visa. Their assistance is completely unnecessary as all aspects can be handled by yourself and it is highly likely that they will charge you a fee or load your bags into their friend's truck, where you will be charged an excessive fee.

Taxi and pick-up scams Taxis and pick-ups routinely overcharge for the trip from Poipet to Siem Reap (it should be ฿1000 for the full car or ฿250 per person). It is best to find some fellow travellers going in the same direction, as you will have more bargaining power in a group. If you are paying full fare for the taxi, don't let them sneak anyone else in without your knowledge. Both taxi and pick-up drivers have been known to ask for payment (usually half) beforehand and then stop half-way, refusing to go any further until you pay them a new, inflated fare. To avoid this don't pay a cent until you have arrived at your destination, regardless of their protests. If you are travelling by pick-up you will need to change vehicles at Sisophon so only pay for the trip to Sisophon, around ฿30-60. You will need to negotiate the next leg once you hit Sisophon (Sisophon to Siem Reap ฿50-200, depending on where you are sitting in the vehicle). Try not to separate yourself from your bags, either by taxi or pick-up, as theft is common (particularly if your bags are in the back of a pick-up).

Guesthouse scam Most drivers will have pretty set ideas about where they want you to stay in Siem Reap – usually the place that pays them the highest commission. They have been known to stall the trip to Siem Reap so tourists arrive in Siem Reap late and disorientated and will stay at their selected place without debate. Many will try to tell you that the guesthouse you wish to stay at is 'full', or 'closed' or 'dangerous'. Taxis have been known to drop people at guesthouses and when those concerned have decided that they wish to move elsewhere, the guesthouse proprietors have seized their luggage. Select a guesthouse/hotel from the guide and inform your driver you have a booking at a certain guesthouse already – this they can't dispute.

Note that these scams aren't exclusive to Poipet – they are also known to occur around O'Smach, Pailin and Koh Kong. It would be very unlucky to encounter every one of these scams in a single trip and for the most part the Bangkok to Siem Reap trip is a breeze.

hence the need for a guide. Whilst this may be enough to keep most people away, the birds, the clear, cooling pools at the foot of each fall, and the surrounding unspoilt forest makes this an adventure not to be missed. The drive into the mountains is spectacular. You can tour the countryside by yourself, but stick to the main roads. Thailand is a 24-km drive from town, but note that the border is not a legal crossing point for westerners. As at Poipet, there is a casino, called **Caesar International Casino**, on the border.

Sisophon and around → *See listings, pages 157-164.*

Sisophon lies at the junction of Route 5 to Phnom Penh, Route 6 up to Siem Reap, the road north into the Dangrek Mountains and the pot-holed highway to Poipet and Thailand. Formerly part of Battambang Province, Sisophon is now the provincial capital of Banteay

Meanchey Province. There are a handful of temples – two are very pleasant and are built next to lakes – some parks, a sleepy market, and a couple of comfortable and well-equipped hotels. Sisophon's former role as a stopover on the route from Siem Reap to Thailand has now been massively diminished due to the quality of the new road linking Poipet and Siem Reap. Unless you're visiting the local sights there is now no need to stop here.

Sights

Sisophon is small enough to explore on foot, although there are plenty of moto drivers willing to persuade you otherwise! There are two parks in town; both are on the main road that runs from Siem Reap to Poipet. The larger and scruffier one has a small **pavilion**, and comes alive at night with food vendors, lights, music and dancing. **Thien Po Park** alongside has well-tended lawns and shrubs, an elephant fountain and a plethora of benches and swings inside. However, the gate always seems to be locked and the park is deserted.

Around Sisophon

There is a temple complex at **Banteay Chhmar** ① *61 km north of Sisophon on Route 69, a moto should cost around US$6 round trip.* Banteay Chhmar was one of the capitals of Jayavarman II. It was rebuilt by Jayavarman VII and dedicated to his sons and four generals who were killed in battle repelling a Cham invasion in 1177. Banteay Chhmar, because of its secluded location, is rarely visited. This remoteness has made the temple particularly vulnerable to looting and in July 1994 valuable 12th-century carvings were stolen from the site. Local officials say that Cambodian army units were involved in the looting using trucks to pull statues from their pedestals and then transport them the short 30-minute journey across the Thai border for sale. In 1998, the plunder of Banteay Chhmar reached a new peak with the boldest and best organized temple robbery of recent times. More than 500 sq ft of bas-relief was hacked off and discovered in a fleet of trucks en route for Thailand. The Cambodian army was, once again, implicated in the vandalism and theft.

Poipet → See listings, pages 157-164.

Poipet is not a good introduction to Cambodia. To say the place is an unattractive town is a major understatement. The dusty streets are pockmarked by casinos, brothels, massage parlours, karaoke bars and all with an overriding sewer stench. To make matters worse, more than Cambodia's fair share of corrupt officials, hustlers, thieves, pimps, scamming touts, beggars, gamblers and prostitutes have chosen this mini hell as their haven. Scratch below the surface and the town's folk are as nice as anywhere else and Poipet isn't particularly dangerous for those passing through. Just keep your eye on the scammers (see box, page 154). The best thing that has ever happened to Poipet is the recent completion of the Thai-built road to Siem Reap – journey times between the two have been cut to around just two hours. This means, of course, there is no need to spend any more than a few minutes in Poipet. The town is hoping to become the Las Vegas of Cambodia – they have even erected a sign declaring a street Las Vegas Boulevard. Not quite there yet, but casinos continue to crop up to satisfy the never-ending supply of Thais willing to cross the border to win or lose their fortunes (gambling is illegal in Thailand). One of the more bizarre sights in Poipet is the gathering of various casinos located in no man's land between the two immigration posts. Built mostly by Thai companies predominately for Thais they feature blackjack, roulette, standard casino games, an array of fruit machines and restaurants.

For Sleeping and Eating price codes and other relevant information, see Essentials pages 22-23.

⊜ Sleeping

Kompong Chhnang *p146, map p147*

D-F Asia Hotel, next door to **Sovann Phum Hotel**, T012-405010. This well-run friendly, quirky hotel hosts the usual smattering of spotless fan and a/c rooms complete with cable TV, hot water and en suite bathrooms.
D-F Sovann Phum Hotel, Route 5, just south of Victory Monument, T011-886572. Variety of spotless fan and a/c rooms in this recently built hotel. There's free Wi-Fi, cable TV, en suite hot water facilities throughout and a central location. Attached restaurant (see Eating) offers decent food too. Friendly.
E-F Samrongsen, setback from road on way to lake, T011-975609. Largish, hotel complex set in quiet grounds. The airy upstairs rooms come complete with nice veranda areas. Rooms are a/c, all with hot water and ensuite facilities and cable TV.
E-G Sokha Guesthouse, T026-988622. A 2-storey white house down a leafy lane in a peaceful location – a 5- to 10-min walk from the centre of town and 3 km from the lake. Reopened in 1997 and popular with NGO staff with large garden with swings and benches, basic rooms with fan only but clean (some have attached and some shared bathroom).
F-G Holiday Guesthouse, on the road to Phnom Penh, T012 508732. Basic rooms though a little run down – a long way out of the town centre though. Friendly owner, if you can find them.

Pursat *p148*

D-F Khsach Meas, before bridge on main road, T092-379783. Decent enough choice with friendly staff and clean en suite fan and a/c rooms complete with TVs.
D-F Pursat Century Hotel, 239A Route 5 (opposite Sokimex petrol station), T017-286281. Biggest and newest hotel in town

this friendly place has everything from flat-screen TVs in the VIP suite through to free Wi-Fi and choice of fan and a/c throughout. Good value.
E-F Phnom Pich Guest- house, on Rd 1, near the bridge, T052-951515. The staff are exceptionally friendly, the rooms are clean with TV, big bathroom and a/c or fan. Great restaurant attached. Nice views of the river.
E-F Tounsour Hotel, on Rd 2, off Route 5, behind the sculptural school, T052-951506. Clean, some well-sized and some small rooms all in a wooden structure with hot water, fan, a/c and TV. Despite the kitsch 1970s feel to this place the lobby has some very impressive wooden carved apsaras. Motorbike hire US$5 a day.
E-F Vimean Tip Guest- house, on Rd 3, just off Highway 5, T012-836052. Slightly worn out rooms that include a large bath and granite basin. The staff are a bit of a bungling bunch but nice enough. A/c and fan rooms available.

Battambang *p149, map p150*

There is quite a lot of accommodation in town with 1 or 2 guesthouses overlooking the river. The quality of this accommodation has also improved and some excellent places have opened up recently.
A-B La Villa, riverfront, T012-991801, www.lavilla-battambang.com. Wonderfully restored art deco colonial villa. There are only 6 rooms here so you'll need to book in advance if you want a room in this groovy little hotel. All rooms have bathroom, and a/c or fan. Restaurant and bar attached. Great place to sup evening cocktails.
A-C Stung Sangke Hotel, just by new stone bridge on Route 5 in town centre, T053-953495, www.stungsangkehotel.com. Opening in late 2008 this is Battambang's 1st real business-class hotel, with all the trimmings of pool, fitness suite, good service that you'd expect. All rooms are a/c with minibar, TV and en suite hot-water facilities. There's a café, free Wi-Fi in the lobby and

prices can be haggled down during quieter times. Outside guests can also use the pool and fitness centre for US$5 a day. Breakfast is included.

A-D Khemara Battambang, St 515, north of town centre, T053-737878, www.khemarahotel.com. This is a massive almost resort-style complex located on the northern fringes of Battambang complete with pool, restaurants, marble flooring and friendly vibe. The en suite rooms are comfy – if a little dated – with a/c, hot water and breakfast included in the rate. Outside guests can use the pool for US$3 a day plus they rent bicycles to guests for US$4 per day.

B-C Ma Maison, 169 Lor et Village, on road on east side of river about 2 km from town centre, T011-876322. This gorgeous 2-room lovingly restored French colonial era villa set in its own private grounds in a quiet part of Battambang has to be one of the nicest places to stay in Cambodia. Beautiful tiling, 4-poster beds, yummy breakfast and dinner made to order. There's Wi-Fi, an iPod player, ensuite bathrooms and a very friendly welcome at this community-run project that is linked to **Colors & Tents** (see below). If you're going to splurge anywhere do it here. Highly recommended.

D-E President Hotel (no address, see map), T053-952456, www.presidentbattambang city.com. Big brand-new, garish hotel set back about 300 m from the eastern side of the river. Rooms are clean and well appointed, all with a/c, free Wi-Fi, en suite facilities with the more expensive options have flat-screen TVs. There's an extrernal glass elevator which has great views of next door's crocodile farm.

D-F Spring Park Hotel, Rom Chek 4, T053-730999. Quiet, well-run hotel in a good spot just over the river from the town centre. All rooms come with bathtubs, fridge and cable TV and there's a choice of fan and a/c.

D-F Star Hotel, near the taxi stand, T012-894862, www.asrhotel.com. Clean and well-appointed fan and a/c rooms, all with TV and en suite. Can be a bit noisy but a good location for the centre of town.

D-G Royal, T016-912034, royal_asiahotelbb @hotmail.com. What sets this hotel apart from the others in this price range is the small rooftop terrace with restaurant where you can enjoy the sunset and panoramic views of the outlying countryside. The 42 rooms, all of which have attached bathrooms, are clean with a/c and fan. At the ferry port and bus terminal a representative from the hotel will usually meet you. Recommended.

E Golden Land Hotel, east side of river in town centre, T077-993277. Ask for a room overlooking the river and you'll land yourself a real bargain in this friendly new, clean and well appointed hotel. TVs, hot water, fridge and a/c are in each room. Recommended.

E-F Bus Stop Guesthouse, 149, Rd 2, T053-730544, www.busstopcambodia.com. Western-run guesthouse in the centre of town with spotless fan or a/c rooms, cable TV and private bathrooms. Wi-Fi and breakfast also available.

E-F Colors & Tents, 32 Lor et Village, on road on east side of river about 1.5 km from town centre, T011-876344, www.colorsof battambang.hi5.com. Funky little guesthouse set in own garden a little bit before **Ma Maison** (see above)– each room is themed with different colours – Voodoo Red, Black and White, Ocean Blue, etc – and comes with en suite facilities and Wi-Fi. There's a small bar area and a very friendly vibe. Part of a community-run tourist project – they also rent out tents if you're on a lower budget.

E-F Park Hotel, Rattanak Village (on the east side of the river), T053-953773. Very clean, with good amenities and friendly staff. Rooms include TV, wardrobe, fan and hot water. A/c available.

E-F Seng Hout, 1008B, Rd 2, T053-952900. One of the best mid-range options the rooms here come with fan or a/c, TV and hot water. The ones on the upperfloors lead out onto huge roof terraces give great views of the city. There's Wi-Fi, a quiet but central locaction and a very friendly welcome as well. Recommended.

E-G Asia Hotel, St Lar A, T053-953523, www.asrhotel.com. Sister hotel to **Royal**.

Everything from cheap, fan rooms with cold water showers to pretty plush affairs with a/c and TV. Popular with tour groups. Good location and there's Wi-Fi on the ground floor.

F-G Chhaya Hotel,118 Rd 3, T012-733204. This large, older-style hotel, situated just off the market, is popular with travellers. The fan and a/c rooms are clean with attached bathrooms and Western toilets. Lots of tourist services available.

Pailin p153

In Pailin there isn't a great selection of hotels to choose from, most of them rate somewhere between horrendous and average.

F-G Kim Young Heng Guesthouse, near truck station on the road into town, T016-727343. A film of dust covers the rooms and it is a bit noisy but is better than some of the other alternatives. TV, fan and attached bathroom.

G Ponleu Pich Pailin, near the market, next to **Lao Lao Keng Guesthouse**. Very friendly owner. Clean rooms with fan and bathroom. Attached bathrooms.

Sisophon p155

There are several spots to stay in Sisophon but most of them are quite dubious. With the new road to Siem Reap now providing a quick exit few people stay here. There are however, a couple of decent places should you decide to rest up

D Bambous 215, St 5, T012-313259, www.bambous-sur-pieds.com. Excellent little homestay-style guesthouse with 3 lovely rooms, each kitted out in an engaging "bamboo" style. The people who run this place are very friendly and you can arrange tours and buy bus tickets here. There's cable TV, cute veranda and breakfast and dinner available for a small extra charge. Highly recommended.

D Botoum Hotel, on road to Poipet almost opposite the provincial hall, T097-886 9868. Friendly, eccentric hotel with clean rooms complete with cable TV and hot water/ en suite facilities. The upstairs rooms also have balconies. There's a small coffee shop and restaurant attached.

Poipet p156

An overnight stop in Poipet is not advised and should not be necessary – you can easily reach Bangkok or Siem Reap from here.

B-D Grand Diamond City Hotel, in the casino area. Dodgy but cleanish modern rooms with all facilities. Patrons can be noisy.

D Holiday Palace Casino, in the casino area. Although the room rate is ฿1000 guests are given ฿400 worth of non-redeemable vouchers which can be used for gambling. The rooms are of a better standard here and reasonably well-equipped.

F Poypad Phnom Pich Guesthouse, on the main road up from immigration. Red tiled throughout, clean but small rooms with basic facilities and attached bathroom. A lack of windows in some rooms make the place a little gloomy. Family run. For ฿350 you can get a room with a/c and TV.

F-G Poipet Pass Guesthouse. Reasonably good value as most rooms have fridge, attached bathroom and TV. A few extra dollars gets you hot water. The on-premises karaoke can be a bit grating.

G Bayon Guesthouse, is a basic guesthouse offering good, clean rooms, with fan, windows (a big plus compared to other places) and bathroom. One of the best restaurants in town, the **Hang Neak Restaurant**, is on the premises.

🍴 Eating

Kompong Chhnang p146, map p147
Considering the number of guesthouses in town, there aren't an awful lot of restaurants that cater for tourists. At the time of writing a new **Sarmarkey Restaurant** was under construction slightly up and across from the Victory Monument. It is possible to get spring rolls and other snacks down by the river.

🍴 **Metapheap Restaurant**, on the corner opposite the Victory Monument. English menu, but little English is spoken. Chinese and Khmer dishes with an emphasis on soup, bit pricey.

♦ **Sovann Phum**. Open 0600-2200. Attached to the hotel of the same name (see Sleeping) this welcoming and affordable restaurant offers a huge range of Khmer and Western food.

♦ **Soksen Restaurant**, on the corner beside the Sokimex Petrol Station. The name and menu are all in Khmer and the staff speak no English, so it can be tricky. But they do very good, cheap Khmer food, ie noodles and vegetables. Best bet is to point at what another customer is having.

Pursat *p148*

The market on the west side has food stalls where it is possible to pick up a tasty meal or snack and there are various restaurants along the main road. Also a number of *tikalok* (fruit shakes) vendors.

♦♦♦ **Magic Fish/Tepmachha Restaurant**, located on the riverbank about 1.5 km from the bridge, T012-832309. Open 1000-2100. Variety of Khmer dishes including plenty of eel from the local river. Great breezy riverside setting and popular with locals.

♦ **Borei Thmei Restaurant**, on the corner of Rd 4 and Route 5, T012-838332. Good little Khmer restaurant offering all the staples, fried fish, etc. Most dishes come in under US$1.50.

♦ **Lamb Sewing**, on Route 5 as you come in from Phnom Penh. Beer garden atmosphere with little thatched huts in a garden setting. Fantastic selection of Khmer food, though one must watch the beer girls hovering. The jovial, old one-legged owner is very accommodating.

♦ **Phnom Pich**. Part of the hotel (see Sleeping) you'll find simple rice and noodle dishes served here from 0600-2200 plus coffees and breakfasts.

Battambang *p149, map p150*

The best place to start is around the market where a number of stalls and small restaurants are open during the day and evening. Many have pans with ready cooked dishes. Just point to what you want. Rice, meat and vegetables costs US$0.50-0.80.

♦♦ **Madison Corner**, St 3, couple of streets down from the market. Open 0900-0100. Friendly and tasty small café/diner/bar, selling Khmer food, burgers, ice cream, pancakes and beer. Also screens videos. Perfect hang-out for wasted backpackers.

♦♦ **Pkay Proek**, St 3, west of Battambang Ct, T012- 571579. Large restaurant (with further extensions planned) offering a range of Cambodian, Chinese and Thai dishes. Considered the best Khmer food in town. Beer garden. Somewhat of a Khmer franchise, restaurants of the same name can be found in Phnom Penh, Pailin, Poipet and Banteay Meanchey.

♦♦ **Riverside Balcony Bar**, located just down from the Governor's Residence where the road turns off for Pailin, this attractive wooden terraced bar, overlooks the river and is the best place to go if the ebb and flow of river life, particularly as dusk descends, is your idea of entertainment. Open from 1800, the comfortable bar is lit up by fairy lights. The menu is predominantly American and Mexican. Good value. Highly atmospheric. Recommended.

♦♦ **Sunrise Coffeehouse**, slightly down from the Royal Hotel. Attempt at a French-style bakery serving falls a bit flat in this foreign-owned NGO hang out.

♦♦♦ **Bamboo Train Café**, just over Hinsen Bridge (see map). Open 0700-2200.You can find ok Khmer and Western food here but there is a free pool table, cocktails and draught beer as well. Plus they run tuk tuks to the real bamboo train.

♦♦♦ **City Cafe**, just before Stung Sangke Hotel on Route 5, 0600-2200. Great combination of Wi-Fi, ice cream and very affordable Khmer food in this clean, new and stylish little spot. Cake and decent coffee are good too. Recommended.

♦♦♦ **Espresso Coffee**, next to Royal Hotel. Open 0600-2200. Excellent fresh coffee, some Western snacks and great, basic Khmer food. Cheap, friendly and Khmer-owned. Recommended.

ᵀᵀ-ᵀ Mariyan Pizza House, next door to **Bamboo Train Café**. Open 0700-2100. Small Khmer-themed pizzas here plus shakes and some Asian food. You get to sit in small, private, open booths set around a courtyard on either the floor or at tables.

ᵀᵀ-ᵀ Tho Ny, just opposite **Bamboo Train Café**, 0600-2100. Simple Khmer dishes and good coffee in this brand-new a/c spot.

ᵀᵀ-ᵀ White Rose is just up from the **Angkor Hotel**. It specializes in great fruit shakes (US$0.50- 0.60) but also has an extensive selection of dishes (predominantly Cambodian and Thai), 1 or 2 words of English spoken but for non-speakers of Khmer the best option is look and point.

Pailin *p153*

There are lots of cheap stalls and restaurants in the market area which are good for breakfast noodles and cool drinks. If you are in search of a quiet beer in the evening, head for the bottom of the hill on the road into town. Here there are numerous thatched drinking huts where you can perch on a stool.

ᵀᵀ Bamboo Restaurant, on the main road towards the Thai border, T012-405818. Quite atmospheric with open salas and romantically lit gardens. Good selection of fish dishes, slightly on the pricey side. Over zealous beer girls. Also a popular drinking hole.

ᵀᵀ Reksmei Phnom Yat Restaurant. The owner of this place clearly couldn't decide whether to open a restaurant or a furniture shop specializing in teak products. The house speciality is the local smoked fish and the owners are planning to expand their rooftop empire.

ᵀᵀ-ᵀ Phkay Phreauk Restaurant, on Highway 10, towards the pagoda. This restaurant's brilliant food and extensive menu has easily made it the best restaurant in town. Very reasonable prices.

Sisophon *p155*

There really isn't a brilliant selection of restaurants in town. Surprisingly, eating at the street stalls is probably the best option, as the kids are extraordinarily bright and the food and service is usually nothing short of exceptional. At night the main park is packed with food vendors selling sweet desserts, sour wine, noodles, soup and rice. There is also a line of food and shake stalls lining the south and west side of Thien Po Park.

ᵀᵀ-ᵀ Peng Hour, just behind the market and is hard to miss as it is lit up by flashing lights. Little Chinese restaurant-cum-coffee shop. English menu offering noodles, stir fries and other Sino-Khmer meals. Unexciting and expensive dishes.

Poipet *p156*

There are plenty of noodle soup stalls around and inside the market. The restaurant at the **Bayon Guesthouse** is very popular and extremely good value.

ᵀᵀ Srah Trocheck, on the main road. A favourite, serving very good Khmer and Thai food.

⊕ Entertainment

Battambang *p149, map p150*
Phare Ponleu Selpak circus. This French-run circus training project is worth a visit. The circus is an initiative by a number of NGOs and organizations to provide opportunities for disabled children and those coming from underprivileged backgrounds. Starting at 2000, the circus includes trapeze artists, mono-cyclists, jugglers, clowns and scores of other entertaining acts. The circus is located 3 km out of town and runs infrequently (dependent on numbers) so it is best to check beforehand with **Asian Trails**, No 111 E1, St 2, T053-73008, asiantrails@online.com.kh.

○ Shopping

Pursat *p148*
Aside from the local market which stocks most products, Pursat is famous for its marble carvings. There is a marble carving workshop in the centre of town.

Battambang *p149, map p150*

A range of shops selling local souvenirs can be found along Street 1 on the riverfront.

The **Central Market**, Phsar Nath, sells clothes, film and gems. Around its precinct there are several film shops.

Near Pailin is one of the central gem-mining areas in Cambodia so there are many gem dealers sprinkled around Battambang. There are some exceptionally good deals as well as some outright scams (heated stones, glass, etc). Most of the gemmologists can be found around the Central Market area.

Danine mini-mart behind the **Chaya Hotel** stocks a wide range of foreign foodstuffs and other goods.

Pailin *p153*

The local market is stocked with a good variety of supplies due to the town's proximity to Thailand. Prices are usually quoted in baht. The signature trade business of Pailin is gems and there are a multitude of places where you can buy them around town, usually sapphires and rubies, though other precious and semi precious stones are in abundance. Watch out for artificially coloured gems – mostly through intensive heating (bright blues and reds are a tell-tale sign).

▲ Activities and tours

Battambang *p149, map p150*

Intrepid, Rd 2, www.intrepidtravel.com, and **Asian Trails**, T053-730088, www.asiantrails.travel, run tours of the region. There is no shortage of well-briefed moto-dop drivers who speak good English. They usually hang around the **Royal Hotel** and **Chaya Hotel**. The standard tour includes a trip to some outlying villages, a trip to Phnom Sampeu and Wat Banon and a short ride on the Bamboo Train back to town again. Allocate a day for the tour and expect to pay US$6-8.

Mr Pou, T012 895442, is possibly one of the best guides in the country and arranges explorations around the circuit for US$7 a day.

Therapies

Seeing Hands Massage, 10 m down from the corner of St 3. Massage is US$4 for 1½ hrs.

⊖ Transport

Kompong Chhnang *p146, map p147*
Boat

The boat between Phnom Penh and Siem Reap will stop in Kompong Chhnang sometimes if you request. Catching it from Kompong Chhnang is quite tricky. Climb down the bank opposite the **Rithisen Hotel** to the police jetty. When you can see the boat (boat to **Siem Reap** is around 0830), hop onto a nearby craft, US$0.50-1, to take you into the middle of the lake. The fast boat should then stop, allowing you to board – but not always! The fee is usually the same as the whole journey (Phnom Penh–Siem Reap) ie US$35. Buy your ticket on board the boat; don't, despite their protests, pay your money to the marine policemen on the jetty.

Bus/pickup/taxi

Kompong Chhnang lies about 91 km from Phnom Penh and 201 km from Battambang along Route 5. The truck stop in Kompong Chhnang is opposite the Victory Monument. There is a bus station next to Sokimex Petrol Station and buses leave to **Phnom Penh**, invariably every hour (on the hour) from 0800-1600. Buses to **Battambang** can also be arranged here. Pick-up trucks from Phnom Penh onwards to **Pursat**, US$1.30, roughly 2½ hrs, and **Battambang**, US$2.60, 4-5 hrs, pass the roundabout by the petrol station at around 0800.

Pursat *p148*

Shared taxi and pick-ups ply the route from Phnom Penh to Battambang and beyond.

The nearest boat stop is Krakor, 35 km east. It is possible to get to Phnom Penh and to Siem Reap from here. A train departs on alternate days for the north travelling as far as **Battambang** (at around 1300, US$0.40), and for the south down to **Phnom Penh** (at 1100, US$0.80). The train is notoriously unreliable and slow.

GST Buses to **Phnom Penh** depart from Pursat Railway Station at 0630, 0830, 1245 (10,000 riel), 3 hrs. **Phnom Penh Public Transport Buses**, T023-210359, depart for Phnom Penh at 0645, 0730, 1230, 10,000 riel.

Battambang p149, map p150
Boat
River connections to **Siem Reap** daily from the pier just east of Route 5 river crossing. Departs at 0700, 3-4 hrs, US$15. In the dry season the boat can take up to 7 hrs, or longer, and includes a 1-hr trip in the back of a pick-up, when the river becomes too low. From the boat to any hotel a moto should cost US$1.

Bus/pickup/taxi
Bus transport is pretty rough but still reasonably cheap. **Neak Krorhorm Travel**, T023-219496, in Phnom Penh and **Phnom Penh Public Transport Company** run daily buses between Battambang and Phnom Penh (departure times vary but it is usually quite early in the morning).

Most guesthouses in Battambang sell tickets onwards to **Siem Reap** or **Phnom Penh** (12 hrs) or tickets can be bought directly from the **Capital Tour Bus Company** or **Neak Krorhorm Travel**, near the morning market. Buses depart for **Siem Reap**, US$5 at 0700, and **Phnom Penh**, US$4 at 0700, 0730, 0800, 0900, 1200 daily from Psar Nath. GST Buses, T012-895550, runs 3 trips a day each way, US$3 at 0630, 0830, 1245 and departs from Phnom Penh, St 142, near the Central Market. The buses depart from Battambang near Por Khnung Pagoda,

T012-414441, 5 hrs. **Phnom Penh Public Transport Buses**, T023-210359, depart from Battambang near Thmor Thmey Bridge. They depart 3 times a day to **Phnom Penh** at 0645, 0730, 1230, US$3.

Pick-ups and shared taxis depart from Boeung Choeuk Market, shared taxi US$7 per person to **Phnom Penh**, a 5-hr hard slog, **Sisophon**, US$4, and **Poipet**, US$6. Pick-ups to **Pailin** depart from Loeu Market at the western end of town, US$3. The roads are okay for about half the trip and horrible for the rest, so allow around 3 hrs for the trip from Battambang.

Train
At time of publication all rail travel in Cambodia had been suspended. This situation is likely to change. There is, however, a rail line to Phnom Penh should rail services resume.

Pailin p153
Bus/pickup/taxi
There is only 1 way into Pailin on the Cambodian side and that is the 83 km along Route 10 from Battambang. Pick-ups leave all day (0600-1600) from the bus station next to the market at **Battambang**, US$3 inside. It is also possible to organize a motodop to take you for the night for around US$30-40.

There is an **international border crossing** 20 km from Pailin, identifiable by the tell-tale casino-out-in-the-middle-of-nowhere. You will need to bring passport photographs with you as there is no photography processing facility here. From Pailin it is ฿50 per person in a shared taxi to the border which is around 20 km away. There are usually motos and taxis at the border crossing to take tourists at Pailin. From the Thai side it is a ฿20 motorbike ride to the *songthaew* station – which has *songthaews* to the nearest bus station at Chantaburi. It takes 1½ hrs to reach Chantaburi bus station and costs ฿35.

Sisophon p155

Bus

The trip between Sisophon and **Phnom Penh** takes 6 hrs. The buses depart from Sisophon Market bound for Phnom Penh, 18,000 riel at 0645, 0715, 0745. **Phnom Penh Public Transport Buses**, T023-210359, depart from Sisophon's central market, 0700, 20,000 riel.

To **Poipet**, 48 km, 40 mins: pick-ups can be caught on the main road near the park and Provincial Offices. To **Battambang**, 69 km, 2 hrs, leaves from the truck station, US$2 inside. There are also vehicles travelling the 360 km to **Phnom Penh** (9-12 hrs). Route 5 to Battambang is poor. To **Siem Reap**, 105 km, 75 mins, US$5 inside.

Poipet p156

To **Siem Reap**, 153 km, 90 mins to 2 hrs. Pick-ups converge on the Cambodian side of the border to collect passengers going to Siem Reap. Plenty of minibuses and taxis. Some hotels in Siem Reap will arrange pick-ups for a fee.

Border with Thailand The border crossing is open daily 0730-1700. The last bus from Aranya Prathet to Bangkok departs at 1700. The immigration officials at the Poipet border can be difficult.

⊙ Directory

Kompong Chhnang p146, map p147
Banks The Acleda Bank, Route 5, on the way to Phnom Penh (2 blocks past the Victory Monument). Mon-Fri 0800-1600. Western Union money transfer but no credit card advances or TC exchange. **Internet** You can find free Wi-Fi at the **Sovann Phum** hotel. **Telephone** Phone booths are scattered

around the town, particularly concentrated around the bus station (Sokimex Petrol Station) and Psar Leu.

Battambang p149, map p150
Banks Most of the banks exchange TCs and change money but are closed frequently. Several banks around town now have ATMs. Money-changers/goldsellers are concentrated around the market with a few along Rd 1. There are a number of banks in town but they are often shut so for simple exchange purposes the gold and gem shops are the best bet. **Internet** There are numerous internet cafés scattered around the market and along Rd 1 (River Rd) and Rd 3 (search around for the cheapest as the rates range from US$1-2). **Telephone** The post office provides international connections as do a few of the better hotels. Telephone booths are scattered all over the town and internet cafés now offer net calls for a very cheap rate.

Pailin p153
Banks Canadia Bank has an outlet on Highway 10 towards the pagoda. Mon-Fri 0800-1600 and Sat until 1200.

Sisophon p155
Bank Canadia Bank, one street south of the park. **Internet** There are a couple of internet cafés on the road running parallel to Thien Bo Park.

Poipet p156
Banks There is an Acleda bank in town, which will do Western Union transfers only. **Telephone** Interphone shops with IDD facility are dotted around the town (around US$1 per min). Code for interphones here is 037.

Contents

Footprint features

The Northeast

★ **Don't miss ...**
1 **Irrawaddy dolphins**, see page 170.
2 **Ethnic minority villages**, see pages 176 and 182.
3 **Yaek Lom**, see page 180.
4 **Say San River**, see page 181.

LAOS

Virachey
National Park

Eastern Highlands

Voen
Kham

Dom
Kralor

STUNG TRENG

Veng Xai

RATANAKIRI

O Chum

Ta Veng

13

Ban Lung

*Yaek Lom
Lake*

Bokeo

Stung Treng

19

Lumphat

MONDULKIRI

Boos Ra

KRATIE

Phnom
Santok

Sen Monorom

Kratie

Dak Dam

13

Potang

Mekong

Chhlong

Snuol

VIETNAM

Kompong
Cham

7

13

KOMPONG CHAM

N

PREY VANG

7

30 km

30 miles

A wild and rugged landscape, consisting of the three provinces of Ratanakiri, Mondulkiri and Stung Treng, greets any visitor to Cambodia's remote northeast region. Vast forested swathes of sparsely inhabited terrain spread north and eastwards toward Vietnam and Laos and are home to several distinct ethnic groups, notably the Tampuan, Jarai and Kreung. The thick jungles also provide sanctuary to the majority of Cambodia's few remaining tigers.

During the civil war, the Northeast was cut off from the rest of the country. Then came years of bad transport links, with only the most committed making the arduous run up from up Phnom Penh. Yet the Northeast, much like the rest of the country, is now developing. A brand new Chinese-built road, including an arcing road bridge over the river in Stung Treng, forms a strong link between Cambodia and Laos, cutting hours off the journey time. A tarmaced road is now under construction to Ratanakiri and guesthouses and traveller facilities are firmly asserting themselves throughout the region.

Framing its western edge, and cutting it off from the rest of the country, is the Mekong River. It bifurcates, meanders and braids its way through the country and represents in its width a yawning chasm and watery superhighway that connects the region with Phnom Penh. Stung Treng and Kratie are located on this mighty river and despite the lack of any kind of riverboat service are still becoming excellent places to view the elusive Irrawaddy River Dolphin.

The dust-blown and wild frontier town of Ban Lung, the capital of Ratanakiri, is slowly emerging as a centre of trekking and adventure travel while in Mondulkiri, Sen Monorom is a more elegant introduction to Cambodia's hinterland.

Background

Northeast Cambodia was, alas, unwittingly sucked into the Second Indochina War. The Ho Chi Minh Trail snaked south, concealed in remote passes and dense jungle. Viet Cong cadres, holed up in pockets on the border beyond the reach of foot patrols, attracted the deadly attention of US bombers. Aerial bombing left the Viet Cong largely unscathed but inflicted untold destruction and damage on the local population.

The region has a very primitive economic base, primarily it is shifting cultivation: clearings in the forest are often hewn using hand tools. These are cultivated with rice, corn, root crops and vegetables and, increasingly, a few cash crops such as cashews and coffee. In the 1960s the French attempted to establish rubber plantations here but there was never sufficient labour for them to be profitable. Today, wealth accumulates in the hands of a few influential politicians and businessmen as a result of gem mining and illegal logging. The remoteness of the area and the fact that vast tracts of land are controlled by the army make this ideal territory for illicit activities, far from the eyes of investigative journalists, but the swathes of cleared land cannot be concealed from the all-seeing eye of orbiting satellites. Nor can the huge volume of logging trucks rumbling down the roads to Vietnam be kept a secret for long, no matter how strenuously the two governments may try to deny such awkward facts. Having said this, the region is slowly undergoing huge improvements in infrastructure with roads being built and airstrips planned for re-opening. There is no doubt that this will be a game-changer for the Northeast with the all attendant positive and negative consequences that usually follow.

The ethnic minorities are evicted from their ancestral lands as companies coerce them into signing documents, which they do not understand, in exchange for a pittance. Governor of Ratanakiri, Kep Chutkema, lamented: "They will strip away all the trees … everything will be gone." And he should know – it was he who granted logging rights to three companies to export timber to Vietnam. Yet, predictably, it is the minorities who get the blame for deforestation.

Mekong Provinces

Kompong Cham, Kratie and Stung Treng make up the Mekong Provinces. Despite the Mekong River, its waterway and perpetual irrigation, these provinces are surprisingly economically unimportant and laid back. But with the new Chinese-built road now open and fully functioning – its easily one of the best in the country – the Northeast's provincial charms may soon be eradicated. ▶▶ *For listings, see pages 172-175.*

Kompong Cham and around → *For listings, see pages 172-175.*

Kompong Cham is the fourth largest town in Cambodia and is a town of some commercial prosperity owing to its thriving river port and also, it is said, as a result of preferential treatment received from local boy made good, the prime minister, Hun Sen. Town and province have a combined population of more than 1.5 million people.

There is nothing in or around Kompong Cham to detain the visitor for long, most merely pass through, en route for Stung Treng and the northeast, but it is a pleasant enough town to rest awhile. In common with a lot of riverside towns, it has retained a good deal of its **colonial shophouse architecture** and there are a couple of places of interest. **Wat Nokor** is a well preserved 11th-century monument several kilometres west of town off Route 7. At **Phnom Pros** and **Phnom Srei** ('Man and Woman Hill'), 5 km from town on highway Number 7, are the foundations of two early temples. The site reportedly gets its name from the legend of a competition between the town's men and women as to who could build the biggest hill (the women won). Here also are mass graves in which victims of the Khmer Rouge are buried. All three places can be visited in a couple of hours.

A short trip down the Tonle Tuok tributary is the **Maha Leap Pagoda**, a complex that survived the Khmer Rouge and has since been ascribed magical powers. The rare wooden pagoda features intricately adorned teak columns, a lovely pond and a modern concrete pagoda and reclining Buddha near the rear. Nearby is **Prey Chung Krap Weaving Village**, an epicentre for fine, detailed silk that has attracted the attention of many silk traders. The **Koh Pen Bamboo Bridge**, 10 minutes' walk down the river, is constructed every year during the low season and is worth a quick visit. Small villages and sandy beaches surround the area.

The small town of **Chhlong** ⓘ *get there by minibus, 4 hrs, US$5*, between Kompong Cham and Kratie is one of Cambodia's best kept secrets. The small town, nestled on the banks of the Mekong, 41 km from Kratie and 82 km from Kompong Cham, is one of the few places that survived the Khmer Rouge's ransacking and contains a multitude of crumbling French colonial buildings and traditional wooden Khmer houses. Of particular interest are the foundations of 120 antique houses and a 19th-century wooden Khmer house supported by 100 columns. Formerly a base for workers from surrounding rubber plantations, it is easy to feel nostalgic for a bygone era in Chhlong, with its wats and monasteries, an old school and charming market set in a colonial-style building. There's a couple of basic guesthouses on the riverfront road should you want to stop here for a night or two: E **Penh Chet**, T012-690354, with simple clean rooms, and E **Mekong Guesthouse**, T012-203896, which is a lovely old atmospheric wooden house although rooms are a bit dirty. There's also a small market with a few stalls selling noodle and rice dishes. At the time of going to press a new road linking Kompong Cham and Kratie, and passing just outside Chhlong, is near completion. This would not only shave about 90 minutes off the original journey time but could place Chhlong on a new travellers' route.

Kratie (pronounced 'Kratcheay') is a port town on the Mekong roughly halfway between Phnom Penh and Laos. In many ways it is a delightful place with a relaxed atmosphere and some good examples of shophouse architecture but there is a discernible nefarious undercurrent due to Kratie's reputation as a centre of organized crime and corruption. With the murky majesty of the Mekong dominating the town, sunset is a real highlight in Kratie, as the burning red sun descends slowly below the shore line. The central market sells most things and there are a couple of pharmacies in town.

Koh Trong Island, directly opposite Kratie town, has a lovely 8-km stretch of sandy dunes (in the dry season) where you can swim and relax. Aside from the beach, the island consists of small market farms and a simple, laid-back rural life – highly recommended for those who want to chill out. On the south side is a small Vietnamese floating village.

Kratie's main claim to some modicum of fame are the **Irrawaddy dolphins** ⓘ *go by moto, US$4-5 return, boats then cost US$9 per person or US$7 per person if there is 3 or more, at the official viewpoint (signposted on the left of the road)*, which inhabit this portion of the Mekong (Kampi Dolphin pool), 15 km north of the town on the road to Stung Treng. The best time to glimpse these rare and timid creatures is at sunrise or sunset when they are feeding. Verdant country-side surrounding the river provides romantic rural scenery with children on buffalos, cows munching haystacks, old men sorting out their fishing nets, lovers doubling on bicycles and people waving you through.

Kampi Rapids ⓘ *3 km north of Kampi Dolphin Pool, 1000 riel*, (also known as Kampi resort), provides a refreshing and picturesque area to take a dip in the clear Mekong waters (during the dry season). A bridge leads down to a series of scenic thatched huts which provide shelter for the swimmers.

Twenty-one kilometres further north of the Kampi pool is **Sambor**, a pre-Angkorian settlement, but today unfortunately not a single trace of this ancient heritage exists. The highpoint of a trip to Sambor is more in the getting there, as you pass through beautiful countryside, than in the temples themselves. Replacing the ancient ruins are two temples. The first and most impressive is the 100-column pagoda, rumoured to be the largest new pagoda in the country. It is a replica of the 100-column, wooden

Kratie

To Snuol & Stung Treng

To Koh Trong Island & Vietnamese Floating Village

Mekong

Ferry Port

Pagoda Wat

Taxis

Food Stalls

Hour Lean Bus Station

Phnom Penh Public Transport Co

Acleda

Street 5
Street 6
Street 7
Street 8
Street 9
Street 10
Street 11
Street 12

Preah Soramarit St

To Phnom Penh

N

Not to scale

Sleeping
Balcony Guesthouse 9
Heng Heng 6
Heng Heng II 7
Heng Oudom 2
Oudom Sambath 4
Riverside Guesthouse 5
Santhepheap 3
Star Guesthouse 1
You Hong Guesthouse 8

Eating
Mekong 2
Red Sun Falling 1

original, which was built in 1529. During the war, Pol Pot based himself out of the complex, killing hundreds of people and destroying the old pagoda. The new one was built in 1985 (perhaps the builders were slightly overzealous – it features 116 columns). Sitting 300 m behind the gigantic pagoda is a much smaller and arguably more interesting temple. The wat still contains many of its original features including a number of wooden pylons which date back 537 years. Originally built in 1648 by the king, the temple has received a number of facelifts benefiting its beautiful Buddhist murals. The paintings, which depict the birth and life of Buddha, are believed to be about 400 years old.

Stung Treng

Tonlé Sekong

To Stung Treng Women's Development Centre (5km)

River Rd
☐ Taxis

❹ ❹
@ ❿
❺ ❶ ❸ ❻
❺ ❷
Ⓜ ❼
@ ❶
❾ ☐ Kodak Shop

🚌

✉

To Kratie & Ban Lung

N

100 metres
100 yards

Sleeping 😴
Dara Guesthouse **6**
Gold River **3**
Ly Ly Guesthouse **7**
Ratana Sambath **5**
Riverside **1**
Sekong **4**
Sok Sambath **2**
Sok San **9**
Stung Treng Guesthouse **10**

Eating 🍴
Dara **3**
Prochum Tonle **4**
Sophakmukal **1**
Stung Treng Burger **2**
Sun Tha **5**

Stung Treng → *For listings, see pages 172-175.*
Yet another eponymous provincial capital set at the point where the Sekong River cuts away from the Mekong, Stung Treng is just 40 km from Laos and a stopping-off place on the overland route to Ratanakiri. The town still maintains a wild frontier feel despite losing much of its edge due to the building of the mammoth Chinese road and a striking bridge that has created good links to Laos (see Transport, page 175). Pigs, cows and the odd ox-cart still wander through the town's busy streets but there isn't a lot for tourists around Stung Treng. Tour guides can organize boat runs to a local river dolphin project, cycling trips along the river banks and excursions to some waterfalls, making it a friendlier alternative to Kratie. **Lbak Khone**, the 26 km rocky area that the Mekong rapids flow through en route to the Laos border, is one of the country's most stunning areas.

The **Stung Treng Women's Development Centre** on Street 1 is 1 km from Stung Treng Airport. It is a local NGO helping to train women in a variety of skills. They make some beautiful silk and welcome visitors. Some tour operators can also organize a trip to Siem Pang, where you can travel through to Virachey National Park, see page 182.

For Sleeping and Eating price codes and other relevant information, see Essentials pages 22-23.

● Sleeping

Kompong Cham and around *p169*

D-E Monorom 2 VIP Hotel, Mort Tunle St, waterfront, T092-777102, www.monorom viphotel.com. With a perfect Mekong setting this brand new hotel is easily the best in town. Get a room at the front and you'll have a balcony overlooking the river; each comes with bathtub, hot water, cable TV, tea-making facilities and there's free Wi-Fi/internet for guests on the ground floor. Recommended.

D-G Leap Viraksar, big yellow building on right just before bridge on way to Kratie, T042-633 7778. Range of rooms from grim-looking fan rooms through to accommodation replete with a/c, TV and bathtubs. Friendly, and mini-mart attached.

E Mekong, T042-941536. This long-established hotel was undergoing renovations at the time of writing and may re-open later in 2010 or 2011.

E Pounleau Ramsey, T042-941324, pounleaurasmey@yahoo.com. Good central location near the market area. Rooms have a/c, fan and attached bathroom. Not the most helpful staff.

E Rana, T012-696340. Set in a small village just outside Kampong Cham, this is a well-run and engaging homestay programme run by Kheang and her American husband, Don. Set up more for educational purposes than as a business you can get a real insight into rural life here. Rates include full-board but accommodation is basic. They offer free moto pick up from Kampong Cham if you book for 2 or more nights. Recommended.

F-G Kim Srun Guesthouse, on the river road, T042-941507. Scantily decorated, cell-like rooms but clean nonetheless. Separate bathrooms with squat toilet. Foyer eerily decorated with a gamut of wooden-carved moose-heads. Good views from communal balcony. Small family hotel.

Kratie *p170, map p170*

E Santepheap, on the river road, T072-971537. Rooms are adequate in this reasonable hotel. It has a quiet atmosphere and the clean and airy rooms come with attached bathrooms, fridge, fan or a/c.

E-F Heng Heng Hotel II, 2 shops up from the original hotel, T012-929943, hengheng2hotel @yahoo.com. Well-furnished, clean rooms, with fan, TV and hot water. There's also a great balcony for taking in the wonderful red sunsets.

E-F Heng Oudom, near the market, opposite the Star Guesthouse, T072-971629. Relative newcomer to the Kratie hotel scene and you can tell. The rooms are impeccable, clean, TV, attached bathrooms and fan but the service isn't quite up to scratch.

E-F Oudom Sambath, on the river road (No 439), T072-971502. This is a well-run place with a friendly English-speaking Chinese-Khmer owner. The rooms are huge, with a/c, TV, hot water, etc. The more expensive rooms are fit for royalty with large ornate bathtub and regal-looking furniture. The huge rooftop balcony is a perfect spot for sunset gazing with the best views of the Mekong in town.

E-G Balcony Guesthouse, riverfront road, T01-604036, www.balconyguesthouse.net. There are several, airy, clean and basic rooms in this villa overlooking the river. There is, of course, a giant, communal balcony which is a great place to lounge and watch Mekong sunsets.

F-G Heng Heng, T072-971405. This is a small hotel, with only 11 rooms, some over-looking the Mekong. The rooms are a bit cramped and furnished with 1970s wallpaper, but they are clean with fan or a/c and have attached bathrooms.

F-G Riverside Guesthouse, on the riverfront next door to **Oudom Sabath**. The basic rooms have all the necessary facilities but are a bit dingy. On the upside it's one of the cheaper places to stay on the waterfront.

F-G Star Guesthouse, T072- 971663. Situated beside the market, this has gained the reputation of being the friendliest guesthouse in town. It's very popular with travellers and its rooms are well appointed.

F-G You Hong Guesthouse, between the taxi rank and the market, T012-957003. Clean rooms with attached bathroom and fan. US$1 extra gets you cable TV. The owners are friendly and helpful. The restaurant is often filled with drunk backpackers.

Stung Treng *p171, map p171*

C-E Hotel Gold River, riverfront, T012-980678. This brand new 4-storey hotel has splendid river views and the only lift in Northeastern Cambodia. Each spotless and comfortable room has a hot water bathtub, cable TV and a/c; those at the front offer the river as backdrop. It has friendly service and is a bargain, given the location. Recommended.

D-F Ly Ly Guesthouse, opposite the market, T012-937859. Decent Chinese-style hotel with varying types of rooms – all come with private shower/toilet and cable TV. The ones at the back of the building have balconies and are the best value; option of a/c or fan throughout. Friendly with some English spoken. Recommended.

D-F Nature Lodge, a few kilometres north of Stung Treng town, T074-637 7767. A gorgeous location set in a nook of the Sekong River is offset by the tired-looking rooms and bungalows. It's been recently taken over by a local community group who hope to help this wonderfully sited resort-type set-up reach its full potential. Check in Stung Treng at the **XploreAsia** office; see Activities and tours, below, for details.

D-F Sok Sambath, near the market, T016-746666. Decent enough place in good location. The more expensive rooms are well furnished with a/c, TV and good bathrooms with hot water.

D-F Sok San, on main road near the river, T092-799108. Decent enough a/c and fan rooms although service is incredibly ropey; leaving surly teenagers to run a guesthouse is never the best option.

D-F Stung Treng Hotel and Guest House, on main road near the river, T092-999566.

This is a reasonable second option with decent enough rooms in a good location.

E-F Ratana Sambath, opposite the market, T012-755469. In a noisy but central location, the clean and basic en suite rooms vary from fan and no hot water to a/c and hot water. It also sells bus tickets.

E-F Sekong, on the river road, T012-931884. The shabby en suite fan and a/c rooms have seen better days but this would make for a good fallback option in the unlikely event everywhere else is full. It has a good location and restaurant though.

F-G Dara Guesthouse, on the river road near the taxi stand, T011-693429. The friendly French-speaking Khmer owner provides dingy though incredibly cheap rooms. Good if you're very, very skint. The food isn't too bad either.

F-G Riverside, opposite taxi stand, T012-439454. Dingy rooms with squat toilet and crude furniture. The restaurant's food is about the same quality as its rooms. Not the best option in town; there is a renovation planned for late 2010.

🍴 Eating

Kompong Cham *p169*

🍴 Ho An, Monivong St, T042-941234. This large Chinese restaurant has a good selection of dishes and friendly service.

🍴 Mekong Crossing, on the riverfront, T012-432427. Friendly restaurant and bar, though it does seem to have seen better days. Proprieter, Joe, is a great source of local information. It serves Western dishes: hamburgers, sandwiches and steaks (US$2-4). There's a good selection of magazines and board games.

🍴-🍴 Lazy Mekong Daze, on the riverfront. British owner Simon provides alcohol, cakes, fish and chips and Khmer food in this new and friendly riverside establishment. He also has a free pool table and you can catch the latest football on his TV.

🍴 Fresh Coffee, same block as **Monorom 2 VIP Hotel** on the riverfront. Open 0700-2100.

Small new coffee shop selling burgers, cakes and some Khmer food.

₹ **Smile**, same block as **Monorom 2 VIP Hotel** on the riverfront. Open 0630-2200. There's a huge Khmer menu with some Western dishes in this new and excellent NGO-connected eatery that helps orphans and kids with HIV. Free Wi-Fi. Recommended.

Kratie p170, map p170

There are a number of foodstalls set up along the river at night serving great fruit shakes. The market also sells simple dishes during the day.
₹₹ **Balcony Guesthouse**, see page 172. From its huge balcony overlooking the river, this place serves up an excellent fried English breakfast and various other Western and Khmer dishes. It's a good spot for a drink as well. Recommended.
₹₹ **Red Sun Falling**, on the river road. Closed Sun. This is probably the best restaurant in town and offers a variety of excellent Western dishes and a few Asian favourites. The full monty breakfast is fantastic. Good cocktails. The very friendly proprietor, Joe, also runs a very good bookshop on premises. Recommended.
₹₹ **Star Guesthouse**. This place has a decent enough menu but sometimes the prices (almost US$1 for a squeeze of honey) and quality let the place down. Good array of Western food and the homemade bread is excellent.
₹ **Mekong**, just off St 9 (near the river). A cheap selection of Khmer staples.
₹ **You Hong Guesthouse** (see above). Has a diverse menu in town, from muesli through to *amok*.
Santhepeap Hotel and **Heng Heng Hotel** restaurants both serve delicious Khmer food (and a sprinkling of Western dishes) at very reasonable prices.

Stung Treng p171, map p171

There isn't a whole lot of choice when it comes to restaurants in Stung Treng. Most visitors choose to eat in their hotels. The market offers the usual array of foodstalls serving simple but good 1-dish meals.
₹ **Dara**, opposite the taxi stand. An extensive menu of Khmer food plus a few Western

dishes (omelettes, etc). Outdoor seating. Reasonably friendly.
₹ **Prochum Tonle**, at the Sekong Hotel. There's some of the best Khmer food in town at this locally renowned restaurant.
₹ **Sophakmukal**, near the market. Beer garden-style restaurant with very good, cheap Cambodian food, curry, *amok*, soup (all under US$1) and a very friendly owner. Recommended.
₹ **Stung Treng Burger**, in a side street near the market. Daily 0630-2100. Friendly owners, fresh decor and good food make this place one of the best spots in town. Great burgers and even pizza supplement excellent Khmer food; there are decent breakfasts too. Recommended.
₹ **Sun Tha**, opposite the bus station. Very cheap soup shop popular with the locals. Soup costs US$0.50. Next door is a fruit shake shop with a name in Khmer. It serves great fruit shakes and fruit salads for under US$0.25. If you don't like your fruit salad smothered with ice and condensed milk you may need to indicate this beforehand.

▲ Activities and tours

Stung Treng p171, map p171

Tour company **XploreAsia** opened a small office in late 2009 on the riverfront near **Hotel Gold River**. They are working in conjunction with various local community projects and offer a variety of tours including river excursions, trips to see the dolphins and cycling and kayaking tours. You should also be able to find out about other tours at the **Riverside Guesthouse**.

⊙ Transport

Kompong Cham p169

Due to improved roads the boat service to and from Kompong Cham is non-existent. The boat service from Phnom Penh has also been curtailed. The town is 120 km northeast of Phnom Penh via the well-surfaced Routes 5, 6 and 7. There are regular connections with **Phnom Penh** by shared taxi and numerous bus companies run regular services. Buses also connect to all points north including Chhlong, Kratie, Stung Treng and Ban Lung. Pickups and shared taxis plough through to **Sen Monorom**, via **Snuol**, 2 hrs, US$3-4.

Local transport is by moto, tuk-tuk or taxi. A moto for a day is between US$6-8 and between 500-1000 riel for short trips. Local tuk-tuk driver and guide **Mr Vannat** has an excellent reputation and is fluent in French and English, T012-995890. It's US$20 a day for a boat ride.

Kratie p170, map p170
Roughly 4 buses a day run to **Phnom Penh** (4-5 hrs, US$5/US$8) stopping off at **Kompong Cham** en route. **Stung Treng** is served by regular minibuses 0800-1400 (2 hrs, US$6) and at least 1 daily bus (2½ hrs, US$4), while there is at least 1 minibus a day to **Ban Lung** (6 hrs, US$12). Many of these buses depart from the bus stand near the river but you might want to ask at your accommodation if this has changed. You can also find shared taxis plying routes to all destinations, though prices fluctuate according to season, road condition and fuel prices.

Local transport by motodop US$1 per hr or US$6-7 per day.

Stung Treng p171, map p171
Before the bridge opened in 2008, Stung Treng used to be the staging post for travel to Laos with regular boats plying the few kilometres upriver to the border. This situation, however, has now completely changed with most travellers heading south from Pakse in Laos (see box, page 18 for details of this border crossing) no longer stopping in Stung Treng, preferring instead to take through buses direct to Kratie and Phnom Penh. Most hotels (such as Sekong, Riverside, etc) can organize tickets. Alternatively, you can go directly to the taxi/bus rank.

At present there is at least 1 bus a day to **Pakse** (4½ hrs, US$6) in Laos and through

ticketing to **Vientiane** (change in Pakse) is also available (US$35) should you wish to connect directly to the Laos capital. There are a couple of buses to **Phnom Penh** daily (9 hrs, US$7.50) and the same bus will stop at **Kratie**, US$5. Plenty of minibuses also ply this route.

Pickups and shared taxis connect regularly with **Phnom Penh** via **Kratie** and with recent road construction the roads should be fine to travel along (if a little bumpy). Shared taxis to **Phnom Penh** leave at 0600 from the taxi rank near the river, 7 hrs, US$15. To **Ban Lung** at 0700 from the taxi rank and the trip takes 4-5 hrs, US$10.

Directory

Kompong Cham p169
Banks There are 2 banks in town – **Acleda** and **Canadia Bank**. Acleda will do Western Union transfers and Canadia will do advances on Visa and MasterCard. 0800-1600.
Internet ABC computers, in the centre of town, was the only internet shop operating at the time of writing, US$1 per hr and overse as phone calls available. A new internet café was due to open on Pasteur St, opposite the Mekong Crossing.

Kratie p170, map p170
Banks There is an **Acleda Bank** half way down St 11. It does not do advances on Visa or MasterCard but is a subsidiary for Western Union. **Internet** You Hong guesthouse offer a good, cheap connection. **Three Star Internet** US$4 per hr. There is another internet café near **Phnom Penh Transport** bus office; at the time of writing it was US$4 per hr.

Stung Treng p171, map p171
Banks There are no banks in town.
Internet Internet is available at the computer shop opposite the market and the **Sekong Hotel**, US$4 per hr.
Telephone There are telephone shops all over town.

The borderlands

Mondulkiri and Ratanakiri are very different with their green rolling hills, lush jungle areas and cascading falls. Many compare them to the green pastures of England or Tasmania. Here ethnic minorities comprise the majority of the population and a great fusion of diverse cultures and peoples populate the region. There are a great deal of natural attractions in the area, such as pristine lakes, national parks and beautiful rivers. During the dry season, the areas around Ban Lung and Sen Monorom appear windblown with stark earth-red roads snaking through desiccated landscapes. ▶▶ *For listings, see pages 184-188.*

Mondulkiri Province → For listings, see pages 184-188.

One of the most frequent epithets used to describe Mondulkiri is 'the Wild East'. Although this is one of Cambodia's largest provinces, it is also its most sparsely inhabited and at present the region is still underdeveloped. It does have the potential to become a major ecotourism Mecca but, sadly, not enough people make it here as the roads are pretty tricky – in the wet season hideously slippery and in the dry season considerably dusty. However, they are a lot better now than they were a few years ago and things are changing. A diamond in the rough, Mondulkiri's barren, harsh and burnt out landscape conceals virgin jungle, ethnic minority villages and some of the country's most unique flora and fauna. With an average elevation of 800 m, it is also a lot cooler than most other parts of Cambodia.

Ins and outs

Getting there Despite some minor improvements in infrastructure getting to Mondulkiri is still a bit tricky with no completely paved road in and out. At present there are only two daily direct connections with Phnom Penh – minibus and standard bus – with other regular links to Kratie and Kompong Cham. Like much else in this rapidly developing region this is likely to change so for more precise information check upon arrival. Share taxis are also available though, like elsewhere, you may have to wait until they are full. ▶▶ *See Transport, page 187.*

Getting around Most guesthouses and hotels in Sen Monorom can recommend a well-briefed, English-speaking guide/moto driver for around US$15 and a few dollars more if lengthy trips are required.

Sen Monorom

Sen Monorom is the provincial capital of Mondulkiri. It is particularly quaint and the surrounding country is breathtaking. Overshadowing the town, **Dakramon Mountain** is a large, auspicious hill and a major place of worship for villagers. It is believed a wise old man called 'Ta Dakramon' who was a traditional healer, healed the masses up there. **Dam Nok Old Royal Palace**, 3 km southwest of town and built in the 1960s, was pretty much destroyed during the Vietnam War. Once the holiday home for Sihanouk, only remnants of walls exist today.

Ethnic minority villages and elephant treks in Mondulkiri

The province of mountains and rainforests is dotted with hundreds of ethnic minority villages. Here, the term 'ethnic minority' is a misnomer, with the majority of the population (80%) comprising 12 different ethnic groups. The largest ethnic group is the Phnong, 'the people of the mountain' which make up about 70% of the province's population and the indigenous people of Cambodia. Visiting a local minority village is a completely captivating experience and is highly recommended. Most tour guides or guesthouses can arrange a visit to a village. It is best to stick with a local organization who is working alongside these groups who ensure the locals benefit from tourist visits and support the sustainability of cultures and development. Other minorities include Tampeun, Jarri, Krow, Steeng, Sumray and Rodai.

The best village to visit is **Potang Village**, one of the closest and largest Phnong villages, with about 140 families spread across the area. The village consists of a collection of the unique traditional Phnong thatched huts and raised wooden houses. The residents are very hospitable, inviting tourists into their surprisingly large abodes for a drink of rice wine or something to eat. It is still possible here to see some of the elders in their traditional attire including the not so politically correct elephant tusk earrings. The village

Sen Monorom

To Phulung Village & Boos Ra Waterfall (38km)

To Boos Ra (38km)

To ⑥ ⑦

Dakramon Mountain

Airstrip (Not in use)

Taxis

To Dak Dam Village (17km), Troy Tom Waterfall & Vietnam Border (35km)

To Dam Nok Old Royal Palace (3km) & Sen Monorom Waterfall

Wat Sen Monorom

To Potang Village, Kbal Prehear Waterfall, Putro Village, Rum Near Falls & Phnom Penh

N

800 metres
800 yards

Sleeping
Bou Sra Guesthouse 2
Holiday Guesthouse 3
Long Vibal 1
Nature Lodge 6
Phanyro Guesthouse 7

Pitch Kiri Guesthouse 5
Sovannkiri 4

Eating
Arun Reah II 6
Bamboo Bar 2

Chom Nor Thmei 1
Green House 5
Orameas 4
Sen Monorom II 7

is home to 15 elephants, making it the most popular launching pad for elephant treks. It is usually possible to stay the night at a villager's abode for US$1-2. Aside from elephant treks the main income base for this village is the collection of resin.

Phulung Village, 8 km northwest of town, is home to about 80 families and four elephants used for trekking. The Potang and Phulung villages hold **cultural shows** for around US$30 per group. You can't be sure how culturally sensitive it is going to one of these 'shows', though it is a good way for the groups to benefit from tourism directly, while retaining their culture. The performance includes a large amount of dancing and singing in traditional attire while people play pipes, gongs and bells. The performance lasts for about two hours and a guide/moto can organize the day beforehand. Performances are usually held in the afternoon.

Dak Dam Village is 17 km east of town and home to a whopping 250 families of Phnong, Khmer and Vietnamese people. The village is renowned locally for its handicrafts, particularly bags and scarves. The **Tray Tom Waterfall** is 2 km from the village and its cascade can measure up to 15 m in the wet season (see below).

Elephant treks can be organized by most guesthouses/hotels (such as **Long Vibol, Pich Kiri, The Nature Lodge** and **Green House restaurant**, etc) or motodops/guides. The treks start at one of the ethnic minority villages, typically Potang Village or Phulung Village. Treks can also be organized from Putru Village and Dak Dam Village. The pachyderms are not the most comfortable means of transport (expect a sore bottom for weeks to come) but offer a unique opportunity to explore the surrounding jungle, habitat and villages. The slow-moving creatures have the added benefit of transcending areas not usually accessible by motor vehicles. The elephant's 'passenger' basket fits up to two people and a day trek costs around US$25 (which is half the price of treks in Mondulkiri). Tourists also have the option of two- or three-day treks which usually involve camping by a lakeside or in jungle, romantically lit with fireflies. Routes vary depending on which village you start in.

Waterfalls

There are over 100 waterfalls in the area. **Sen Monorom Waterfall**, 5 km northwest of Sen Monorom, is the closest and most popular with tourists. The fall plunges 6 m into a lovely turquoise pool – perfect for a dip when the water levels are high enough. **Boos Ra Waterfall**, 35 km from town, is one of the region's best and the firm Khmer favourite. The fall became legendary when one of Cambodia's most famous singers, Sen Sisamoth, declared in tune that it was "the most beautiful waterfall in Cambodia". Unfortunately the singer was killed during the Pol Pot regime but the waterfall's legacy continues. From the summit, the water plunges 15 m to a second tier, where people can shower under the spray. The next tier features an even larger drop which plummets into an 8-m-deep bottle-green pool which is perfect for bathing in. The fall is surrounded by dense foliage and chirping cicadas. There is a good new road to the waterfall. **Boos Ra Village**, 4 km from the waterfall, has a small handicraft shop and run-down guesthouse for US$2.50 a night.

Kbal Prehear Waterfall is 27 km from Sen Monorom and 18 km from the ethnic minority settlement of Potang Village (see above). Kbal Prehear means 'Head of God' and the waterfall is so named because of its large breadth and 7-m drop. At its base is a large swimming pool.

Ol Leng Tang Waterfall, 40 km from Sen Monorom, near Memong Village, is possibly the province's most beautiful, with exceptionally clean water and a lovely spot to take a dip.

Dak Dam Waterfall, also known as **Tray Tom**, is 30 km from Sen Monorom, near the Phnong Village of Dak Dam. The provincial tourist office has heavily promoted this fall as

The Phnong

The Phnong revere their elephants, holding an enormous amount of respect for these colossal creatures. Phnong legend states that the elephants were once Phnong people but after eating fish they transformed into their current mammoth form. They are considered the most sacred of all creatures and because of this the Phnong do not let their village elephants breed as it is viewed as evil, akin to incest (ironic, considering the Phnong people will often marry their cousins). If a baby elephant is born in a village it is considered a very bad omen and large amounts of animals (ie four dogs, two buffalos, eight chickens, etc) are sacrificed to appease the spirits.

To avoid this dilemma, musking bull elephants are tied to trees in the jungle, away from the village, until their sexual urges desist. This age-old custom presumably derives from the destruction caused by very aggressive, sexually-driven bull elephants. They know when their elephants are musking by a gland behind the restless creature's eye that starts oozing oil. In 2001, a musking elephant killed two local Phnong people and destroyed many villagers' houses. The elephant was shot and local Sen Monorom sources say that the elephant's owner died the next day. The whole incident was considered a seriously bad omen and the whole village moved, many burning their houses.

The downside of this animistic belief system is that the Phnong capture their elephants from the wild, which is depleting the natural supply. In Mondulkiri the current wild elephant population is believed to be around 60 (the second biggest animal populace in the country).

Traditionally elephants were used for transport and to clear forests but this tradition has died out. Most Phnong villages now employ their elephants for tourist treks and a few years ago impoverished locals sold their elephants to companies in Siem Reap where they are now used to transport tourists around Angkor Wat.

---

an alternative to Boos Ra, due to the former's inaccessibility during the wet season. The large fall has a 15-m drop and runs 2 m across but is difficult to find on your own. In nearby Dak Dam Village (2 km away) visitors can stop off for refreshments or purchase some locally produced handicrafts.

Rum Near Waterfall is not as impressive or large as its counterparts (it only has a 6-m drop) but has the added bonus of being close to town (13 km) and is on the way to the major Phnong settlement of Putru Village, 18 km from Sen Monorom. The fall has its own charm and is surrounded by large shady trees and jungle with a nice pool at the bottom.

Ratanakiri Province → For listings, see pages 184-188.

Ratanakiri is like another planet compared to the rest of Cambodia: dusty, red roads curl through the landscape in summer, while in the rainy season the area becomes lush and green. Adventure enthusiasts won't be disappointed, with waterfalls to discover, ethnic minorities to meet, elephants to ride, river trips to take and the beautiful Yaek Lom volcanic lake to take a dip in. Be warned – get there soon as a major new road linking Ban Lung to the outside world is now under construction. Once this has been completed Ban Lung is likely to obscure into just another provincial town.

Ins and outs

Getting there Ban Lung is a back-jarring, bottom-bruising, brain-wobbling 13 hours from Phnom Penh. It is better to break your journey in Kratie and Stung Treng and take a pickup/taxi from there. There is a small airstrip in Ban Lung but at present it has no regular flights.

Getting around The chief mode of transport is the motorbike which comes with a driver, or not, as required (usually US$5 without driver and US$15 with, but you'll have to haggle). Bus services are sporadic. Cars with driver can be hired for US$40-50 a day.

Ban Lung and around

Ban Lung has been the dusty provincial capital of Ratanakiri Province ever since the previous capital Lumphat was flattened by US bombers trying to 'destroy' the footpaths and tracks that made up the Ho Chi Minh Trail. In comparison with Sen Monorom, Ban Lung is considered cosmopolitan. To the outside world, however, the town is of such insignificance that most refer to it as 'Ratanakiri'. The dirt tracks that used to suffocate the town with their dry season dust and wet season mud have now been mostly paved, making a visit here more amenable. The town is situated on a plateau dotted with lakes and hills, many of great beauty, and serves as a base from which visitors can explore the surrounding countryside. The Vietnamese in the east building a road from the nearby Le Thanh/O Yadao border crossing, plans to pave the existing roads into and out of Ban Lung, and a burgeoning tourist market mark this part of Cambodia for dramatic change. At present you'll find basic guesthouse accommodation, and food and drink can be obtained in town.

Sights around Ban Lung

The name Ratanakiri means 'jewel mountains' in Pali, and presumably comes from the wealth of gems in the hills, but it could just as easily refer to the beauty of the landscape. **Yaek Lom** ① *US$1 and a parking charge of 500 riel, all of which goes into a fund to promote the conservation of the area,* is a perfectly circular volcanic lake about 5 km east of town and easily reached by motorbike. The crystalline lake is rimmed by protected forest dominated by giant emergents (dipterocarps and shoreas) soaring high into the sky. Around the feet of these giant trees are a dense tangle of smaller woods and bamboos which filter the late afternoon sun into gorgeous hues of green and dappled patterns of light and shade. It takes about one hour to walk around the lake: in doing so you will find plenty of secluded bathing spots, a couple of small jetties and, given the lack of water in town, it is not surprising that most locals and visitors bathe in the wonderfully clear and cool waters. There is a visitor centre which serves as an ethnic minority museum with a collection of instruments, baskets, tools and other curios.

There are three **waterfalls** ① *all 2000 riel, follow Highway 19 out of town and branch off 2 km out on the main road in the first village out of Ban Lung: Chaa Ong Falls are 9 km northwest at the intersection, turn right at the village and head for about 5 km to head to Katien Waterfall (follow the signs), the same road heads to Kachaang Waterfall,* in close proximity to Ban Lung town. **Kachaang Waterfall** is 6 km away. The 12-m-high waterfall flows year round and is surrounded by magnificent, pristine jungle and fresh mist rising from the fall. **Katien Waterfall** is a little oasis 7 km northwest of Ban Lung. Believed to have formed from volcanic lava hundreds of years ago, the 10-m plunging falls are sheltered from the outside world by a little rocky grotto. It is one of the better local falls to swim in as it is very secluded (most people will usually have the area to themselves), the water is completely clean and the bunches of vines hanging from its summit providing good swinging potential. Amongst the dotted ferns, rocky boulders and large meandering fig trees, the 40 m-wide pool peters off into a delicate brook, an offshoot of the Koutung Stream. Katien flows all year round and is a favourite of elephant trekkers. However, the best waterfall is arguably **Chaa Ong Falls**, with the 30-m falls plunging into a large pool. Those game enough can have a shower behind the crescent-shaped ledge.

Veng Xai is a small village 35 km northwest of Ban Lung that straddles the charming **Say San River**. The trip here along the green, curling road speckled with the odd basket-carrying family or lazy buffalo, offers plenty of wonderful distractions for passengers. Veng Xai itself is an itty-bitty town consisting of a few shops and outdoor foodstalls. A **Tampeun Village** is about 20 km up the Say San (a one-hour boat ride up glassy green waters). The village of about 200 Tampeun, Lao and Khmer isn't particularly noteworthy, but the **Tampeun cemetery**, 200 m from the village, is rather fascinating. The cemetery holds the graves of around 200 people and provides quite a colourful contrast to its Western counterparts. Each memorial site houses two graves, usually those

Ban Lung

Lake Konsaign

Wat Phnom Svay

To Stung Treng

CIC

To 3, Lake Komsam & O Chum

Virachay National Park Headquarter

To 6 7, Yaek Lom Lake & Vietnam (63km)

Taxis

ATM

Psar Ban Luang

To 11

N

200 metres
200 yards

Sleeping
Borann Lodge 1
Cheng Luk 2
Lakeside Chenglock 8
Lake View Lodge 3
Norden House 6
Sopheap Guesthouse 10

Sovannikiri 5
Tree Top Eco
Lodge 11
Tribal 4
Yaklom Hill Lodge 7

Eating
A'Dam 2
Apocalypse Bar 5
Beoung Kamsan 3
Chum Nor Beoung
Konsaign 4

of man and wife. And the sites are decorated with an elaborately painted small pagoda with large wooden-carved male and female effigies marking the front corners. Whoever dies first will have their effigy placed on the right-hand side. Some of the more noteworthy effigies are the mushroom-headed man (who died from eating a poisonous mushroom); a Western-like couple towards the back (distinguished by their large noses), and the military man, with CB radio, and his wife, with several big hearts.

Most people in this area belong to the Kreung minority. **Kreung villages** are often built around large and venerable trees such as flame trees and mango trees. One notable feature is the brides' and grooms' houses which are built on stilts 5-10 m off the ground and reached via a rickety ladder. These are actually separate houses for teenagers to entertain prospective spouses.

The woods, where slash and burn agriculture is increasingly common, are a twitcher's paradise: stand near a tall flame tree or fruit tree and listen to the cries, calls and songs of the birds. There are also trees of commercial value such as the sandalwood tree, the heart of which fetches thousands of dollars per kilo in Arab states. Out towards the south of Ban Lung you will come across rubber plantations where you can rest in the dappled light.

The drive from Ban Lung to **Ta Veng** is roughly twice as long and certainly twice as pretty as that to Veng Xai. Beyond the tiny hamlet of **O Chum** there is nothing: no water, no petrol, no puncture repair services – so go well prepared. The road undulates and winds and for much of its length it runs through dense forest providing welcome relief from sun or rain. Occasionally you will see a family marching in file or workers returning from the fields and there are a few villages built by the roadside. Much the best option, however, is to be bold and steer your Honda down one of the many small tracks leading off to the side. After a while you will probably come into a village or pass an isolated house. Your reception will vary from warm to indifferent. Your presence may be regarded as an intrusion so it always a good idea to hover in a public area while gauging the response to your unannounced arrival. Expect no English to be spoken, those with a smattering of Khmer or Vietnamese will fare best.

Virachey National Park is the country's largest national park and contains some of the nation's best forested areas. Organized tours are still being refined by local government officials. There are four national park headquarters, at Veng Xai, Lumphat, Ta Veng and Ban Lung. As the majority of guides/rangers at the smaller posts don't speak English it is probably better to organize treks from the main ranger office in Ban Lung (see box, page 183). The park is host to a number of rare and not-so-rare animal species including wild cats, wild pigs, Asian elephants, the gau, and possibly the rare douc langur. Animal sightings are a lot more common during the wet season. The park also contains ancient rock formations, extinct volcanoes, the only high elevation forest in Cambodia and the Se Cong and Se San river catchments.

The trip to **Ou'Sean Lair Waterfall**, 35 km from Ban Lung, is a wonderful day excursion offering a fantastic cross-section of what is essentially Ratanakiri's main attractions (without the riverside element). From Ban Lung, fields of wind-bent, spindly rubber trees provide a canopy over the road's rolling hills, a legacy left from the French in the 1960s. The kindly government has built a minority 'camp' near the rubber factory, to ensure they have a cheap labour force at hand to collect the rubber (with around 300 riel paid per litre of rubber, with 30-50 litres yielded daily in the wet and dry season respectively). The natural archway created by the surprisingly beautiful rubber trees provides a magical entrance into the oncoming territory. As the landscape transforms, so does the road, degenerating into a bumpy, sandy nightmare (which would be extremely difficult to navigate during the wet

Ecotourism in Virachey National Park

Virachey National Park has been recognized by international conservation experts as one of the top conservation priorities in Asia. The national park extends over three districts – Veng Xai, Taveng and Siem Pang in two provinces – Ratanakiri and Stung Treng. The park is bordered by Laos to the north and Vietnam to the east and is bound by two major rivers, the Sekong River in the west and the Se San River in the south.

The national park has relatively low population density. Most of those living in the park are ethnic minority peoples. Ethnic minorities comprise 4% of Cambodia's total population, and of this, 16% live in Ratanakiri.

A lot of tour operators are offering trips into Virachey National Park via the district ranger stations. These trips should be avoided as they are undermining local authorities in the effective management of the park. Those wishing to explore the area should contact the Biodiversity Protected Area and Management Project (BPAMP) who have been actively developing an ecotourism programme for Virachey National Park. The project focuses on small scale, low impact, culture, nature and adventure trekking-based tourism which benefits and involves local communities. They currently offer and are developing a number of different tours which combine jungle trekking with overnight camping, river journeys and village-based accommodation. These include a day trip from Ban Lung to the national park for a short forest walk, lunch and swim in the river; mountain biking to the national park boundary (a short two-hour ride from Ban Lung), trekking and overnight stay beside a jungle waterfall in a known gibbon area, with a kayak return (three days, two nights); a river journey and trekking in Veng Xai district with village homestay (four days, three nights); extended wilderness trekking with patrolling rangers to a natural grassland deep in Taveng area (seven to eight days).

All visitors to the park require a permit which can be obtained from the national park headquarters either in Ban Lung (for Veng Xai and Taveng) or Stung Treng (for Siem Pang). For further information contact Ban Lung head office, T075-974176, virachey@camintel.co.kh. Some excellent information on the park is available here http://viracheyecotourism.blogspot.com/.

season). Here the scenery morphs from little fish farms and rugged jungle to bushy cashew nut farms and verdant mango plantations with hacked-up, depleted, slash and burn areas interspersed amongst the beautiful countryside (which some guides may try to tell you is a result of people 'recklessly throwing their cigarettes away'). Punctuating the mottled natural vista is an equally diverse range of ethnic minority settlements. Tampeun and Kreung villages are dotted along the road and about half way (17 km from Ban Lung), in a lovely valley, is a tiny Cham village. The village has a small sugarcane drink stand and is an ultra-friendly spot to break the journey. From here the landscape becomes a bit more barren and burnt out, with old gem shafts producing dips in the surface of the land all along on the road. The township of **Bei Sruk Chomrom**, 32 km from Ban Lung and 3 km from the falls, is the epitome of hardship. The town could come straight from a country and western movie with its tough feel, wooden shopfronts and gales of dust blowing through. Here the townsfolk are seriously poor but still wear the bling you would expect from a mining town. They are largely a friendly mob who don't mind tourists poking around the mine shafts that have been burrowed absolutely anywhere and everywhere a hole can be dug. Amethyst is their holy grail and one must pity the poor miners who are sent down the extremely thin (60-70 cm) and deep (10-15 m) claustrophobic holes in searing temperatures – for the most part, bearing very little. The town has four cheap foodstalls-cum-restaurants that actually provide very good food (although the hygiene of the buffets are a tad dubious). Food for the most part is pork, pork or … pork. Some 3 km from the mining town and the perfect end to the journey is the seven-tiered Ou'Sean Lair falls. The falls were reportedly 'discovered' by a Tampeun villager five years ago, who debated as to whether he should tell the Department of Tourism of their existence. In return for turning over the falls, they were named after him. The falls are most spectacular in the wet season but are still pretty alluring during the dry season. Shaded by large Ta Prohm-like fig trees the pool at the bottom of the fall provides a nice swimming area (there is some rubbish but not too much). The ropey, sturdy roots of these gigantic trees provide good leverage into the 3-m-deep pool.

Bokeo is a gem mining town some 30 km east down Highway 19 on the road to Vietnam. This place was eclipsed by Pailin, close to the Thai border, but years of heavy duty mining there during the Khmer Rouge period means that Bokeo is now reputed to be a richer source of precious stones. Gem rushes are much like gold rushes and gem miners are equally careless about the effects of their actions on the environment. The rather unattractive town is booming as hopeful miners make their way here. The road is atrocious so few people make it. There is reported to be a guesthouse near the market.

Lumphat ⓘ *the most common way to arrive is with a motodop, US$15 (unless you are lucky enough to get a lift on one of the rare pickups heading this way); it's also possible to catch a boat down the river from Veng Xai but some tough negotiating may be required as the longboat drivers can be quite mercenary (the trip could cost up to US$30),* is approximately a two-hour drive south of Ban Lung (45 km). It is described as a 'ghost town' but occupies an attractive spot on the Se San River and boats can be hired for around US$15 to visit some of the nearby Lao villages. Before the war Sihanouk pumped loads of money into the town and some of the 1960s-era hospitals and school survived the massive bombing campaign. But for the most part, the place has been destroyed – buildings have been blown up and craters pockmark the small town. Some tourists like to visit the now derelict and decrepit airport, once a major Khmer Rouge base.

◉ The borderlands listings

For Sleeping and Eating price codes and other relevant information, see Essentials pages 22-23.

◉ Sleeping

Sen Monorom *p176, map p177*
Electricity is irregular but better than it was.
E-F Bou Sra Guesthouse, in front of the market, on the road to Phnom Penh, T012-527144. Needing a clean and updating, some rooms with a TV, which is great when the town's limited electricity supply is on.
E-F Long Vibal, 900 m past the roundabout in the town centre, T012-944647. These beautiful

bungalows in a lush garden setting have rooms with fan and attached bathroom. Triple rooms are available. The owner is an excellent source of local information and staff speak good English. There is also a restaurant. They have a generator so you are not stuck bumbling around your room during the night. Recommended.
E-F Phanyro Guesthouse, on a winding road near town, T017-770 8697. These newly built, clean bungalow-style rooms overlook the hillside. There's ample car parking and monthly rates for volunteers. The owner Mr Net has good English and shares the accommodation with his family.

E-F Pitch Kiri Guesthouse, on a bend in the main road, behind the market, T012-932102. A newly built extension offers 40 spacious rooms with traditional Khmer furniture and decoration, each twice the size of other hotel rooms in Sen Monorom. Run by Madame Deu and her daughter, it's one of the longest-running and biggest places offering accommodation. The old rooms in the guesthouse are run down and the bungalows are only marginally better. Internet is available at US$1 per hr.

F Holiday Guesthouse, on the main road to Phnom Penh, T012-588060. Rooms are comfortable but on the smallish and dusty side, with bathroom and shared facilities. TV, mosquito nets and candles supplied.

F Nature Lodge, just outside the town centre, T012-230272. Set in beautiful countryside and farmland, this budget resort focuses on utilizing its natural surroundings to provide quirky accommodation options, including outdoor bathrooms. The bar, restaurant and general hang-out area is a huge treehouse slung with hammocks to relax in.

F-G Homestays. It's possible to stay in the home of one of the local ethnic minorities for around US$2 a night. You will need a moto or guide to arrange this prior to your stay; don't expect to turn up and arrange it on the spot and make sure it is the family who benefits from you being there and not the moto driver who took you there. The huts or houses usually feature wooden beds with no mattress or linen, so you'll need to bring what you need (including mosquito nets). A welcome gesture would be to bring some food with you to share with the family at your homestay.

F-G Sovannkiri, on the main road to Phnom Penh to the east of the market, T017-472769. As this doubles as the bus terminal most people are put off, but the big, airy rooms are extremely good value with attached bathroom, mosquito nets, candles and free bottled water.

Ban Lung *p180, map p181*

C-E Borann Lodge, no address, see map, T012-959363, www.yaklom.com. This huge, chalet-style villa set down a Ban Lung side street has 6 rooms of varying sizes. Each has a/c or a fan and an en suite bathroom with hot water. The owners and staff are very friendly and Borann feels more like a homestay than a guesthouse. Massive wooden model of Angkor and various over-the-top wooden furniture items add to the character. Affiliated with **Yaklom Hill Lodge**. Recommended.

C-E Norden House, on road to Yaklom Lake, T012-880327, www.nordenhouseyaklom.com. The nearest accommodation to the Yaklom Lake offers a collection of spotless, well-appointed bungalows with a/c, TV and en suite hot-water facilities. There are attractive gardens, a decent restaurant, free Wi-Fi plus they can arrange bus tickets. The Swedish and Khmer owners also rent out the best motorbikes in town. Recommended.

C-F Sovannkiri, on the outskirts of town, T075-974001. This hotel, which seems a bit ostentatious for Ban Lung, has a choice of rooms (and rates), from basic ones with TV, fan and attached bathroom to the VIP suite, with grandiose wooden furniture, a hot-water bath (great after a day's hiking) and fridge. The staff are rigidly formal but very helpful and friendly.

C-F Tribal Hotel, 200 m from the centre of town, behind the post office, T075-974074, tribal_hotel@yahoo.com. A reasonable place that does seem to have seen better days and management. There is a variety of rooms, from gloomy cells to those with en suite, hot water and a/c.

D-F Lakeside Chenglock Hotel, beside the smaller Lake Konsaign, T012-957422. An exponential improvement on its town counterpart. The rooms are very comfortable; the cheapest is spacious, with fan and attached bathroom, and the more expensive bungalow-type rooms offer lovely wooden furniture, attached bathroom with hot water and bath, a/c and a beautiful view over the lake. Good value. Recommended.

D-F Yaklom Hill Lodge, near Yaklom Lake, 6 km east of Ban Lung, T012-644240, www.yaklom.com. Set in a private forest, this rustic ecolodge is a bit out of town. Bungalows have balconies and hammocks and are well decorated with local handicrafts and fabrics. They have fan, mosquito net, attached bathroom and shower. Power is supplied via generator and solar panels. The friendly owner, Sampon, arranges all manner of tours and treks and is the only operator in the area who uses local ethnic minority peoples as guides. It's affiliated with **Borann Lodge**, see above. The food is a bit ropey but still this place is recommended.

E-F Cheng Luk Hotel, near the roundabout, in the town centre, T075-974121. Clean rooms with TV, fan and attached bathroom. Hot water and a/c available. This hotel receives mixed reports but is generally a good fall back if other places are full.

E-F Lake View Lodge, overlooking the lake, Old Governors House, T092-785259. The rooms are nothing to get too excited about – from fan and cold-water bathrooms through to a/c, TV and hot water – but the welcome is exceptional. Sophat will pick you up from the bus station in the middle of the night, provides internet access, decent food and trekking tours to outlying villages. There's even a small restaurant attached.

E-F Sopheap Guesthouse, next to the market, T012-958746. Clean rooms have hot water, fan or a/c, cable TV and a noisy and lively central location. Get one with a balcony and you'll have a great view of the market life unfolding below you.

F-G Tree Top Eco Lodge, no address so see map, T011-600381, www.treetop-ecolodge.com. Lovely set of large wooden bungalows overlooking a valley on the edge of town. The interiors are well decorated and each room has adjacent huge balconies and en suite hot-water bathrooms. There are some attractive communal areas and verandas, a restaurant/bar and free transfers to the bus station. Recommended.

⊙ Eating

Sen Monorom *p176, map p177*
Compared to the number of guesthouses there are relatively few restaurants.

❡ **Bamboo Bar Tours and Restaurant**, next to the bus station, T012-234177. This place offers a welcome retreat with free hot Khmer tea, traditionally served in a coconut shell, and free internet if you eat there. Reasonably priced mix of Khmer and Western foods.

❡ **Chom Nor Thmei**, on the main road to Phnom Penh, in front of the market. The best restaurant in town by a long shot. Cheap Khmer food and a few Western dishes (omelettes and French fries). Good, fresh orange juice and scrumptious guacamole (when in season). The lovely owners go well out of their way to satisfy customers. Recommended.

❡ **The Green House Restaurant**, on the other side of the bus station opposite the **Holiday Guesthouse**, T017-905659. This friendly restaurant run by Mr Sam Nang ('Lucky') serves good, cheap Cambodian and Western foods, such as tasty fried noodles with fresh vegetables, US$2. Promoting responsible tourism, Mr Nang can book a variety of sustainable tours in the area, including elephant trekking, and he rents out motos for around US$8 a day.

❡ **Orameas**, further out on the road to Phnom Penh past the hospital. Khmer and Western food. Good *lok lok*. Very cheap and popular with the locals. The owner generates hydroelectric power.

❡ **Sen Monorom Restaurant II**, just up from the taxi/pickup drop-off point. Khmer restaurant offering simple Cambodian dishes.

A number of guesthouses have restaurants including **Pitch Kiri** , **Arun Reah II** (locals refer to it as very Khmer karaoke style) and **Long Vibol** (recommended). There are a number of good fruit shake shops around the market.

Ban Lung p180, map p181

Food options are now improving in Ban Lung with a greater range of fresh fruit and other produce on sale at the market and various small bakeries opening up, offering Khmer-style cakes and breads.

ŦŦŦ-ŦŦ Terres Rouges Lodge Restaurant. Once considered the 'in' place to eat but the food is nothing exceptional, the service can be dodgy and they do charge very high corkage (US$10) should you decide to bring your own wine.

ŦŦ Tribal Hotel Restaurant (see page 185). This place has lost some of its previous reputation for good food at equally good prices. It might be worth a visit if you've tried everywhere else in town.

ŦŦ-Ŧ Beoung Kamsan Restaurant, beside Lake Kamsan. The place offers a fantastic selection of Cambodian food including its own delicious speciality, chicken with cashew nuts (US$3) and the famous local delicacy, volcanic beef. They seem genuinely grateful to see foreign customers and the swift, attentive service reflects this.

Ŧ A' Dam, on the same road as **Borann Lodge** and **Tree Top Eco Lodge**. Open 1100(ish)-2400. It's understandable why A'Dam is popular with both Ban Lung locals and expat NGO workers. Great Khmer and Western food is piled high and served cheap by the friendly Khmer owners. It also doubles as a bar. Recommended.

Ŧ Apocalypse Bar, no address so see map. You can get decent coffee and tea plus breakfast at this small eatery attached to the **Dutch Couple** tour agency.

Ŧ Chum Nor Beoung Konsaign, situated on the bend in the road around Lake Konsaign. This restaurant is not as atmospheric as its counterpart but offers a good selection of Khmer and Chinese food.

Ŧ Tree Top Eco Lodge, see page 186. Great location for both dinner and a drink but the food isn't all that it could be.

⊙ Shopping

Sen Monorom p176, map p177

The central market in town has some useful products (eg batteries) and it is also possible to pick up ethnic minority handicrafts in some villages. An interesting ethical stop-off in town is **The Middle of Nowhere** craft shop, T012-474879, selling traditional handicrafts and locally produced wild honey.

Ban Lung p180, map p181

Ban Lung market is the largest market in this area and from 0600-0700 is a hive of activity as nearby villagers come to sell their honey, nuts and other produce and catch up on the morning gossip while eating their breakfast. From 1700-1800 the food market opens at the back and, if you can face it, you can try their specialities.

▲ Activities and tours

Sen Monorom p176, map p177

A good tour guide is **Ok Sambol**, T012-944647, US$15 a day.

Ban Lung p180, map p181

Dutch Couple, see Apocalypse Bar, above, T099-531745, www.ecotourismcambodia.info. This is a small and recently opened eco-tourism outfit offering well-equipped, upmarket and pricey tours to various destinations in Northeast Cambodia.
Lake View Lodge, T092-785259. Offer a variety of tours and other adventures. They can also procure motos and dirt bikes of varying quality for rent.

⊖ Transport

Sen Monorom p176, map p177

Local transport is US$10-15 a day with moto guide.

It's 370 km from Phnom Penh to Sen Monorom. The trip takes between 6-8 hrs, depending on the speed of your car and the weight of the local's unusual luggage and goods (but this time will be greatly reduced once the road is fixed).The bus leaves for **Phnom Penh** at 0730, 8 hrs, US$6-9. The Phnom Penh bus goes via **Snuol** which is a staging post for buses and pickups to other destinations. Bus ticket to Snuol US$5. If you want to go to **Kratie** (change at Snuol), US$8, or **Stung Treng**, US$12. At present there is no direct transportation from Siem Reap to Sen Monorom; however, you can purchase a bus ticket for US$14 and change in Skun.

Pick-ups and shared taxis are probably the most comfortable option (particularly if you buy extra space). They depart from the morning market between 0700-0800. The cost of a shared taxi per seat costs US$9-12. In Phnom Penh see the ever-smiling Mr Pheat, the **Happy River Agent**, T012-247793, on the riverfront.

Ban Lung *p180, map p181*

With the route from Kompong Cham to Kratie being both shortened and improved plus the plans to upgrade the road into Ban Lung, journey times between Ratanakiri and Phnom Penh (and places en route) could be significantly reduced in the near future. Regular daily buses to **Stung Treng** (3 hrs, US$6), **Kratie** (5-6 hrs, US$7), **Kompong Cham** (6-8 hrs, US$9), **Siem Reap** (change in Skon, 14 hrs, US$16), **Phnom Penh** (9-11 hrs, US$9-14) and to the **Vietnamese border** (see box, page 18, 2½ hrs, US$10) are all available in a variety of mini and larger buses. Share and private taxis are also available, with prices fluctuating depending on season, road conditions and price of fuel; ask at your guesthouse/hotel for price approximations on arrival.

Tourists commonly ask about travelling between Ban Lung and **Sen Monorom**. The roads are almost impassable and difficult to navigate. Only experienced dirt-bike riders with excellent local knowledge should attempt this trip. Several guesthouses have motorbikes for hire, or can arrange hire, for around US$5 per day without driver and triple that with a driver. There are no garages/petrol stops outside the town of Ban Lung, though there are a few roadside places offering bottles of fuel of dubious quality, so it is advisable to set off with a full tank. **Lake View Lodge** can also arrange moto and dirtbike for US$5-10 per day. Norden House (see page 185) has a few top-class 250cc and 400cc dirtbikes for rent, from US$25 to US$50 per day.

⊙ Directory

Sen Monorom *p176, map p177*
Banks There is one **Acleda** bank available with an ATM available to withdraw cash, a slight walk away from the town centre. **Internet** Try Bamboo Restaurant next door to the bus stop. There are a few places in town charging around US$1 an hour.

Ban Lung *p180, map p181*
Banks ANZ bank have opened an ATM near the airport though it is not certain if it is always stocked with sufficient cash. The **Mountain Guesthouse** and the **Ratanak Hotel** both change TCs but allow at least 3 days for your cheques to clear. **Internet** CIC near Sovannikiri Hotel. **Medical services** The hospital is on the road north towards O Chum. **Dr Vannara**, T012-970359, speaks very good English. **Post office** In the centre of town.

Contents

Footprint features

The South

Don't miss ...

★ 1 Kampot, see page 199.
2 Bokor Hill Station, see page 200.
3 Kep, see page 201.

With the opening of the Vietnamese border near Kampot at Ha Tien, southern Cambodia is now firmly grasping its tourist potential as a staging post for overland travellers. Yet, in many ways it manages to encompass the worst and best of what tourism can offer to a developing country such as Cambodia. Take Sihanoukville. It's not so long ago that the beaches around this sleepy port town could be described as idyllic. Now, with human waste pouring directly into the sea from dozens of generic backpacker shanty bars and flophouses, Sihanoukville could almost offer a textbook study in environmental catastrophe. Things have slightly improved though sustainable and equitable development still seems like a long way off.

Travel down the coast to Kep and Kampot, and things couldn't be more different. An old French trading port overlooking the Prek Kamping Bay River and framed by the Elephant Mountains, low-key Kampot, is filled with decrepit dusty charm. Just outside Kampot is Kep, the resort of choice for France's colonial elite, which is now slowly reasserting its position as a place for rest and recuperation. Don't go to Kep expecting wild nights or even a great beach, but perfect views, good seafood and serenity are on offer here.

Northwest from Sihanoukville is Koh Kong province, a vast, wild and untamed expanse of jungle that smothers the stunning Cardamom Mountain range in a thick green blanket. There's now a sealed road through here linking Sihanoukville with Thailand. With logging companies waiting in the wings, this area is now facing an uncertain future.

With the best bus services in the country linking Sihanoukville to Phnom Penh, the resort town has now established itself as the gateway to southern Cambodia. There is now a fledgling bus service linking Sihanoukville to Kampot and Kep, but this can depend on season and demand making the journey along the shoreline not always the easiest (though there are plentiful buses from Phnom Penh to these coastal jewels). You can also travel to Koh Kong via the brand new road from Sihanoukville or Hat Lek, Thailand. With the new road and bridges finally completed the boat from Sihanoukville to Koh Kong is very likely to disappear.

Sihanoukville → See listings, pages 204-216.

Sihanoukville, or Kompong Som as it is called during the periods the king is in exile or 'out of office', was founded in 1964 by Prince Sihanouk to be the nation's sole deep-water port. It is also the country's prime seaside resort. In its short history it has crammed in as much excitement as most seaside towns see in a century – but not of the sort that resorts tend to encourage. Sihanoukville was used as a strategic transit point for weapons used in fighting the USA during the Vietnam War. In 1975, the USA bombed the town when the Khmer Rouge seized the container ship *SS Mayaguez*.

Sihanoukville has now turned a corner, however, and with rapid development has firmly secured its place in Cambodia's 'tourism triangle', alongside Phnom Penh and Angkor Wat. Not much of this development is sustainable and seems more to do with 'cleaning' ill-gotten gains from the international criminal community than anything else. Nearly every single island has now been bought up by Koreans and Russians, with incredibly bad taste, tacky and overpriced resorts already being built. If you scratch the surface in this town a rotten web of corruption, paedophilia and other nefarious activities emerges. And while a liberal attitude towards the smoking of marijuana attracts a youthful crowd, no amount of intoxicants can cover up the fact that Sihanoukville is rapidly becoming an environmental stain on this already horribly scarred country. By late 2009 massive off-shore sand-dredging was also having an impact on this fragile coastline – the beaches here were slowly being eroded with high tides swamping many of the beachside bars and restaurants. If it all becomes too much there are vast unspoiled areas close by in the coastal Preah Sihanouk 'Ream' National Park.

Ins and outs

Getting there There are several regular bus services direct from/to Phnom Penh ranging in price from US$3 to US$7 each way. Journey time is four hours and all of them arrive in Sihanoukville at the bus station near the new market. - as do the share taxis. A seat in a share taxi should cost about US$7 to/from Phnom Penh and a private taxi US$35 to US$50. For travel to/from Siem Reap your best bet is to break your journey in Phnom Penh – new national airline Cambodia Angkor Air has plans to operate a route between Sihanoukville and Siem Reap at some point in the future; visit www.cambodiaangkorair.com for details. For the two-hour journey to Kampot there is no official bus service though local business owners have now established a couple of services that operate sporadically. There are regular share taxis to/from Kampot US$4 to US$5 while private taxis cost US$20 to US$25. With the road now fully complete to/from Koh Kong the boat service has been suspended. There are now two or three

1 Sihanoukville

➡ **Sihanoukville maps**
1 Sihanoukville, page 193
2 Sihanoukville centre, page 194

To Koh Kong ►

Victory Beach

Weather Station Hill

Wat Lau

To Phnom Penh & Kampot

Ekareach St

Vietnamese Consulate

Bus & Taxi Station for South

Independence Beach

Park Beach

Sokha Beach

Lions Statue

Casino

Top Cat Cinema

Serendipity Beach

Ochheuteal Beach

Kanda St

Tola St

Mithona St

To ② ② ② ② ⑦

N

200 metres
200 yards

Sleeping 🛏
Beach Road **1** *C2*
Bungalow Village **3** *A2*
Castaways (Otres) **2** *C3*
Chez Claude **4** *B2*
Chez Mari-yan **5** *A2*
Cloud 9 **6** *C2*

Coasters Guesthouse **7** *C2*
Crystal **8** *C3*
Deva Raja Villa
  & Bungalows **13** *C2*
Golden Sand **10** *C3*
GST Guesthouse **27** *C2*
Holiday Palace
  & Casino **12** *A2*
Independence Boutique
  Resort & Spa **14** *B1*
Mealy Chenda **15** *A2*
Mean Mean (Otres) **9** *C3*
Mick & Craig's **11** *C2*
Monkey Republic **23** *C2*

Motel 7 **24** *C3*
New Beach **16** *A2*
Nika Guesthouse **17** *A2*
Ocean Front (Otres) **28** *C3*
Orchidée Guesthouse **18** *C3*
Reef Resort **25** *C2*
Sakal Bungalows **19** *A2*
Sea Garden (Otres) **29** *C3*
Seahorse Bungalows **30** *C2*
Seaside **20** *C3*
Snake House **31** *A2*
Sokha Beach Resort **21** *C2*
Sunset Garden Inn **22** *A2*
Utopia **32** *C2*

Zen Garden **26** *B3*

Eating 🍴
Cabbage Garden **3** *B3*
Cantina del Mar (Otres) **7** *C3*
Chhner Molop Chrey **1** *A2*
Corner Bar **2** *A2*
Escape **9** *C2*
Le Vivier de la Paillote **4** *A2*

Bars & clubs 🍸
Airport **10** *A2*

buses a day making the four-hour journey – there are also numerous share and private taxis. ▸▸ *See Transport, page 214.*

Getting around Motos and tuk tuk drivers are numerous in Sihanoukville and with some restrictions on motorcycle rental (see below) these are now the preferred modes of transport for many visitors. Expect to pay US$2 to Serendipity Beach with a tuk tuk from the bus station – this may fluctuate according to fuel prices. If you find a good reliable tuk tuk driver get their name and number and use them again – many will also offer a full-day hire for US$10 to US$15. If you decide on renting a motorbike be warned – there are now regular crackdowns on unlicensed tourists riding on motorcycles and you may find yourself being flagged down and the bike impounded. The bike shops can reclaim the bikes so don't accept any extra charges and be especially wary of police on the make here – avoid stopping for them unless you have no alternative Within any given beach area everything is close enough to reach on foot but from beach to beach or beach to town it is definitely a ride... Don't ride with your bag strap across your shoulder as it screams 'pull me off my bike'.

Sights
If Sihanoukville was being tended with care it would occupy a lovely site on a small peninsula whose nobbly head juts out into the Gulf of Thailand. The first-rate beaches, clean waters, trees and invigorating breezes are slowly being replaced with human effluvia, piles of stinking rubbish and nasty flophouses. Cambodia's beaches could be comparable to those in Thailand but are slowly being horribly degraded. Most people head for beaches close to the town which, starting from the north, are Victory, Independence, Sokha, Ochheauteal and, a little further out, Otres. Sihanoukville's layout is unusual, with the 'town' itself, acting as a satellite to the roughly equidistant three beaches. The urban area is pretty scattered and has the distinct feel of a place developing on an ad hoc basis. It has a few large Chinese hotels, a market, petrol stations and a couple of bars.

Victory Beach is a thin, 2-km-long beach on the north of the peninsula, just down from the port, and at its extremes offers reasonably secluded beaches. Beach hawkers are ubiquitous and outnumber tourists at a ratio of about three to one. The area does afford a good sunset view, however. A rocky point at the south end divides the beach. Here is another small streak of sand referred to as **Hawaii Beach**

2 Sihanoukville centre

➡ **Sihanoukville maps**
1 Sihanoukville, page 193
2 Sihanoukville centre, page 194

To Victory Beach
Sopheakmongkol W St
Street 109
Ekareach St
Sopheakmongkol E St
Street 108
Caltex
Fishermen's Den
Main St
Makara St
Samudera Supermarket
Shell
Seeing Hands Massage
G & A Bookshop
Towards Bus Taxi Stand
To Ochenial Beach

N

100 metres
100 yards

Sleeping 🛏
Asean Guesthouse 1
G'Day Mate 9
Geckozy 2
New Paris 4
Oasis 5
Small 6

Eating 🍴
Café Colonia 1
Espresso Kampuchea 2
Holy Cow 4
Starfish Café 5

or Lamherkey Beach. This quiet spot was a bustle of activity during the 1950s when French and Cambodian workers laid the groundwork for construction of the new Port of Kampong Som. North of the beach is the shipping port and a park. **Weather Station Hill**, above the beach, is now slowly transforming into a destination for sex tourists and there are a large number of bars here. There are still a couple of decent places to stay and eat.

Independence Beach was at one time the sole preserve of the once bombed and charred – and now beautifully restored – **Independence Hotel**. The location of the hotel is magnificent and the grounds are a reminder of the place's former grandeur. With the restoration of this sleek hotel complete, its re-opening will do a lot to revive Independence Beach's fortunes.

Sokha Beach is arguably Sihanoukville's most beautiful beach. The shore laps around a 1-km arc and even though the large **Sokha Beach Resort** has taken up residence it is very rare to see more than a handful of people on the beach. It is said that Sihanouk used to import sand to local beaches and looking at the picture-perfect powdery sand of Sokha one wouldn't be surprised if this practice still occurs. Early risers will see why the beach is so perfect, every morning a troupe of sweepers rid the beach of debris. It is best to swim between the centre and the end closest to Ochheauteal Beach, as the Sam At waterway appears to be leaking some rather dubious content into the farther end of the beach.

Ochheauteal Beach lies to the south and, bizarrely, is the most popular with hordes of backpackers and 'sex-pats'. What was once a sparkling stretch of white sand has been reduced to an unending dustbin of rickety, badly planned budget bars, restaurants and accommodation. Much of this has been built directly on the beach, with concrete foundations poured into what could be a stunning waterfront. Coupled with this is a complete lack of proper sewerage and stinking waste pours straight into the sea. Even more astonishing are the tourists and travellers who seem content to swim opposite the pipe openings, the once white foam of the waves turning a yucky brown. If all this isn't enough to put you off, then there is the unrelenting hassle you will get from hawkers and hordes of child vendors pursuing sales very aggressively. Watch your stuff as theft is also common here.

The beach commonly referred to as **Serendipity Beach** is at the very north end of Ochheauteal and is basically Ochheauteal-lite, complete with stinking sewer pipes. This little strand has gained favour with travellers due in part to being the first beach in Sihanoukville to offer a wide range of budget accommodation. Several of these places have now been cleared out and this stretch of beach is attempting to move upmarket. Along the beach front road here keep a look out for Hun Sen's massive and impregnable residence.

Otres Beach is a couple of kilometres south of Ochheauteal and is, at least for the moment, relatively quiet and undeveloped. The stretch of sand here is probably Sihanoukville's longest and it is easy to find a spot for yourself. There are now a number of budget guesthouses opening up here should you wish to stay here. To reach here you'll need to take a moto or tuk tuk (US$3-4). Be careful of walking the long road out here or passing through the local fishing village – several tourists have been robbed, threatened and even a stabbing has been reported.

Around Sihanoukville

Preah Sihanouk 'Ream' National Park ⓘ *HQ 18 km north of Sihanoukville, opposite the airport, T012-875096, daily 0700-1715. You can explore the park either by taking a boat trip (half or 1 day, US$30 for 4 people) or on foot with a guide (US$5 per person for a 3- to 5-hr nature trek). To arrange a guided tour visit the park office in Ream or arrange one through a*

Sihanoukville's islands

More than 20 beautiful islands and pristine coral reefs lie off Sihanoukville's coastline. Most of the islands are uninhabited except Koh Russei (Bamboo Island), Koh Rong Salaam and a few others that contain small fishing villages.

Diving and snorkelling around the islands is pretty good. The coast offers an abundance of marine life including star fish, sea anemones, lobsters and sponge and brain coral. Larger creatures like stingrays, angel fish, groupers, barracuda, moray eels and giant clams are ubiquitous. Baby whale sharks and reef sharks also roam the waters. More elusive are the black dolphins, pink dolphins, common dolphins and bottle-nosed dolphins but they are sighted from time to time. It is believed that further afield (closer to Koh Kong) are a family of dugongs (sea cows). No one has sighted these rare creatures except for one hotel owner who sadly saw a dugong head for sale in Sihanoukville's market.

The islands are divided into three separate groups: the Kampong Som Group, the Ream Group and the Royal Islands. The **Kampong Som Islands** are the closest to Sihanoukville and have quite good beaches. Here the visibility stretches up to 40 m. Koh Pos is the closest island to Sihanoukville, located just 800 m from Victory Beach. Most people prefer Koh Koang Kang also known as Koh Thas, which is 45 minutes from shore. This island has two beautiful beaches (with one named after Elvis) and the added attraction of shallow rocky reefs, teeming with wildlife, which are perfect for snorkelling. More rocky reefs and shallow water can be found at the **Rong Islands**. Koh Rong is about two hours west of Sihanoukville and has a stunning, 5-km-long sand beach (on the southwest side of the island). To the south of the Koh Rong is Koh Rong Salaam, a smaller island that is widely considered Cambodia's most beautiful. There are nine fantastic beaches spread across this island and on the east coast, a lovely heart-shaped bay. It takes about 2½ hours to get to Koh Rong from Sihanoukville. Koh Kok, a small island off Koh Rong Salaam, is one of the firm favourite dive sites, warranting it the nickname 'the garden' and takes 1¾ hours to get there.

During winter (November to February) the **Ream Islands** are the best group to visit as they are more sheltered than some of the other islands but they are a lot further out. The Ream Islands encompass those islands just off the Ream coast: Prek

guesthouse in Sihanoukville. Basic accommodation is available at the park headquarters for US$5 per person. To get there it is probably best to hire a motorbike or a moto driver from Sihanoukville. Head north on Route 4 out of Sihanoukville until you get to a major intersection at around 15 km. Turn right here and onto the road that was resurfaced by the Petroleum Authority of Thailand (PTT) in 1996. The road follows the coastline until you get to the PTT plant and the park can be accessed from here. This beautiful park is a short 30-minute drive from Sihanoukville. The park was set up in 1993 and hugs the coastline of the Gulf of Thailand. It includes two islands and covers 21,000 ha of beach, mangrove swamp, offshore coral reef and the Prek Tuk Sap Estuary. Samba deer, endangered civet species, porcupines and pangolin are said to inhabit the park, as well as dolphins.

Kbal Chhay Waterfall ① *at Khan Prey Nup Village, 8.5 km from downtown Sihanoukville. Follow Highway 4 for 1 km until you have passed the 'Welcome to Sihanoukville' sign, turn left*

Mo Peam and Prek Toek Sap, which don't offer the clearest waters. The islands of Koh Khteah, Koh Tres, Koh Chraloh and Koh Ta Kiev are best for snorkelling. Giant mussels can be seen on the north side of Koh Ta Kiev island. Some 50 km out are the outer Ream Islands which, without a doubt, offer the best diving in the area. The coral in these islands though has started to deteriorate and is now developing a fair bit of algae. Kondor Reef, 75 km west of Sihanoukville, is a favorite diving spot. A Chinese junk filled with gold and other precious treasures is believed to have sunk hundreds of years ago on the reef. Famous underwater treasure hunter, Michael Archer, has thoroughly searched the site but no one can confirm whether he struck gold.

Koh Tang, Koh Prins and Paulo Wai are seven hours away to the southwest. These islands are believed to have visibility that stretches for 40 m and are teeming with marine life. These islands are recommended as some of the best dive sites. It is believed that Koh Prins once had a modern shipwreck and sunken US helicopter but underwater scavengers looking for steel and US MIA guys have completely cleared the area. Large schools of yellow fin tuna are known to inhabit the island's surrounding waters. Koh Tang is worth a visit but is quite far from the mainland so an overnight stay on board might be required. Many local dive experts believe Koh Tang represents the future of Cambodia's diving. The island became infamous in May 1975 when the US ship *SS Mayaguez* was seized by the Khmer Rouge just off here. The area surrounding Paulo Wai is not frequently explored, so most of the coral reefs are still in pristine condition.

Closer to Thailand lies Koh Sdach ('King's Island'), a stop off on the boat ride between Sihanoukville and Koh Kong. This undeveloped island is home to about 4000 people, mostly fishing families. The beaches are a bit rocky but there is some fabulous snorkelling. At the time of publication a guesthouse was being built on the island so it should be possible to stay.

The Cambodian diving industry is still in its fledgling years. The positive in this is that most of the islands and reefs are still in relatively pristine condition and the opportunities to explore unchartered waters limitless.

Some of the islands mentioned above now have guesthouses and hotels – see page 207 for details.

page 207 for details.

and follow this road for another 7.5 km until you reach the falls. This place is near the top of the motos and local tour operator 'must-see' list. The multiple falls are pleasant enough but don't live up to their reputation as one of the area's premier tourist attractions (funnily enough one tour operator refers to it as "something out of Hollywood"). The falls are at their best in the wet season with deeper swimming areas and clean flushes of water. In the drier months they're reduced to a stream, dotted with a few small pools in desperate need of a good clean. The waterfall was 'discovered' in 1960 but plans to establish it as Sihanoukville's primary reservoir were thwarted when the Khmer Rouge seized the area during the war. There are a number of food and drink vendors near the falls but try to avoid a visit on weekends when scores of picnickers descend on the site.

Stung Hav ① *take Hun Sen Beach Dr out past the Sokimex terminal*, is a small fishing village approximately 25 km north of Sihanoukville. The settlement isn't exactly a tourist site but a place where visitors can experience an authentic taste of Khmer life – watching fishing boats come and go, buyers checking out the catch of the day and other platitudes from waterfront life. Sometimes it reeks here due to the prahok factory – a less than palatable, pungent fermented fish paste (see page 24).

For those not wanting to venture out of Sihanoukville, there is also a small fishing port, 2 km north of the ferry dock. Here, the motley collection of wharves comes alive at daybreak, when colourful fishing boats dock and the fish are sorted and bought by wheeling dealing merchants.

At the top of **Sihanoukville Mountain** ① *follow Route 4 about 2.5 km north of town and turn right at the brewery and follow the road up the hill*, is **Wat Leu**, a pretty but rather unexciting modern temple. Of more interest is the nearby **Chinese Cemetery**, which juts from the hillside. The hill's 145-m-high pinnacle affords brilliant panoramic views of Sihanoukville and the islands, particularly at sunset.

The dozens of beautiful **islands** off the coast of Sihanoukville are now being sold off for development – mostly to Korean and Russian businesses. At present many of them still remain untouched and there are a few small bungalow operations that you can stay at (see Sleeping, page 207) – they will also organize transport for you. The first island to be fully developed is on **Koh Dek Koul** where the incredibly gaudy, tasteless Russian-owned Mirax resort has just opened. It looks like a Bond-villain's lair and, to be honest, it probably is.

Koh Kong and around → See listings, pages 204-216.

Dusty Koh Kong is better known for its brothels, casinos and 'Wild West' atmosphere than for lying at the heart of a protected area with national park status (granted by Royal Decree in 1993). It is also often confused with its beautiful offshore namesake Koh Kong Island. The town is also reputed to have the highest incidence of HIV infection of anywhere in Cambodia and is a haven for members of the Thai mafia trying to keep their heads down and launder large sums of money through the casino. The place is only really used by travellers as a transit stop on the way to and from Thailand or two of the most scenic places in Cambodia – Koh Kong Island and the Cardamom Mountains. Due to its border location most people in Koh Kong will accept Thai baht as well as the usual US dollar and Cambodian riel.

Central Cardamoms Protected Forest

① *The area remains relatively inaccessible but over the next few years it is anticipated that ecotourism operators will flock to the area. For now, it is best to make short trips into the park as the area is sparsely populated and heavily mined (so stay on clearly marked paths). Take a motorbike (with an experienced rider) or a boat. The latter option is more convenient in Koh Kong. There are usually several men with boats willing to take the trip down the Mohaundait Rapids, cutting through the jungled hills and wilderness of the Cardomoms. The cost of the trip is US$25-30.*

In 2002, the government announced the creation of the **Central Cardamoms Protected Forest**, a 402,000-ha area in Cambodia's Central Cardamom Mountains. With two other wildlife sanctuaries bordering the park, the total land under protection is 990,000 ha – the largest, most pristine wilderness in mainland Southeast Asia. The extended national park reaches widely across the country, running through the provinces of Koh Kong, Pursat, Kompong Speu and Battambang. Considering that Cambodia has been severely deforested and seen its wildlife hunted to near-extinction, this park represents a good opportunity for the country to regenerate both flora and fauna. The Cardamoms are home to most of Cambodia's large mammals and half of the country's birds, reptiles and amphibians.

The mountains have retained large populations of the region's most rare and endangered animals, such as the Indochinese tigers, Asian elephants and sun bears. Globally threatened species like the pileated gibbon and the critically endangered Siamese crocodile, which has its only known wild breeding population here, exist in the Cardamoms. Environmental surveyors have identified 30 large mammal species, 30 small mammal species, more than 500 bird species, 64 reptiles and 30 amphibians, which reside in the park. Conservationists are predicting they will discover other animals that have disappeared elsewhere in the region such as the Sumatran rhinoceros. With virgin jungles, waterfalls, rivers and rapids this area represents a huge untapped ecotourism potential. However, tourist services to the area are still quite limited.

Koh Kong Island

ⓘ *About 60-90 mins by boat from Koh Kong town. Boats from town usually charge ฿1000 per round trip. Koh Kong Divers, see page 214, offer diving and snorkelling trips to Koh Kong.*
The island (often called Koh Kong Krau) is arguably one of Cambodia's best islands. There are six white powdery beaches each stretching kilometre after kilometre, while a canopy of coconut trees shade the glassy-smooth aqua waters. It's a truly stunning part of the country and has been earmarked by the government for further development, so go now, while it's still a little utopia. There are a few frisky dolphin pods that crop up from time to time – both from the black and the white species. Their intermittent appearances usually take place in the morning and in the late afternoon. You could feasibly camp on the island though would likely need to bring all supplies with you, including drinking water.

Kampot and around → *See listings, pages 204-216.*

Kampot is a charming riverside town that was established in the 19th century by the French. The town lies at the base of the Elephant Mountain Range, 5 km inland on the River Prek Thom and was for a long time the gateway to the beach resort at Kep, see page 201. On one side of the river are tree-lined streets, crumbling mustard yellow French shopfronts and a sleepy atmosphere while on the other side you will find locals working in the surrounding salt pans. The town feels like it's from another era – with a dabbling of Chinese architecture but an overall French colonial influence. With a bit of restoration work it could easily be compared to UNESCO World Heritage sites such as Hoi An in Vietnam and Luang Prabang in Laos. Life is very laid back in Kampot and the town has become a regular expat retreat with Phnom Penh-ites ducking down here for a breath of fresh air and the cooler climate. And with Bokor Mountain National Park close by, Kampot has plenty to offer visitors.

Bokor Mountain National Park

ⓘ *US$5. Bokor is 42 km and 90 mins from Kampot. Head back 6 km towards Sihanoukville then take a right. In 2009 work began on a new road to Bokor and a new Korean-owned casino project on the plateau top. At present the road-builders are allowing some road traffic through though this is intermittent and likely to be with local tour operators only. This situation could also change and you should check with locals when you arrive in Kampot. The old abandoned French-built resort complex (see below) is likely to be demolished.*

Bokor Mountain National Park's plateau, at 1040 m, peers out from the southernmost end of the Elephant Mountains with a commanding view over the Gulf of Thailand and east to Vietnam. Bokor Hill (Phnom Bokor) is densely forested and in the remote and largely untouched woods scientists have discovered 30 species of plant unique to the area. Not for nothing are these called the 'Elephant Mountains' but besides Asian elephants there are tigers, leopards, wild cows, civets, pigs, gibbons and numerous bird species.

At the peak of the mountain is **Bokor Hill Station** where eerie, abandoned, moss-covered buildings sit in dense fog. The buildings were built by the French who, attracted by Bokor's relative coolness, established a 'station climatique' on the mountain in the 1920s. In the grand old days there was a casino, a hotel, villas and a church with a graveyard for those for whom even the cool mountain air proved too oppressive. King Monivong established a residence which his son, Sihanouk, was later pleased to use. In 1970 Lon Nol shut it down and Bokor was quickly taken over by communist guerrillas; it later became a strategic military base for the Khmer Rouge. In more recent years there was a lot of guerrilla activity in the hills, but the area is now safe, with the exception of the ever-present danger of landmines.

The ruins are surprisingly well preserved but bear evidence of their tormented past. Many of the lower windows are bricked up, sandbags are packed into the lower floors and the walls are scarred by bullet holes. You could spend plenty of time poking around in the old settlement speculating where the king may once have lain his royal head, who lost

Kampot

Sleeping
Blissful Guesthouse 3
Bodhi Villa 6
Bokor Mountain Lodge 9
Borey Bokor 1 1
Hang Guesthouse 11
Kampot Guesthouse 2

Les Manguiers 12
Little Garden Bar 5
Long Villa 13
Molieden 7

Eating
Epic Arts Café 2

Jasmine 3
Rusty Key Hole 4

N

200 metres
200 yards

what to whom in the casino, and who wed whom in the church. Then there are lovely walks down into the forest. There is a double waterfall called **Popokvil Falls**, a 2-km walk from the station, which involves wading through a stream, though in the wet season this is nigh on impossible.

Kbal Romeas caves and temple

Some 10 km or so out of Kampot on both the roads to Phnom Penh and to Kep, limestone peaks harbour interesting caves with stalactites and pools. It is here that you can find one of Cambodia's hidden treasures – an 11th-century temple slowly being enveloped by stalactites and hidden away in a cave in **Phnom Chhnok**, next to the village of Kbal Romeas. The temple, which is protected by three friendly monks, was discovered by Adhemer Leclere in 1866. It was closed off because of thieving and now lies virtually forgotten by all bar the villagers who live here. The temple is on the road towards Kep but directions on how to get there are fairly complex and many of the motos (US$3-4) and cars (around US$10) now do trips out there. If caves are more your cup of tea, take the Phnom Penh road out of town and turn right into the cement factory and head for the peaks; there are caves all around. About 8 km along the road to Kep under **Phnom Siap Ta'aun**, there are yet more caves, called Kbal Meal.

Kompong Trach and White Mountain

ⓘ *Bear left at the White Horse Statue and follow the road. The road is a combination of well graded and badly potholed. A torch and good shoes are required for serious exploring.*
Although Kompong Trach, 35 km east of Kep, is best known for being the area where three foreign tourists were held captive by the Khmer Rouge in 1994, it makes for an interesting day trip out of either Kampot or Kep. The main reason people visit this area is to see the impressive limestone caves of the White Mountain which lie a few kilometres outside the town (look out also for the limestone kilns on the outskirts of Kompong Trach). Water erosion has created large outcrops of caves. The White Mountain has been an important religious pilgrimage spot for hundreds of years and local rumour maintains there are several long forgotten Hindu temples within the caves which tunnel deep into the mountain. More easily accessible are the reclining Buddhas and shrines found in many of the cave entrances. As well as Kompong Trach's caves, the area has another reason to stand tall: it is the durian-growing centre of the country.

Kep

Tucked in on the edge of the South China Sea, Kep was established in 1908 by the French as a health station for their government officials and families. Being the nearest beach to Phnom Penh, Kep was once very popular with the elite of Cambodian and French society. The ruins of their holiday villas stand along the beachfront and in the surrounding hills. They were largely destroyed during the civil war under Lon Nol and by the Khmer Rouge. They were then further ransacked during the famine of the early 1980s when starving Cambodians raided the villas for valuables to exchange for food. The white villa on the hill is said to be Sihanouk's. In the past Sihanouk also had his own private island here – Ile des Ambassadeurs – where he entertained guests. Khmers will tell you that the name originates from the legend of Sa Kor Reach who cast a spell on the King of Angkor, stole the king's white horse, and rode to Kep where he was forced out of town by the king's soldiers leaving behind his saddle (Kep She which literally translates to 'horse seat' in Khmer). The horsey statue on the way into town lends weight to this eponymous name.

At the time of publication, Kep still hadn't hit the radar of many international tourists. It is very popular on weekends with holidaying Cambodians who have managed to keep this idyllic town one of the country's best kept secrets. Beautiful gardens and lush green landscape juxtaposed with the blue waters makes it one of the most wonderfully relaxing places in the country. The town itself only has one major beach, a pebbly murky pool which doesn't really compare with Sihanoukville beaches, but they can be found at almost all of the 13 outlying islands, see below. Kep is considerably more beautiful than Sihanoukville and much more relaxing. It is famous for the freshly caught crab, which is best eaten on the beach (US$1.50 per kg), and the drink *tik tanaout jiu*, a palm wine. Along the waterfront lie a number of ruined holiday homes – testament to the town's wonderful past.

The town is divided into two parts. The beach area features a **pier** with a large-buttocked mermaid statue, the best crab restaurants and the ruined colonial villas. It is here that you will find the sand. The **beachfront** is pleasant with plenty of shady trees and benches, but the beach itself can be quite dirty. From July to October Kep is subject to the southeast monsoon, occasionally rendering the beach unswimmable because of the debris brought in. About 2 km further on, where the beach is stoney, is the administrative area and the **market**.

There are 13 islands off Kep's shore: Koh Trangol, Koh Korang, Koh Mtes, Koh Kok, Koh Svay, Koh Tbol, Koh Hal Trey, Koh Makprang, Koh Ses, Koh Sngout, Koh Pou, Koh Angkrang and Koh Toensay. From Kep it is possible to hire a boat to **Koh Toensay** (Rabbit Island) ① *expect to pay about US$10 to hire a boat for the day*. There are four half-moon beaches on this island which boast much finer, whiter sand than Kep beach. Note that the snorkelling and diving is not as good as it is around Sihanoukville's islands. Further out is **Snake Island** ① *local craft are generally too small to make the journey so it might be better to take a larger boat from Kampot,* which has beautiful white sandy beaches and coral. The Kampot to Kep road has some good caves about 8 km out of Kampot.

Takeo and around → *See listings, pages 204-216.*

There isn't a whole lot drawing tourists to Takeo. Most find themselves coming here to visit nearby sites such as Angkor Borei or Phnom Da. It's hard today to imagine Takeo being the powerhouse scholars presume it was. Third-century Chinese merchants referred to this area as the mighty Funan Kingdom and archaeological evidence discovered at Angkor Borei substantiates the theory that the area was probably an epicentre of some kind around AD 300-400.

Modern-day Takeo might lack the chutzpah of an ancient kingdom but is still delightful in its own way – bright red flame trees bloom about the town, these are charming parks and a very serene, lotus-filled lake. During the wet season Takeo becomes a wetlands almost overnight with over half the local land mass dedicated to rice cultivation. When heavy rains fall the hilltop of Phnom Da becomes a little island approachable by boat only. When the roads become impassable, a nifty canal system acts as a substitute.

Sights

① *Getting to Angkor Borei and Phnom Da is half the fun, taking a boat down the local canals and meandering down the river. The day excursion should cost US$20 by boat and is a scenic 40-min trip through the rice fields, marshlands and criss-crossing the ancient canals.*

Angkor Borei is a lovely little settlement on the banks of the Prek Angkor, a tributary from the Bassac. The ancient Funan ruins here have attracted worldwide acclaim as research

The legend of Phnom Da

The mighty King of Champassack had a beautiful daughter, Princess Ak Or. As a young woman the princess fell hopelessly in love with a poor villager and the pair secretly married. The king was enraged when he found out and banished them from the kingdom, sailing them down the river on a small raft with only a few morsels to eat. They drifted for months and eventually washed up at Phnom Borei.

Poor, hungry and tired they immediately set about creating a new life, building a house and planting some crops. But they were desperately poor and nothing could quell Ak Or's pining for her old life. She prayed to the spirits every night for some luck and one night in her dream a man said: "I am an honest man. From now on I will watch over you and your fortunes will change. You will be rich and famous."

The next day, when her husband collected wood, she went to check, only to find he was collecting precious sandalwood. She was ecstatic and Ak Or's husband, desperate to keep her happy, went deeper into the forest, stumbling across a pile of colourful stones. He took them back to their house and Ak Or immediately knew he had found precious gems.

Eventually some traders came through and the couple sold their precious commodities and became very rich. Eventually Ak Or inherited the throne and as king and queen they constructed a huge castle out of bricks and stones and called it Da – the word for rock. Once their castle was completed they asked their subjects to build a small but beautiful stone temple on the mountain to pay tribute to the honest man who had kept his word. The temple they built was Phnom Da.

indicates the ancient walled city of Angkor Borei could date as far back as 2000 years. There were probably hundreds of temples once but today there is not much for tourists to see. The major draw card is the nearby **museum** ① *US$1, 0830-1630 (with a 2-hr lunch break in the middle of the day)*. Housed in a small colonial building, the museum has several reproductions of sculptures, statues, beads, rocks and inscriptions from the nearby ruins of Phnom Da. Many of these artifacts have been carbon-dated, some as far back as the fourth century. There is also small photography exhibition showing the extensive excavations undertaken by the University of Hawaii team to find out more about the Funan era.

Ten minutes away from the museum is **Phnom Da** ① *US$2*, the oldest historical site in Cambodia. This site was a place of worship prior to the erection of the first temple here in the sixth century. There are two 45-m high hills and at the peak of one sits Prasat Phnom Da. On the way up the hill there are four caves used as shrines. Phnom Da is a square laterite tower with four doorways. Most of the precious artifacts have been relocated and false carvings and embellishments have been substituted (except for the east side).

For Sleeping and Eating price codes and other relevant information, see Essentials pages 22-23.

Sleeping

Sihanoukville *p192, maps p193 and p194*

There is a lot of accommodation in Sihanoukville and not all of it good, but the situation is developing. The future of Sihanoukville's guesthouses is somewhat insecure. Many small operators will be cleared out (especially those on the beachfront) as bigger developers move in. Plenty of new businesses are also opening up and then going bust within a year or 2. We've listed our pick of the best that Sinahoukville has to offer.

Town centre

Travellers en route for Kampot or Thailand may choose to stay in town, otherwise one of the beach areas represents a more pleasant alternative.

C-E New Paris Hotel, corner of Sopheakmongkol and Ekareach St. Passable rooms with a/c, hot water, TV and fridge. Clean but nondescript and a serious overuse of wood panelling. Khmer and Thai restaurant with large menu of dishes charging between US$5-8.

E Asean Guesthouse, corner of Ekareach St and Makara St. Decent, clean a/c rooms in this central and sometimes noisy location. The Khmer owners are friendly enough and the rooms at the back are quieter. Will also offer long-stay rates.

E-F G'Day Mate, Ekareach St, T012-280947. Decent enough rooms, fan and a/c, all with TV and fridge. They run a good bar and restaurant and also a (sporadic) bus service to Kampot and Kep.

E-F Oasis Hotel, Ekareach St, T092-274021. Large rooms with TV, a/c, fridge and hot water. Very large building with cavernous lobby behind the restaurant/ bar and mammoth staircase. Restaurant with large bar, Western breakfast, pizza and generic Asian food. Ping pong, pool and big TV available.

E-F The Small Hotel, a block off Ekareach St, T012-794637, thesmallhotel@yahoo.com. As the name indicates this place is not big. Nonetheless it still manages to deliver much more than its name suggests and is very clean and friendly. Good-sized, bright rooms are spotlessly clean and offer a/c or fan, en suite, fridge, TV, new fixtures and big balconies. Swedish and Khmer restaurant. Recommended.

F-G Geckozy, 2 blocks back from Ekareach St, T012-495825, www.geckozy-guesthouse. com. Brightly painted guesthouse set in lovely gardens. Mid-sized rooms colourfully decorated in a beach theme with fan and balcony. Attached toilet. Great restaurant with modern Japanese and Western cuisine. Travel services and motorbike rental.

F-G Zen Garden, just south of downtown area, T011-262376. Nice setting in an old wooden building in a relaxed back street. Rooms are very basic but very cheap. Good budget option. Also have dorms and serve food.

Victory Beach Area and Weather Station Hill

Weather Station Hill is now becoming a haven for sex tourists.

A-D Holiday Palace Hotel and Casino, near the Victory Monument, T034-933808. 140 rooms with a/c, TV, fridge and hot water. This is quite a good hotel for the rates, which are usually quite low in order to attract casino-goers. Has a slightly dodgy atmosphere which is in keeping with Sihanoukville's general vibe.

A-D New Beach Hotel, T034-933822. Quite ostentatious, with an overly decorated lobby. Decent rooms with particularly good ocean views, well furnished, a/c, hot water and TV. Breakfast included. Bar and restaurant opens right onto the shore and the menu features typical Western breakfasts, seafood dishes and a whole 'intestinal' section.

A-D Snake House, Soviet St (between North and South Victory Beach) attached to the restaurant of the same name, T012-673805. Collection of musty, overpriced, non-descript, bungalows and rooms, all a/c, TV and with en suite hot-water facilities, set amid thick foliage, a distance from the beach. The extraordinary collection of snakes, insects and giant crocodile pit, plus a smattering of Russians and bargirls make the experience here uniquely Sihanoukville.

C-F Chez Mari-yan, Sankat 3, Khan Mittapheap, T034-933709. Currently the best bungalow-style place to stay in this end of town. It offers a block of hotel rooms and simple wooden and concrete bungalows perched on stilts at the top of a hill affording nice sea views. It is family-run (Swiss and Khmer). Occupants need to be nimble footed to scramble over the maze of pathways to get to their bungalow. Restaurant sports a short menu which features fish, squid and crab.

D-G Mealy Chenda, on the crest of Weather Station Hill on the triangle road, T034-933472. Very popular hotel offering accommodation to suit a wide range of budgets from dorm rooms through to a/c double rooms. Sparkly clean with fantastic views from the restaurant (the Korean BBQ is highly acclaimed here).

D-G Nika Guesthouse, Ekareach St, T012-286191. Newly refurbished rooms come complete with a/c and fan. Great views from the rooftop restaurant which serves Khmer and French-inspired grub. Haggle if you're planning to stay long-term.

E-G Bungalow Village, halfway down Weather Station Hill, T012-490293, bungalowvillage@hotmail.com. Managed by a French chap – cheap clean rooms in a mild state of disrepair but the atmospheric restaurant affords lovely sea views and has quite nice food.

E-G Sakal Bungalows, near the end of Weather Station Hill, T012-806155, www.sakal bungalows.com. A mix of fan and a/c rooms and bungalows available in this spotless and well-run mini-resort. Restaurant, bar and cheap internet also available. Closest bungalows to Victory Beach. Popular and cheap.

E-G Sunset Garden Inn, near Mealey Chenda, T012-562004. 3-storey guesthouse on the hill with an unobstructed view of the ocean. Restaurant with not-so-impressive backpacker-orientated meals. Exceptionally clean, simple rooms with TV, Western bathroom and fan. Very friendly, family-run Khmer hotel. Recommended.

Sokha and Independence Beach

LL-AL The Independence Boutique Resort and Spa, T034-934300, www.independence hotel.net. Undoubtedly the most groovy and gorgeous hotel in town, **The Independence** has been beautifully restored to all its modernist glory. The rooms are minimalist and chic and complete with a/c, TV, bathtub and other luxuries. Great views over the sea from the hilltop perch and it's also set in some pleasing gardens with a pool. This is exactly the kind of thing Sihanoukville needs to pull itself out of its current malaise. You can also haggle the rates down when it is quiet. Highly recommended.

LL-AL Sokha Beach Resort and Spa, St 2 Thnou, Sangkat 4, T034-935999, www.sokha hotels.com. A de luxe, 180-room beachfront resort and spa, set amidst an expansive 15 ha of beachfront gardens fronting pristine white sandy beach. Guests have a choice between hotel suites or private bungalows dotted in the tropical gardens. Rooms are quite impressive, with beautiful Italian linen and lovely bathtubs. The hotel has very low occupancy, so it is worthwhile checking if it can offer a discount as it's always running special deals.

B-C Chez Claude, between Sokha Beach and Independence Beach, on the hilltop, T012-824870. 9 bungalows occupy a beautiful hillside spot just behind Sokha Beach. The accommodation represents a cross-section of Indonesian-, Lao- and Khmer-style bungalows. Good for those with kids as it offers 2-room bungalows with Western toilet, hot water and fan. The restaurant (see page 211) has fantastic views and is great (but pricey). Excellent selection of wines. Recommended.

Ochheuteal and Serendipity beach area

A-C Crystal Hotel, Ochheuteal Beach, T034-933881. The stylish rooms on the inside belie the garish exterior of this friendly Khmer-owned hotel set on the beach road. All the usual facilities of hot-water bathrooms, a/c and free Wi-Fi are on offer as are views of Hun Sen's massive palatial mansion next door.

A-C Golden Sand, corner of Tola St, T034-933607, www.hotelgoldensand.com.kh. Large hotel with nice pool but somewhat soulless rooms, but at this price, it beats its competition, the **Sokha Hotel**. Nice views from some of the upper floors. Includes buffet breakfast. The restaurant serves Khmer, Chinese and Thai food.

A-F Coasters Guesthouse, near the end of the cove, T034-933776, coasters@ camintel.com. The bungalows are pretty basic but have Western toilet and fan. The hotel rooms are good and have hot water and a/c. It boasts a restaurant right on the beach with a patio with lovely views.

B Seaside Hotel, Mithona St, a block from the traffic circle, T034-933641, www.seasidehotel.com.kh. The building is designed to look like a wat. Some large, decent rooms with a/c, hot water, bath and fridge, some overlooking the beach. Price varies according to floor. Restaurant with large Khmer menu, which is seafood intensive, gift shop and internet. Some guests have complained about this hotel and you may want to have a good look around before booking a room.

B-C Deva Raja Villa and Bungalows, T012-1600374, www.devarajavilla.com. Great little boutique-type affair with stylish rooms, en suite facilities with stylish bathtubs, a/c. Good restaurant. Recommended.

B-D Reef Resort, T012-315338, www.reef resort.com.kh. Well-run, small hotel at the top of the hill near the garish golden lions roundabout. Rooms are a touch overpriced but there is a nice little pool and mammoth breakfast included. One of the better mid-range places in town and always full, so book ahead. Has a bar and restaurant which serves average food.

B-E Beach Road Hotel, Serendipity Rd, T017-827677, www.beachroad-hotel.com. Excellent-value well-run and maintained hotel with a large range of rooms to fit most budgets – prices drop during low season. All rooms are en suite, with TV, a/c, free Wi-Fi and hot water. The clincher is the gorgeous pool. There's a reasonable and decent bar attached.

C-F Cloud 9, on the hill above Serendipity Beach (at the very end of the beach), T012-479365, www.cloud9bungalows.com. Basic wooden bungalows (the nicest 'huts' on the beach). Prices vary according to view, with Western toilet and fan.

D-E Orchidée Guesthouse, Tola St, T034-933639, www.orchidee-guesthouse.com. This place does not belie its name and the courtyard full of beautiful orchids provides an auspicious welcome. It is well-run, properly maintained and clean, offering well-aired rooms, a/c and hot water. Restaurant with Khmer and Western seafood. Nice pool area, a 5-min walk to the beach. Great value. Highly recommended.

E Monkey Republic, Serendipity Rd. T012-490290. Notorious backpacker hangout which is more renowned for the party atmosphere and cocktail menu than for the quality of its accommodation. Rooms are simple affairs and could be cleaner. There are better deals to be had elsewhere.

E-F Motel 7, Ochheuteal Beach, T015-207719. Set just back from the beach on the road, this is a brand new, stylish and simple guesthouse. All rooms have ensuite facilities, cable TV and free Wi-Fi – the pricier ones also have a/c and hot water. Friendly owners were planning to set up a small coffee and ice cream parlour.

E-G GST Guesthouse, Mithona St, T016-210222. Popular guesthouse, in part because it is where the bus terminates and in part because they pay motos quite good commission for dropping you here. Regardless, the place is clean (fan, attached bathroom), cheap and reasonably close to the beach.

F Mick & Craigs, Serendipity Rd, T012-727740. Nicely decorated small rooms set around the back of a restaurant of same name on hill above beach. The rooms only have cold water and fan but are excellent value for the location.

G Seahorse Bungalows, Serendipity Rd, T012-597161. Simple basic rooms, with mosquito nets and fans, plus shared cold water bathrooms in this rustic, wooden house. Hippy atmosphere might not be for everyone but this is a friendly and reasonably well-run operation.

G Utopia, Serendipity Rd, T034-934319, www.utopiacambodia.com. It's hard to figure out if this is a new concept in budget travel – the bunks in the dorm rooms are completely free (they also have private rooms for US$5) – or if it's the beginning of some kind of *Beach*-like cult. The avowed aim here is partying with poolside raves and an endless supply of fries and burgers. There's nothing remotely Khmer about the experience on offer here but it might indicate one possible future for budget travel.

Otres Beach

There are several new places opening up along about 1 km of this stretch of beach but most seem like temporary affairs - we've listed the best here. Facilities are also basic with limited electricity and running water. All those listed here run restaurants and bars.

E Ocean Front, T012-478531. Reasonably well-run place with the glass-fronted rooms laid out looking onto the beach. The rooms are a bit dingy though. Claim to have electricity all day in high season. Every room has fan and cold-water en suite bathrooms.

E-F Castaways. Friendly place with basic bungalows and rooms directly on the beach.

All are en suite and have fans. Good electricity supply that should be 24 hrs in high season.

F Mean Mean. One of the longest established operations on Otres you'll find the usual simple fan bungalows and rooms complete with coldwater bathrooms. Cosy communal areas plus they also host a number of water sports. Electricity all night.

F Sea Garden. Nice rustic bungalows, some with 4-poster beds. Also serve pretty good food and cold beer. Shared bathrooms.

Islands

The islands close to Sihanoukville are slowly getting developed.

L Mirax Resort, Koh Dek Koul Island, T012-966503, www.miraxresort.com. Grotesque island resort that epitomises everything nasty about Cambodian tourism.

C-E EcoSea Bungalows, Koh Rung Samloem Island, office is at **Reef Resort** (see page 206), T012-606646, wwwecoseadive.com. Small group of 4 basic bungalows and a couple of family rooms on this remote and beautiful island. Food is also available.

D Lazy Beach, Koh Rung Samloem Island, booking office is just past **Seahorse Bungalows** (see page above), T016-214211, www.lazybeach cambodia.com. Simple, clean bungalows set by a stunning beach. They charge US$10 per person per single boat transfer to reach the island. Serve up a good array of food as well.

D-F Jonty's Jungle Camp, Koh Ta Kiev Island, T092-502374, www.jontysjungle camp.com. Basic, hammock-style camping accommodation in this gorgeous island retreat. They also have a few treehouses if you don't fancy a hammock. Don't come expecting any mod cons but you will be given a mosquito net. Price drops if you stay for more than one night. Great snorkelling nearby, idyllic if you like this sort of thing. Serve their own basic food. Price includes long-tail to and from the island.

E-G Koh Ru, Koh Russie Island, booking office just past **Sea Horse Bungalows**, T012-388860. This is a quaint collection of simple fan bungalows and dormitory rooms in a lovely beachside location. Totally relaxed and quiet, this is a decent spot to really get away from it all. Also serve food and drinks. Boat transfers US$10.

Koh Kong and around *p198*

With the road to Phnom Penh and Sihanoukville now completed, accommodation and other facilities in Koh Kong are improving.

D-E Apex Koh Kong, St 8, T016-307919, www.apexkohkong.com. With a swimming pool, free Wi-Fi, friendly staff and good food this is easily one of the best places to stay in Koh Kong. The bright, fresh rooms, all set around a courtyard, have cable TV, hotwater and a/c. Excellent value and recommended.

D-E Asean Hotel, riverfront, T012-936667. Nice rooms with a/c, bathtubs, cable TV. The ones at the front have balconies and river views. There's a decent internet café downstairs. Friendly owners and well run. Recommended.

D-E Koh Kong City Hotel, riverfront, T035-936777, http://kkchotel.netkhmer.com. This biggish hotel by the river has decent, clean rooms, the best of which have great river views. Staff are a little indifferent but it makes for a good place to stay. Rooms are a/c with cable TV and hot-water en suite facilities throughout.

E Bopha Koh Kong, 2 blocks east of the boat pier, T035-936073. Good, clean rooms with all amenities – a/c, cable, fridge. More expensive rooms have bathtub and hot water. Pretty good value. Restaurant also.

F Koh Kong Guest House, riverfront, T011-821525. The pleasant veranda where drinks and food are served doesn't really make up for the slightly dingy fan-only rooms. Although this place has a reputation as a travellers' hang-out you can find better deals elsewhere in town.

F-G Otto's, a block south of the boat pier, T012-924249. Basic fan rooms in a wooden house. Shared bath, fan, mosquito net, rather random and kitsch decor. Old wooden structure, feels like a bungalow, bit dirty, good size though.

Kampot and around *p199, map p200*

There is now a good range of accommodation in Kampot. Some guesthouses seem to have been set up to indulge their owners' ganja smoking habits and you may feel left out if you're not interested in engaging in this past-time.

B-D Bokor Mountain Lodge, T033-932314, www.bokorlodge.com. Old colonial property on the riverfront that has had several incarnations and was once even a HQ for the Khmer Rouge. It has bags of atmosphere and is probably the best spot in town for an icy sundowner. All rooms have en suite, a/c, cable TV. Recommended.

B-D Les Manguiers, 2 km north of town, T092-330050, mango@mfone.com.kh, www.mangokampot.com. Cute little French-run guesthouse. Set by the river amidst paddies and swaying tropical trees this is a relaxing place to spend a couple of days. Nice bungalows with fans or a/c – some rooms also in main building. Offers free bicycles to guests.

B-D Rikitikitavi, T012-235102. A recently opened riverfront, Western-owned, guesthouse. The rooms are nice enough, a/c, TV, en suite, with cute touches, though the management is soporific at best and indifferent at worst. There are better options in town in this price range.

D-E Little Garden Bar, T012-427572, www.littlegardenbar.com. Basic, clean rooms, fan and bathroom. Restaurant offering panoramic views of Mount Bokor.

D-F Borey Bokor Hotel 1, T092-978168, boreybokorhotel@yahoo.com. In an ostentatious style with all rooms offering a/c, TV, fridge and comfy beds.

E-F Hang Guesthouse, T016-389170, www.hang.esmartweb.com. Sweet guesthouse set by the river a little further south along the estuary than the main drag. Pretty gardens, free bicycles and a friendly vibe enhance the small rooms. Fan and cool water only.

E-F Molieden, a block away from the main bridge, T012-820779, mailmoliedenkampot@

yahoo.com. A surprisingly good find, its hideous façade gives way to a very pleasant interior. Large, tastefully decorated modern art deco rooms with TV and fan. The rooftop restaurant also serves some of the best Western food in town (see Eating). Very good value, with free Wi-fi.

E-G Blissful Guesthouse, next to Acleda Bank, T092-494331, www.blissfulguesthouse. com. Converted colonial building with lovely surrounding gardens and relaxing public areas. Rooms are simple with mosquito net, fan and attached bathroom. High on atmosphere and very popular with locals and expats alike. Recently refurbished, they have even created a disabled-access room – the only one in Kampot. One of the best guesthouses in this part of Cambodia. Recommended.

E-G Bodhi Villa, 2 km north west of town on Teuk Chhou Rd, T012-728884, www.bodivilla.com. Cheap and popular budget guesthouse in nice location just outside town, set on the river bank. Owners seem well-intentioned, linking into local volunteer projects, though the hedonistic atmosphere and roaring speed boat which they've introduced to the peaceful river detracts from their efforts. Basic rooms, simple bungalows and US$1 a night dorm.

E-G Long Villa, T092-251418 or T012-731400, www.longvillaguesthouse.com. Very friendly, well-run guesthouse. The unspectacular though functional rooms vary from en suite with a/c and TV through to fan with shared facilities. Recommended.

F Kampot Guesthouse, T012-956040 or T077-483377. Converted from a private house, this guesthouse has a welcoming atmosphere with quiet, plain but comfortable fan or a/c rooms and attached bathrooms. It is tucked away on a small road 200 m from the taxi station. Offers internet free of charge.

Bokor Mountain National Park *p199*
The park rangers run a simple guesthouse at the hill station – youth hostel style. There are bunk beds (US$5) and doubles (US$20), with clean, shared toilets and showers. There is no restaurant so you bring your own food: there is a large kitchen available for guests. Pack warm clothes and waterproofs.

Kep *p201*
The accommodation standards in Kep are higher than the rest of the country and are still considerably cheaper.

LL-AL Knai Bang Chatt, T012-349742, www.knaibangchatt.com. Set in a splendidly restored 20th-century modernist villa, this property seeks to recreate an elitist, and arguably, colonial atmosphere. High walls keep the locals and other undesirables out, while the infinity pool and hackneyed contemporary Asian designer trim of dark woods and white walls offers nothing particularly original. Some people will love the banality of exclusivity – others may judge that the money used to pay for the incredibly high rates would be better spent elsewhere. All rooms, as would be expected, come with all the usual luxury amenities.

A-B La Villa, T012-1702648, www.lavillakep. com. An interesting old French villa forms the centrepiece of this brand-new bungalow operation set by the sea. It's worth just taking a look at the villa if you're passing by. A giant tree grows through the back of the structure much like Ta Prohm in Angkor and the whole restored edifice seems to defy gravity. The bungalows are well-appointed with verandas, a/c, en suite bathrooms, Wi-fi and cable TV. There are plans to open a restaurant and art space in the villa. Recommended.

A-D Veranda Resort and Bungalows, next door to N4, further up Kep Mountain, T012-888619 or T033-399035, veranda resort@gmail.com. Superb accommodation. Large wooden bungalows set in an enchanting garden of ripe fruits, vines and tropical flowers which weave around the stairways criss-crossing the hillside. Each bungalow includes a good-sized balcony, fan, mosquito net and nicely decorated mosaic bathroom. The more expensive of these include very romantic open-air beds.

A few extra upmarket bungalows are about to be built (a/c and hot water). The restaurant offers the perfect vista of the ocean and surrounding countryside. Epicureans will love the variety of international cuisines including poutine of Quebec, smoked ham linguini, fish fillet with olive sauce (all under US$3). Recommended.

B The Beach House, T012-712750 www.thebeachhousekep.com. Arguably the nicest spot to stay in Kep. Great rooms, nearly all of which look out onto the mesmeric ocean – all have a/c, hot water, TV. They even have a small pool and soothing chill-out area. Unpretentious and good value. The staff can sometimes appear to be half-asleep but are very friendly when provoked. Recommended.

D Le Bout Du Monde, to get to the hotel turn left onto the small road going up hill just before the APSECA orphanage, in the first part of town, T011-964181, www.leboutdu mondkep.com. Basic accommodation under a thatched roof, rattan-style walls, simple wooden beds, mosquito nets provided and attached shower and toilet (no fans). There are hammocks out on the front to relax and read while enjoying panoramic views. Comfortable restaurant area with a selection of Western and seafood specialities. No electricity after 2300.

E The Vana Guesthouse, TT012-755038, www.vannabungalows.com. On the hill before Le Bout Du Monde this guesthouse comprises 4 attractive thatch-roofed bungalows with attached bathrooms and Western toilet. They are clean but simple with double beds, mosquito nets and little more. The open, thatched restaurant and eating terrace has a friendly and sedate atmosphere and the food is also good. Staff are friendly and more than willing to organize boat trips to the offshore islands.

E-F Seaside Guesthouse, the 1st right-hand turn as you enter Kep, before the APSECA turn-off, T012-684241. Owned by the Governor of Kep this waterfront concrete hotel lacks the ambience of some of those placed on the hill but is still clean, with fan, attached bathroom.

Takeo and around *p202*
D-E Boeung Takeo Guesthouse, near the park, T032-931306. Reasonably good rooms with fan and Western toilet and a nice view of the lake.
E Phnom SonLonng Guesthouse, near the boat dock. Wide variety of rooms. Ask for one with en suite bathroom and TV.

❼ Eating

Sihanoukville *p192, maps p193 and p194*
Town centre
⫷ **Cafe Colonia**, Ekareach St, T092-529292. Open 1000-2200. New, very sleek looking Khmer-owned café selling ice cream, hot dogs and coffee. Neat hang-out spot away from the backpackers.
⫷ **Geckozy**, in a small street down from the petrol stations, see Sleeping. A lovely German-Japanese restaurant set in a large garden with nifty selection of fare at very reasonable prices. Recommended.
⫷ **Holy Cow**, Ekareach St. Ambient restaurant offering a selection of healthy, Western meals – pasta, salads, baked potatoes. The English owner is a long-term resident and very good source of local information. To his credit he has created a lovely atmosphere and provides impeccable working conditions for his staff. Highly recommended.
⫷ **Starfish Café**, behind Samudera Supermarket, T034-952011. Small café-cum-bakery in a very peaceful garden setting. Here you can eat great food while knowing that you are supporting a good cause. The organization was originally established to help rehabilitate people with disabilities and has extended their services to cover a whole range of poverty-reducing schemes. A very positive place that oozes goodness in its food, environment and service – good Western breakfasts, cakes, sandwiches, salads and coffees. A non-profit massage business has also opened on the premises. Recommended.
⫷-⫷ **Espresso Kampuchea**, Sopheakmôgkol St, T012-478139. Open 0630-2000. Best coffee in

town and the owner is good for a chat. Decent breakfast menu and good hang-out spot.

Victory Beach Area

♦♦♦ **Chez Mari-yan**, see page 205. Has a good seafood restaurant with probably the nicest setting in Sihanoukville, US$4-5 per dish.
♦♦♦-♦♦ **Le Vivier de la Paillote**, at the top of Weather Station Hill. This is the finest dining establishment in town and one of the best in the country. They have everything right: the service can't be surpassed and it is high on atmosphere – cocooned from the noisy street and lit by soft glowing candles. The modern Asian-European fusion menu changes regularly. Recommended.
♦♦ **Chhner Molop Chrey Restauraunt**, across the road from the casino, T034-933708. Big Khmer restaurant with a wide-open platform overlooking the beach. One of the most beautiful locations in town (perfect for a sunset drink). Specializing in some very delicious Cambodian, Thai and Vietnamese seafood dishes (US$2-5). Its menu also emphasizes a 'meat for drinking' section and a wide range of raw fish cuisines (non-Japanese).
♦♦ **The Corner Bar**, T012-479395. Open 1200-0200. Its pizzas have a reputation as the best in town. It also offers salads and baguettes for around the same price. Home delivery available.
♦♦ **The Snake House**, Soviet St (between North and South Victory Beach) attached to the hotel of the same name, T012-673805. The biologist owner of this Russian restaurant has created a unique and captivating place to dine especially if snakes are your thing. A huge King Cobra and a multitude of enclosed vipers and pythons can provide hours of endless fascination. The fantastic staff can provide a miscellany of anecdotes about the reptiles. A particularly good place to bring children (but monitoring would be required). There is a wide range of traditional Russian dishes offered, some a tad too stodgy for the weather but otherwise very good. Recommended.

Ochheuteal and Serendipity beach areas

Almost all the hotels and guesthouses here double as places selling food. It's the usual unadventurous travellers fare. There are a couple of Khmer-style restaurants by the Golden Lions roundabout and a small local market has been established here as well.
♦♦ **Mick and Craig's**. Thankfully, the menu here is a lot more creative than the venue's name. Sufficiently large meals with a bit of pizzazz – pizzas, burgers, hummus, etc. The restaurant also offers 'themed food nights' Sunday roast, BBQ and 'all you can eat' nights.
♦♦-♦ **Cabbage Garden**, T011-940171, down a back lane between Golden Lions and town centre, see map. Open 1000-2300. This restaurant is rightly famous with both locals and resident expats for its incredible Khmer food. The spicy shrimp mango salad is essential. Little tricky to find but a real discovery when you do. Highly recommended.
♦♦-♦ **Escape**, opposite **Reef Resort** (see Sleeping), 0700-2200. Ice cream, cookies, shakes, cakes, coffee, cocktails and books create a decent and distracting combination in this cute little place. It also has a/c, which can provide welcome relief.

Sokha Beach

♦♦♦♦-♦♦ **Chez Claude**, on the hill above Sokha Beach, see Sleeping page 205. Claude has been running a very popular restaurant for years. French, seafood dishes. Provencal-style. Good wine list. Nice view from the restaurant.

Otres Beach

♦♦-♦ **Cantina del Mar**, owned by the same people who run the restaurant of the same name in Phnom Penh. You should find authentic Mexican food and cold Mexican beer here.

Koh Kong p198

There are several places around town that sell Thai food – most of the Khmer-owned hotels listed in Sleeping also serve food or have a restaurant attached. The market is also a good place to pick up fruit and street food.

ffff-f Cafe Laurent, next to **Koh Kong City Hotel**, T011-590168. Open Mon-Sat, 0700-2400. This new bistro serves excellent breakfasts, pastas and pizzas. The coffee and bread are also superb and the pastries are not bad either. Highly Recommended.

ff-f Aqua Sunset Bar and Restaurant, riverfront, T035-6378626. Open 0700-2400. Average Thai, Western and Khmer food served here. They also plan to run river sunset cruises every day at 1700. It's still a great spot to sup a sundowner even if the boat is not running.

ff-f Dug Out. Great Western breakfasts. Also serve other meals but it's at its best first thing. Recommended.

f Otto's Restaurant, big menu with Western breakfasts, baguette sandwiches, schnitzels, seafood, soups, Khmer standards and lots of vegetarian options.

Kampot and around p199, map p200

ffff Molienden Restaurant, see Sleeping page 208. On the roof of the guesthouse of the same name. Extensive selection of pastas, spaghetti, soup and Italian seafood dishes. Fantastic food. Recommended.

ff Bokor Mountain Lodge, see Sleeping page 208. Has recently relaunched its entire menu. Great sandwiches made with the best ingredients – the fish and chicken *amok* is also divine. Recommended.

ff Jasmine, is an excellent riverside eaterie set up by a switched-on Khmer woman (Jasmine) and her American photographer partner. They offer a slightly more up-market experience than many of the other places along the riverfront and the food ain't bad as well. Khmer and Western dishes. Recommended.

ff Phnom Kamchay, beside the bridge on the river offering an English menu, Khmer, Chinese and Western dishes. Considered the best Khmer restaurant in town (free from the monotony of stand-over-beer-girl tactics). Good seafood, friendly staff.

ff Rusty Key Hole Bar and Restaurant, River Rd, past **Bamboo Light**. Run by the very

down-to-earth Mancunian, Christian, **Rusty's** is now something of a local legend. Western food served. Friendly and the best place to watch football in town. The BBQ seafood and ribs come highly recommended.

ff-f Epic Arts café, T092-922069, www.epicarts.org.uk. A brilliant little NGO-run establishment in the centre of Kampot. Set up as a project to employ local disabled people, they produce some incredibly delicious cakes. Highly recommended.

ff-f Little Garden Bar, T012-427572, littlegardenbar@gmail.com. This is an attractive and relaxed bar and restaurant on the riverfront offering delicious Khmer and Western food for reasonable prices. The rooftop bar is the place to be for the spectacular sunset descending over the Elephant Mountains.

Kep p201

There are scores of seafood stalls on the beach, just before the tourist centre, that specialize in cooking freshly caught crab. At the tourist office itself there is also a row of restaurants serving crab, shrimp and fish. Nearly every hotel or guesthouse also serves food – see also Sleeping entries.

ff-f The Riel, T017-902771, www.kep-riel-bar.com. This is now Kep's only proper restaurant-cum-café-cum bar. Great friendly atmosphere and decent food should make this establishment a winner. Good rock 'n' roll stories from the owner as well.

Takeo and around p202

f Grand Café Chisor. Bakery, Khmer and Western food. Very good.

🍸 Bars and clubs

Sihanoukville p192, maps p193 and p194
Most resorts, guesthouses and hotels are also home to some kind of bar. In the Serendipity/Ochheuteal beach area 2 of the most infamous night-time hang-outs are **Monkey Republic** and **Utopia**. For a Khmer

alternative head to one of the Khmer restaurants near the Golden Lions where you will very likely be serenaded by Khmer singers.
Airport, Victory Beach. Set up by the same Russians who own **Snake House**, this massive night club is located inside a fake aircraft hangar which is home to an actual, real aircraft. Decent beachside spot and free entry make this place doubly popular when Sihanoukville is busy.
Sokha Beach Resort. Has a live Filipino band perform every night from 1800.
Top Cat, at the top of the hill near the Golden Lions roundabout, this cinema has been opened by an American ex-pat. They show a variety of films and will even let you use the screen to play Play Station games should the urge overcome you. It's normally US$2 entry but the owner will even let you book out the entire place should you want a romantic evening with your loved one. The seats are all soft furnishings and you can lie, flop or go to sleep if the movie is bad. Recommended.

O Shopping

Sihanoukville *p192, maps p193 and p194*
You should find all the usual traveller items easily in Sihanoukville. A few other places selling slightly more upmarket handmade items have recently emerged but whether they will survive more than a few months is debatable. Petrol stations, especially **Caltex** and **Shell**, have excellent convenience stores attached wherein most little luxuries and necessaries can be bought.
Casablanca, near the Golden Lions Roundabout, has a very good selection of second-hand books to cater for almost all literary tastes. There is also a small boutique at the back of the store which stocks some fashionable clothes and jewellery items. Very quick (but more expensive) email here.
Q & A Book Cafe, near the **Holy Cow** (see Eating), 95 Ekareach St. Great little book shop that also doubles as a café.

Samudera Supermarket, 7 Makara St. Stocks everything and anything a person could possibly want – Western foodstuffs through to toiletries.

Kampot and around *p199, map p200*
Kepler's Books, stocks a decent selection of novels, guidebooks and non-fiction. They buy, sell and exchange books as well. You can also find DVDs here. Recommended.

▲ Activities and tours

Sihanoukville *p192, maps p193 and p194*
Diving and snorkelling
Chez Claude, was the 1st diving operator in Sihanoukville. These days he caters mostly to experienced divers but also offers training. US$60-125 a day. Open water US$350. Snorkelling trips are roughly half the price.
Diving and more, Victory Beach, T034-960625, www.divingandmore.com. A relative newcomer. It markets its dives towards already certified divers. US$70 for a couple of dives.
Scuba Nation Diving Centre, Weather Station Hill, T012-604680, www.divecambodia.com, has the best reputation in town and is the longest established PADI dive centre. It runs the complete range of PADI courses and offers PADI insurance. Prices vary depending on what you want. Open water Course (US$350) through to dive trips (US$70). It has a custom-built dive boat. Recommended.

Fishing
Tradewinds Charters, at The Fishermen's Den Sports Bar, Ekareach St, T01-2702478. Runs daily fishing trips. If you have caught something worth eating, the proprietor, Brian, will organize the restaurant to prepare a lovely meal from the catch.

Massage
Seeing Hands Massage, next to Q&A Book Café on Ekareach St. Open 0900-2100. US$6 per hr. Have a soothing Japanese-style shiatsu massage from the trained blind masseurs.

Koh Kong *p198*
Diving and tours.
Koh Kong Divers, 243 Riverfront Rd, T035-690 0073, www.kohkongdivers.com. The only dive shop in Koh Kong is a professional and well-run operation offering the usual PADI courses, diving and snorkelling trips. They also offer several day trips to local islands, 4WD vehicle sojourns into the nearby Cardamom Mountains and numerous other boat excursions up river to waterfalls and into mangroves. Recommended.

Kampot and around *p199, map p200*
Massage
There are a couple of great blind masseuse places in town, the best being the **Kampot 5 Seeing Hands**, just back from the river near the **Bokor Mountain Lodge**. The people here are incredibly warm and friendly and at US$4 an hr, it's a great way to relax.

Tour operators
Cheang Try, is a local Khmer who runs both a motorcycle rental outlet in the centre of Kampot town (T012-974698) and also does guided tours. At 17 Mr Try's entire family was murdered by the Khmer Rouge and he was forced to live alone in the jungle on Elephant Mountain, near Bokor for 18 months. He then returned to fight the Khmer Rouge. If you take a tour with Mr Try to Bokor his experiences really bring the place alive – rather than getting some wooden tourist tour you'll come away with some redolent and powerful memories. Highly recommended.
Sok Lim Tours, on the riverfront, T012-719872, www.soklimtours.com. Organize tours to surrounding sites. Make sure you get a good guide as it really makes a difference. A scam among the guides is the 'bait and switch', where you arrange the tour with one of their knowledgeable guides only to have them drive round the corner and switch to an average guide/driver at the last minute.

◒ Transport

Sihanoukville *p192, maps p193 and p194*
Sihanoukville is 230 km south of Phnom Penh on Route 4. To get there independently from Phnom Penh you will need to follow the airport road from town and take a right-hand turn at the main intersection between Route 3 and Route 4.

Boat
Fishermen will take visitors out to the **islands** (fee negotiable). The cheapest way to get out to the islands is to try and bargain with the captain from a pre-arranged tour from Ochheuteal Beach at around 0800. Most boats don't usually mind taking an extra passenger for US$5-10. With roads now improving, the boat to and from Koh Kong was suspended at time of writing and is unlikely to return to service.

Bus
All buses depart from the main bus station near the new market unless otherwise stated. Many guesthouses and local tour operators may also offer minibus services but these vary in price and scheduling according to season. Around Khmer New Year and during the peak season you will need to book tickets the day before travel. **Phnom Penh Sorya** and **Paramount** run several services 0700-1400, US$4-5. **Mekong Express** runs at 0745 and 1430, US$6. Route 4 is quick and comfortable and the trip takes about 4 hrs.

Bus services to **Koh Kong** are improving with roughly 2 morning departures a day, 4 hrs, US$13. The Thai border is open until 2000 and buses depart until 2330 from Trat to **Bangkok**.

Minibuses to/from **Kampot** are presently run on a somewhat ad hoc basis by the **G'Day Mate** guesthouse (see Sleeping) US$7.50, 0830 departure and the **Peppercorn Express**, T017-921990, 0830, US$7.50. Both will also pick you up from your guesthouse and need to be booked in advance.

Taxi
Seats in shared taxis are available to **Phnom Penh** (US$7), **Koh Kong** (US$9) and **Kampot** (US$5). All depart from the taxi stand near the bus station. Private taxis are available and according to the quality of the car vary - Phnom Penh (US$35 to US$50), Koh Kong (US$60) and Kampot (US$20 to US$25).

Koh Kong and around *p198*
International connections to **Thailand**. The border crossing is 12 km from Koh Kong, across the river (15-20 mins), see page 18.

Bicycle
Rental from **Otto's** and **Cheap Charlie's** for ฿50 per day.

Boat
At time of publication the boat service between Koh Kong and Sihanoukville was suspended and unlikely to be reinstated.

Bus
Bus tickets are available from most main guesthouse and hotels with buses departing from bus station 1 km out of town down St 3.

There are presently about 2 or 3 departures a day to/from **Sihanoukville**, US$13, 4 hrs; and **Phnom Penh**, US$8 to US$10, 5 hrs. There are also numerous minibus services to destinations in Thailand including **Trat**, **Pattaya** and **Bangkok** but almost all require a change of bus at the border.

Moto
About ฿10 to anywhere in town or ฿40 per hr or ฿250 per day.

Motorbike
Rental from **Otto's** and **Motobar** for ฿150-200 per day.

Shared taxi
To **Sihanoukville**, 5-6 hrs, leaves from market, US$9 person (6 per car), US$60 own car, from 0600 onwards, leaves when full.

Taxi
US$1-2 around town, about US$20 per day, 110 cc.

Kampot and around *p199, map p200*
Bus
There are 2 buses in both directions run by the **Phnom Penh Sorya Transport Co.** between Kampot and **Phnom Penh**. These services also stop in **Kep**. They depart the bus station on Blvd Charles de Gaulle near the central market in Phnom Penh at 0730 and 1315, returning at 0730 and 1230 from Kampot bus stand, US$4.

To/from Sihanoukville see Sihanoukville bus listings in Transport, above.

Motos
Motos usually charge 1000 riel for short trips across town. There are usually a few gathered around the Sokimex petrol station on the way into town.

Shared taxi
From **Phnom Penh**, 3 hrs to Kampot. Leaving from Doeum Kor Market on Mao Tse Tung Blvd and not the central market in Phnom Penh, US$3-4, 3 hrs. To **Phnom Penh**, vehicles leave from the truck station next to the **Total** gas station at 0700-1400, US$3.50, private taxi US$20. To **Sihanoukville**, US$4, private US$20-25, 2 hrs. To **Kep**, US$8, return US$14-15.

There are a few early-morning pickups from the market to Kep, US$3 or else you can hire a moto, US$2-3, US$5-6 return or car, US$14 return.

You can now cross the border into **Vietnam** at Ha Tien, see page 18. As this exit/entry point is so new, fares have not been decided on. They should settle at roughly US$5 for a moto and US$10 for a tuk tuk. Sok Lim tours are now also offering shared-car transport from US$4.

Kep *p201*
Kep is only 25 km from Kampot. The road is good and the journey can be made in

30-45 mins. A large white horse statue marks the turn-off to Kep. Buses now run twice a day between Kep/**Kampot** and **Phnom Penh** (see page 215).

Takeo and around *p202*
Bus
Buses leave Takeo market for **Phnom Penh** every hour 0700-1600, 6000 riel, 2½ hrs.

Directory

Sihanoukville *p192, maps p193 and p194*
Banks There are 4 banks in town (often shut): Acleda, Canadia, Mekong Bank and UCB. All 4 are on Ekareach St in downtown. Acleda does Western Union money transfer and UCB and Canadia do Visa/MasterCard cash advances. Cash advances are also available at Samudera Supermarket, in town, 5% commission. Lucky Web, on Weather Station Hill, charges 4% commission. The gold traders at the market are often more convenient and can offer a better exchange rate on cash than some of the banks.
Embassies and consulates Vietnamese Consulate, 'Main Street' in town for visa business. **Internet** All tourist areas in Sihanoukville have internet within 1-2 mins' walking distance. Prices vary from 3000-8000 riel per hr. See also Telephone below. **Post office** There are 2 post offices: 1 opposite the central market and another behind the casino at Victory Beach. **Telephone** Larger hotels have IDD facilities and most major

internet cafés let you make internet calls: Casablanca, Ana, Lucky Web, etc.

Koh Kong and around *p198*
Banks There is now an ATM at the Acleda Bank on St 5. **Internet** Most accommodation now has Wi-Fi. Good coffee and some tourism info available. **Koh Kong Computer**, on road southwest from traffic circle between Ramsay Bun Thaim Guesthouse and Pailin Guesthouse, internet ฿120 per hr, overseas calls ฿10 per min, CD burning, printing, scanning. **Otto's Restaurant** has internet. **Sohka Internet**, on St 2 near riverside (intersection with St 1), internet ฿180 per hr, overseas calls.
Telephone Calls within Cambodia can be made from the phone boxes scattered around town. **Camintel Office**, near the post office, charges US$2 a min for international calls.

Kampot and around *p199, map p200*
Banks Acleda Bank, T033-932880, offers a Western Union Service. Canadia Bank is close to the Blissful Guesthouse. Cash advances on Visa and MasterCard (with no commission fee). Money changers are concentrated at the traffic circle by the market. **Internet** Numerous internet cafés have cropped up around town. There is a cluster of them on the road between the river and the central roundabout, US$1 per hr. International calls can be made and vary between 600-900 riel per min. **Post office** On the river road in town. There are many print and phone shops around town where you can fax and make international phone calls.

Contents

Footprint features

Background

History

Pre-history

Archaeological evidence suggests that the Mekong Delta and the lower reaches of the river – in modern-day Cambodia – have been inhabited since at least 4000 BC. But the wet and humid climate has destroyed most of the physical remains of the early civilizations. Excavated remains of a settlement at Samrong Sen on the Tonlé Sap show that houses were built from bamboo and wood and raised on stilts – exactly as they are today. Where these people came from is uncertain but anthropologists have suggested that there were two waves of migration; one from the Malay peninsula and Indonesia and a second from Tibet and China.

Rise of the Lunar and Solar Dynasties

For thousands of years Indochina was isolated from the rest of the world and was virtually unaffected by the rise and fall of the early Chinese dynasties. India and China 'discovered' Southeast Asia early in the first millennium AD and trade networks were quickly established. The Indian influence was particularly strong in the Mekong basin area. The Khmers adopted and adapted Indian script as well as their ideas about astrology, religion (Buddhism and Hinduism) and royalty (the cult of the semi-divine ruler). Today, several other aspects of Cambodian culture are recognizably Indian in origin – including classical literature and dance. Religious architecture also followed Indian models. These Indian cultural influences which took root in Indochina gave rise to a legend to which Cambodia traces its historical origins. An Indian Brahmin called Kaundinya, travelling in the Mekong Delta area, married Soma, daughter of the Naga (the serpent deity), or Lord of the Soil. Their union, which founded the 'Lunar Dynasty' of Funan (a pre-Angkorian Kingdom), symbolized the fertility of the kingdom and occupies a central place in Khmer cosmology. The Naga, Soma's father, helpfully drank the floodwaters of the Mekong, enabling people to cultivate the land.

Funan

The kingdom of Funan – the forerunner of Kambuja – was established on the Mekong by tribal people from South China in the middle of the third century AD and became the earliest Hindu state in Southeast Asia. Funan was known for its elaborate irrigation canals which controlled the Mekong floodwaters, irrigated the paddy fields and prevented the incursion of seawater. By the fifth century Funan had extended its influence over most of present day Cambodia, as well as Indochina and parts of the Malay peninsula. Leadership was measured by success in battle and the ability to provide protection, and in recognition of this fact, rulers from the Funan period onward incorporated the suffix 'varman' (meaning protection) into their names. Records of a third century Chinese embassy give an idea of what it was like: "There are walled villages, places and dwellings. The men ... go about naked and barefoot. ... Taxes are paid in gold, silver and perfume. There are books and libraries and they can use the alphabet." Twentieth-century excavations suggest a seafaring people engaged in extensive trade with both India and China, and elsewhere.

Chenla

The 'Solar Dynasty' of Chenla was a vassal kingdom of Funan, probably first based on the Mekong at the junction with the Mun tributary, but it rapidly grew in power, and was centred in the area of present day southern Laos. It was the immediate predecessor of Kambuja and the great Khmer Empire. According to Khmer legend, the kingdom was the result of the marriage of Kambu, an ascetic, to a celestial nymph named Mera. The people of Chenla – the Kambuja, or the sons of Kambu – lent their name to the country. In AD 540 a Funan prince married a Chenla princess, uniting the Solar and Lunar dynasties. The prince sided with his wife and Funan was swallowed by Chenla. The first capital of this fusion was at **Sambor**. King Ishanavarman (AD 616-635) established a new capital at Sambor Prei Kuk, 30 km from modern Kompong Thom, in the centre of the country (the monuments of which are some of the best preserved of this period). His successor, Jayavarman I, moved the capital to the region of Angkor Borei near Takeo.

Quarrels in the ruling family led to the break-up of the state later in the seventh century: it was divided into 'Land Chenla', a farming culture located north of the Tonlé Sap (maybe centred around Champassak in Laos), and 'Water Chenla', a trading culture based along the Mekong. Towards the end of the eighth century Water Chenla became a vassal of Java's powerful Sailendra Dynasty and members of Chenla's ruling family were taken back to the Sailendra court. This period, from the fall of Funan until the eighth century, is known as the pre-Angkorian period and is a somewhat hazy time in the history of Cambodia. The Khmers remained firmly under Javanese suzerainty until Jayavarman II (AD 802-850), who was born in central Java, returned to the land of his ancestors around AD 800 to change the course of Cambodian history.

Angkor and the god-kings

Jayavarman II, the Khmer prince who had spent most of his life at the Sailendra court, claimed independence from Java and founded the Angkor Kingdom to the north of the Tonlé Sap in AD 802, at about the same time as Charlemagne became Holy Roman Emperor in Europe. They were men cast in the same mould, for both were empire builders. His far-reaching conquests at Wat Phou (Laos) and Sambhupura (Sambor) won him immediate political popularity on his return and he became king in AD 790. In AD 802 he declared himself a World Emperor and to consolidate and legitimize his position he arranged his for coronation by a Brahmin priest, declaring himself the first Khmer devaraja, or god-king, a tradition continued today. From then on, the reigning monarch was identified with Siva, the king of the Hindu gods. In the centuries that followed, successive devaraja strove to outdo their predecessors by building bigger and finer temples to house the royal linga, a phallic symbol which is the symbol of Siva and the devaraja. The god-kings commanded the absolute allegiance of their subjects, giving them control of a vast pool of labour which was used to build an advanced and prosperous agricultural civilization. For many years historians and archaeologists maintained that the key to this agricultural wealth lay in a sophisticated hydraulic – that is irrigated – system of agriculture which allowed the Khmers to produce up to three harvests a year. However, this view of Angkorian agriculture has come under increasing scrutiny in recent years and now there are many who believe that flood-retreat – rather than irrigated – agriculture was the key. Jayavarman II installed himself in successive capitals north of the Tonlé Sap, secure from attack by the Sailendras, and he ruled until AD 850, when he died on the banks of the Great Lake at the original capital, Hariharalaya, in the Roluos area (Angkor).

A Chinese emissary's account of his stay at Angkor (1296-1297)

One of the most interesting documents relating to the great empire of Angkor is the Chinese emissary Chou Ta-kuan's short account of his stay there entitled *Notes on the customs of Cambodia*. The book was written in the late 13th or early 14th century, shortly after he had returned to China from a sojourn at Angkor between 1296 and 1297. His book describes the last days of the kingdom and his role as companion to the Chinese ambassador.

The book is divided into 40 short 'chapters' dealing with aspects of everyday and royal life ranging from childbirth, to justice, to clothing. The account also details aspects of the natural environment (fish and reptiles, birds), the economy of the empire (agriculture, trade, products), and technology (utensils, boats and oars). What makes the account so useful and unusual is that it describes not just the concerns and actions of great men and women, but of everyday life too. The extracts below are just a sample of the insights into everyday Cambodian life during the waning days of the Angkorian Empire. For those intending to visit the site of Angkor, the book (see page 276) is highly recommended. It brings to life the ruins of a city, helping you to imagine the place – now so empty – full of people and life.

Cambodian dwellings Out of the [royal] palace rises a golden tower, to the top of which the ruler ascends nightly to sleep. It is common belief that in the tower dwells a genie, formed like a serpent with nine heads, which is Lord of the entire kingdom. Every night this genie appears in the shape of a woman, with whom the sovereign couples. Not even the wives of the king may enter here. At the second watch the king comes forth and is then free to sleep with his wives and his concubines. Should the genie fail to appear for a single night, it is a sign that the king's death is at hand.

Straw thatch covers the dwellings of the commoners, not one of whom would dare place the smallest bit of tile on his roof.

Clothing Every man or woman, from the sovereign down, knots the hair and leaves the shoulders bare. Round the waist they wear a small strip of cloth, over which a large piece is drawn when they leave their houses. Many rules, based on rank, govern the choice of materials. Only the ruler may wear fabrics woven in an all over pattern.

Women Generally speaking, the women, like the men, wear only a strip of cloth, bound round the waist, showing bare breasts of milky whiteness. As for the concubines and palace girls, I have heard it said that there are from three to five thousand of these, separated into various categories. When a beautiful girl is born into a family, no time is lost in sending her to the palace.

Childbirth Once a Cambodian woman's child is born, she immediately makes a poultice of hot rice and salt and applies it to her private parts. This is taken off in 24 hours, thus preventing any untoward after-effects and causing an astringency which seems to renew the young mother's virginity. When told of this for the first time, my credulity was sorely taxed. However, in the house where I lodged a girl gave birth to a child, and I was able to observe beyond peradventure that the next day she was up carrying the baby in her arms and going with him to bathe in the river. This seems truly amazing!

Everyone with whom I talked said that the Cambodian women are highly sexed.

One or two days after giving birth they are ready for intercourse: if a husband is not responsive he will be discarded. When a man is called away on matters of business, they endure his absence for a while; but if he is gone as much as 10 days, the wife is apt to say, "I am no ghost; how can I be expected to sleep alone?"

Slaves Wild men from the hills can be bought to serve as slaves. Families of wealth may own more than 100; those of lesser means content themselves with 10 or 20; only the very poor have none. If a slave should run away and be captured, a blue mark would be tattooed on his face; moreover, an iron collar would be fitted to his neck, or shackles to his arms or legs.

Cambodian justice Points of dispute between citizens, however trifling, are taken to the ruler. In dealing with cases of great seriousness, recourse is not had to strangulation or beheading; outside the West Gate, however, a ditch is dug into which the criminal is placed, earth and stones are thrown back and heaped high, and all is over. Lesser crimes are dealt with by cutting off feet or hands, or by amputation of the nose.

When a thief is caught red-handed, he may be imprisoned and tortured. Recourse is also had to another curious procedure. If an object is missing, and accusation brought against someone who denies the charge, oil is brought to boil in a kettle and the suspected person forced to plunge his hand into it. If he is truly guilty, the hand is cooked to shreds; if not, skin and bones are unharmed. Such is the amazing way of these barbarians.

Products of Cambodia Many rare woods are to be found in the highlands. Unwooded regions are those where elephants and rhinoceros gather and breed. Exotic birds and strange animals abound. The most sought-after products are the feathers of the kingfisher, elephant tusks, rhinoceros horns, and beeswax.

Trade In Cambodia it is the women who take charge of trade. For this reason a Chinese arriving in the country, loses no time in getting himself a mate, for he will find her commercial instincts a great asset.

Utensils For sleeping only bamboo mats are used, laid on the wooden floors. Of late, certain families have adopted the use of low beds, which for the most part are made by the Chinese.

A prodigy Within the Walled City, near the East Gate, a Cambodian man committed fornication with his younger sister. Their skin and their flesh were fused beyond the power of separating them. After three days passed without food, both parties died. My compatriot Mr Hsieh, who spent 35 years in this country declares he has known this to happen twice. If such be the case, it shows how well the Cambodians are policed by the supernatural power of their holy Buddha.

Notes on the customs of Cambodia was translated from the Chinese original into French by Paul Pelliot. J Gilman d'Arcy Paul translated the French version into English, and the Siam Society in Bangkok have republished this version with colour photographs and reproductions of Delaporte's fine lithographs of the monuments. The *Customs of Cambodia*, Siam Society: Bangkok, 1993.

Jayavarman III (AD 850-877) continued his father's traditions and ruled for the next 27 years. He expanded his father's empire at Hariharalaya and was the original founder of the laterite temple at Bakong. **Indravarman (AD 877-889)**, his successor, was the first of the great temple-builders of Angkor and somewhat overshadowed the work of Jayavarman III. His means to succession are somewhat ambiguous but it is generally agreed that he overthrew Jayavarman III violently. Unlike his predecessor, Indravarman was not the son of a king but more than likely the nephew of Jayavarman's II Queen. He expanded and renovated the capital, building Preah Ko Temple and developing Bakong. Indravarman is considered one of the key players in Khmer history. Referred to as the "lion among kings" and "prince endowed with all the merits", his architectural projects established precedents that were emulated by those that followed him. After Indravarman's death his sons fought for the King's title. The victor, at the end of the ninth century was **Yasovarman I (AD 889-900)**. The battle is believed to have destroyed the palace, thus spurring a move to Angkor. He called his new capital Yasodharapura and copied the water system his father had devised at Roluos on an even larger scale, using the waters of the Tonlé Sap. After Yasovarman's death in AD 900 his son **Harshavarman (AD 900-923)** took the throne, until he died 23 years later. Harshavarman was well regarded, one particular inscription saying that he "caused the joy of the universe". Upon his death, his brother **Ishanarvarman II**, assumed the regal status. In AD 928, **Jayavarman IV** set up a rival capital about 65 km from Angkor at Koh Ker (see page 127) and ruled for the next 20 years. After Jayavarman IV's death there was a period of upheaval as **Harsharvarman II** tried unsuccessfully to lead the empire. **Rajendravarman (AD 944-968)**, Jayarvarman's nephew, managed to take control of the empire and moved the court back to Angkor, where the Khmer kings remained. He chose to build outside of the former capital Bakheng, opting instead for the region south of the East Baray. Many saw him as the saviour of Angkor with one inscription reading: "He restored the holy city of Yashodharapura, long deserted, and rendered it superb and charming." Rajendravarman orchestrated a campaign of solidarity – bringing together a number of provinces and claiming back territory, previously under Yasovarman I. From the restored capital he led a successful crusade against the Champa in what is now Vietnam. A devout Buddhist, he erected some of the first Buddhist temples in the precinct. Upon Rajendravarman's death, his son **Jayavarman V (AD 968-1001)**, still only a child, took the royal reigns. Once again the administrative centre was moved, this time to the west, where Ta Keo was built. The capital was renamed Jayendranagari. Like his father, Jayavarman V was Buddhist but was extremely tolerant of other religions. At the start of his tenure he had a few clashes with local dissidents but things settled down and he enjoyed relative peace during his rule. The next king, **Udayadityavarman I**, lasted a few months before being ousted. For the next few years Suryavarman I and Jayaviravarman battled for the King's title.

The formidable warrior **King Suryavarman I (1002-1049)** won. He may originally have come from the Malay peninsula. He was a determined leader and made all of his officials swear a blood oath of allegiance. He undertook a series of military campaigns geared towards claiming Mon territory in central and southern Thailand and victoriously extended the Khmer empire into Lower Menam, as well as into Laos and established a Khmer capital in Louvo (modern day Lopburi in Thailand). Suryavarman holds the record for the greatest territorial expansion ever achieved in the Khmer Empire. The Royal Palace (Angkor Thom), the West Baray and the Phimeanakas pyramid temples were Suryavarman's main contributions to Angkor's architectural heritage (see page 101). He continued the royal Hindu cult but also tolerated Mahayana Buddhism.

On Suryavarman's death, the Khmer Kingdom began to fragment. His three successors had short, troubled reigns and the Champa kingdom captured, sacked and razed the capital. When the king's son, **Udayadityavarman II (1050-1066),** assumed the throne, havoc ensued as citizens revolted against him and some of his royal appointments.

When Udayadityavarman II died, his younger brother, **Harsharvarman III** (1066-1080), last in the line of the dynasty, stepped in. During his reign, there were reports of discord and further defeat at the hands of the Cham.

In 1080 a new kingdom was founded by a northern provincial governor claiming aristocratic descent. He called himself **Jayavarman VI (1080-1107)** and is believed to have led a revolt against the former king. He never settled at Angkor, living instead in the northern part of the kingdom. He left monuments at Wat Phou in southern Laos and Phimai, in Thailand. There was an intermittent period where Jayavarman's IV brother, **Dharanindravarman (1107-1112)** took the throne but he was overthrown by his grand-nephew **Suryavarman II (1113-1150),** who soon became the greatest leader the Angkor Empire had ever seen. He worked prolifically on a broad range of projects and achieved some of most impressive architectural feats and political manoeuvres seen within the Angkorian period. He resumed diplomatic relations with China, the Middle Kingdom, and was held in the greatest regard by the then Chinese Emperor. He expanded the Khmer Empire as far as Lopburi, Siam, Pagan in Myanmar, parts of Laos and into the Malay peninsula. He attacked the Champa state relentlessly, particularly Dai Vet in Northern Vietnam, eventually defeating them in 1144-1145, and capturing and sacking the royal capital, Vijaya. He left an incredible, monumental legacy behind, being responsible for the construction of Angkor Wat, an architectural masterpiece that represented the height of the Khmer's artistic genius, Phnom Rung temple (Khorat) and Banteay Samre. A network of roads was built to connect regional capitals.

However, his success was not without its costs – his widespread construction put serious pressure on the general running of the kingdom and major reservoirs silted up during this time; there was also an intensified discord in the provinces and his persistent battling fuelled an ongoing duel between the Cham and Khmers that was to continue (and eventually be avenged) long after his death.

Suryavarman II deposed the King of Champa in 1145 but the Cham regained their independence in 1149 and the following year, Suryavarman died after a disastrous attempt to conquer Annam (northern Vietnam). The throne was usurped by **Tribhuvanadityavarman** in 1165, who died in 1177, when the Cham seized their chance of revenge and sacked Angkor in a surprise naval attack. This was the Khmer's worst recorded defeat – the city was completely annihilated. The 50-year-old **Jayavarman VII** – a cousin of Suryavarman – turned out to be their saviour. He battled the Cham for the next four years, driving them out of the Kingdom. In 1181 he was declared king and seriously hit back, attacking the Chams and seizing their capital, Vijaya. He expanded the Khmer Kingdom further than ever before; its suzerainty stretched from the Malay peninsula in the south to the borders of Burma in the west and the Annamite chain to the northeast.

Jayavarman's VII's first task was to plan a strong, spacious new capital – Angkor Thom; but while that work was being undertaken he set up a smaller, temporary seat of government where he and his court could live in the meantime – Preah Khan meaning 'Fortunate City of Victory' (see page 110). He also built 102 hospitals throughout his kingdom, as well as a network of roads, along which he constructed resthouses. But because they were built of wood, none of these secular structures survive; only the foundations of four larger ones have been unearthed at Angkor.

Angkor's decline

As was the case duuring Suryavarman II's reign, Jayavarman VII's extensive building campaign put a large amount of pressure on the kingdom's resources and rice was in short supply as labour was diverted into construction.

Jayavarman VII died in 1218 and the Kambujan Empire fell into progressive decline over the next two centuries. Territorially, it was eroded by the eastern migration of the Siamese. The Khmers were unable to prevent this gradual incursion but the diversion of labour to the military rice farming helped seal the fate of Angkor. Another reason for the decline was the introduction of Theravada Buddhism in the 13th century, which undermined the prestige of the king and the priests. There is even a view that climatic change disrupted the agricultural system and led to Kambuja's demise. After Jayavarman VII, no king seems to have been able to unify the kingdom by force of arms or personality – internal dissent increased while the king's extravagance continued to place a crippling burden on state funds. With its temples decaying and its once-magnificent agricultural system in ruins, Angkor became virtually uninhabitable. In 1431 the royal capital was finally abandoned to the Siamese, who drove the Khmers out and made Cambodia a vassal of the Thai Sukhothai Kingdom.

Explaining Angkor's decline

Why the Angkorian Empire should have declined has always fascinated scholars in the West – in the same way that the decline and fall of the Roman Empire has done. Numerous explanations have been offered, and still the debate remains unresolved. As Anthony Barnett argued in a paper in the *New Left Review* in 1990, perhaps the question should be "why did Angkor last so long? Inauspiciously sited, it was nonetheless a tropical imperium of 500 years' duration."

There are essentially five lines of argument in the 'Why did Angkor fall?' debate. First, it has been argued that the building programmes became simply so arduous and demanding of ordinary people that they voted with their feet and moved out, depriving Angkor of the population necessary to support a great empire. Second, some scholars present an environmental argument: the great irrigation works silted-up, undermining the empire's agricultural wealth. (This line of argument conflicts with recent work that maintains that Angkor's wealth was never based on hydraulic – or irrigated – agriculture, see pages 102 and 103.) Third, there are those who say that military defeat was the cause – but this only begs the question: why were they defeated in the first place? Fourth, historians with a rather wider view, have offered the opinion that the centres of economic activity in Southeast Asia moved from land-based to sea-based foci, and that Angkor was poorly located to adapt to this shift in patterns of trade, wealth and, hence, power. Lastly, some scholars argue that the religion which demanded such labour of Angkor's subjects became so corrupt that it ultimately corroded the empire from within.

After Angkor – running scared

The next 500 years or so, until the arrival of the French in 1863, was an undistinguished period in Cambodian history. In 1434 the royal Khmer court under Ponheayat moved to Phnom Penh, where a replica of the cosmic Mount Meru was built. There was a short-lived period of revival in the mid-15th century until the Siamese invaded and sacked the capital again in 1473. One of the sons of the captured King Suryavarman drummed up enough Khmer support to oust the invaders and there were no subsequent invasions during the

16th century. The capital was established at Lovek (between Phnom Penh and Tonlé Sap) and then moved back to the ruins at Angkor. But a Siamese invasion in 1593 sent the royal court fleeing to Laos; finally, in 1603, the Thais released a captured prince to rule over the Cambodian vassal state. There were at least 22 kings between 1603 and 1848.

Politically, the Cambodian court tried to steer a course between its powerful neighbours of Siam and Vietnam, seeking one's protection against the other. King **Chey Chetta II** (1618-1628), for example, declared Cambodia's independence from Siam and in order to back up his actions he asked Vietnam for help. To cement the allegiance he was forced to marry a Vietnamese princess of the Nguyen Dynasty of Annam, and then obliged to pay tribute to Vietnam. His successors – hoping to rid themselves of Vietnamese domination – sought Siamese assistance and were then forced to pay for it by acknowledging Siam's suzerainty. Then in 1642, **King Chan** converted to Islam, and encouraged Malay and Javanese migrants to settle in Cambodia. Considering him guilty of apostasy, his cousins ousted him – with Vietnamese support. But 50 years later, the Cambodian **Ang Eng** was crowned in Bangkok. This see-saw pattern continued for years; only Siam's wars with Burma and Vietnam's internal disputes and long-running conflict with China prevented them from annexing the whole of Cambodia, although both took territorial advantage of the fragmented state.

By the early 1700s the kingdom was centred on Phnom Penh (there were periods when the king resided at Ondong). But when the Khmers lost their control over the Mekong Delta to the Vietnamese in the late 18th century, the capital's access to the sea was blocked. By 1750 the Khmer royal family had split into pro-Siamese and pro-Vietnamese factions. Between 1794-1811 and 1847-1863, Siamese influence was strongest; from 1835-1837 the Vietnamese dominated. In the 1840s, the Siamese and Vietnamese armies fought on Cambodian territory, devastating the country. This provoked French intervention – and cost Cambodia its independence, even if it had been nominal for several centuries anyway. On 17 April 1864 (the same day and month as the Khmer Rouge soldiers entered Phnom Penh in the twentieth century) King Norodom agreed to French protection as he believed they would provide military assistance against the Siamese. The king was to be disappointed: France honoured Siam's claim to the western provinces of Battambang, Siem Reap and Sisophon, which Bangkok had captured in the late 1600s. And in 1884, King Norodom was persuaded by the French governor of the colony of Cochin China to sign another treaty that turned Cambodia into a French colony, along with Laos and Vietnam in the Union Indochinoise. The establishment of Cambodia as a French protectorate probably saved the country from being split up between Siam and Vietnam.

The French colonial period

The French did little to develop Cambodia, preferring instead to let the territory pay for itself. They only invested income generated from tax revenue to build a communications network and from a Cambodian perspective, the only benefit of colonial rule was that the French forestalled the total disintegration of the country, which would otherwise have been divided up between its warring neighbours. French cartographers also mapped Cambodia's borders for the first time and in so doing forced the Thais to surrender the northwestern provinces of Battambang and Siem Reap.

For nearly a century the French alternately supported two branches of the royal family, the Norodoms and the Sisowaths, crowning the 18-year-old schoolboy **Prince Norodom Sihanouk** in 1941. The previous year, the Nazis had invaded and occupied France and

French territories in Indochina were in turn occupied by the Japanese – although Cambodia was still formally governed and administered by the French. It was at this stage that a group of pro-independence Cambodians realized just how weak the French control of their country actually was. In 1942 two monks were arrested and accused of preaching anti-French sermons; within two days this sparked demonstrations by more than 1000 monks in Phnom Penh. These demonstrations marked the beginning of Cambodian nationalism. In March 1945 Japanese forces ousted the colonial administration and persuaded King Norodom Sihanouk to proclaim independence. Following the Japanese surrender in August 1945, the French came back in force; Sihanouk tried to negotiate independence from France and they responded by abolishing the absolute monarchy in 1946 – although the king remained titular head of state. A new constitution was introduced allowing political activity and a National Assembly elected.

Independence and neutrality

By the early 1950s the French army had suffered several defeats in the war in Indochina. Sihanouk dissolved the National Assembly in mid-1952, which he was entitled to do under the constitution, and personally took charge of steering Cambodia towards independence from France. To publicize the cause, he travelled to Thailand, Japan and the United States, and said he would not return from self-imposed exile until his country was free. His audacity embarrassed the French into granting Cambodia independence on 9 November 1953 – and Sihanouk returned, triumphant.

The people of Cambodia did not want to return to absolute monarchy, and following his abdication in 1955, Sihanouk became a popular political leader. But political analysts believe that despite the apparent popularity of the former king's administration, different factions began to develop at this time, a process which was the root of the conflict in the years to come. During the 1960s, for example, there was a growing rift between the Khmer majority and other ethnic groups. Even in the countryside, differences became marked between the rice-growing lands and the more remote mountain areas where people practised shifting cultivation, supplementing their diet with lizards, snakes, roots and insects. As these problems intensified in the late 1960s and the economic situation deteriorated, the popular support base for the Khmer Rouge was put into place. With unchecked population growth, land ownership patterns became skewed, landlessness grew more widespread and food prices escalated.

Sihanouk managed to keep Cambodia out of the war that enveloped Laos and Vietnam during the late 1950s and 1960s by following a neutral policy – which helped attract millions of dollars of aid to Cambodia from both the West and the Eastern Bloc. But when a civil war broke out in South Vietnam in the early 1960s, Cambodia's survival – and Sihanouk's own survival – depended on its outcome. Sihanouk believed the rebels, the National Liberation Front (NLF) would win; and he openly courted and backed the NLF. It was an alliance which cost him dear. In 1965-1966 the tide began to turn in South Vietnam, due to US military and economic intervention. This forced NLF troops to take refuge inside Cambodia (in 1966 half of Cambodia's rice supplies, normally sold abroad, were distributed to the NLF agents inside Cambodia). When a peasant uprising in northwestern provinces in 1967 showed Sihanouk that he was sailing close to the wind his forces responded by suppressing the rebellion and massacring 10,000 peasants.

Slowly – and inevitably – he became the focus of resentment within Cambodia's political élite. He also incurred American wrath by allowing North Vietnamese forces to use Cambodian territory as an extension of the **Ho Chi Minh Trail**, ferrying arms and men into South Vietnam. This resulted in his former army Commander-in-Chief, **Marshal Lon Nol** masterminding Sihanouk's removal as Head of State while he was in Moscow in 1970. Lon Nol abolished the monarchy and proclaimed a republic. One of the most auspicious creatures in Khmer mythology is the white crocodile. It is said to appear 'above the surface' at important moments in history and is said to have been sighted near Phnom Penh just before Lon Nol took over.

The Third Indochina War and the rise of the Khmer Rouge

On 30 April 1970, following the overthrow of Prince Norodom Sihanouk, US President Richard Nixon officially announced **Washington's military intervention in Cambodia** – although in reality it had been going on for some time. The invasion aimed to deny the Vietnamese Communists the use of Sihanoukville port through which 85% of their heavy arms were reaching South Vietnam. The US Air Force had been secretly bombing Cambodia using B-52s since March 1969. In 1973, facing defeat in Vietnam, the US Air Force B-52s began carpet bombing Communist-controlled areas to enable Lon Nol's inept regime to retain control of the besieged provincial cities.

Historian David P Chandler wrote: "When the campaign was stopped by the US Congress at the end of the year, the B-52s had dropped over half a million tons of bombs on a country with which the United States was not at war – more than twice the tonnage dropped on Japan during the Second World War.

The war in Cambodia was known as 'the sideshow' by journalists covering the war in Vietnam and by American policy-makers in London. Yet the intensity of US bombing in Cambodia was greater than it ever was in Vietnam; about 500,000 soldiers and civilians were killed over the four-year period. It also caused about two million refugees to flee from the countryside to the capital."

As Henry Kamm suggested, by the beginning of 1971 the people of Cambodia had to face the terrifying realisation that nowhere in the country was safe and all hope and confidence in Cambodia's future during the war was lost. A year after the coup d'etat the country was shattered: guerrilla forces had invaded Angkor, the country's primary oil refinery, Lol Non had suffered a stroke and had relocated to Hawaii for months of treatment, Lol Non's irregularly paid soldiers were pillaging stores at gunpoint and extreme corruption was endemic.

By the end of the war, the country had become totally dependent on US aid and much of the population survived on American rice rations. Confidence in the Lon Nol government collapsed as taxes rose and children were drafted into combat units. At the same time, the **Khmer Rouge** increased its military strength dramatically and began to make inroads into areas formerly controlled by government troops. Although officially the Khmer Rouge rebels represented the Beijing-based Royal Government of National Union of Cambodia (Grunc), which was headed by the exiled Prince Sihanouk, Grunc's de facto leaders were Pol Pot, Khieu Samphan (who, after Pol Pot's demise, became the public face of the Khmer Rouge), Ieng Sary (later foreign minister) and Son Sen (Chief of General Staff) – all Khmer Rouge men. By the time the American bombing stopped in 1973, the guerrillas dominated about 60% of Cambodian territory, while the government clung tenuously to towns and cities. Over the next two years the Khmer Rouge whittled away Phnom Penh's defence perimeter to the point that Lon Nol's government was sustained only by American airlifts into the capital.

Some commentators have suggested that the persistent heavy bombing of Cambodia, which forced the Communist guerrillas to live in terrible conditions, was partly responsible for the notorious savagery of the Khmer Rouge in later years. Not only were they brutalized by the conflict itself, but they became resentful of the fact that the city-dwellers had no inkling of how unpleasant their experiences really were. This, writes US political scientist Wayne Bert, "created the perception among the Khmer Rouge that the bulk of the population did not take part in the revolution, was therefore not enthusiastic about it and could not be trusted to support it. The final step in this logic was to punish or eliminate all in these categories who showed either real or imagined tendencies toward disloyalty". And that, as anyone who has watched *The Killing Fields* will know, is what happened.

The 'Pol Pot time': building year zero

On 1 April 1975 President Lon Nol fled Cambodia to escape the rapidly advancing Khmer Rouge. Just over two weeks later, on 17 April, the victorious Khmer Rouge entered Phnom Penh. The capital's population had been swollen by refugees from 600,000 to over two million. The ragged conquering troops wearing Ho Chi Minh sandals made of used rubber tyres – which were de rigueur for guerrillas in Indochina – were welcomed as heroes. None in the crowds that lined the streets appreciated the horrors that the victory would also bring. Cambodia was renamed Democratic Kampuchea (DK) and Pol Pot set to work establishing a radical Maoist-style agrarian society. These ideas had been first sketched out by his longstanding colleague Khieu Samphan, whose 1959 doctoral thesis – at the Sorbonne University in Paris – analysed the effects of Cambodia's colonial and neo-colonial domination. In order to secure true economic and political independence he argued that it was necessary to isolate Cambodia completely and to go back to a self-sufficient agricultural economy.

Within days of the occupation, the rubber sandalled revolutionaries had forcibly evacuated many of the inhabitants of Phnom Penh to the countryside, telling citizens that the Americans were about to bomb the capital. A second major displacement was carried out at the end of the year, when hundreds of thousands of people from the area southeast of Phnom Penh were forced to move to the northwest.

Prior to the Khmer Rouge coming to power, the Cambodian word for revolution (*bambahbambor*) had a conventional meaning, 'uprising'. Under Pol Pot's regime, the word *pativattana* was used instead; it meant 'return to the past'. The Khmer Rouge did this by obliterating everything that did not subscribe to their vision of the past glories of ancient Khmer culture. Pol Pot wanted to return the country to '**Year Zero**' – he wanted to begin again. One of the many revolutionary slogans was "we will burn the old grass and new will grow"; money, modern technology, medicine, education and newspapers were outlawed. Khieu Samphan, who became the Khmer Rouge Head of State, following Prince Sihanouk's resignation in 1976, said at the time: "No, we have no machines. We do everything by mainly relying on the strength of our people. We work completely self-sufficiently. This shows the overwhelming heroism of our people. This also shows the great force of our people. Though bare-handed, they can do everything".

The Khmer Rouge, or *Angkar Loeu* ('The Higher Organization') as they touted themselves, maintained a stranglehold on the country by dislocating families, disorientating people and sustaining a persistent fear through violence, torture and death. At the heart of their strategy was a plan to unfurl people's strongest bonds and

Pol Pot – the idealistic psychopath

Prince Norodom Sihanouk once referred to Pol Pot as "a more fortunate Hitler". Unlike his erstwhile fascist counterpart, the man whose troops were responsible for the deaths of perhaps two million fellow Cambodians has managed to get away with it. He died on 15 April 1998, either of a heart attack or, possibly, at his own hands or somebody else's.

Pol Pot's real name was Saloth Sar – he adopted his nom de guerre when he became Secretary-General of the Cambodian Communist Party in 1963. He was born in 1928 into a peasant family in Kompong Thom, central Cambodia, and is believed to have lived as a novice monk for nine months when he was a child. His services to the Democrat Party won him a scholarship to study electronics in Paris. But he became a Communist in France in 1949 and spent more time at meetings of Marxist revolutionary societies than in classes. In his 1986 book *Sideshow*, William Shawcross notes that at that time the French Communist Party, which was known for its dogmatic adherence to orthodox Marxism, "taught hatred of the bourgeoisie and uncritical admiration of Stalinism, including the collectivization of agriculture". Pol Pot finally lost his scholarship in 1953.

Returning to newly independent Cambodia, Pol Pot started working as a school teacher in Phnom Penh and continued his revolutionary activities in the underground Cambodian Communist Party (which, remarkably kept its existence a secret until 1977). In 1963, he fled the capital for the countryside, fearing a crackdown of the left by Sihanouk. There he rose to become Secretary-General of the Central Committee of the Communist Party of Kampuchea. He was trained in guerrilla warfare and he became a leader of the Khmer Rouge forces, advocating armed resistance to Sihanouk and his 'feudal entourage'. In 1975 when the Khmer Rouge marched into Phnom Penh, Pol Pot was forced out of the shadows to take the role of leader, 'Brother Number One'. Although he took the title of prime minister, he ruled as a dictator and set about reshaping Cambodia with his mentor, Khieu Samphan, the head of state. Yet, during the years he was in power, hardly any Cambodians – save those in the top echelons of the Khmer Rouge – had even heard of him.

The Vietnam-backed Hun Sen government, which took over the country after the overthrow of the Khmer Rouge in December 1978, calculated that by demonizing Pol Pot as the mastermind of the genocide, it would avert the possibility of the Khmer Rouge ever making a comeback. The Hun Sen regime showed no interest in analysing the complex factors which combined to bring Pol Pot to power. Within Cambodia, he has been portrayed simply as a tyrannical bogey-man. During the 1980s, 20 May was declared National Hate Day, when everyone reaffirmed their hatred of Pol Pot.

In a review of David Chandler's biography of Pol Pot (*Brother Number One: A Political Biography of Pol Pot*, Westview Press, 1992), Peter Carey – the co-director of the British-based Cambodia Trust – was struck by what he called "the sinister disjunction between the man's evident charisma ... and the monumental suffering wrought by his regime". Carey concludes: "one is left with the image of a man consumed by his own vision, a vision of empowerment and liberation that has little anchorage in Cambodian reality".

loyalties: those that existed between family members. The term *kruosaa*, which traditionally means 'family' in Khmer, came to simply mean 'spouse' under the Khmer Rouge. In Angkar, family no longer existed. *Krusosaa niyum*, which loosely translated to 'familyism' (or pining for one's relatives) was a criminal offence punishable by death. Under heinous interrogation procedures people were intensively probed about their family members (sisters, brothers, grandparents and in-laws) and encouraged to inform on them. Those people who didn't turn over relatives considered adversaries (teachers, former soldiers, doctors, etc) faced odious consequences, with the fate of the whole family (immediate and extended) in danger.

Memoirs from survivors detailed in the book *Children of Cambodia's Killing Fields* (see page 276) repeatedly refer to the Khmer Rouge dictum "to keep you is no benefit to destroy you is no loss." People were treated as nothing more than machines. Food was scarce under Pol Pot's inefficient system of collective farming and administration was based on fear, torture and summary execution. A veil of secrecy shrouded Cambodia and, until a few desperate refugees began to trickle over the border into Thailand, the outside world was largely ignorant of what was going on. The refugees' stories of atrocities were, at first, disbelieved. Jewish refugees who escaped from Nazi occupied Poland in the 1940s had encountered a similarly disbelieving reception simply because (like the Cambodians) what they had to say was, to most people, unbelievable. Some left wing academics initially viewed the revolution as an inspired and brave attempt to break the shackles of dependency and neo-colonial domination. Others, such as Noam Chomsky, dismissed the allegations as right wing press propaganda.

It was not until the Vietnamese 'liberation' of Phnom Penh in 1979 that the scale of the Khmer Rouge carnage emerged and the atrocities witnessed by the survivors became known. The stories turned the Khmer Rouge into international pariahs – but only until 1982 when, remarkably, their American and Chinese sympathizers secured them a voice at the United Nations. Wives had been encouraged to denounce their husbands; children their mothers. Anyone who had smoked an American cigarette was a CIA operative; anyone with a taste for café crème was a French collaborator. During the Khmer Rouge's 44-month reign of terror, it had hitherto been generally accepted that around a million people died. This is a horrendous figure when one considers that the population of the country in 1975 was around seven million. What is truly shocking is that the work undertaken by a team from Yale University indicates that this figure is far too low.

Although the Khmer Rouge era in Cambodia may have been a period of unprecedented economic, political and human turmoil, they still managed to keep meticulous records of what they were doing. In this regard the Khmer Rouge were rather like the Chinese during the Cultural Revolution, or the Nazis in Germany. Using Australian satellite data, the team was expecting to uncover around 200 mass graves; instead they found several thousand. The Khmer Rouge themselves have claimed that around 20,000 people died because of their 'mistakes'. The Vietnamese have traditionally put the figure at two to three million, although their estimates have generally been rejected as too high and politically motivated (being a means to justify their invasion of the country in 1978/79 and subsequent occupation). The Documentation Center of Cambodia, involved in the heavy mapping project, said that 20,492 mass graves were uncovered containing the remains of 1,112,829 victims of execution. In addition, hundreds of thousands more died from famine and disease; frighteningly, the executions are believed to only account for about 30-40% of the total death toll.

How such a large slice of Cambodia's people died in so short a time (between 1975 and the end of 1978) beggars belief. Some were shot, strangled or suffocated; many more starved; while others died from disease – malaria was rife – and overwork. The Khmer Rouge transformed Cambodia into what the British journalist, William Shawcross, described as: "a vast and sombre work camp where toil was unending, where respite and rewards were non-existent, where families were abolished and where murder was used as a tool of social discipline ... The manner of execution was often brutal. Babies were torn apart limb from limb, pregnant women were disembowelled. Men and women were buried up to their necks in sand and left to die slowly. A common form of execution was by axe handles to the back of the neck. That saved ammunition".

The crimes transcended all moral boundaries known to mankind – soldiers cooked and ate the organs of victims, removed while they were still alive. Sydney Schanberg's forward to *Children of Cambodia's Killing Fields* says of the memoirs: "painful though it may be to contemplate these accounts of young survivors, they desperately need to be passed, whole and without softening, from generation to generation. For it is only by such bearing of witness that the rest of us are rendered unable to pretend that true evil is exceedingly rare in the world, or worse, is but a figment".

The Khmer Rouge revolution was primarily a class-based one, fed by years of growing resentment against the privileged élites. The revolution pitted the least-literate, poorest rural peasants (referred to as the "old" people) against the educated, skilled and foreign-influenced urban population (the "new" people). The "new" people provided an endless flow of numbers for the regime's death lists. Through a series of terrible purges, the members of the former governing and mercantile classes were liquidated or sent to work as forced labourers. But Peter Carey, Oxford historian and Chairman of the Cambodia Trust, argues that not all Pol Pot's victims were townspeople and merchants. "Under the terms of the 1948 Genocide Convention, the Khmer Rouge stands accused of genocide," he wrote in a letter to a British newspaper in 1990. "Of 64,000 Buddhist monks, 62,000 perished; of 250,000 Islamic Chams, 100,000; of 200,000 Vietnamese still left in 1975, 100,000; of 20,000 Thai, 12,000; of 1800 Lao, 1000. Of 2000 Kola, not a trace remained." American political scientist Wayne Bert noted that: "The methods and behaviour compare to that of the Nazis and Stalinists, but in the percentage of the population killed by a revolutionary movement, the Khmer Rouge holds an unchallenged record."

It is still unclear the degree to which these 'genocidal' actions were controlled by those at the centre. Many of the killings took place at the discretion of local leaders, but there were some notably cruel leaders in the upper echelons of the Khmer Rouge and none can have been ignorant of what was going on. Ta Mok, who administered the region southwest of Phnom Penh, oversaw many mass executions for example. There is also evidence that the central government was directly involved in the running of the Tuol Sleng detention centre in which at least 20,000 people died. It has now been turned into a memorial to Pol Pot's holocaust (see page 51).

In addition to the legacy left by centres such as Tuol Sleng, there is the impact of the mass killings upon the Cambodian psyche. One of which is – to Western eyes – the startling openness with which Khmer people will, if asked, matter-of-factly relate their family history in detail: this usually involves telling how the Khmer Rouge era meant they lost one or several members of their family. Whereas death is talked about in hushed terms in Western society, Khmers have no such reservations, perhaps because it touched, and still touches, them all.

King Norodom Sihanouk: latter-day god-king

An uncomplimentary profile of Prince Norodom Sihanouk in *The Economist* in 1990 said that over the preceding 20 years, he "twisted and turned, sulked, resigned many times, [was] humiliated and imprisoned. In one thing, however, he [was] consistent: his yearning to recover the face he lost in 1970, and return to Phnom Penh in triumph". The following year, on 14 November, Prince Sihanouk did exactly that, arriving in his former royal capital to a rapturous welcome, after 13 years of exile. In November 1991, as in 1953 when he returned from exile at Independence, he represented the one symbol Cambodia had of any semblance of national unity.

Norodom Sihanouk was crowned King of Cambodia at the age of 18 in 1941. He owed his accession to the throne to a method of selection devised by the French colonial regime who hoped that the young, inexperienced Sihanouk would be a compliant puppet-king. But in the event he turned out to be something very different. Using his position to great advantage, he became a nationalist leader and crusaded for independence in 1953. But following independence, his royal title worked against him: the 1947 constitution restricted the role the monarch could play in politics. So, he abdicated in favour of his father, Norodom Suramarit, in 1955 and, as Prince Sihanouk, was free to enter politics. He immediately founded the Sangkum Reastr Niyum – the Popular Socialist Community (PSC). The same year, the PSC won every seat in the National Assembly – as it did in subsequent elections in 1958, 1962 and 1966.

The old king died in 1960, but Sihanouk side-stepped the problem of succession by declaring himself Head of State, without ascending to the throne. Michael Leifer, a British political scientist, writes: "As Head of State, Prince Sihanouk became literally the voice of Cambodia. He articulated its hopes and fears within the country and to the outside world... He appeared as a popular figure revered especially in the rural areas as the father figure of his country." He was a populist of the first order.

Someth May, in his autobiography *Cambodian Witness*, describes Phnom Penh in the early 1960s: "Sihanouk's portrait was everywhere around town: in uniform with a sword, in a suit, in

The Vietnamese invasion

The first border clashes over offshore islands between Khmer Rouge forces and the Vietnamese army were reported just a month after the Khmer Rouge came to power. These erupted into a minor war in January 1977 when the Phnom Penh government accused Vietnam of seeking to incorporate Kampuchea into an Indochinese federation. Hanoi's determination to oust Pol Pot only really became apparent however, on Christmas Day 1978 when 120,000 Vietnamese troops invaded. By 7 January (the day of Phnom Penh's liberation) they had installed a puppet government which proclaimed the foundation of the People's Republic of Kampuchea (PRK): Heng Samrin, a former member of the Khmer Rouge, was appointed president. The Vietnamese compared their invasion to the liberation of Uganda from Idi Amin – but for the Western world it was an unwelcome Christmas present. The new government was accorded scant recognition monk's robes, dressed in white with a shaved head like an achar; on posters, on notebooks; framed in every classroom above the teacher's head; in the shops and offices. In the magazine that he edited himself we saw him helping a farmer dig an irrigation canal, reviewing the troops, shooting a film (for he was also a film-maker), addressing the National Assembly, giving presents to the monks, opening the annual regatta with his wife, Monique. On the radio we heard his speeches, and one year when he had a craze for singing you could hear his songs more than 10 times a day."

Sihanouk liked to run the show single-handedly and he is said to have treated his ministers like flunkies. In *Sideshow*, William Shawcross paints him as being vain – "a petulant showman who enjoyed boasting of his sexual successes. He would not tolerate criticism or dissent ... At the same time he had enormous political skill, charm, tenacity and intelligence."

With an American-backed right-wing regime in power after the coup in 1970, the former king went into exile in China, where his supporters formed an alliance with his former enemies, the Khmer Rouge: the Royal Government of National Union of Cambodia – otherwise known as the Grunc. When the Khmer Rouge marched into Phnom Penh in 1975, they restored Prince Sihanouk as Head of State.

He resigned in April 1976 as he became increasingly marginalized, and the Grunc was dissolved. Sihanouk was kept under house-arrest until a few days before the Vietnamese army occupied Phnom Penh in January 1979, whereupon he fled to Beijing. There Sihanouk and his supporters once again joined forces with the Khmer Rouge in a tripartite coalition aimed at overthrowing the Hanoi-backed government.

The peace settlement which followed the eventual Vietnamese withdrawal in 1989 paved the way for Sihanouk's return from exile. His past association with the Khmer Rouge had tarnished the prince's image, but to many Cambodians, he represented their hopes for a stable future. Following the elections of 1993, Sihanouk returned from Beijing to be crowned King on 24 September, thus reclaiming the throne he relinquished in 1955. In 2004 the King abdicated, making way for his son Sihamoni to fill his shoes.

abroad, while the toppled government of Democratic Kampuchea retained the country's seat at the United Nations.

The country's 'liberation' by Vietnam did not end the misery; in 1979 nearly half Cambodia's population was in transit, either searching for their former homes or fleeing across the Thai border into refugee camps. The country reverted to a state of outright war again, for the Vietnamese were not greatly loved in Cambodia – especially by the Khmer Rouge. American political scientist Wayne Bert wrote: "The Vietnamese had long seen a special role for themselves in uniting and leading a greater Indochina Communist movement and the Cambodian Communists had seen with clarity that such a role for the Vietnamese could only be at the expense of their independence and prestige."

Under the Lon Nol and Khmer Rouge regimes, Vietnamese living in Cambodia were expelled or exterminated. Resentment had built up over the years in Hanoi – exacerbated by the apparent ingratitude of the Khmer Rouge for Vietnamese assistance in fighting

Lon Nol's US-supported Khmer Republic in the early 1970s. As relations between the Khmer Rouge and the Vietnamese deteriorated, the Communist superpowers, China and the Soviet Union, polarized too – the former siding with the Khmer Rouge and the latter with Hanoi. The Vietnamese invasion had the full backing of Moscow, while the Chinese and Americans began their support for the anti-Vietnamese rebels.

Following the Vietnamese invasion, three main anti-Hanoi factions were formed. In June 1982 they banded together in an unholy and unlikely alliance of convenience to fight the PRK and called themselves the Coalition Government of Democratic Kampuchea (CGDK), which was immediately recognized by the United Nations. The Communist **Khmer Rouge**, whose field forces recovered to at least 18,000 by the late 1980s. Supplied with weapons by China, they were concentrated in the Cardamom Mountains in the southwest and were also in control of some of the refugee camps along the Thai border. The National United Front for an Independent Neutral Peaceful and Co-operative Cambodia (Funcinpec) – known by most people as the **Armée Nationale Sihanoukiste** (ANS) was headed by Prince Sihanouk although he spent most of his time exiled in Beijing. The group had fewer than 15,000 well-equipped troops – most of whom took orders from Khmer Rouge commanders. The anti-Communist **Khmer People's National Liberation Front** (KPNLF), headed by Son Sann, a former prime minister under Sihanouk. Its 5000 troops were reportedly ill-disciplined in comparison with the Khmer Rouge and the ANS.

The three CGDK factions were ranged against the 70,000 troops loyal to the government of President Heng Samrin and Prime Minister Hun Sen (previously a Khmer Rouge cadre). They were backed by Vietnamese forces until September 1989. Within the forces of the Phnom Penh government there were reported to be problems of discipline and desertion. But the rebel guerrilla coalition was itself seriously weakened by rivalries and hatred between the different factions: in reality, the idea of a 'coalition' was fiction. Throughout most of the 1980s the war followed the progress of the seasons: during the dry season from November to April the PRK forces with their tanks and heavy arms took the offensive but during the wet season this heavy equipment was ineffective and the guerrilla resistance made advances.

The road towards peace

In the late 1980s the Association of Southeast Asian Nations (ASEAN) – for which the Cambodian conflict had almost become a raison d'être – began steps to bring the warring factions together over the negotiating table. ASEAN countries were united primarily in wanting the Vietnamese out of Cambodia. While publicly deploring the Khmer Rouge record, ASEAN tacitly supported the guerrillas. Thailand, an ASEAN member-state, which has had a centuries-long suspicion of the Vietnamese, co-operated closely with China to ensure that the Khmer Rouge guerrillas over the border were well-supplied with weapons.

After Mikhail Gorbachev had come to power in the Soviet Union, Moscow's support for the Vietnamese presence in Cambodia gradually evaporated. Gorbachev began leaning on Vietnam as early as 1987, to withdraw its troops. Despite saying their presence in Cambodia was 'irreversible', Vietnam completed its withdrawal in September 1989, ending nearly 11 years of Hanoi's direct military involvement. The withdrawal led to an immediate upsurge in political and military activity, as forces of the exiled CGDK put increased pressure on the now weakened Phnom Penh regime to begin power-sharing negotiations (see page 236).

Modern Cambodia

Until the mid-19th century, the outside world knew almost nothing of the interior of Cambodia. From the 16th and 17th centuries, rumours began to surface in Europe – based on tales from Portuguese and French missionaries – about a magnificent city, hidden somewhere in the middle of the jungle. It is usually claimed that the ruins of Angkor were 'discovered' by the French naturalist and explorer Henri Mouhot in 1861. This is a travesty of history: Southeast Asians never forgot that Angkor existed. Truth, as they say, is determined by the powerful, and in this case the West determined that a Westerner should 'discover' what was already known. In a sense, Angkor is a great weight on the collective shoulders of the Cambodian people. The usual refrain from visitors is: 'How could a people who created such magnificence have also nurtured Pol Pot and the Khmer Rouge?' A simple answer might be that only despotic rule could create anything on the scale of Angkor. The totalitarianism of the Khmer Rouge echoed that of the Khmer kings, but as the kings built, so the Khmer Rouge destroyed. Nonetheless, it is easy enough to see a stark disjuncture between the glory of Angkor and the horrors of recent history. As Elizabeth Becker wrote at the beginning of 1995: "Cambodia's recent history is one of breathtaking tragedy; by comparison its immediate future looks small and venal. Today Cambodia resembles many of the striving, corrupt, developing nations trying to make up for time lost behind the iron curtain. The nation that bore the horrors of the Khmer Rouge seemed ready for a kinder if not a more prosperous transformation."

In his book *Sideshow*, the British journalist William Shawcross says the diplomats, journalists and tourists who visited Cambodia in the 1950s and 1960s described it as "an idyllic, antique land unsullied by the brutalities of the modern world". Paddy farmers laboured in their ricefields, mystical ruins lay hidden in the jungle, the capital had the charm of a French provincial town and pagodas dotted the landscape. "Such was the illusion," writes Shawcross, of "bucolic plenty, Buddhist serenity, neutralist peace". This was an illusion because for centuries Cambodia had been in a state of continuous social and political upheaval. Since the demise of the Angkorian Empire in the 15th century, the country has been at the mercy of its much larger neighbours, Siam (Thailand) and Vietnam, and of various foreign powers – China, France, the USA and the former Soviet Union. This history of foreign domination is starkly overshadowed by the so-called 'Pol Pot time'. Between 1975 and 1979, Cambodians suffered one of the worst human tragedies to afflict any country since the Second World War – as we have seen, over a million people died out of a total population of about seven million. If the preceding period, during America's involvement in Indochina, is also taken into account, it is possible that around a fifth of Cambodia's population was killed.

The relics and reminders of those days are now firmly on the tourist's sightseeing agenda. These include the chilling Tuol Sleng Genocide Museum (see page 51), in the former high school where the Khmer Rouge tortured and killed at least 20,000 people and Choeung Ek (see page 53), a series of mass graves, the 'Killing Fields', 15 km southwest of Phnom Penh.

Politics

For a lengthy period from the mid-1960s Cambodian politics was chaotic, with warring and bickering factions, backed by different foreign powers and domestic cliques, and shifting alliances. The groups which battled for power following the Vietnamese invasion in 1979 are still in the political arena and although the country may have held several democratic elections since peace returned, civil society remains poorly developed.

The road to peace (of a kind), 1989-1993

In September 1989, under pressure at home and abroad, the Vietnamese withdrew from Cambodia. The immediate result of this withdrawal was an escalation of the civil war as the rebel factions (see page 234) tried to take advantage of the supposedly weakened Hun Sen regime in Phnom Penh. The government committed itself to liberalizing the economy and improving the infrastructure in order to undermine the political appeal of the rebels – particularly that of the Khmer Rouge. Peasant farmers were granted life tenancy to their land and collective farms were substituted with agricultural co-operatives. But because nepotism and bribery were rife in Phnom Penh, the popularity of the Hun Sen regime declined. The rebel position was further strengthened as the disparities between living standards in Phnom Penh and those in the rest of the country widened. In the capital, the government became alarmed; in a radio broadcast in 1991 it announced a crackdown on corruption claiming it was causing a "loss of confidence in our superb regime... which is tantamount to paving the way for the return of the genocidal Pol Pot regime".

With the withdrawal of Vietnamese troops, the continuing civil war followed the familiar pattern of dry season government offensives, and consolidation of guerrilla positions during the monsoon rains. Much of the fighting focused on the potholed highways – particularly Highway 6 which connects the capital with Battambang – with the Khmer Rouge blowing up most of the bridges along the road. Their strategy involved cutting the roads in order to drain the government's limited resources. Other Khmer Rouge offensives were designed to serve their own economic ends – such as their capture of the gem-rich town of Pailin.

The Khmer Rouge ran extortion rackets throughout the country, even along the strategic Highway 4 which ferried military supplies, oil and consumer goods from the port of Kompong Som (Sihanoukville) to Phnom Penh. The State of Cambodia – or the government forces, known as SOC – was pressed to deploy troops to remote areas and allot scarce resources, settling refugees in more secure parts of the country. To add to their problems, Soviet and Eastern Bloc aid began to dry up.

Throughout 1991 the four warring factions were repeatedly brought to the negotiating table in an effort to hammer out a peace deal. Much of the argument centred on the word 'genocide'. The Prime Minister, Hun Sen, insisted that the wording of any agreement should explicitly condemn the former Khmer Rouge regime's 'genocidal acts'. But the Khmer Rouge refused to be party to any power-sharing deal which labelled them in such a way. Fighting intensified as hopes for a settlement increased – all sides wanted to consolidate their territory in advance of any agreement.

Rumours emerged that China was continuing to supply arms – including tanks, reportedly delivered through Thailand – to the Khmer Rouge. There were also accusations that the Phnom Penh government was using Vietnamese combat troops to stem Khmer Rouge advances – the first such reports since their official withdrawal in 1989. But finally, in June 1991, after several attempts, Sihanouk brokered a permanent ceasefire during a meeting of the Supreme National Council (SNC) in Pattaya, South Thailand. The SNC had been proposed by the United Nations Security Council in 1990 and formed in 1991, with an equal number of representatives from the Phnom Penh government and each of the resistance factions, with Sihanouk as its chairman. The following month he was elected chairman of the SNC, and resigned his presidency of the rebel coalition government in exile. Later in the year, the four factions agreed to reduce their armed guerrillas and militias by 70%. The remainder were to be placed under the supervision of the United Nations Transitional Authority in Cambodia (UNTAC), which supervised Cambodia's transition to multi-party democracy. Heng Samrin's decided to drop his insistence that reference should be made to the former Khmer Rouge' "genocidal regime". It was also agreed that elections should be held in 1993 on the basis of proportional representation. Heng Samrin's Communist Party was promptly renamed the Cambodian People's Party, in an effort to persuade people that it sided with democracy and capitalism.

The Paris Peace Accord

On 23 October 1991, the four warring Cambodian factions signed a peace agreement in Paris which officially ended 13 years of civil war and more than two decades of warfare. The accord was co-signed by 15 other members of the International Peace Conference on Cambodia. There was an air of unreality about the whole event, which brought bitter enemies face-to-face after months of protracted negotiations. There was, however, a notable lack of enthusiasm on the part of the four warring factions. Hun Sen said that the treaty was far from perfect because it failed to contain the word 'genocide' to remind Cambodians of the atrocities of the former Khmer Rouge regime and Western powers obviously agreed. But in the knowledge that it was a fragile agreement, everyone remained diplomatically quiet. US Secretary of State James Baker was quoted as saying "I don't think anyone can tell you there will for sure be lasting peace, but there is great hope."

Political analysts ascribed the successful conclusion to the months of negotiations to improved relations between China and Vietnam – there were reports that the two had held secret summits at which the Cambodia situation was discussed. China put pressure on Prince Norodom Sihanouk to take a leading role in the peace process, and Hanoi's new understanding with Beijing prompted Hun Sen's participation. The easing of tensions between China and Moscow – particularly following the Soviet Union's demise – also helped apply pressure on the different factions. Finally, the United States had shifted its position: in July 1990 it had announced that it would not support the presence of the Khmer Rouge at the UN and by September US officials were talking to Hun Sen.

On 14 November 1991, Prince Norodom Sihanouk returned to Phnom Penh to an ecstatic welcome, followed, a few days later, by Son Sen, a Khmer Rouge leader. On 27 November Khieu Samphan who had represented the Khmer Rouge at all the peace negotiations, arrived on a flight from Bangkok. Within hours mayhem had broken out, and a lynch mob attacked him in his villa. Rumours circulated that Hun Sen had orchestrated the demonstration, and beating an undignified retreat down a ladder into a waiting armoured personnel carrier, the bloodied Khmer Rouge leader headed back to Pochentong Airport. The crowd had sent a clear signal that they, at least, were not happy to see him back. There were fears that this incident might derail the entire peace process – but in the event, the Khmer Rouge won a small public relations coup by playing the whole thing down. When the Supreme National Council (SNC) finally met in Phnom Penh at the end of December 1991, it was unanimously decided to rubberstamp the immediate deployment of UN troops to oversee the peace process in the run-up to a general election.

Cambodia 1953-2010

1953	Cambodian independence from France.
1965	Prince Sihanouk's government cuts links with the United States following deployment of US troops in Vietnam.
1966	Right-wing beats Sihanouk in the election; Lon Nol elected prime minister.
1967	Lon Nol toppled following left-wing demonstrations.
1969	Lon Nol becomes prime minister again.
1970	Lon Nol topples Sihanouk in US-backed coup; US bombs Communist bases in Cambodia.
1972	Lon Nol becomes first president of the Khmer Republic.
1975	Lon Nol flees as Khmer Rouge seizes power; Sihanouk made head of government. December: Vietnam invades.
1976	Cambodia renamed Democratic Kampuchea; Sihanouk resigns and Khieu Samphan becomes head of state, with Pol Pot as prime minister. Government moves people from towns to labour camps in the countryside.
1981	Cambodia renamed the People's Republic of Kampuchea (PRK).
1982	Coalition government-in-exile formed by anti-Hanoi resistance comprising Sihanoukists, Khmer Rouge and KPNLF. Sihanouk appointed President; Khieu Samphan, Vice-President and Son Sann, Prime Minister. Coalition backed by China and ASEAN.
1984	Vietnam gains rebel-held territory along Thai border; Vietnamese civilians settle in Kampuchea.
1989	People's Republic of Kampuchea renamed the State of Cambodia. September: last of the Vietnamese troops leave.
1991	International Conference on Cambodia in Paris leads to peace treaty and deployment of UNTAC.
1993	In May elections were held under the auspices of the United Nations Transitional Authority in Cambodia. A coalition government was formed and Norodom Sihanouk was re-crowned King in September.
1996	Ieng Sary (Brother Number Two) splits from Khmer Rouge and is granted a royal pardon.
1997	Hun Sen's coup ousts Ranariddh and Funcinpec from government.
1998	Pol Pot dies. Elections and Hun Sen becomes sole prime minister.
1999	Cambodia joins ASEAN.
2001	Cambodian Senate approves a law to create a tribunal to bring genocide charges against Khmer Rouge leaders.

The UN peace-keeping mission

The UN mission "...conducted a brief, profound and very welcome social revolution [in Cambodia]" (William Shawcross, *Cambodia's new deal: a report*, 1994).

The UN mission favoured "Phnom Penh's profiteers, the Khmer Rouge utopists, the Chinese businessmen of Southeast Asia, the annexationist neighbours..." (Marie Alexandrine Martin, *Cambodia: a shattered society*, 1994).

Yasushi Akashi, a senior Japanese official in the United Nations, was assigned the daunting task of overseeing the biggest military and logistical operation in UN history. UNTAC comprised an international team of 22,000 peacekeepers – including 16,000

2002	First multi-party commune elections; the incumbent Cambodian People's Party wins in all but 23 out of 1620 communes.
2003	Major diplomatic upset with Thailand in January over comments attributed to a Thai TV star that the Angkor Wat temple complex was stolen from Thailand. Angry crowds attack the Thai embassy and Thai-based businesses in Phnom Penh.
2003	Prime Minister Hun Sen's Cambodian People's Party wins the election in July but fails to secure sufficient majority to govern alone. A political deadlock arises.
2004	After nearly a year of political stalemate, Prime Minister Hun Sen is re-elected after his ruling Cambodian People's Party (CPP) forms a coalition with the royalist Funcinpec party.
2004	In August the parliament ratifies Cambodia's entry into World Trade organization (WTO).
2004	King Sihanouk abdicates in October and is succeeded by his son Norodom Sihamoni.
2005	Opposition leader Sam Rainsy flees the country after his parliamentary immunity is stripped.
2006	Hun Sen releases political detainees and allows Sam Rainsy to return to the country.
2007	Local elections pass off peacefully and give Hun Sen's CPP 61% of the vote. The Khmer Rouge trial's finally get underway and all the main targets, including Pol Pot's second in command, Brother No 2, Nuon Chea, are arrested.
2008 July	Hun Sen's Cambodian People's Party wins elections. Opposition threaten to boycott national assembly but back down.
2008 Oct	Thailand and Cambodia troops clash at disputed Preah Vihear temple.
2009 Nov	Trial of Kaing Guek Eav aka Comrade Duch, the infamous chief of the Tuol Sleng death camp is completed. Ex-Thai prime minister Thaksin Shinawatra is made economic adviser to Cambodia; this almost provokes war with Thailand.
2010	Duch is convicted and sentenced to 35 years in prison. Trials of other senior Khmer Rouge figures begin. Sporadic, though minor, armed clashes continue along Thai border.

soldiers from 22 countries; 6000 officials; 3500 police and 1700 civilian employees and electoral volunteers. The first 'blue-beret' UN troops began arriving in November 1991, even before the SNC had agreed to the full complement of peacekeepers. The UN Advance Mission to Cambodia (UNAMIC) was followed four months later by the first of the main peacekeeping battalions. The odds were stacked against them. Shortly after his arrival, Akashi commented: "If one was a masochist one could not wish for more".

UNTAC's task

UNTAC's central mission was to supervise free elections in a country where most of the population had never voted and had little idea of how democracy was meant to work. The UN was also given the task of resettling 360,000 refugees from camps in Thailand and of demobilizing more than a quarter of a million soldiers and militiamen from the four main factions. In addition, it was to ensure that no further arms shipments reached these factions, whose remaining forces were to be confined to cantonments. In the run-up to the elections, UNTAC also took over the administration of the country, taking over the defence, foreign affairs, finance, public security and information portfolios as well as the task of trying to ensure respect for human rights.

By early 1993, UN electoral workers had successfully registered 4.7 million of roughly nine million Cambodians – about 96% of the population of voting age. With a US$2 billion price-tag, this huge operation was the most expensive mission ever undertaken by the UN. At the time, the UN was running 12 peacekeeping operations throughout the world, but two-thirds of its peacekeeping budget was earmarked for Cambodia. Over the months a steady stream of VIPs arrived to witness the operation – they included the UN Secretary-General, Boutros-Boutros Ghali, the Chinese Foreign Minister, Qian Qichen and President François Mitterrand of France.

UNTAC's job would have been easier if the different guerrilla factions and militias had stopped fighting once the Peace Accord was signed. In the months after their arrival UN troops had to broker successive ceasefires between government forces and the Khmer Rouge. During 1992, the Khmer Rouge refused to demobilize their fighters as required by the Accord and attempted to gain a foothold in the strategic central province of Kompong Thom in advance of the full deployment of UN peacekeeping forces. This prompted further scepticism among observers as to their commitment to the peace process. The Khmer Rouge – which was by then referred to (in politically neutral parlance) as the Party of Democratic Kampuchea, or the DK – made it as difficult as possible for the UN. It refused UN soldiers, officials and volunteers access to areas under its control. On a number of occasions in the months running up to the elections, UN military patrols were held hostage after entering Khmer Rouge-held territory.

The Khmer Rouge pulls out

At the beginning of 1993 it became apparent that the Khmer Rouge had no intention of playing ball, despite its claim of a solid rural support base. The DK failed to register for the election before the expiry of the UN deadline and its forces stepped up attacks on UN personnel. In April 1993 Khieu Samphan and his entire entourage at the Khmer Rouge compound in Phnom Penh left the city. It was at this stage that UN officials finally began expressing their exasperation and anxiety over the Khmer Rouge's avowed intention to disrupt the polls. It was well known that the faction had procured fresh supplies of Chinese weapons through Thailand – although there is no evidence that these came from Beijing – as well as large arms caches all over the country.

By the time of the elections, the group was thought to be in control of between 10% and 15% of Cambodian territory. Khmer Rouge guerrillas launched attacks in April and May 1993. Having stoked racial antagonism, they started killing ethnic Vietnamese villagers and settlers, sending up to 20,000 of them fleeing into Vietnam. In one particularly vicious attack, 33 Vietnamese fishermen and their families were killed in a village on the Tonlé Sap. The Khmer Rouge also began ambushing and killing UN soldiers and electoral volunteers.

The UN remained determined that the elections should go ahead despite the Khmer Rouge threats and mounting political intimidation and violence between other factions, notably the Cambodian People's Party and Funcinpec. But it did not take any chances: in the week before the elections, 6000 flak jackets and helmets were flown into the country and security was tightened. In the event, however, there were remarkably few violent incidents and the feared co-ordinated effort to disrupt the voting failed to materialize. Voters took no notice of Khmer Rouge calls to boycott the election and in fact, reports came in from several provinces of large numbers of Khmer Rouge guerrillas and villagers from areas under their control, turning up at polling stations and casting their ballots.

The UN-supervised elections

The voting was by proportional representation, province by province. The election was conducted under the aegis of 1400 International Polling Station Officers from more than 40 countries. The Cambodian people were voting for a 120-member Constituent Assembly to write a new constitution.

The days following the election saw a political farce – Cambodian style – which, as Nate Thayer wrote in the *Far Eastern Economic Review* "might have been comic if the implications were not so depressing for the country's future". In just a handful of days, the Phnom Penh-based correspondent went on, Cambodia "witnessed an abortive secession, a failed attempt to establish a provisional government, a royal family feud and the manoeuvres of a prince [Sihanouk] obsessed with avenging his removal from power in a military coup more than 20 years [previously]". The elections gave Funcinpec 45% of the vote, the CPP 38% and the BLDP, 3%. The CPP immediately claimed the results fraudulent, while Prince Norodom Chakrapong – one of Sihanouk's sons – announced the secession of the country's six eastern provinces. Fortunately, both attempts to undermine the election dissolved. The CPP agreed to join Funcinpec in a power sharing agreement while, remarkably, the Khmer Rouge were able to present themselves as defenders of democracy in the face of the CPP's claims of vote-rigging. The new Cambodian constitution was ratified in September 1993, marking the end of UNTAC's involvement in the country. Under the new constitution, Cambodia was to be a pluralistic liberal-democratic country. Seventy-year-old Sihanouk was crowned King of Cambodia, reclaiming the throne he relinquished in 1955. His son Norodom Ranariddh was appointed First Prime Minister and Hun Sen, Second Prime Minister, a situation intended to promote national unity but which instead lead to internal bickering and dissent.

An uncivil society?

Almost from day one of Cambodia's rebirth as an independent state espousing the principles of democracy and the market, cracks began to appear in the rickety structure that underlay these grand ideals. Rampant corruption, infighting among the coalition partners, political intrigue, murder and intimidation all became features of the political landscape – and have remained so to this day. There are three bright spots in an otherwise pretty dismal political landscape. First of all, the Khmer Rouge – along with Pol Pot – is dead and buried. Second, while there have been coups, attempted coups, murder, torture and intimidation, the country does still have an operating political system with an opposition of sorts. And third, the trajectory of change since the last edition of this guide was published has been upwards. But, as the following account shows, politics in Cambodia makes Italy seem a model of stability and common sense.

From the elections of 1993 through to 1998, relations between the two key members of the ruling coalition, the CPP and Funcinpec, went from bad to quite appalling. At the end of 1995 Prince Norodom Sirivudh was arrested for plotting to kill Hun Sen and the prime minister ordered troops and tanks on to the streets of Phnom Penh. For a while the capital had the air of a city under siege. Sirivudh, secretary-general of Funcinpec and King Norodom Sihanouk's half brother, has been a vocal critic of corruption in the government, and a supporter of Sam Rainsy, the country's most outspoken opposition politician and the bane of Hun Sen's life. The National Assembly voted unanimously to suspend Sirivudh's immunity from prosecution. Few commentators really believed that Sirivudh had plotted to kill Hun Sen. Though he had been outspoken, and occasionally rather injudicious in his public remarks, Sirivudh was not seen to be someone who would involve himself in such a serious conspiracy. The assumption, then, was that Hun Sen – a 'notorious bully' in the words of The Economist – was merely playing politics Cambodia-style. In the end Hun Sen did not go through with a trial and Sirivudh went into self-imposed exile.

In 1996, relations between the CPP and Funcinpec reached another low. First Prime Minister Prince Norodom Ranariddh joined his two exiled brothers – princes Chakkrapong and Sirivudh – along with Sam Rainsy, in France. Hun Sen smelled a rat and when Ranariddh threatened in May to pull out of the coalition his worries seemed to be confirmed. Only pressure from the outside prevented a meltdown. Foreign donors said that continuing aid was contingent on political harmony, and ASEAN sent the Malaysian foreign minister to knock a few heads together. Some months later relations became chillier still following the drive-by killing of Hun Sen's brother-in-law as he left a restaurant in Phnom Penh.

Things, it seemed, couldn't get any worse – but they did. In February 1997 fighting between forces loyal to Ranariddh and Hun Sen broke out in Battambang. March saw a grenade attack on a demonstration led by opposition leader Sam Rainsy outside the National Assembly leaving 16 dead and 150 injured – including Rainsy himself who suffered minor injuries. In April, Hun Sen mounted what became known as the 'soft coup'. This followed a complicated series of defections from Ranariddh's Funcinpec party to the CPP which, after much to-ing and fro-ing overturned Funcinpec's small majority in the National Assembly. In May, Hun Sen's motorcade was attacked and a month later, on 16 June, fighting broke out between Hun Sen and Ranariddh's bodyguards leaving three dead. It was this gradual decline in relations between the two leaders and their parties which laid the foundations for the coup of 1997.

In July 1997 the stage was set for Cambodia to join ASEAN, along with Laos and Myanmar (Burma). This would have marked Cambodia's international rehabilitation. Then, just a month before the historic day, on 5-6 June, Hun Sen mounted a coup and ousted Norodom Ranariddh and his party, Funcinpec, from government. It took two days for Hun Sen and his forces to gain full control of the capital. Ranariddh escaped to Thailand while the United Nations Centre for Human Rights reported that 41 senior military officers and Ranariddh loyalists were hunted down in the days following the coup, tortured and executed. In August the National Assembly voted to withdraw Ranariddh's immunity from prosecution. Five months later, in January 1998, United Nations High Commissioner for Human Rights Mary Robinson visited Cambodia and pressed for an investigation into the deaths – a request that Hun Sen rejected as unwarranted interference. ASEAN, long used to claiming that the Association has no role interfering in domestic affairs, found it had no choice but to defer Cambodia's accession.

The coup was widely condemned and on 17 September the UN decided to keep Cambodia's seat vacant in the General Assembly.

Following the coup of 1997 there was some speculation that Hun Sen would simply ignore the need to hold elections scheduled for 26 July. In addition, opposition parties threatened to boycott the elections even if they did occur, claiming that Hun Sen and his henchmen were intent on intimidation. But despite sporadic violence in the weeks and months leading up to the elections, all parties ended up participating. It seems that intense international pressure got to Hun Sen who appreciated that without the goodwill of foreign aid donors the country would simply collapse. Of the 4.9 million votes cast – constituting an impressive 90% of the electorate – Hun Sen's Cambodian People's Party won the largest share at just over 41% while Ranariddh's Funcinpec secured 31.7% of the vote and the Sam Rainsy Party (SRP), 14.3%.

Hun Sen offered to bring Funcinpec and the SRP into a coalition government, but his advances were rejected. Instead Rainsy and Ranariddh encouraged a series of demonstrations and vigils outside the National Assembly – which quickly became known as 'Democracy Square', à la Tiananmen Square. At the beginning of September 1998, following a grenade attack on Hun Sen's residence and two weeks of uncharacteristic restraint on the part of the Second Prime Minister, government forces began a crack down on the demonstrators. A week later the three protagonists – Ranariddh, Sam Rainsy and Hun Sen – agreed to talks presided over by King Sihanouk in Siem Reap. These progressed astonishingly well considering the state of relations between the three men and two days later the 122-seat National Assembly opened at Angkor Wat on 24 September. Shortly before the talks, Cambodia's Queen Monineath put forward the suggestion that the three leaders should play more golf together – believing that this might lead to greater co-operation. (Southeast Asian leaders are great believers in the diplomatic powers of golf.) In mid-November further talks (it was not made clear whether these were before, during or after any golf match) between the CPP and Funcinpec led to the formation of a coalition government. Hun Sen became sole prime minister and Ranariddh chairman of the National Assembly. While the CPP and Funcinpec took control of 12 and 11 ministries respectively, with Defence and Interior shared, the CPP got the lion's share of the key portfolios. Sam Rainsy was left on the opposition benches. Even so King Sihanouk could say, before embarking on another round of medical tests in Beijing in November 1998 that "The big political crisis in our country has been solved, the political deadlock is over". It was only after the political détente that followed the elections that Cambodia was given permission to occupy its UN seat in December 1998. At a summit meeting in Hanoi around the same time, ASEAN also announced that they had agreed on the admission of Cambodia to the grouping – which finally came through on 30 April 1999.

The press and the King

The years since the UN-supervised elections in 1993 have seen, in the eyes of some commentators, a gradual erosion of press freedoms as the government has become becoming increasingly authoritarian. In July 1995 a new press law gave additional powers to a state which has too often resorted to thuggery to convince its opponents. As one observer was quoted as saying in the *Far Eastern Economic Review* at the beginning of 1996, "many people's initial reactions in Cambodia are still violent". At times the sensitivity of politicians has descended into farce. In March 1995, Cambodian newspaper editor Chan Rottana was sentenced to a year in gaol for writing a "false and defamatory statement" that First Prime Minister Prince Norodom Ranariddh was "three times more stupid" than Second Prime Minister Hun Sen. In mid-1995 former foreign minister Sam Rainsy summed up the state of political affairs in the country when he said: "If you are satisfied with cosmetics, everything is OK, like some Americans tell me. But if you scratch a little bit below the surface, there is nothing democratic about the government. The parliament is a rubber stamp. The press is being killed ... The judiciary is far from independent."

There is no doubt that by the mid-1990s the job of being a newspaper editor with opposition leanings was becoming increasingly dangerous. In May 1995, the *Khmer Ideal* newspaper was closed down and its publisher fined; in the same month, the editor of *New Liberty* was jailed for a year for penning an editorial entitled 'Nation of thieves', alluding to corruption in government ranks; a week after this, the government began proceedings against the editor of the *Morning News* – a man who was jailed in 1994 for a previous offending article. Human Rights Watch Asia reported that this series of actions "represent one of the most serious assaults yet on freedom of expression". In January 1996 the offices of the opposition Khmer Nation Party were raided by police, and in the following month Ek Mongkol, a radio commentator and Funcinpec member, was shot and seriously injured. In May 1996 anti-government newspaper editor Thun Bunly was gunned down in Phnom Penh and later died. Human Rights Watch reported that in 2003, Chou Chetharith, the deputy editor at royalist radio station, *Ta Prohm*, was shot and killed outside his office after Hun Sen publicly warned the station to stop broadcasting insults directed at the CPP. However, local journalists today claim they have more "press freedom" or as one Khmer journalist aptly put it "the party you are aligned with protects you". Many media outlets depend on financial support from political parties. Not surprisingly, Prime Minister Hun Sen and his allies control several broadcasters. A report by the United States Agency for International Development (USAID) into corruption in 2004 indicated that the media is far from free of bias – politicians will regularly pay journalists to run certain stories and pay them to not run others. It was reported that at the Poipet border, a quagmire of trafficking, corruption and lawlessness, journalists clued up on the pay-offs, regularly gather by the border and wait for officials to come and pay them off for not reporting the terrible border stories.

Most commentators also viewed former King Norodom Sihanouk as part of the problem, simply because he was so revered. He interfered in the political process, changed his mind constantly, and exasperated government ministers. Yet the respect held for him by Cambodians meant that he could not be ignored, or easily contradicted.

Nonetheless, in 1995 the government apparently had a stab at trying to reduce his influence and role. For a start the police confiscated all copies of a booklet entitled *Only the King can save Cambodia* – reputed to call for the return of King Sihanouk to politics. But this council consists of a myriad of competing factions.

In 1996 William Shawcross returned to Cambodia and spent two hours with Sihanouk. The former King "was his usual charming and voluble self", Shawcross wrote of the meeting, "offering Tattinger champagne and chocolates". But he was also, apparently, a saddened man as he watched his country lurch from crisis to crisis. Sihanouk explained to Shawcross: "I am like a piece of ham in a sandwich, but not a delicious sandwich like those created by Lord Sandwich. I'm stuck instead between the government and the opposition. I am very miserable. Very, very miserable. I would like to conciliate. I cannot. I cannot reunite the two sides. My hope for Cambodia to become one of the world's most advanced liberal democracies is finished" (*The New York Review*, 14 November 1996).

After countless threats, on 7 October 2004, King Sihanouk abdicated; requesting by letter that all "compatriots please allow him [sic] to retire". Sihanouk's long-time battle with cancer was cited as his motivation. It is said that a fortune teller once predicted that he would not live past his 74th birthday, so he was already defying the odds. On his website the King explained: "My abdication allows me to give our country, our nation and our people a serious opportunity to avoid mortal turmoil the day after my death."

On October 14, the Cambodian Throne Council selected Prince Norodom Sihamoni to succeed Sihanouk as King. King Norodom Sihamoni officially ascended the throne in a coronation ceremony held on 29 October.

Even though Cambodia's constitution states that the king officially reigns as head of state but does not govern, Sihanouk king never stayed far from politics. Unlike his father, Sihamoni has no background in politics nor appears likely to head that way. Instead, the new King is renowned for his ballet prowess, having trained as a dancer in Prague in the 1970s. He later studied film in North Korea and served as Cambodia's envoy to the UNESCO in Paris.

Sihanouk, based in Beijing in 2005, continued to prove that out of sight wasn't out of mind, retaining an omnipresent voice. Having tried his hand as author, film maker, song writer, actor, and of course king, the serial multi-tasker, Sihanouk assumed a new hobby – blogging.

A return to some kind of normality

The year 1997 was the low point in Cambodia's stuttering return to a semblance of normality. The Asian economic crisis combined with the coup (see above) to rock the country back on its heels. On 3 February 2002 free, fair and only modestly violent local commune elections were held. The CPP won the vote by a landslide and although there is little doubt that Hun Sen's party used a bit of muscle here and there, foreign election observers decided that the result reflected the will of the 90 per cent of the electorate who voted. The CPP, despite its iron grip on power, does recognize that democracy means it has to get out there and make a case. Around one third of the CPP's more unpopular commune chiefs were replaced prior to the election. Funcinpec did badly, unable to shake off the perception that it sold out its principles to join the coalition in 1998. The opposition Sam Rainsy Party did rather better, largely for the same reason: the electorate viewed it as standing up to the might of the CPP, highlighting corruption and abuses of power.

In July 2002 Hun Sen took on the rotating chairmanship of ASEAN and used a round of high-profile meetings to demonstrate to the region, and the wider world, just how far the country has come. Hun Sen, who hardly has an enviable record as a touchy-feely politician, used the chairmanship of ASEAN to polish his own as well as his country's credentials in the arena of international public opinion. But despite the PR some Cambodians are concerned that Hun Sen is becoming a little like Burma's Ne Win. Like Ne Win, Hun Sen seems to be obsessed with numbers. His lucky number is 9; in 2002 he brought the local elections forward by three weeks so that the digits in the date would add up to 9. In 2001 he closed down all Cambodia's karaoke bars; fine if he was closing down drug dens, but karaoke bars? With over 20 years as prime minister there is no one to touch Hun Sen and he seems to revel in his strongman reputation. Judges bow to his superior knowledge of the judicial system; kings and princes acknowledged his unparalleled role in appointing the new king; many journalists are in thrall to his power. Hun Sen once said to foreign monitors that "international standards exist only in sports" (*The Economist*, 2 May 2002). If even the most fundamental of rights are negotiable then it would seem that only Cambodia's dependence on foreign largesse constrains his wilder impulses.

Compared to its recent past, the last 10 years has been a period of relative stability for Cambodia. Political violence and infighting between parties continues to be a major problem – by international standards the elections were borderline unacceptable, although most of the major parties were reasonably satisfied with the results which saw Hun Sen's landslide victory. The 2003 election wasn't smooth-sailing either. Prior to the June 2003 election the alleged instructions given by representatives of the CPP to government controlled election monitoring organizations were: "If we win by the law, then we win. If we lose by the law, we still must win." Nonetheless a political deadlock arose, with the CPP winning a majority of votes but not the two-thirds required under the constitution to govern alone. The incumbent CPP-led administration assumed power and took on a caretaker role, pending the creation of a coalition which would satisfy the required number of National Assembly seats to form government. Without a functioning legislature, the course of vital legislation was stalled. After almost a year-long stalemate, the National Assembly approved a controversial addendum to the constitution, which allowed a new government to be formed by vote. The vote took place on 15 July 2004, and the National Assembly approved a new coalition government, an amalgam of the CPP and FUNCINPEC, with Hun Sen at the helm as Prime Minister and Prince Norodom Ranariddh as President of the National Assembly.

The government's democratic principles came under fire once again in February 2005, when opposition leader Sam Rainsy fled the country after losing his parliamentary immunity from prosecution. Rainsy is perceived as something of a threat due to his steadily gaining popularity with young urban dwellers, whose growing disenchantment with the current government he feeds off. On the one hand, his 'keep the bastards honest' style of politics has added a new dimension of accountability to Cambodian politics, but on the other, his nationalist, racist rantings, particularly his anti-Vietnamese sentiments, could be a very bad thing for the country. In May, 2005 Hun Sen said that Sam Rainsy would have to wait until the "next life" before he would guarantee his safety. However, having received a pardon in February 2006, he returned to the political fray soon thereafter.

The lingering death of the Khmer Rouge

What many outsiders found hard to understand was how the Khmer Rouge enjoyed such popular support among Cambodians – even after the massacres and torture. UN officials working in Phnom Penh in 1992 and 1993 found this disquieting. In June 1994, the retiring Australian ambassador to Cambodia, John Holloway, in a leaked account of his 2½ years in Phnom Penh wrote: "I was alarmed in a recent dialogue with about 100 students from different groups at the University of Phnom Penh to hear them espousing a return to government by the Khmer Rouge… They estimated that 60% of the student body favoured Khmer Rouge participation in government… It is necessary for outsiders to understand, that for most Cambodians, the Vietnamese are a far more traumatic issue than the Khmer Rouge."

The Khmer Rouge was not, of course, just a political force. Its political influence was backed up and reinforced by military muscle. And it has been the defeat of the Khmer Rouge as an effective fighting force which seems to have delivered the fatal blow to its political ambitions.

In mid-1994 the National Assembly outlawed the Khmer Rouge, offering a six-month amnesty to rank and file guerrillas. By the time the six months was up in January 1995, 7,000 Khmer Rouge had reportedly defected to the government, leaving at that time somewhere between 5000 and 6000 hardcore rebels still fighting. A split in this core group can be dated to 8 August 1996 when Khmer Rouge radio announced that former 'brother number two', Ieng Sary, had betrayed the revolution by embezzling money earned from mining and timber contracts, and branded him a traitor.

This was the first evidence available to Western commentators that a significant split in the Khmer Rouge had occurred. In retrospect, it seems that the split had been brewing for some years – ever since the UN-sponsored elections had revealed a division between 'conservatives' and 'moderates'. The latter, apparently, wished to co-operate with the UN, while the former group desired to boycott the elections. In 1996 the moderate faction, headed by Ieng Sary, finally broke away from the conservatives led by Pol Pot and hardman General Ta Mok. Hun Sen announced soon after the radio broadcast in August 1996 that two Khmer Rouge commanders, Ei Chhien and Sok Pheap had defected to the government. At the end of September Ieng Sary held a press conference to declare his defection. He told an incredulous audience that he "had nothing to do with ordering the execution of anyone, or even the suggestion of it". On 14 September King Norodom Sihanouk granted Ieng Sary a royal pardon.

The Cambodian government's conciliatory line towards Ieng Sary seemed perplexing given the man's past. Although he cast himself in the mould of 'misguided and ignorant revolutionary', there are few who doubt that he was fully cognisant of what the Khmer Rouge under Pol Pot were doing even if, as Michael Vickery argues, he was not Brother Number Two, just Brother Number Four or Five. Indeed he has admitted as much in the past. Not only is he, as a man, thoroughly unpleasant – or so those who know him have said – but he was also a key figure in the leadership and was sentenced to death in absentia by the Phnom Penh government. Stephen Heder of London's School of Oriental & African Studies was quoted as saying after the September press conference: "It's totally implausible that Ieng Sary was unaware that people were being murdered [by the Khmer Rouge]". This was confirmed in October 1996 when Laurence Piq, formerly married to Suong Sikoeun an aide to Ieng Sary, wrote: "As in The Little Red Riding Hood, the hand he [Ieng Sary] extends for photographs is the better to grab you with. The jovial demeanour he affixes to his mouth is the better to bite you with. The red carpet is laid out. Abominable crimes are being erased. All shame is swallowed. The world's nations accept this under the pretext of peace. What kind of peace? A peace à la Khmer Rouge, dripping with the blood of genocide." The split in the Khmer Rouge and the defection of Ieng Sary deprived the Khmer Rouge of 3000-5000 men – halving its fighting force – and also denied the group important revenues from key gem mining areas around Pailin and many of the richest forest concessions.

The disintegration of the Khmer Rouge continued in 1997 after a complicated deal involving Pol Pot, Khieu Samphan, Son Sen and Ta Mok, as well as members of Funcinpec, collapsed. In early June Khieu Samphan, the nominal leader of the Khmer Rouge, was thought to be on the verge of brokering an agreement with Funcinpec that would give Pol Pot and two of his henchmen (Son Sen and Ta Mok) immunity from prosecution. This would then provide the means by which Khieu Samphan might enter mainstream Cambodian politics. It seems that Hun Sen, horrified at the idea of an alliance between Khieu Samphan and Funcinpec, mounted the coup of June 1997 to prevent the deal coming to fruition. Pol Pot was also, apparently, less than satisfied with the terms of the agreement and pulled out – killing Son Sen in the process. But before Pol Pot could flee, Ta Mok captured his erstwhile leader on June 19th at the Khmer Rouge stronghold of Anlong Veng.

A little more than a month later the 'Trial of the Century' began in this remote jungle hideout. It was a show trial – more like a Cultural Revolution lynching. A crowd of a few hundred people were on hand to shout slogans like "Crush, crush, crush Pol Pot and his clique". Pol Pot offered the usual Khmer Rouge defence: the revolution made mistakes, but its leaders were inexperienced. And, in any case, they saved Cambodia from annexation by Vietnam. (There is an argument purveyed by some academics that the Khmer Rouge was essentially involved in a programme of ethnic cleansing aimed at ridding Cambodia of all Vietnamese people and influences.) Show trial or not, few people had any sympathy for Pol Pot as he was sentenced by the Khmer Rouge 'people's' court to life imprisonment for the murder of Son Sen. A Khmer Rouge radio station broadcast that with Pol Pot's arrest and sentencing, a 'dark cloud' had been lifted from the Cambodian people.

Confirmation of this bizarre turn of events emerged in mid-October when journalist Nate Thayer of the *Far Eastern Economic Review* became the first journalist to interview Pol Pot since 1979. He reported that the former Khmer Rouge leader was "very ill and perhaps close to death". Even more incredibly than Ieng Sary's defence, Pol Pot denied that the Cambodian genocide had ever occurred and told Nate Thayer that his 'conscience was clear'. "I came to carry out the struggle, not to kill people", he said, adding "Even now, and you can look at me, am I a savage person?".

In March 1998 reports filtered out of the jungle near the Thai border that the Khmer Rouge was finally disintegrating in mutinous conflict. The end game was at hand. The government's amnesty encouraged the great bulk of the Khmer Rouge's remaining fighters to lay down their arms and in December 1998 the last remnants of the rebel army surrendered to government forces, leaving just a handful of men under hardman 'The Butcher' Ta Mok still at large. But even Ta Mok's days of freedom were numbered. In March 1999 he was captured near the Thai border and taken back to Phnom Penh.

The death of Pol Pot

On 15 April 1998 unconfirmed reports stated that Pol Pot – a man who ranks with Hitler, Stalin and Mao in his ability to kill – had died in a remote jungle hideout in the north of Cambodia. Given that Pol Pot's death had been announced several times before, the natural inclination among journalists and commentators was to treat these reports with scepticism. But it was already known that Pol Pot was weak and frail and his death was confirmed when journalists were invited to view his body the following day. Pol Pot was reported to have died from a heart attack. He was 73.

A new era?

The question of what to do with Ieng Sary was the start of a long debate over how Cambodia – and the international community – should deal with former members of the Khmer Rouge. The pragmatic, realist line is that if lasting peace is to come to Cambodia, then it may be necessary to allow some people to get away with – well – murder. As one Western diplomat pondered: "Do you owe fealty to the dead for the living?" This would seem to be Hun Sen's preferred position.

By late 1998, with the apparent end of the Khmer Rouge as a fighting force, the government seemed happy to welcome back the rank and file into mainstream

Cambodian life – and even into the armed forces – while putting on trial key characters in the Khmer Rouge like Ta Mok, Khieu Samphan and Nuon Chea. While the government was considering what to do, former leaders of the Khmer Rouge were busy trying to rehabilitate their muddied reputations. After years of living pretty comfortable lives around the country, particularly in and around Pailin, by the end of 2007 the old guard of the Khmer Rouge were finally being brought to book. This turn of events was finally set in motion in March 2006 with the nomination of seven judges by the then Secretary General of the United Nations, Kofi Annan for the much anticipated Cambodia Tribunal. With Ta Mok dying in prison in early July 2006 the first charges were laid against the notorious head of the Tuol Sleng prison, Khang Khek leu – aka 'Comrade Duch' (his trial was completed in July 2010, see box, page 250). Yet it was with the arrests in late 2007 of Ieng Sary, Nuon Chea and Khieu Samphan that the tribunal finally began to flex its muscles. Each of these arrests made international news and it seems, almost 30 years after the Vietnam invasion ended the abhorrent Khmer Rouge regime, that Cambodia may finally be coming to terms with its horrific past (for more information on the Tribunal see box, page 250).

However, with only the few living key Khmer Rouge figures standing trial most of the minor – and probably equally murderous – cadre are still in circulation. It could be argued that the Tribunal is purely a diversion that allows this coterie of killers and Hun Sen's nefarious past to remain hidden from scrutiny.

What is obvious is that as the Tribunal progressed, many of the old divisions that have riven Cambodian society for generations where taking hold again. In late 2007 Cambodia was officially and internationally recognized as one of the most corrupt countries in history. Spend five minutes in Phnom Penh and this air of corruption is staring you in the face – Toyota Land Cruisers, giant, black Lexus SUVs and Humvees plough through the streets without regard for anyone or anything. When these vehicles do crush or kill other road users, the driver's well-armed body guards hop out, pistols waving, and soon dissuade any eager witnesses. This kind of event is commonplace and the poorer locals know this. Speak to a moto or tuk tuk driver and you'll soon sense the resentment, "We hate the corrupt and we'd be happy to see them die", is a frequent comment reminiscent of Cambodia's darker times. The establishment of a new, rich elite is not leading to the trickle down of wealth but the entrenchment of certain groups who have no regard at all for building a new society. Even the aid community is complicit in this – one senior worker from a massive donor to Cambodia made this damning off-the-record comment, "We view corruption as the only stabilising factor in Cambodian society. It is awful but what else is there?"

The July 2008 general election changed little. Hun Sen was returned with an enlarged majority after a campaign that drew both praise and criticism from EU observers. On the upside the election was seen as being 'technically proficient' and possibly the best-run vote in Cambodia's history. Not that that's saying much – Hun Sen's ruling CPP was seen to have abused its position and not only dominated the media but also disenfranchised tens of thousands of opposition voters. Yet the same EU observers also felt the CPP would have won despite any machinations by Hun Sen and the vote was accepted in the international community. At the same time the election was taking place a row began to brew with Thailand over the contested Preah Vihear temple near the Thai/Cambodian border. In early July the Cambodian-led effort to turn the revered Preah Vihear into a UNESCO World Heritage Site was greeted by huge celebrations in Phnom Penh. For the Cambodians this meant that the long-contested temple was now firmly recognized as

Cambodia Tribunal

In 1997, with the country's interminable civil war set to end, the Cambodian government made an official approach to the United Nations to establish a court to prosecute the senior members of the Khmer Rouge. The thinking at the time was that Cambodia lacked the institutions and know-how to handle such a big trial and that outside expertise would be needed.

At first, things for the prosecution looked promising, with an agreed handing over of Pol Pot (was holed up in northern Cambodia in Anlong Veng), set to take place in April 1998. But he never made it to court, mysteriously dying the night before his supposed arrest. Some say from a heart attack, others that he took his own life.

In 1999, Kaing Guek Eav aka 'Comrade Duch', the commandant of the infamous Tuol Sleng prison camp in Phnom Penh, surrendered to the Cambodian authorities. In the same year, Ta Mok, another blood-soaked Khmer Rouge leader, was also arrested (he died in custody seven years later in 2006). Initially, however, no power or legal authority existed to try them and it wasn't until 2001 that the Cambodian government agreed to pass a law setting up what came to be known as the 'Extraordinary Chambers in the Courts of Cambodia for the Prosecution of Crimes Committed during the Period of Democratic Kampuchea' or, for short, the Cambodia Tribunal.

Several more years passed, with the sometimes indifferent Cambodians stating that they had no money to finance the trials and the international community unwilling to fund a process in a country where corruption was so rampant. But despite this, in early 2006, buildings just outside Phnom Penh were requisitioned, the UN nominated its judges and by July of the same year a full panel of 30 Cambodian and UN judges were fully sworn in. A list of five main suspects was drawn up in July 2007 and the first person formally charged was the already incarcerated Comrade Duch on 31 July 2007.

Then, in late 2007, after years of snail-like progress, and with the main protagonists approaching their twilight years, a flurry of dramatic arrests occurred. Former Khmer Rouge ideologue and Foreign Minister Ieng Sary and his wife, the Minister of Social Affairs, Ieng Thirith, former Chief of State and Pol Pot's number two, Khieu Samphan, were all taken into custody and charged with war crimes and crimes against humanity.

The first trial of Extraordinary Chambers in the Courts of Cambodia for the Prosecution of Crimes Committed during the Period of Democratic Kampuchea began with Comrade Duch in February 2009. By the end of the same year his trial was over and in July 2010 he received a 35-year sentence (reduced to 19 years due to his pre-trial incarceration). Also in 2010 trials against many other senior Khmer Rouge figures began.

There's no doubt that Duch's public trial marked a turning point for Cambodia. For the first time the Khmer Rouge's crimes were aired in the cold, calculated and unambiguous efficiency of a courtroom. Victims confronted their tormentor and saw Duch express remorse and, more bizarrely, ask to be released by the court.

With the first trial completed a giant psychological hurdle was taken in its stride by the Cambodian people. Finally, after almost 40 years, it seems like justice will be delivered – this can only bode well for Cambodia's future.

being in their territory. By early October 2008 a troop build-up escalated into an exchange of fire that led to a tense two-week stand and resulted in several deaths. Eventually, after pressure from the international community, both sides backed down but the dispute is still not settled and, at present, one of the region's most spectacular sites is off-limits.

It wasn't all bad news though as on 17 February 2009, 30 years after the fall of the Khmer Rouge regime, the first trial against one of its former commanders, Kaing Guek Eav AKA Comrade Duch, the infamous chief of the Tuol Sleng death camp, finally began.

As it progressed through 2009, Duch's trial attracted a huge amount of international attention, not least for the extraordinary plea the accused made in November 2009 to be released. While it must be said Duch has been one of the few senior Khmer Rouge leaders to have expressed any regret, this was still a staggering moment. By July 2010 Duch was convicted of crimes against humanity, murder and torture. He received a 35-year sentence but this was tempered with a 16-year reduction due to the lengthy time Duch had been incarcerated before the trial began – in effect he could be released, aged 87, in 2029. This twist on the length of imprisonment caused much distress to the families of Duch's victims. Furthermore, by the end of 2010 Duch's status of being the only other senior Khmer Rouge figure to be fully indicted for crimes perpetrated during the Pol Pot era finally came to an end. In September 2010 several other high profile senior Khmer Rouge figure, including their chief idealogue, Nuon Chea, their former head of state, Khieu Samphan, and Ieng Sary and his wife, Ieng Thirith (both Khmer Rouge ministers), were formerly charged with crimes against humanity and genocide with their trial timetabled to begin in early 2011.

The other main issue that has dominated Cambodia over the last period has been its relations with its neighbour, Thailand. Ostensibly focused on the disputed Preah Vihear temple, this dispute has already reached the shooting stage on several occasions with soldiers on both sides being killed. There's also little doubt that the appointment of deposed Thai prime minister Thaksin – who is loathed by the controlling Thai elite and has been defined as a wanted "criminal" by the Thai state – as an economic adviser by Hun Sen only exacerbated the situation. After Thaksin arrived in Cambodia in late 2009 the Thais withdrew their ambassador, threatened to tear up long-standing trade agreements and demanded that Cambodia, an ASEAN partner, arrest Thaksin and extradite him to Thailand to face a prison cell.

Hun Sen, with some justification, refused, citing that Thaksin's criminal conviction in Thailand was politicized and that Cambodia could choose who it wanted as an economic adviser. After the Thais threw a few more toys out of the pram, things calmed down enough for Hun Sen to visit Thailand for an ASEAN meeting and by mid-2010 it seemed as though the Thaksin element in Thai/Cambodia relations was no longer a defining factor.

Yet the Preah Vihear issue remains (see box, page 126), as does the need for both governments to have an issue around which they can raise nationalistic sentiment and support. While Cambodia under Hun Sen's rule has made huge advances in recent years, and the Khmer Rouge trials clearly point to the nation finally coming to terms with itself, there is still a strong warrior streak running the Cambodian leader's character – maintaining peaceful relations with its turbulent and troublesome neighbour is key to Cambodia's ongoing development.

People and society

Before 1975, Cambodia had a population of about 7.2 million; within four years this had dropped to around six million (some were the victims of genocide, others became refugees). The population topped 10 million in 1995 and according to the CIA Factbook in 2010 (www.cia.gov), the figure now stands at about 14.5 million. The Khmers are the dominant group (about 85% of the total population) but there are significant Chinese and Vietnamese minorities as well as a small percentage of tribal groups – most of whom suffered badly during the Pol Pot years.

Khmers
The Khmers are believed to have lived in the region from about the second century AD but there is some argument as to where they migrated from. Some anthropologists suggest that they are a fusion of Mongul and Melanesian elements. They have been mainly influenced over the centuries by the powerful Indian and Javanese kingdoms.

Khmer Loeu
The Khmer Loeu, or Upland Khmer (divided into the Saoch, Pear, Brao and Kui), are one of the main tribal groups and live in the forested mountain zones, mainly in the northeast. The Saoch live in the Elephant Mountains to the southwest; the Pear occupy the Cardamom Mountains to the west; while the Brao are settled along the Lao border to the northeast. Traditionally the Khmer Loeu were semi-nomadic and practised slash and burn agriculture. Like many tribal groups in Southeast Asia they were also mainly animist. In recent years, however, increasing numbers have turned to settled agriculture and adopted many of the customs of the lowland Khmers.

Chinese
In the 18th and 19th centuries large numbers of ethnic Chinese migrated to Southeast Asia, where most became involved in commerce. Until the Khmer Rouge take-over in 1975, the Chinese played a central role in the economy, controlling trade, banking and transport. As in neighbouring Thailand, they assimilated to a greater degree than in other parts of Southeast Asia. In recent decades, most of Cambodia's urban and governing élite has had at least some Chinese blood – Lon Nol, for example had a Chinese grandparent. The Chinese started leaving the country when civil war broke out in 1970 – and many of those who did not get out before 1975 were killed during the Pol Pot years. The few who survived the Khmer Rouge era emigrated during the first months of the pro-Vietnam PRK rule. Officially, the Chinese population of Cambodia today constitutes around 1% of the total.

Vietnamese
The southern part of Cambodia, particularly along the Mekong, has always had many inhabitants of Vietnamese descent, as well as the area around Phnom Penh. The Vietnamese live very separate lives to the Cambodians due to centuries of mistrust and animosity between the two groups. They are known by the Khmers as 'youn', a derogatory term meaning 'people from the north' and it is hard to find other Cambodians who have anything positive to say about Vietnamese settlers in the country. One human rights official was quoted as saying "Given a choice, a lot of people in this country would

expel every single Vietnamese". And if the nationalistic fervour of Sam Rainsy ever comes to fruition, this could potentially happen. This dislike of the Vietnamese stems partly from historical fears – Vietnam absorbed large areas of the former Cambodian Empire in the 18th and 19th centuries; partly from Vietnam's role in Cambodia between 1979 and 1989; and partly from the sheer size of Vietnam – some 70 million inhabitants – when set against Cambodia's population of 10 million. As a result anti-Vietnamese sentiment is mainstream politics in the country. Inventing fanciful stories about Vietnamese commandos infiltrating the country, or Vietnamese control of the economy, is never likely to do harm to a budding populist politician. Many Vietnamese (and Cham) live in floating villages due to the foreign ownership laws relating to property.

Cham-Malays

There are about 200,000 Cham-Malays, descended from the Cham of the royal kingdom of Champa based in present-day central Vietnam. They now constitute the single largest ethnic minority in the country. In the 15th century the Vietnamese moving south drove many of the Cham living in the lower Mekong area into Cambodia. They now mainly live along the Mekong, north of Phnom Penh. The Chams were badly persecuted during the Pol Pot years and their population more than halved. They are Muslim and their spiritual centre is Chur-Changvra near Phnom Penh. They adopted their faith and script from Malays who settled in Kampot and interior regions on the invitation of the Muslim Khmer King Chan in 1642, after he had converted to Islam. The Cham are traditionally cattle traders, silk weavers and butchers – Theravada Buddhism forbids the Khmer to slaughter animals. Their batik sarongs are very similar to those found in Malaysia.

Although the Cham are now free to pursue their faith largely free from persecution, they still suffer from the stigma of being viewed, by many Cambodians, as second-class citizens. There is a close affinity between Christians and Muslims in Cambodia – in the face of an overwhelmingly dominant Buddhist faith.

Other groups

There are also a small number of Shans, Thai and Lao, most who live near Battambang, the descendants of miners and jewellers who came to work the ruby mines of Pailin during the French colonial era.

Women in Cambodia

Many academics have heralded the fact that a large proportion of Cambodian women control the finances at home as a measure of equality. And yes, on many fronts Khmer women are equal: it is not uncommon to see female labourers constructing new buildings, nor is it odd to see women heaving around big boulders to build the country's roads. In total, it is believed that Khmer women account for 65% of agricultural labour and 80% of food production.

However, like most undeveloped countries it's women and children that carry the biggest burden of poverty. Oxfam reports that 80% of males are literate yet only 22% of Cambodia women could read a newspaper or write a simple letter in 2003. Many Cambodian families, particularly in rural areas still arrange marriages for their daughters – most of the time trading them off to the highest bidder. The Cambodian League for the Promotion and Defence of Human Rights (LICADHO, www.licadho.org) reported that even the upper echelons of society are perpetuating this practice, where public figures have arranged the marriages of their children.

On almost every social indicator front, Cambodian women rank worse-off than males but perhaps most alarming, is the amount of violence targeted at them. In 2005 there was a general consensus among NGOs and the government that the incidence of rape was increasing. A particularly disturbing report, *Princelings and Paupers by Gender and Development Cambodia* (2003) brought to light the insidious spread of gang-rape across urban areas. It is referred to as *bauk*, which means 'plus'.

Prostitution

In 2003, a survey put the number of prostitutes in the country as a whole at 55,000 prostitutes. Of those 35% are children under the age of 16. Many of the women and girls working in these establishments are from poor farming families: many are also Vietnamese. In 2004 research indicated that 64.45% of prostitutes had been forced into this work; including 52.9% who were duped by the prospect of a good job, and 11.04% who were sold.

Trafficking is a huge problem in Cambodia with the number of trafficked women and children in country estimated to be anywhere between 2000 and 100,000. Inter-country trafficking is also an issue. It is estimated that 88,000 Cambodian bonded workers (not necessarily sex slaves) are in Thailand at any given time. Hundreds of these people are deported every month, half of which are children. Many are then retrafficked back to Thailand and the cycle is repeated.

On paper at least, the prostitution industry in Phnom Penh should now be history: in August 1994 the Mayor of Phnom Penh banned brothels from operating in the city, threatening a fine of one million riel (US$250) to any brothel owners discovered ignoring the ban. However this edict did little to stop prostitution, and many commentators saw it as just a wheeze so that the police could extort money from brothel owners, sex workers, and their clients. There were numerous reports of plainclothes policemen entering brothels, having sex, and then whipping out their police ID cards before demanding a payment. Other stories tell of prostitutes being arrested by the police for illegally plying their trade, and then being 'sold' to another brothel. According to LICADHO's *Project Against Torture* report, "The flesh trade is lucrative business and, like most lucrative businesses in Cambodia, is controlled by people with weapons and influence. Police, military police, army and other state personnel are deeply enmeshed in the trade, actively running or protecting trafficking rings and brothels."

Child prostitution is also rife and more than one half of commercial prostitutes are thought to be underage. In one village, young girls who have been sold into prostitution for as little as US$300 by their destitute parents are paraded for clients from the Cambodian military and government, and for European and American paedophiles. In 2002 it was reported that underage virgins were being sold to foreign visitors for US$1000 – and after their ordeal, tattooed with a butterfly to indicate their loss of virginity before being sent to brothels. An article in the *Phnom Penh Post* in mid-1997 claimed that tourist buses from the state-owned Phnom Penh Tourism had been seen in villages which specialize in child prostitution.

Child sex tourism is flourishing in Cambodia – a result, in part, of the number of abandoned children in the country. This, in turn, can be linked back to the corrosive effects that the Khmer Rouge period had on family structures. Until late 2000 the government did little to stamp out child sex tourism. But even now it is firmly on the government agenda, the problem is proving to be an intractable one. Not only is there a large pool of vulnerable children who can be tempted into the industry, but corruption in the police force means that many paedophiles can buy their way out of trouble. However, the authorities do now have the power to deport or deny entry to anyone suspected of being a paedophile.

Adoption of children

The problems that have led to a flourishing child prostitution industry also fuelled an adoption racket. Until 2000 when the laws were tightened, Cambodia was possibly the easiest place to adopt a child. The infamous baby brokering by Lauryn Galindo, between 1997-2001, is believed to have been responsible for the 'sale' of over 700 Cambodian children. (Galindo was an Hawaiian who took children from families and then represented them as orphans needing to be adopted with people paying big fees for the adoption – up to US$3500 per child.) The *Cambodia Daily* suggested that government officials, the major profiteers of the scheme, netted themselves up to US$2.45 million from her business alone.

Many children put up for adoption, like many of those sold into prostitution, come from families so mired in poverty that they see no option but to sell their babies. Foreigners pay US$5000-15,000 to officials to grease the process of adoption while poor villagers, it has been said, sell their babies to orphanages for as little as US$100. A fallacy often reported, which spurs on the business, is that Cambodia has over half a million orphans. These figures are largely sensationalized; the *Cambodia Daily* said in April 2005 that of 670,000 children, 85% have at least one parent. In 2005, it was estimated that there were 12,000 orphans in institutionalized care.

HIV and AIDS

Like some other countries of Southeast Asia, Cambodia is thought to be in the midst of an AIDS epidemic. Although the first AIDS case was only diagnosed in 1993 and even by September 1996 there were just 240 reported cases, since then the scale of HIV infection has increased very rapidly.

Most AIDS researchers believe that Cambodia is likely to follow the path that Thailand has already forged – towards an AIDS epidemic of increasingly serious proportions. (The Cambodia-Thailand border is porous and the employment of Cambodian women in Thai brothels is helping Thailand 'export' its problem to Cambodia.) Past claims that two million Cambodians could die of AIDS seem highly excessive on current evidence and projections but sexual culture in Cambodia provides a fertile environment for rapid spread. A study undertaken by the Cambodian AIDS Social Research Project revealed that 80% of young men have had sex with a prostitute and 10% with other men. Another survey, undertaken in 2000, revealed that almost half of men who had had anal sex with other men in the month prior to the survey had also had sex with women during the same period. In other words, and this also extends to the intravenous drug-using population, unlike in the West, in Cambodia many of those men who engage in homosexual anal sex also have sex with women and a significant proportion also take drugs intravenously. They are far from being discrete populations.

The UN study noted above tried to put a price tag on Cambodia's AIDS problem: between US$1.97bn and US$2.82bn, or between four and six times the country's total annual aid budget in 1996. The challenge facing Cambodia is the need to inform people of the dangers of unprotected sex and multiple partners particularly between husbands and wives when education levels and facilities are poor and resources comparatively paltry. Thailand offered an insight into the AIDS problem, where an innovative and broad-based AIDS education programme increased the number of prostitutes using condoms from virtually zero a few years back to more than 90% by 1998. This model for dealing with the epidemic was adopted by Cambodia and was largely facilitated by the mega "Number One" condom campaign, run by Population Services International. The campaign was so successful that "number one" has become a household phrase and the majority of sex workers are now practicing safe sex. The hope is that just as Cambodia has tracked Thailand's trajectory of increase in the use of condoms, it will also mirror that country's continued stabilization.

Culture

Language and literature

The Khmer language
The Khmer language belongs to the Mon-Khmer family, enriched by the Indian Pali and Sanskrit languages and peppered with Thai and French influences. The use of Sanskrit in royal texts became more widespread after the introduction of Mahayana Buddhism in the 12th century (although there are inscriptions dating from the sixth century) and the Pali language spread into Cambodia via Siam with Theravada Buddhism. Khmer is related to languages spoken by hill tribe people of Laos, Vietnam and even Malaysia – but is very different to Thai or Lao. Khmer has no tones, no tenses, and words are attached to the masculine or feminine genders. But Khmer does have 23 vowel-sounds and 33 consonants; it is also a very specific language – for instance, there are 100 different words for types of rice. The Khmer language is written from left to right often with no separation between words. ▶▶ *For a list of Khmer words and phrases, see page 280.*

French was widely spoken by the intelligentsia before 1975 and is still spoken by a few elderly Cambodians. But these days most people seem to want to learn English, and there are informal pavement English schools setting up on Phnom Penh's streets. This has led to some Franco-Anglophone friction. Understandably, the French government – one of Cambodia's largest aid donors – would like to see the French language sustained, perhaps even developed. In 1995 this led to the strange spectacle of language riots on the campus of Phnom Penh's Cambodian University of Technology as students burnt French text books in protest at being forced to learn a language which, they said, 'got them nowhere'.

Cambodian literature
Religious literature comprises works of religious instruction, derived from the Sanskrit and Pali texts of the Theravada Buddhist canon, the *Tripitaka*. The *Jataka* tales are well known in Cambodia and several modern adaptations have been made from these texts. The *Jatakas* recount the former lives of the historic Buddha and were probably first introduced to Cambodia from Laos. Most of the stories tell of how the Buddha – then a prince – managed to overcome some defect by the use of magic or the assistance of some god, enabling him to be born higher up the scale of birth and re-birth on his long road to nirvana.

The two Khmer epics are the poem of Angkor Wat and the *Reamker* (or Ramakerti), derived from the Indian Ramayana. Traditionally the literature was recorded by incising palm leaf manuscripts with a sharp stylus, the incisions then being blackened to make them easily visible. From around the 17th century, **chap** poetry, an import from Thailand, became popular. The poetry took root in monasteries as a means by which

The Cambodian Ramayana: the *Reamker*

The *Reamker* – 'The Story of Rama' – is an adaptation of the Indian Hindu classic, the *Ramayana*, which was written by the poet Valmiki about 2000 years ago. This 48,000 line epic odyssey – often likened to the works of Homer – was introduced into mainland Southeast Asia in the early centuries of the first millennium. The heroes were simply transposed into a mythical, ancient, Southeast Asian landscape.

In Cambodia, the *Reamker* quickly became highly influential. The scenes carved in stone at Angkor, many of the murals painted on monastery walls, and the tales enacted in shadow theatre (*nang sbaek*) all derive inspiration from the *Reamker*. The Cambodian *Ramayana* dates back to the Angkor period, although the earliest existing written work only dates back to 1620.

In the first part of the story, Rama – who in the Cambodian version is depicted as the Buddha – renounces his throne following a long and convoluted court intrigue, and flees into exile. With his wife Sita and trusted companion Hanuman (the monkey god), they undertake a long and arduous journey. In the second part, his wife Sita is abducted by the evil king Ravana, forcing Rama to wage battle against the demons of Langka Island (Sri Lanka). He defeats the demons with the help of Hanuman and his monkey army, and recovers his wife. In the third and final part of the story – and here it diverges sharply from the Indian original – Sita and Rama are reunited and reconciled with the help of the gods (in the Indian version there is no such reconciliation). Another difference from the Indian version is the significant role played by Hanuman – here an amorous adventurer who dominates much of the third part of the epic.

There are also numerous sub-plots which are original to the *Reamker*, many building upon events in Cambodian history and local myth and folklore. In tone and issues of morality, the Cambodian version is less puritanical than the Indian original. There are also, of course, differences in dress, ecology, location and custom.

Hanuman

Adapted from Hallet, Holt (1890) *A Thousand miles on an elephant in the Shan States*, William Blackwood: Edinburgh

monks could more easily teach the laity the lessons of the Buddhist texts. However, over time, they also took on a secular guise and became a means by which more everyday homilies were communicated.

Most of the early literature has been destroyed but there are surviving Sanskrit inscriptions on stone monuments dating from the sixth century and some early palm leaf manuscripts. Many of these are contained in the Bibliothèque Nationale in Paris – the Khmer Rouge managed to destroy most of those housed in monasteries and museums in Cambodia itself.

Historical literature consists largely of inscriptions from Angkor Wat as well as the Cambodian royal chronicles. Fictional literature is diverse in Cambodia and includes the lpaen folk stories written in prose. French literature has had a profound influence on modern Cambodian literature. The first modern Cambodian novel was *Sophat* published in 1938. It, and the novels and short stories that followed it, represented a break with the past. The authors wrote of ordinary people, used natural conversation, and wrote in prose. Most of the recent Cambodian novels have been written by Cambodians living abroad – most writers and journalists were either killed by the Khmer Rouge or fled the country.

Arts and architecture

Indian origins

The art of modern Cambodia is almost completely overshadowed by its past. The influence of the Khmers at the height of the empire spread as far as the Malay peninsula in the south, to the Burmese border in the west and the Vietnamese frontier in the north and east. But ancient Khmer culture was itself inherited. Indian influence was particularly strong in the Mekong basin area and the Khmers accepted Indian ideas about astrology, religion and royalty – including the cult of the god-king (*devaraja*). Other elements of Cambodian culture which are recognizably Indian in origin include classical literature and dance, as well as religious architecture. Hindu deities inspired the iconography in much of Cambodian art and Sanskrit gave the Khmers access to a whole new world of ideas. Cambodian influence is very strong in Thai culture as Siam's capture of a large part of the Khmer Empire in the 15th century resulted in many of Cambodia's best scholars, artists and craftsmen being transported to Siam (Thailand).

Artistic revival

The richness of their culture remains a great source of pride for the Khmer people and in the past it has helped forge a sense of national identity. There has been an artistic revival since 1979 and the government has devoted resources to the restoration of monuments and pagodas. (Many local wats have been repaired by local subscription; it is estimated that one-fifth of rural disposable income is given to the upkeep of wats.) The resurgence of Buddhism has been paralleled in recent years by a revival of traditional Khmer culture, which was actively undermined during the Pol Pot years. Today Phnom Penh's two Fine Arts Schools are flourishing again; one teaches music and dance, the other specializes in architecture and archaeology. There is a surprisingly good collection of artefacts in the National Museum of Arts even though huge quantities of treasure and antiques have been stolen and much of the remainder destroyed by the Khmer Rouge.

Angkor period

The Angkor period (ninth-13th centuries) encapsulated the greatest and best of Cambodia's art and architecture. Much of it shows strong Indian influence. The so-called 'Indianization' of Cambodia was more a product of trade than Hindu proselytism; there was no attempt made at formal conquest, and no great emigration of Indians to the region. In order to meet the Romans' demand for exotic oriental merchandise and commodities, Indian traders ventured into the South China Sea, well before the first century AD when it was discovered that monsoon winds could carry them to the Malay Peninsula and on to Indochina and Cambodia. Because of their reliance on seasonal winds, Indian navigators were obliged to while away many months in countries with which they traded and the influence of their sophisticated culture spread.

But although Khmer art and architecture was rooted in Indian prototypes, the expression and content was distinctively Cambodian. Most of the art from the Angkor period is Hindu although Mahayana Buddhism took hold in the late 12th century. Some Buddhist figures have been dated to as early as the sixth century – the standing Buddhas were carved in the same style as the Hindu deities, minus the sensuous voluptuousness.

The ancient kingdoms of Funan (the Chinese name for the mercantile state encompassing the area southwest of the Mekong Delta, in what is now southern Vietnam and southern Cambodia. First century AD 613) and Chenla (a mountain kingdom centred on northern Cambodia and southern Laos, AD550-eighth century) were the first to be artistically and culturally influenced by India. In *The Art of Southeast Asia* Philip Rawson wrote that the art styles of Funan and Chenla were "the greatest phase of pre-Angkor Khmer art, and... we can treat the evolution under these two kingdoms together as a stylistic unity. It was the foundation of classic Khmer art, just as archaic Greek sculpture was the foundation of later classical Greek art".

The Angkor region was strategically important to the Funan Empire as it helped control the trade routes around the region – specifically the Malay Peninsula and the Mekong Delta. The only traces of the kingdom of Funan – whose influence is thought to have spread as far afield as southern Burma and Indonesia – are limited to four Sanskrit inscriptions on stelae and a few sculptures. The earliest surviving Funanese statues were found at Angkor Borei and have been dated to the sixth century. Most represent the Hindu god, Vishnu (patron of King Rudravarman), and their faces are distinctly Angkorian. Scattered remains of these pre-Angkorian periods are all over southern Cambodia – especially between the Mekong and the Tonlé Sap. Most of the earliest buildings would have been made of wood rotted away – there being a paucity of stone in the delta region.

The kingdom of Chenla, based at Sambor and later at Sambor Prei Kuk (see page 124), expanded at the expense of Funan, which gradually became a vassal state. In the sixth century evidence of a new Chenla Kingdom started to appear in local inscriptions. Chenla inherited Funan's Indianized art and architectural traditions. Some buildings were built of brick and stone and typical architectural relics are brick towers with a square (or sometimes octagonal) plan: a shrine set atop a pedestal comprising of mounting tiers of decreasing size – a style which may have been structurally patterned on early Pallava temples in southeast India. The sculptural work was strongly rooted in Indian ideas but carved in a unique style – many of the statues from this era are in the museum at Phnom Penh (see page 47). Rawson wrote: "Among the few great stone icons which have survived are some of the world's outstanding masterpieces, while the smaller bronzes reflect the same sophisticated and profound style."

In the late eighth century the Chenla Kingdom collapsed and contact with India came to an end. Chenla is thought to have been eclipsed by the increasingly important Sumatran-based Srivijayan Empire. Jayavarman II, who had lived most of his life in the Sailendra court in Java but who was of royal lineage, returned to Cambodia in about AD 790. Jayavarman II's reign marked the transition period between pre-Angkorian and Angkorian styles – by the ninth century the larger images were recognizably Khmer in style. From Jayavarman II onwards, the kings of Cambodia were regarded as god-kings – or *devaraja* (see page 219).

Jayavarman II established a royal Siva-lingam (phallic) cult which was to prove the inspiration for successive generations of Khmer kings. "He summoned a Brahmin learned in the appropriate texts, and erected a lingam... with all the correct Indian ritual," Rawson said. "This lingam, in which the king's own soul was held to reside, became the source and centre of power for the Khmer Dynasty. At the same time – and by that act – he severed all ties of dependence upon Indonesia." To house the sacred lingam each king in turn built a new temple, some of the mightiest and finest of the monuments of the Khmer civilization.

Angkor temples

The temples at Angkor were modelled on those of the kingdom of Chenla, which in turn were modelled on Indian temples. They represent Mount Meru – the home of the gods of Indian cosmology. The central towers symbolize the peaks of Mount Meru, surrounded by a wall which represents the earth. The moats and basins represent the oceans. The *devaraja* was enshrined in the centre of the religious complex, which acted as the spiritual axis of the kingdom. The people believed their apotheosized king communicated directly with the gods.

The central tower sanctuaries housed the images of the Hindu gods to whom the temples were dedicated. Dead members of the royal and priestly families were accorded a status on a par with these gods. Libraries to store the sacred scriptures were also built within the ceremonial centre. The temples were mainly built to shelter the images of the gods. Unlike Christian churches, Muslim mosques and some Buddhist pagodas, they were not intended to accommodate worshippers. Only priests, the servants of the god, were allowed into the interiors. The 'congregation' would mill around outside in open courtyards or wooden pavilions. The first temples were of a very simple design but with time they became more grandiose and doors and galleries were added. Most of Angkor's buildings are made from a soft sandstone which is easy to work. It was transported to the site from Phnom Kulen, about 30 km to the northeast. Laterite was used for foundations, core material and enclosure walls as it was widely available and could be easily cut into blocks. The Khmer sandstone architecture has echoes of earlier wooden structures: gallery roofs are sculpted with false tiles, while balustred windows imitate wooden ones. A common feature of Khmer temples was false doors and windows on the sides and backs of sanctuaries and other buildings. In most cases there was no need for well-lit rooms and corridors as hardly anyone ever went into them. That said, the galleries round the central towers in later temples, such as Angkor Wat, indicate that worshippers did use the temples for ceremonial circumambulation when they would contemplate the inspiring bas-reliefs from the *Ramayana* and *Mahabharata*.

In Europe and the Middle East the arch and vault were used in contemporary buildings but at Angkor architects used the false vault – also known as corbelling. It is strange that, despite the architectural innovation of the Khmer, the principle of the arch, used to such great effect in Christian and Muslim architecture, should have eluded them. Corbelling is a fairly primitive vaulting system so the interiors of sanctuaries could never be very large. The stones were often laid without staggering the vertical joints and mortar was not used. The builders relied on the weight of the structure, gravity and a good fit between the stones to hold their buildings together. This is why so many of the temples have collapsed.

Despite the court's conversion to Mahayana Buddhism in the 12th century (under Jayavarman VII) the architectural ground-plans of temples did not alter much – even though they were based on Hindu cosmology. The idea of the god-king was simply grafted onto the new state religion and statues of the Buddha rather than the gods of the Hindu pantheon were used to represent the god-king (see Bayon, page 96). One particular image of the Buddha predominated at Angkor in which he wears an Angkor-style crown, with a conical top which is encrusted with jewellery.

There are some scholars who maintain that Angkor has, perhaps, been over praised. Anthony Barnett in the *New Left Review* in 1990, for example, wrote: "...to measure [Angkor's] greatness by the fact that it is nearly a mile square is to deny it a proper admiration through hyperbole. Thus the Church of Saint Sophia, to take one example, was for nearly a millennium the largest domed space in the world until St Peter's was constructed. Saint Sophia still stands in Istanbul. It was built 600 years before Angkor Wat, while Khmer architects never managed to discover the principles of the arch." (1990: 103)

Sculpture

The sculpture of the early temples at Angkor is rather stiff and plain, but forms the basis for the ornate bas-reliefs of the later Angkor Wat. Lintel-carving became a highly developed art form at an early stage in the evolution of Khmer architecture. (The lintel is a horizontal supporting stone at the top of a window or door opening.) The use of columns around doorways was another distinctive feature – they too had their antecedents in the earlier Chenla period. Frontons – the masonry covering originally used to conceal the corbelled end gables – were elaborate at Angkor. They were intricately carved and conveyed stories from the *Ramayana* and other great Hindu epics. The carved fronton is still used in temples throughout modern Thailand, Laos and Cambodia. Sanctuary doorways, through which priests would pass to enter the sacred heart of the temple, were an important site for icons. Ornately carved sandstone blocks were placed in front of and above the true lintel.

Angkor's most impressive carvings are its bas-reliefs which, like the fronton, were devoted to allegorical depictions and mostly illustrate stories from the Hindu classics, the *Mahabharata* and *Ramayana*. The latter is best exemplified at the Baphuon (11th century) – see page 104. Details of the everyday lives of the Angkor civilization can be pieced together thanks to these bas-reliefs. Those on the Bayon illustrate the weaponry and armour used in battle, market scenes, fishing and cockfighting – probably the Khmers' favourite excuse for gambling. In contrast to the highly sculpted outer walls of the temples, the interiors were typically bare; this has led to speculation that they may originally have been decorated with murals.

Laterite, which is a coarse soft stone, was excavated to form many of the moats and barays at Angkor. Early structures such as those at Preah Ko in the Roluos group were built in brick. The brickwork was often laid with dry joints and the only mortar used was a type of vegetable-based adhesive. Bricks were sometimes carved in situ and occasionally plastered. In the early temples sandstone was only used for architectural embellishments. But nearly all of the later temples were built entirely of sandstone. Most of the sandstone is thought to have been quarried from the northern hills around Kulen and brought by barge to Angkor.

The post-Angkor period was characterized by wooden buildings and fastidiously carved and decorated sculptures, but the humid climate has allowed little to survive. The contemporary art of 21st-century Cambodia is still redolent of the grandeur of the Angkor era and today, Khmer craftsmen retain their inherent skills and are renowned for their refined carvings. Art historians believe that the richness of Cambodia's heritage, and its incorporation into the modern artistic psyche, has enabled Khmer artists to produce work which is reckoned to be aesthetically superior to contemporary carving and sculpture in Thailand.

Textiles

Cambodia is not well known for the quality and range of its textiles, especially when compared with the industry in neighbouring Thailand and Laos. In Chou Ta-kuan's account of life at Angkor written in 1296-1297, he claimed that "Not only do the Khmer women lack skill with needle and thread for mending and sewing, they only know how to weave fabrics of cotton, not of silk". However by the time the French arrived in the second half of the 19th century, weaving in silk and cotton was well-established. The Cambodian royal court had a large retinue of weavers producing sumptuous, richly patterned and coloured silk cloth. Even as recently as the 1940s, weaving was still a craft practised in just about every village, and every woman worth her salt was expected to be able to weave. Then, in the 1950s, cheap imported silk and cotton cloth began to undermine the local product and people began to turn to other occupations. One elderly silk weaver, Liv Sa Em, explained in 1995, "you could earn more selling cakes in two days than you could earn weaving in five months". But it was the Khmer Rouge period which finally sealed the fate of Cambodia's textile industry. Apart from producing the familiar checked cloth used as a head scarf, or *kramar*, weaving virtually died out between 1975 and 1979. Many of the most skilled weavers, especially those associated with the Cambodian court, were either murdered or fled the country.

Now the government and many NGOs see a bright future for silk weaving and resources are being directed towards its revitalization. Many women find weaving attractive: it can be built around the demands of housework and childcare; it can be done at home; and it can provide an important supplementary source of income. However, because the domestic industry was so withered after years of neglect, NGOs are finding it necessary to bring in foreign weaving experts from Thailand, Laos, Vietnam and China to teach people anew how to raise silkworms and train women in more advanced weaving techniques.

The Cambodian national dress is the *samphot*, a long rectangle of cloth (about twice as long as a sarong) which is wrapped around the body and then taken up between the legs to be tucked in at the waist. Traditionally women wore this with a simple breast cloth and men with a jacket. Samphot are woven in rich, warm colours. Sometimes the warp and weft are different colours giving the finished cloth a shimmering appearance. Weft ikat is used to produce the well-known *samphot hol* and it is thought that this process influenced Thai designs after Siam conquered Angkor in the mid-15th century, taking many of the most skilled weavers back to the capital, Ayutthaya, as booty.

Dance, drama and music

There is a strong tradition of **dance** in Cambodia which has its origins in the sacred dances of the *apsaras*, the mythological seductresses of ancient Cambodia. Classical dance reached its height during the Angkor period; it was based on interpretations of the Indian epics, particularly the Ramayana. Dance also became a religious tradition, designed to bring the king and his people divine blessing. Dancers, nearly all of whom were well born, were central to the royal court and were protected as a separate part of the king's harem; only the god-king could touch them. The dancers became legendary even outside Cambodia: when Thailand invaded, the Khmer classical ballet dancers were part of their war booty and were taken to the Thai court. The decline of Angkor brought the decline of classical dance, although it continued to survive as an art form through the patronage of the royal Thai court. When the French colonialists revived Khmer ballet in the 20th century they initially imported dancers from Thailand.

The dances are very symbolic. Court dances are subject to a precise order, a strict form and a prescribed language of movements and gestures. Most of the dancers are women and the male and female roles are distinguished by costume. All the dancers are barefoot as the unimpeded movement of the feet is very important. The national dance is called the *lamthon* which is characterized by slow graceful movements of the hands and arms. The most highly trained lamthon dancers wear elaborate, tight-fitting costumes of silk and velvet that have to be sewn onto them before each performance.

Due to their close association with the royal family (they were based at the royal palace right up to 1970 and danced regularly for Prince Sihanouk), the once-famous and flourishing National Dance Group was a prime target for the Khmer Rouge regime of the mid-1970s. Many dancers were killed; others fled into exile. Em Tiay was one of the few to survive the killing fields. She began dancing at the age of six in 1937 and the only reason she survived the Pol Pot years was because the headman of the village where she lived was so captivated by her dancing that he protected her. Her two sisters were not so lucky. With the fall of the Khmer Rouge she returned to dancing and became a full-time classical dance teacher at the Bassac Theatre in Phnom Penh. In 1981 the School of Fine Arts was reopened to train new recruits, 80% of whom were orphans. Today the National Dance Group, which made its first tour to the West in 1990, performs for some tour groups.

The government, with the help of overseas cultural groups, has been trying to resurrect Cambodia's classical dance tradition. By 1997 about 50% of the classical Khmer dance repertoire had been recovered. Support has come in from sources as diverse as the Japanese city of Fukuoka and UNESCO. Some 80 elderly Khmer who managed to survive the Khmer Rouge holocaust are being interviewed and their knowledge committed to paper while 4000 dance gestures and positions have been recorded on video. Nonetheless the effort is proving difficult.

Folk dancing has managed to survive the 1970s intact, although as a form of regular village entertainment, it has been undermined by the arrival of TV and video. Unlike the court dances, folk dances are less structured, with dancers responding to the rhythm of drums. The dancers act out tales from Cambodian folk stories; folk dancing can often be seen at local festivals.

Folk plays and **shadow plays** (*nang sbaek*) are also a popular form of entertainment in the countryside. The latter are based on stories from the Ramayana, embroidered with local legends. The characters are cut out of leather and often painted. Wandering shadow puppeteers perform at local festivals.

Because of the importance of dance to the ancient royal Khmer court, **music** – which always accompanied dance routines – was also central to Cambodian court and religious life. Singers and musicians were often attached to specific temples. Cambodian music has evolved from Indian and Indonesian influences and, more recently, Thai. The traditional orchestra consists of three xylophones, *khom thom* (a horseshoe-shaped arrangement with 16 flat gongs), violins, wind instruments including flutes, flageolets and a Khmer version of bagpipes, as well as drums of different shapes and sizes. There are three types of drum: the hand drum, the *cha ayam* drum and the *yike* drum. The drummer has the most important role in folk music as he sets the rhythm. In 1938 a musical scholar estimated that only 3000 melodies were ever employed in Khmer music. There is no system of written notation so the tunes are transmitted orally from generation to generation. There are five tones (compared to seven in Western music) and no real harmony – the melodies are always simple.

Religion

The god-kings of Angkor

Until the 14th century Buddhism and Hinduism existed side-by-side in Kambuja. In the pre-Angkor era, the Hindu gods Siva and Vishnu were worshipped as a single deity, Harihara. The statue of Harihara from Phnom Da (eighth century) is divided in half: the 'stern' right half is Siva (with wild curly hair) and the 'sublime' left half, Vishnu (who wears a mitre). The first city at Angkor, built by Jayavarman II in the early ninth century, was called Hariharalaya after this god. Early Angkor kings promoted various Hindu sects, mainly dedicated to Siva and Vishnu. During the Angkor period, Siva was the most favoured deity but by the 12th century Vishnu replaced him. Jayavarman VII introduced Mahayana Buddhism as the official court religion at the end of the 12th century. The constant chopping, changing and refining of state religion helped sustain the power of the absolute monarch – each change ushered in a new style of rule and historians believe refinements and changes of religion were deliberately imported to consolidate the power of the kings.

One reason the Khmer Empire was so powerful was its basis on the Hindu concept of the god-king or devaraja. Jayavarman II (AD 802-850) crowned himself as a reincarnation of Siva and erected a Siva lingam (a phallic monument to the god) at Phnom Kulen, the source of power for the Khmer Dynasty. Siva-worship was not originally introduced by Jayavarman II, however – it had been previously practised in the old kingdom of Funan. The investiture of power was always performed by a Brahmin priest who also bestowed divinity on the king as a gift from Siva. This ceremony became an essential rite of kingship which was observed continuously – right into the 20th century. The king's spirit was said to reside in the lingam, which was enshrined in the centre of a monumental religious complex, representing the spiritual axis of the kingdom. Here, the people believed, their divinely ordained king communicated with the gods. Succeeding monarchs followed Jayavarman II's example and continued to install themselves as god-kings, evoking the loyalty of their subjects.

Very few of the statues of Vishnu and Siva and other gods left by the Khmer Empire were traditional representations of the deities. The great majority of the images were portraits of kings and princes and high dignitaries, each represented as the god into whom they would be absorbed at the end of their earthly existence. That the names given to the statues were usually a composite of the names of the man and the god, indicates that men were worshipped as gods.

The installation of the devaraja cult by Jayavarman II took place on the summit of Phnom Kulen. Under subsequent kings, it was transferred, in turn, to Bakong, Phnom Bakheng, Koh Ker and Phimeanakas. At the end of the 11th century, the Baphuon was constructed to house the golden lingam. The tradition of the god-king cult was so deeply rooted in the court that even Theravada Buddhism introduced in the 14th century bowed to its influence. Following the adoption of Mahayana Buddhism in the second half of the 12th century, the god-king left his lingam to enter the statue of the Buddha. Jayavarman VII built the Bayon to shelter the statue of the Buddha-king in the centre of the city of Angkor.

Temple-mountains were built as microcosms of the universe, with Mount Meru, the home of the gods, at the centre, surrounded by oceans (followed most perfectly at Angkor Wat, see page 91). This concept was not invented by the Khmers but was part of an inherited tradition from India. At the summit of the cosmic mountain, at the centre of the city, the king, embodied by his own sacred image, entered into contact with the world of gods. Each temple was the personal temple of an individual king, erected by him during his life. When, after his death, his ashes or remains were deposited there (to animate the statue and give the cult a living image), the temple became his mausoleum. His successor always built another sanctuary to house the image of the god-king. During the Angkor period the Khmers did not seem to question this system. It ordered their lives, regulating everything from agriculture to birth and death rites. But the temples were not the products of a popular faith, like Christian cathedrals – they were strictly the domain of royalty and high priests and were reserved for the worship of kings and members of the entourage deified in the form of one of the Hindu or Buddhist gods.

Theravada Buddhism

Despite the powerful *devaraja* cult, most Khmers also practised an amalgam of ancestor worship and animism. As Theravada Buddhism swept through Southeast Asia (well after the adoption of Mahayana Buddhism), propagated by missionary monks, its message of simplicity, austerity and humility began to undermine the cult of the god-king. As a popular religion, it had great attractions for a population which for so many centuries had been denied access to the élitist and extravagant *devaraja* cult. By the 15th century Theravada Buddhism was the dominant religion in Cambodia.

Buddhism shares the belief, in common with Hinduism, in rebirth. A person goes through countless lives and the experience of one life is conditioned by the acts in a previous one. This is the Law of Karma (act or deed, from Pali *kamma*), the law of cause and effect. For most people, nirvana is a distant goal, and they merely aim to accumulate merit by living good lives and performing good deeds such as giving alms to monks. In this way the layman embarks on the Path to Heaven. It is also common for a layman to become ordained, at some point in his life (usually as a young man), for a three-month period during the Buddhist Rains Retreat.

Monks should endeavour to lead stringently ascetic lives. They must refrain from murder, theft, sexual intercourse, untruths, eating after noon, alcohol, entertainment, ornament, comfortable beds and wealth. They are allowed to own only a begging bowl, three pieces of clothing, a razor, needle, belt and water filter. They can only eat food that they have received through begging. Anyone who is male, over 20, and not a criminal can become a monk.

The 'Way of the Elders' is believed to be closest to Buddhism as it originally developed in India. It is often referred to by the term 'Hinayana' (Lesser Vehicle), a disparaging name foisted onto Theravadans by Mahayanists. This form of Buddhism is the dominant contemporary religion in the mainland Southeast Asian countries of Thailand, Cambodia, Laos and Burma.

In Theravadan Buddhism, the historic Buddha, Sakyamuni, is revered above all else and most images of the Buddha are of Sakyamuni. Importantly, and unlike Mahayana Buddhism, the Buddha image is only meant to serve as a meditation aid. In theory, it does not embody supernatural powers, and it is not supposed to be worshipped. But the popular need for objects of veneration has meant that most images are worshipped. Pilgrims bring flowers and incense, and prostrate themselves in front of the image. This is a Mahayanist influence which has been embraced by Theravadans.

In Siddhartha's footsteps: a short history of Buddhism

Buddhism was founded by Siddhartha Gautama, a prince of the Sakya tribe of Nepal, who probably lived between 563 and 483 BC. He achieved enlightenment and the word 'buddha' means 'fully enlightened one', or 'one who has woken up'.

Siddhartha Gautama is known by a number of titles. In the West, he is usually referred to as 'The Buddha', ie the historic Buddha; more common in Southeast Asia is the title 'Sakyamuni', or Sage of the Sakyas (referring to his tribal origins).

Over the centuries, the Buddha's life has become part legend, and the *Jataka* tales which recount his various lives are colourful and convoluted. But, central to any Buddhist's belief is that he was born under a sal tree, he achieved enlightenment under a bodhi tree in the Bodh Gaya Gardens, he preached the First Sermon at Sarnath, and he died at Kusinagara (all in India or Nepal).

The Budda was born at Lumbini (in present-day Nepal), as Queen Maya was on her way to her parents' home. She had had a very auspicious dream before the child's birth of being impregnated by an elephant, whereupon a sage prophesied that Siddhartha would become either a great king or a great spiritual leader.

His father, being keen that the first option of the prophecy be fulfilled, brought him up in all the princely skills – at which Siddhartha excelled – and ensured he only saw beautiful things, not the harsher elements of life.

Despite his father's efforts Siddhartha saw four things while travelling between palaces – a helpless old man, a very sick man, a corpse being carried by lamenting relatives, and an ascetic, calm and serene as he begged for food. The young prince renounced his princely origins and left home to study under a series of spiritual teachers. He finally discovered the path to enlightenment at the Bodh Gaya Gardens in India. He then proclaimed his thoughts to a small group of disciples at Sarnath, near Benares (Varanasi), and continued to preach and attract followers until he died at the age of 81 at Kusinagara.

Buddhism in Cambodia

The Cambodian Buddhist clergy divide into two groups: the Mahanikay and Thommayuth (or Dhammayuttikanikay) orders. The latter was not introduced from Thailand until 1864, and was a reformist order with strong royal patronage. Theravada Buddhism remained the dominant and unchallenged faith until 1975.

It was a demonstration by Buddhist monks in Phnom Penh which first kindled Cambodian nationalism in the wake of World War II (see page 226). According to historians, one of the reasons for this was the intensifying of the relationship between the king and the people, due to the founding of the Buddhist Institute in Phnom Penh in 1930. The Institute was under the joint patronage of the kings of Laos and Cambodia as well as the French. It began printing and disseminating Buddhist texts – in Pali and Khmer. Historian David P Chandler wrote: "As the Institute's reputation grew, enhanced by frequent conferences, it became a rallying point for an emerging intelligentsia." The institute's librarian founded a Khmer-language newspaper (*Nagaravatta* – or 'Angkor Wat') in 1936, which played a critical role in articulating and spreading the nationalist message.

Before 1975 and the arrival of the Khmer Rouge, there were 3000 monasteries and 64,000 monks (*bonzes*) – many of these were young men who had become ordained to

In the First Sermon at the deer park in Sarnath, the Buddha preached the Four Truths, which are still considered the root of Buddhist belief and practical experience: suffering exists; there is a cause of suffering; suffering can be ended; and to end suffering it is necessary to follow the 'Noble Eightfold Path' – namely, right speech, livelihood, action, effort, mindfulness, concentration, opinion and intention.

Soon after the Buddha began preaching, a monastic order – the Sangha – was established. As the monkhood evolved in India, it also began to fragment into different sects. An important change was the belief that the Buddha was transcendent: he had never been born, nor had he died; he had always existed and his life on earth had been mere illusion. The emergence of these new concepts helped to turn what up until then was an ethical code of conduct, into a religion. It eventually led to the appearance of a new Buddhist movement, Mahayana Buddhism which split from the more traditional Theravada 'sect'.

Despite the division of Buddhism into two sects, the central tenets of the religion are common to both. Specifically, the principles pertaining to the Four Noble Truths, the Noble Eightfold Path, the Dependent Origination, the Law of Karma, and nirvana. In addition, the principles of non-violence and tolerance are also embraced by both sects. In essence, the differences between the two are of emphasis and interpretation. Theravada Buddhism is strictly based on the original Pali Canon, while the Mahayana tradition stems from later Sanskrit texts. Mahayana Buddhism also allows a broader and more varied interpretation of the doctrine. Other important differences are that while the Thervada tradition is more 'intellectual' and self-obsessed, with an emphasis upon the attaining of wisdom and insight for oneself, Mahayana Buddhism stresses devotion and compassion towards others.

escape conscription – in Cambodia and rural life was centred around the wat (Buddhist monastery). Under Pol Pot, all monks were 'defrocked' and, according to some sources, as many as 62,000 were executed or died in the ricefields. Monasteries were torn down or converted to other uses, Pali – the language of Theravada Buddhism – was banned, and former monks were forced to marry. Ironically, Saloth Sar (Pol Pot) himself spent some time as a novice when he was a child. Buddhism was revived in 1979 with the ordination of monks by a visiting delegation of Buddhists from Vietnam; at the same time, many of the wats – which were defiled by the Khmer Rouge – were restored and reconsecrated. The two orders of Theravada Buddhism – the Thommayuth (aristocratic) and Mahanikay (common) – previously practised in Cambodia have now merged. The Hun Sen government softened the position on Buddhism to the degree that it was reintroduced as the national religion in 1989 and young men were allowed to be ordained (previously restricted to men over 45 that were no longer able to serve in the army).

Today 90% of Cambodian citizens are Buddhist. In 2004, the country had almost 59,500 monks spread across the country's 3980 wats. Cambodian Buddhism is an easy-going faith and tolerates ancestor and territorial spirit worship, which is widely practised. The grounds usually consist of a *vihara* (Buddhist temple), Sala Thoama *saphea* (the hall where Dharma is taught) and *kods* (the quarters where the monks live). Traditionally, the

Mudras and the Buddha image

An artist producing an image of the Buddha does not try to create an original piece of art; he is trying to be faithful to a tradition which can be traced back over centuries. It is important to appreciate that the Buddha image is not merely a work of art but an object of and for, worship. Sanskrit poetry even sets down the characteristics of the Buddha – albeit in rather unlikely terms: legs like a deer, arms like an elephant's trunk, a chin like a mango stone and hair like the stings of scorpions. The Pali texts of Theravada Buddhism add the 108 auspicious signs, long toes and fingers of equal length, body like a banyan tree and eyelashes like a cow's. The Buddha can be represented either sitting, lying (indicating paranirvana), or standing, and (in Thailand) occasionally walking. He is often represented standing on an open lotus flower: the Buddha was born into an impure world, and likewise the lotus germinates in mud but rises above the filth to flower. Each image will be represented in a particular mudra or 'attitude', of which there are 40. The most common are:

Abhayamudra – dispelling fear or giving protection; right hand (sometimes both hands) raised, palm outwards, usually with the Buddha in a standing position.

Varamudra – giving blessing or charity; the right hand pointing downwards, the palm facing outwards, with the Buddha either seated or standing.

Vitarkamudra – preaching mudra; the ends of the thumb and index finger of the right hand touch to form a circle, symbolizing the Wheel of Law. The Buddha can either be seated or standing.

Dharmacakramudra – 'spinning the Wheel of Law'; a preaching mudra symbolizing the teaching of the first sermon. The hands are held in front of the chest, thumbs and index fingers of both joined, one facing inwards and one outwards.

Bhumisparcamudra – 'calling the earth goddess to witness' or 'touching the earth'; the right hand rests on the right knee with the tips of the fingers 'touching ground', thus calling the earth goddess Dharani/Thoranee to witness his enlightenment and victory over Mara, the king of demons. The Buddha is always seated.

Dhyanamudra – meditation; both hands resting open, palms upwards, in the lap, right over left.

Other points of note:
Vajrasana – yogic posture of meditation; cross-legged, both soles of the feet visible.

Virasana – yogic posture of meditation; cross-legged, but with the right leg on top of the left, covering the left foot (also known as paryankasana).

Buddha under Naga – the Buddha is shown in an attitude of meditation with a cobra rearing up over his head. This refers to an episode in the Buddha's life when he was meditating; a rain storm broke and Nagaraja, the king of the nagas (snakes), curled up under the Buddha (seven coils) and then used his seven-headed hood to protect the Holy One from the falling rain.

Buddha calling for rain – the Buddha is depicted standing, both arms held stiffly at the side of the body, fingers pointing downwards.

Bhumisparcamudra – calling the earth goddess to witness. Sukhothai period, 13th-14th century.

Dhyanamudra – meditation. Sukhothai period, 13th-14th century.

Abhayamudra – dispelling fear or giving protection. Lopburi Buddha, Khmer style 12th century.

Vitarkamudra – preaching, "spinning the Wheel of Law." Dvaravati Buddha, 7th-8th century, seated in the "European" manner.

Abhayamudra – dispelling fear or giving protection; subduing Mara position. Lopburi Buddha, Khmer style 13th century.

The Buddha 'Calling for rain'.

vihara and the Buddha statues contained within them will face east in order to express gratitude to Lord Buddha for enlightenment and guide others toward the path of enlightenment. There are often small rustic altars to the guardian spirits (*neak ta*) in the corner of pagodas. Cambodians often wear *katha* – or charms – which are believed to control external magical forces. Most important ceremonies – weddings, funerals, coming of age – have both Buddhist and animist elements. Wats play an important role in education and it is fairly common to find schools built inside or beside wats.

Other religions

There are around 60,000 Roman Catholics in Cambodia, mainly Vietnamese, and about 2000 Protestants. Islam, of the Sunni sect, is practised by many of the 200,000 (some commentators would say 500,000) Cham. During the Khmer Rouge period it was reported that Cham were forced to eat pork while most Cham mosques were destroyed, and only now are they being slowly rebuilt. A new International Mosque in Phnom Penh, built with Saudi money, was opened in 1994. Almost all the Chinese in Cambodia are Taoist/Confucianist.

Land and environment

Geography

Cambodia is all that remains of the once mighty Khmer Empire. Covering a land area of 181,035 sq km – about the size of England and Wales combined – the country is squeezed in between Thailand to the west, Vietnam to the east and Laos to the north. Cambodia holds many features of international conservation significance. The country has one of the highest proportions of land as natural habitat (forest and wetlands) in the world, and one of the least disturbed coastlines in continental Asia. The coastline stretches along the Gulf of Thailand for 435 km, supports 64 islands and extensive mangroves and coral reefs. The **Mekong** is as central to life in Cambodia as the Nile is to life in Egypt. The river runs through Cambodia for about 500 km, bisecting the east lowlands, north to south. It is navigable by cargo ships from the delta in Vietnam, right up to Phnom Penh and beyond. Near the centre of the country is the **Tonlé Sap** – the 'Great Lake' – the largest freshwater lake in Southeast Asia. It is connected to the Mekong via the short channel-like Tonlé Sap River. The Tonlé Sap basin includes all or part of eight of Cambodia's 24 provinces and covers 80,000 sq km (44% of Cambodia's total area) and is estimated to be home to 3.6 million people, one third of Cambodia's total population. When the Mekong floods between June and October – sometimes these floods can be devastating, as they were in 1991 – the Tonlé Sap River reverses its flow and the floodwaters fill the Great Lake, which doubles in size, covering the surrounding countryside (see page 123).

North of Phnom Penh, the Mekong is known as the Upper Mekong – or just the Mekong; downriver from the capital it divides into the Lower Mekong and the Bassac rivers. These two tributaries then swing to the southeast across the fertile alluvial plain, towards the sprawling delta and the sea. The broad valley of the Mekong is a centuries-old trade route and its fertile central flood-plain is densely populated. The alluvial soils are irrigated but have an even greater potential for agricultural production than is presently being realized. Throughout most of its course in Cambodia the river averages more than 1.6 km in width. There are vicious rapids at Kratie, northeast of Phnom Penh, and a succession of dramatic waterfalls – Li Phi and Khong Phapheng Falls – on the border with Laos.

The **central lowlands** are surrounded by savannah; in south Cambodia these plains run all the way to the Vietnamese border. But to the north, east and west, Cambodia is enclosed by mountain chains: the Cardamom Mountains and Elephant Range to the west and southwest, while the sandstone escarpment of the Dangrek Range forms a natural border with Thailand. The **Cardamom Mountains** (named after the spice) run in a gentle curve from just south of Battambang towards Phnom Penh. Phnom Aoral, in the Cardamoms, is Cambodia's highest peak at 1813 m and in 2004 **Global Witness** detected a large amount of illegal logging in the area. The **Elephant Mountains** run along the south coastline. All these mountains are densely forested and sparsely inhabited, making them perfect operational bases for Cambodia's rebel guerrilla factions, who fought the Phnom Penh government throughout the 1980s. On the south coast around Kompong Som is a lowland area cut off from the rest of the country by mountains. Because the Mekong was a major thoroughfare, the **coastal region** never developed into a centre of trade until a road was built with American aid from Kompong Som to Phnom Penh in the 1960s.

Climate

The monsoons determine rainfall and temperature patterns in Cambodia. The southwest monsoon, from May to October, brings heavy rain throughout the country. This period accounts for between 75% and 80% of the total annual rainfall. The northeast monsoon blows from October to April and ushers in the dry season. In the mountain areas the temperature is markedly cooler and the dry season only lasts three months. Between the heat and rains there are transitional periods and the best time to visit the country is between November and January, before it gets too hot. Rainfall varies considerably from region to region. The Cardamom Mountains are the wettest. The mean temperature for Cambodia is 27.5°C. It is cooler – around 24°C – from November to January and hotter – around 32°C – between February and April. Humidity is generally high.

Flora and fauna

The central plains are a predominantly agricultural area and are sparsely wooded but most of the rest of Cambodia – until recently – was still forested. In 1970, 73% of Cambodia's land area was thought to be forested but by 1995 the figure was less than 40%, and a paper published at the end of 1998 put the area at 30%. So the trend is rapidly down. The reasons for the alarming decline in Cambodia's forests are pretty clear – illegal logging (see below). In the southwest, around the Cardamom and Elephant Mountains, there are still large tracts of primary forest where teak predominates. There are also tracts of virgin rainforest in the west and the northeast. At higher elevations in these mountains there are areas of pine forest and in the north and east highlands, temperate forest.

Cambodia has a wide variety of fauna and, before war broke out in the 1970s, was on the international game-hunters' circuit; there were tigers (now an endangered species), buffalo, elephants, wild oxen, majestic birds, clouded leopards (also endangered) and bears, including Malaysian sun bears. Today, there are 630 types of protected wildlife, including 122 mammal species, 537 bird species, 114 are rodents from the rodent family, 40 are aquatic animals and 300 are insects and butterflies.

Even after all the fighting, game is still said to be abundant in forested areas, particularly in north-eastern provinces of Mondulkiri and Ratanakiri. Smaller animals include monkeys, squirrels, tree rats and shrews, flying foxes and numerous species of reptile, including several varieties of poisonous snake, the most common being Russell's viper, the banded krait, cobra and king cobra. Even around Phnom Penh one can see herons, cranes, grouse, pheasant, wild duck, pelicans, cormorants and egrets. The kouprey (meaning 'jungle cow') is Cambodia's most famous animal and a symbol of the Worldwide Fund for Nature. A wild ox, it was first identified in 1939 but is now virtually extinct worldwide. In 1963, King Sihanouk declared the animal Cambodia's national animal. Small numbers are thought to inhabit the more remote areas of the country, although some experts fear that the last specimens were either killed by guerrillas for meat or are being fatally maimed after treading on anti-personnel mines laid by the Khmer Rouge. An effort to capture and breed the kouprey is underway in Vietnam.

The Tonlé Sap area is particularly rich in fish-eating waterfowl and marine life. It supports possibly the largest inland fishing industry in the world. The lake is the lifeline for about 40% of the Cambodian population and provides almost 60% of the country's protein.

The lower reaches of the Mekong, marking the border between Cambodia and Laos, is also the last place in Indochina where the rare Irrawaddy dolphin (*Orcaella brevirostris*) is to be found. Unfortunately, fishermen in the area took to fishing using dynamite and this threatens the survival of the mammal. Countless numbers were also killed under the

Khmer Rouge regime. It was also once found in Thailand's Chao Phraya River, but pollution put paid to that population years ago.

The poverty of most of Cambodia's population has made the trade in exotic fauna an attractive proposition. By 1997 the trade in wildlife had become 'rampant', according to the environmental NGO Global Witness. A case in point is the plight of the Malayan sun bear (*Helarctos malayanus*), which has been protected in Cambodia since 1992. But its paws and gall bladder are treasured by many Chinese and bear bile is said to command a price of US$100 per gram in China due to its perceived medicinal properties. The animals are captured and caged and the bile siphoned off through a steel tube inserted into the gall bladder. There is also documentary footage of animals having their paws amputated while still alive. Once again, the failure to protect the sun bear, and many other wild animals, is not due to an absence of environmental legislation but due a lack of commitment to its implementation. Giant ibis and black-necked storks are sold for US$400-500 a pair, rewards are put out for black cranes, turtles and pythons are sold to Chinese and Korean restaurants, and the eggs and chicks of water birds are collected for sale in markets. Cambodia's fauna is being caught, sold and slaughtered on a truly grand scale.

Timber tragedy

In 1995 the Cambodian government, to much fanfare, introduced a new environment law. This was heralded as the first step in the sustainable exploitation of Cambodia's forests and other natural resources. The introduction of the law was accompanied by other legislation, including a new Environmental Impact Assessment Law. At the end of 1996 the government seemed to go one step further when they outlawed the export of whole logs. But even in 1995 experts were sceptical about the ability of the Cambodian government to deliver on its environmental promises. The lack of transparency in many of the regulations, and the ease with which companies and individuals with political and economic power could – and still can – circumvent those regulations, makes environmental protection difficult to achieve in any systematic sense.

This scepticism was borne out later, in 1998, when the UK-based environmental group Global Witness claimed that, unless the rate of logging was reduced substantially, Cambodia was "heading toward deforestation of all saleable timber within three to five years". Patrick Alley, who has done much to highlight the plight of Cambodia's wild areas, claimed at a press conference that "the logging situation is out of control". Although Cambodia still has forests, it is believed 40-50% of the country's forests has been logged.

With foreign donors becoming increasingly frustrated at the Cambodian government's lack of commitment to protecting the environment, Prime Minister Hun Sen ordered a crack-down on illegal loggers in March 1999. The fact that some donors were moving towards making further aid dispersal contingent on forestry reform no doubt concentrated the mind of the Prime Minister. The difficulty for one of the poorest countries in the world is that forestry is one of Cambodia's major industries, accounting for 43% of foreign trade and contributing 15% of GDP in 1997. But even more crucial than the fact that forestry is important to the nation is that fact that timber is valuable to individuals.

The problem is that apparently just about everyone from senior government ministers through to senior army officers and foreign governments or their representatives are involved in illegal logging activities. As Ly Thuch, Under-Secretary for State for the Environment, told a meeting at the Foreign Correspondents Club in Phnom Penh, "the main destroyers of the environment are the Khmer Rouge and the rich and powerful". It is doubtful that even Cambodia's aid donors can make a difference. In mid-1996 international aid donors had become so worried about the failure of the Cambodian government to control logging that the IMF suspended a US$20 million budget-support payment. But Cambodia's two prime ministers continued to sign logging contracts – without cabinet discussion and in contravention of their own environmental laws.

In early 2000, Hun Sen vouched: "If I cannot put an end to the illegal cutting of trees, I will resign from my position of prime minister in the first quarter of 2001." True to his word? No. Needless to say the Cambodian government was still entering into illegal logging concessions in 2004-2005, breaking an international moratorium on logging that was due to expire in late 2005. Furthermore, those critical of the government's illegal activities have been threatened and hassled. In April 2002, a senior official with the independent forestry monitor Global Witness was beaten near her office. The next day she was sent an email instructing her to quit. The forestry monitor, Global Witness was later sacked by Hun Sen.

There are major ecological side effects of deforestation, particularly in a country where 80% of the population rely on subsistence agriculture. The ongoing rice crop failure and siltation of the waterways, effecting the valuable fisheries can largely be contributed to the rampant deforestation.

In an interview published in November 1996, William Shawcross suggested that illegal logging was "perhaps the most serious crisis of corruption in the regime". Nothing much has changed in the intervening years.

National parks

Cambodia was the first country in Southeast Asia to establish protected areas, with the forests surrounding the Angkor temples declared a national park in 1925. By 1969, six wildlife sanctuaries had been established covering 2.2 million ha or 12% of the country for the protection of wildlife, in particular large mammals. Towards the end of 1993, King Sihanouk signed a decree to create 23 protected areas, now covering over 21% of the country. Cambodia has one of the highest percentages of national territory within protected areas in the world and had the goal to increase that area to 25% by the end of 2005.

It may be rather ironic, but the dislocations caused by Cambodia's long-running civil war probably helped to protect the environment, rather than destroy it. Although larger animals like the kouprey may have suffered from the profusion of land mines that dot the countryside, other animals have benefited from the lack of development. Unlike Thailand and Vietnam, forest has not been cleared for agriculture and many regions became 'no-go' areas to all except for the foolhardy and the well-armed. This created conditions in which wildlife could survive largely undisturbed by the forces of 'development'. Now wildlife experts and environmentalists are arguing that Cambodia has a unique asset that should be preserved at all costs – and not just because it might be the morally 'right' thing to do. In addition, the growth in eco-tourism worldwide could create a considerable money-spinner for the country.

Books

Southeast Asia

Dumarçay, Jacques *The Palaces of South-East Asia: architecture and customs.* (Singapore: OUP, 1991.) A broad summary of palace art and architecture in both.

Fenton, James *All the Wrong Places: adrift in the politics of Asia.* (London: Penguin, 1988.) British journalist James Fenton skilfully and entertainingly recounts his experiences.

Fraser-Lu, Sylvia *Handwoven Textiles of South-East Asia.* (Singapore: OUP, 1988.) Well-illustrated, large-format book with informative text.

Higham, Charles *The Archaeology of Mainland Southeast Asia from 10,000 BC to the Fall of Angkor.* (Cambridge: Cambridge University Press, 1989.) Best summary of changing views of the archaeology of the mainland.

King, Ben F and Dickinson, EC *A Field Guide to the Birds of South-East Asia.* (London: Collins, 1975.) Best regional guide to the birds of the region.

Osborne, Milton *Southeast Asia: an introductory history.* (Sydney: Allen & Unwin, 1979.) Good introductory history, clearly written, published in a portable paperback edition.

Rawson, Philip *The Art of Southeast Asia.* (London: Thames & Hudson, 1967.) Portable general art history of Cambodia, Vietnam, Thailand, Laos, Burma, Java and Bali; by necessity, rather superficial.

Reid, Anthony *Southeast Asia in the Age of Commerce 1450-1680: the lands below the winds.* (New Haven: Yale University Press, 1988.) Perhaps the best history of everyday life in Southeast Asia, looking at such themes as physical well-being, material culture and social organization.

Reid, Anthony *Southeast Asia in the age of commerce 1450-1680: expansion and crisis.* (Yale University Press: New Haven. Volume 2, 1993.)

Sesser, Stan *The Lands of Charm and Cruelty: travels in Southeast Asia.* (Basingstoke: Picador, 1993.) A series of collected narratives first published in the New Yorker including essays on Singapore, Laos, Cambodia, Burma and Borneo. Finely observed and thoughtful, the book is an excellent travel companion.

Steinberg, DJ et al *In Search of Southeast Asia: a modern history.* (Honolulu: University of Hawaii Press, 1987.) The best standard history of the region; it skilfully examines and assesses general processes of change and their impacts from the arrival of the Europeans in the region.

Tarling, Nicholas *Cambridge History of Southeast Asia.* (Cambridge: Cambridge University Press, 1992.) Two-volume edited study, long and expensive with contributions from most of the leading historians of the region. A thematic and regional approach is taken, not a country one, although the history is fairly conventional.

Novels

See also Cambodian literature, page 256.

Cixous, Helene *The Terrible but Unfinished Story of Norodom Sihanouk, King of Cambodia.* (University of Nebraska Press, 1994.) Avant-garde 20th-century literature associated with recent political history.

Drabble, Margaret *The Gates of Ivory.* (London: Penguin, 1992.) The third part of a trilogy which deals with Cambodia during the period of the civil war while the Vietnamese 'occupied' Phnom Penh and the Khmer Rouge controlled much of the countryside.

Documentation Centre of Cambodia *The Khmer Rouge – From Victory to Destruction.* The compilation of reports, orders and chronological details helps to give an insight into how the Khmer Rouge operated during this period.

Ho, Minfong *Brother Rabbit: A Cambodian Tale*. (Lothrop, Lee and Shepard Books, 1997.) Traditional legend translated into English along with a discussion on the place of folklore in Cambodia, relating themes to Cambodian history.

Koch, Christopher *Highways to War*. (Minerva, 1996.) New novel about wartime Cambodia and Vietnam – part thriller, part mystery, part heroic epic by the author of *The Year of Living Dangerously*.

Ngor, Haing S *Surviving the Killing Fields*. One of the best, first-hand accounts of this terrible period. Recommended.

Pran, Dith *Children of Cambodia's Killing Fields*. (Yale University Press, 1998.) Eyewitness accounts of the Khmer Rouge regime by Cambodian survivors.

Ryan, Paul Ryder *Khmer Rouge End Game*. (Munewata Press, 1999.) Work of 'faction' relating the kidnapping of six foreigners by the one-legged guerrilla leader Ta Mok.

History

Affonco, Denise *To the End of Hell: One Woman's Struggle to Survive Cambodia's Khmer Rouge*. (Reportage Press, 2007.) A bestseller in France, this is the first English translation of the French-born author's time living with her Communist husband in Khmer Rouge-ruled Cambodia.

Bizot, Francois *The Gate*. (Vintage Press, 2004.) This is the author's true story of his capture by the Khmer Rouge guerrilla force in 1971. An archaeologist studying the Angkor temples, Bizot, was held and interrogated by Comrade Duch, the notorious commandant of Tuol Sleng who was convicted and sentenced at the UN Cambodia Tribunal in 2010. Bizot charts his relationship with Duch, becoming the only Westerner to be released alive by the Khmer Rouge.

Chandler, David P *The Tragedy of Cambodian History: politics, war and revolution since 1945*. (Yale University Press: New Haven, 1993.)

Chandler, David P *Brother Number One: a political biography of Pol Pot*. (Colorado: Westview Press, 1992.) Chandler is considered one of the most authoritative academics in the field of Cambodian history.

Chandler, David P *Voices from S-21: terror and history in Pol Pot's secret prison*. (University of California Press, 2000.)

Chanda, Nayan *Brother Enemy: the war after the war*. (New York: Macmillan, 1986.) Exhaustive and engrossing account of 'the third Indochina war' puts Cambodian conflict into regional perspective: vivid journalistic style.

Chou Ta-kuan *The Customs of Cambodia*. (Bangkok: Siam Society, 1993.) Written in 1296-1297 by Chou Ta-kuan, a Chinese emissary to the kingdom of Angkor. It is a potted, first hand account of life and livelihoods in the 13th century. Widely available in Bangkok.

Criddle, Joan & Butt Mam, Tedda *To Destroy You Is No Loss: the odyssey of a Cambodian family*. (Doubleday, 1987.)

Jackson, K (edit) *Cambodia 1975-1978: rendezvous with death*. (Princeton University Press, 1989.)

May, Someth *Cambodian Witness*. (London: Faber and Faber, 1986.) A chilling personal account of the Pol Pot period. Of Someth May's family of 14 only four survived the terrible years of the Khmer Rouge.

Osborne, Milton *Sihanouk*. (Allen and Unwin, 1996.) A biography of the controversial Asian leader chronicling his evolution from a dilettante king to rigorous and ruthless politician.

Pin Yathay *Stay alive my father*. (Touchstone Books, 1998.)

Ponchaud, Francois *Cambodia Year Zero* (translation from French). (London: Penguin, 1978.)

Shawcross, William *Sideshow: Kissinger, Nixon and the destruction of Cambodia*. (London: Chatto & Windus, 1979, revised 1986.) Excellent, balanced and very readable investigative work on American involvement in the Cambodian 'sideshow'; it runs through to cover the Pol Pot period.

Shawcross, William *The Quality of Mercy: Cambodia, holocaust and the modern conscience.* (London: Fontana, 1984.)

Shawcross, William *Cambodia's New Deal* (1994.) A book by Shawcross examining the UN-brokered peace deal and the country's progress since the elections.

Swain, Jon *River of Time.* (London: Minerva, 1995.) Jon Swain was a journalist in Indochina during the Vietnam War and then stayed on to be one of the few foreigners to witness the fall of Phnom Penh to the Khmer Rouge. The chapters on Cambodia are excellent and Swain's account of Indochina during this traumatic period is enthralling.

Szymusiak, Moldya *The stones cry out: a Cambodian childhood.* (London: Jonathan Cape, 1986.) A book recounting the recent tragedy of Cambodia from the perspective of one person.

Ung, Loung *First They Killed My Father: A Daughter Of Cambodia Remembers.* (Harper Perennial, 2001.) The devastatingly sad and true story of what Loung and her family experienced during the Khmer Rouge period.

General

Basan, Ghillie *The Food and Cooking of Cambodia: Over 60 Authentic Classic Recipes from an Undiscovered Cuisine.* (Southwater, 2007.) A Frenchman, Basan is one of the leading experts on Khmer cuisine. Originally published in French this was a bestseller in the author's home country.

Gilboa, Amit *Off the rails in Phnom Penh: into the Dark Heart of Guns, Girls and Ganja.* (1997) Slightly breathless account of some of Phnom Penh's well-known vices.

Gray, Spalding *Swimming to Cambodia* (Theatre Communications Group, 2005.) A re-issue of Gray's cult classic where he charts his involvement in the Oscar-winning movie, *The Killing Fields*.

Livingston, Carol *Gecko Tails.* (Orion Paperbacks, 1997.) A humorous chronicle of the new wave of tourism that followed the demise of the Khmer Rouge.

Oeur, U Sam *Sacred Vows.* (Coffee House Press 1998.) Collection of poems recalling the horror of the author and his family's spell in six different concentration camps.

Jacob, Judith M *The Traditional Literature of Cambodia: A Preliminary Guide.* (OUP, 1996.) Comprehensive survey of ancient Cambodian writing.

Page, Tim *Derailed in Uncle Ho's Victory Garden.* (Scribner Paperback, 1999.) Page's odyssey, 20 years after the liberation of Vietnam, through the land that dominated his life as a wartime photographer.

Poole, Colin (Author) and **Briggs, Eleanor** (Photographer) *Tonlé Sap: The Heart of Cambodia's Natural Heritage.* (River Books, 2005.) A stunning collection of photos that charts the lives of people living on the incredible Tonlé Sap river and lake.

Venn, Savat and Downie, Sue *Down Highway One: Journeys Through Vietnam and Cambodia.* (Allen and Unwin, 1993.) Highway One is one of the longest and most historic roads in Asia. This recounts the author's travels there.

Travel, geography and guides

Hoskins, John *The Mekong.* (Bangkok: Post Publishing, 1991.) A large-format coffee table book with good photographs and a modest text. Widely available in Bangkok.

Jacobson, Matt *Adventure Cambodia.* (Silkworm Books, 2005, 2nd edition.) A good guide for people interested in motorcycling through Cambodia.

Jensen, Carsten and Haveland, Barbara *I Have Seen the World Begin.* (Harvill Press, 2000.) Collection of travel writings with insights into local households, lives and personal points of view.

Lewis, Norman *A Dragon Apparent: travels in Indochina*. (London: Jonathan Cape, 1951.) Possibly Norman Lewis' best-known travel book. Witty and perceptive, about a fifth is based on his travels in Cambodia. Gives a good feel of Cambodia 'before the fall'.

Art and architecture

le Bonheur, Albert *Of Gods, Kings, and Men: Bas-reliefs of Angkor Wat and Bayon*. (Serindia Publications 1995.)
Dumarcay, Jaques and Smithies, Michael *Cultural Sites of Burma, Thailand and Cambodia*. (OUP SE Asia, 1996.) An investigation of the most important historic sites in these countries.
Dumarcay, Jaques and Smithies, Michael *The Site of Angkor*. (OUP SE Asia, 1998.) An introduction to this amazing complex's history and construction.
Giteau, Madeleine and **Gueret, Danielle** and **Renaut, Thomas** and **Keo, Pich** *L'Art Khmer/Khmer Art*. (ASA Editions, 1998.) A representation of more than a millennium of Cambodian art.
Ibbitson Jessup, Helen *Sculpture of Angkor and Ancient Cambodia: Millennium of Glory*. (Thames and Hudson, 1997.) 1000- year artistic legacy of Cambodia displayed in an extensively illustrated volume.
Jaques, Claude and Freeman, Michael *Ancient Angkor*. (Thames and Hudson, 2000.)
Mannikka, Eleanor *Angkor Wat: Time, Space and Kingship*. (University of Hawaii Press, 1996.) An attempt to understand the temple in terms of the measurement systems used by its original builders and uncovering a sophisticated system of philosophical and religious principles within them.
Miyamato, R *Angkor*. (Art Data, 1994.)
Roveda, Vittorio *Khmer Mythology*. (Thames and Hudson, 1997.) The thousands of temples and shrines erected by the Khmer people were carved with stone reliefs. This volume studies these 'stories in stone'.
Werly, Richard, Renaut, Thomas and **Lacouture, Jean** *Eternal Phnom Penh*. (ASA Editions, 1998.) Photographs and descriptions of Phnom Penh of today.
Zephir, Thierry *Khmer*. (Thames and Hudson, 1998.) The Khmer Empire's art and architecture, its influences, rise and fall explained.

Economics, politics, society and development

Becker, Elizabeth *When the War Was Over*. (New York: Simon & Schuster, 1988.)
Brady, Christopher *United States Foreign Policy towards Cambodia, 1977-1992*. (Macmillan Press Ltd, 1999.) A study of US foreign policy that delves into decision making theory and foreign policy analysis. Widely considered one of the best accounts of this historical period. Recommended.
Chandler, David P *Revolution and Its Aftermath in Kampuchea: Eight Essays*. (Yale University. SE Asia Studies, 1983.)
Curtis, Grant *Cambodia Reborn? The transition to Democracy and Development*. (Brookings Institution Press, 1998.) This book examines Cambodia's uneasy renaissance from years of conflict, isolation and authoritarian rule following the UN-sponsored elections of 1993.
Findlay, Trevor *Cambodia*. (Macmillan Press, 1997.) This is an account and analysis of the United Nations peacekeeping operation mounted in Cambodia between 1991 and 1993.
Heininger, Janet E *Peacekeeping in Transition: The United Nations in Cambodia*. (Brookings Institution Press, 1994.) This book investigates the United Nations Transitional Administration in Cambodia's experiences in their entirety arguing that they can make future UN peace-keeping efforts more effective.

Contents

Footnotes

Useful Khmer words and phrases

There are a number of sounds in Khmer, or Cambodian, which have no equivalent in English. The transcription given here is only an approximation of the sound in Khmer and is taken from David Smyth and Tran Kien's (1991) *Courtesy and Survival in Cambodia*, School of Oriental and African Studies: London.

Consonants

bp	is a sharp 'p' somewhere between 'p' and 'b' in English
ch	as in 'chase'
dt	is a sharp 't', somewhere between 't' and 'd'
j	as in 'jump'
g	as in 'get'
kh	a 'k' as in 'kettle'
ng	as in 'ring'
ph	a 'p' sound as in 'pill', not an 'f' sound as in 'phone'

Vowels

a	as in 'ago'
ah	as in 'car'
ai	as in 'Thai'
ao	as in 'Lao'
ay	as in 'pay'
ee	as in 'see'
eu	as in 'uugh'
i	as in 'fin'
o	as in 'long'
oh	as in 'loan'
oo	as in 'boot'
OO	more of a 'u' sound as in 'cook'
u	as in 'run'

Useful words and phrases

yes	baht (male speakers)
	Jah (female speakers)
no	(ot) dtay
please	suom mehta
thank you (very much)	or-gOOn (j'run)
hello	jOOm ree-up soo-a
goodbye	lee-a hai
see you later	juab k'nea ta'ngay krai
how are you?	Tau neak sok sapbay jea teh?
good morning	arun suor sdei
good afternoon	tiveah suor sdei
good evening	sa-yoanh suor sdei
good night	reah-trey suor sdei

excuse me/sorry!...	...som dta(h)
where's the...?	...noev ai nah?
how much is...?	...t'lai bpon-mahn?
it doesn't matter	mun ay dtay
never mind/that's alright	dop bprum moo-ay
I don't understand	mun yoo-ul dtay
I want a...	k'nyom jang baan
what is your name?	Neak ch'muah ei?
my name is...	k'nyom tch much

Basic vocabulary

bank	ta-nee-a-gee-a
doctor	bpairt
hospital	mOOn-dti-bpairt
Khmer Rouge	k-mai gra-horm
market	p'sah
post office	brai-sa-nee-ya-than
toilet	borng-goo-un
water	dteuk

Food

bread	nOOm bpung
chicken	moan
delicious	ch'ngun
fish	dt'ray
food	m'hohp
meat	saich
restaurant	hanng bai
rice	bai
tea	dtai
water	dteuk

Travel

is it far?	Ch'ngai dtay?
turn left/right	bot dtoh kahng ch'wayng/s'dum
go straight	ondtoh dtrong
where is the...?	noev eah nah?
bus	laan ch'nuol
boat	dtook
train station	ra dteah plerng
cyclo	see kloa
will you go for...riel?...	ree-ul bahn dtay?
that's expensive	t'lai na(h)

Time/date

morning	bpreuk
midday	dtrong

night	yOOp
today	t'ngai ni(h)
day	t'ngai
tomorrow	sa-aik
yesterday	m'seri mern
midnight	aa-tree-at
Sunday	t'ngai aa-dteut
Monday	t'ngai jan
Tuesday	t'ngai ong-gee-a
Wednesday	t'ngai bpoot
Thursday	t'ngai bpra-hoa-a
Friday	t'ngai sok
Saturday	t'ngai sao
month	khaeh
year	ch'nam
last year	ch'nam moon
new year	ch'nam thmey
next year	ch'nam groy
January	ma ga raa
February	kompheak
March	mee nah
April	meh sah
May	oo sa phea
June	mi thok nah
July	ka kada
August	say haa
September	kan'ya
October	dto laa
November	wech a gaa
December	t'noo

Numbers

1	moo-ay	20	m'pay
2	bpee	30	sahm seup
3	bay	40	sai seup
4	boo-un	50	hah seup
5	bprum	60	hok seup
6	bprum moo-ay	70	jert seup
7	bprum bpee or	80	bpait seup
	bprum bpeul	90	gao seup
8	bprum bay	100	moo-ay roy
9	bprum boo-un	1000	moo-ay bpohn
10	dop	10,000	moo-ay meun
11	dop moo-ay	100,000	moo-ay sain
12	dop bpee… etc	1,000,000	moo-ay lee-un
16	dop bprum moo-ay	10,000,000	dahp lee-un

Index → *Entries in bold refer to maps*

Advertisers' index

Notes

Notes

Notes

Notes